W9-BVK-113

More Real Life Rock

Also by Greil Marcus

Mystery Train: Images of America in Rock 'n' Roll Music (1975, Folio Society edition, 2015)

Lipstick Traces: A Secret History of the Twentieth Century (1989, 2009)

Dead Elvis: A Chronicle of a Cultural Obsession (1991)

Ranters & Crowd Pleasers: Punk in Pop Music, 1977–1992 (1993, published 1999 as *In the Fascist Bathroom: Writings on Punk, 1977–1992*)

The Dustbin of History (1995)

Invisible Republic: Bob Dylan's Basement Tapes (1997, published 2000 as *The Old Weird America: The World of Bob Dylan's Basement Tapes*)

Double Trouble: Bill Clinton and Elvis Presley in a World of No Alternatives (2000)

"The Manchurian Candidate" (2002)

Like a Rolling Stone: Bob Dylan at the Crossroads (2005)

The Shape of Things to Come: Prophecy and the American Voice (2006)

When That Rough God Goes Riding: Listening to Van Morrison (2010)

Bob Dylan by Greil Marcus: Writings, 1968–2010 (2010)

The Doors: A Lifetime of Listening to Five Mean Years (2011)

The History of Rock 'n' Roll in Ten Songs (2014)

Real Life Rock: The Complete Top Ten Columns, 1986–2014 (2015)

Three Songs, Three Singers, Three Nations (2015)

Under the Red White and Blue: Patriotism, Disenchantment and the Stubborn Myth of the Great Gatsby (2020)

AS EDITOR

Stranded (1979, 2007)

Psychotic Reactions & Carburetor Dung, by Lester Bangs (1987)

The Rose & the Briar: Death, Love, and Liberty in the American Ballad (2004, with Sean Wilentz)

Best Music Writing 2009 (2009)

A New Literary History of America (2009, with Werner Sollors)

More
Real Life
Rock

The Wilderness Years,
2014 — 2021

GREIL MARCUS

Yale

UNIVERSITY PRESS

New Haven & London

Published with assistance from the foundation established in memory of Calvin Chapin of the Class of 1788, Yale College.

Yale University Press books may be purchased in quantity for educational, business, or promotional use. For information, please e-mail sales.press@yale .edu (U.S. office) or sales@yaleup.co.uk (U.K. office).

Designed by Sonia L. Shannon.
Set in Electra and Sans types by Westchester Publishing Services.
Printed in the United States of America.

Library of Congress Control Number: 2021942568
ISBN 978-0-300-26098-4 (hardcover : alk. paper)

A catalogue record for this book is available from the British Library.

This paper meets the requirements of ANSI/NISO Z39.48-1992 (Permanence of Paper).

10 9 8 7 6 5 4 3 2 1

For Emily

Contents

■

Introduction

TOO MANY OF THE BOOKS I've written have had presidents looming behind them. I wrote my first, *Mystery Train,* during the Watergate crisis; I finished it the day Richard Nixon resigned. Driven by love, pessimism, fatalism, and rage, the book was an embrace of the country. My next, *Lipstick Traces,* was a Reagan book from start to finish: I began writing in 1980 and finished it as his second term was ending. As a Californian, I knew what he was about, and how serious he was about leaving the country forever changed. I couldn't bear to look at the nation as it shifted under his hand. People talk all the time during elections about how if so-and-so is elected they'll leave the country. It's self-flattering nonsense, people tending the flame of their own purity. They never do it. But in a way I did. For nine years I left the USA for Europe, at least in the pages I read and those I tried to write, struggling with the half-a-millennium history of the European avant-garde, where such American ideals as equality, democracy, individualism, and a joint-stock world were foreign, where it made sense for those who considered themselves illuminated to speak as if they should legislate the future and the past. Maybe it was a failure of nerve, but it was the only story I could bear to listen to. "I've been stuck in Paris in 1952 for three years and I can't get out," I said to my wife one day in Berkeley in 1987. "There are worse places to be," she said.

I wrote *The Old, Weird America* (which the late Nick Tosches said I said pretended to be about Bob Dylan's basement tapes when it was really about Dock Boggs) in the mid-1990s. It was a Bill Clinton book. I liked him. He let me back into the American story. *The Shape of Things to Come* came out of the terrorist attacks of 2001. To me that was a biblical event. It raised the question of whether America existed at all. I heard the prophetic tradition in American speech, and artists in the present taking up that language, and tried to listen to the different Americas they displayed when they did so—tried to listen to David Thomas's cracker-barrel tall tales and Laura Palmer's screams.

From the middle of Reagan's second term and through the Obama administration, I was writing the column whose later years are collected here. I started it in 1986 at the *Village Voice*, and over the next nearly thirty years it moved to *Artforum* to *Salon* to *City Pages* to *Interview*; when *Interview*'s editor, the late and beloved Ingrid Sischy, absconded into the night, the column found a home at the *Believer* for eight gratifying years. But when the *Believer* suspended publication in 2014—after which I collected all of the columns from the previous years in a book Yale published in 2015—the column went into a wilderness, arriving in one clearing only to have to pack up and move on. It jumped from one place to another every year without a break (I missed only two or three columns during that time, and then only because of mini-strikes over not being paid), from the *Barnes & Noble Review* (until they said they were changing format) to *Pitchfork* (as a Condé Nast publication they required a click count I didn't make) to the *Village Voice* again (in print until it went online only, until that too was soon shut down and the paper disappeared) to rollingstone.com (I'd started writing at *Rolling Stone*, in 1968—they didn't say why they killed the column in 2019 and I didn't ask) to the *Los Angeles Review of Books*, which I will say nothing good about because I'm superstitious. It seemed appropriate, as during that time the country itself was set loose in the wilderness of its own worst self: the Trump years. While I was writing my first book, I wrote on its second page of the Watergate years, "the country came face-to-face with an obscene perversion of itself that could neither be accepted nor destroyed." The good old days.

So if the columns collected here now are not a chronicle of the Trump years, they are, if they have succeeded at all, a chronicle from that time, which as I write now, a few days after writing the last column here, published following the inauguration of Joe Biden, is still a cloud of smoke over the country. And if it is any kind of chronicle, it's because of the many voices speaking here: the voices of people who wrote in of their own accord, treating the column as a kind of forum, of those I asked to cover shows or events I couldn't be present for, or of the countless people, simply speaking in public in whatever manner, in newspapers or on television or during campaigns or on the street, who said things I would never have thought of in words I never could have found but which have always been part of the conversation of the column as I heard it. And that is especially true with columns that had to be written, or really assembled, after great public events. I found long ago that in those moments, I had no interest in whatever I might have to say. I wanted to listen to what other people had to say, and then, as a writer, to put different voices together as if they were all part of the same, immediate conversation, and the greatest privilege was to try to collect what might, someday if not tomorrow, seem like random, even empty lines, but which in the moment, and in the frame of a literary device, were the judgments of history. That's what they sounded like then and that's what they sound like to me now.

Except for some cheating on overused words and phrases, and circling around originally used illustrations and deleted lyric quotes, I haven't rewritten these columns to make them better. I haven't changed any thoughtless opinions. When there were factual errors I left them as they were and noted them in footnotes. Some changes are a matter of clarity of attribution, varying house styles to which I had to adhere but that always sounded wrong to me, editorial changes I didn't have the opportunity to change back, or typographical mistakes from my own uncorrected errors to passages dropped in layouts. From first to last I was lucky to find people I was privileged to work with and who wanted to work with me.

July 26, 2021

Barnes & Noble Review

2014·2016

November 22, 2014

1 ▪ *The Good Wife,* **"Shiny Objects" (CBS, October 19)** The firm's computers are invaded, frozen, held for ransom: $50,000 or everything will be deleted. The clock is ticking: lightning research fingers a Russian hacker. Investigator Kalinda gets the hulking gangster on the screen: when she threatens to report him to the authorities, he laughs. Then she locks Pussy Riot posters and videos onto his home page and he surrenders in terror. What a great joke, I thought, though I thought that was all it was—but when I told Masha Gessen, author of *The Man Without a Face: The Unlikely Rise of Vladimir Putin* and *Words Will Break Cement: The Passion of Pussy Riot,* about the show, she didn't smile. "There's some truth to that," she said. Does that mean Putin has all the power, or that Pussy Riot and any who might follow in their steps have at least a little?

2 ▪ **Skylark Dry Cleaning, St. Paul, Minnesota (November 29)** "The bird is the word," read the headline on an advertising flyer with a cute logo.

The Trashmen, who in 1963 terrorized the country with "Surfin' Bird" and its immortal clarion call, came from Minneapolis—as they used to say, close enough for rock 'n' roll.

3 ▪ **Adia Victoria, comment at "Exploring the Rise and Fall of Paramount Records" (Battell Chapel, Yale University, October 28)** Victoria is a young blues singer, guitarist, and bandleader working out of Nashville and recording on her own rue Didiot label; she has a commanding presence and a little-girl voice. Her scratchy, almost old-timey-sounding "Stuck in the South" and the humid, creeping "Howlin' Shame," which may be a murder ballad or may merely be on the way to one, are as daring as any blues anyone has made in twenty years, each taking in the thinking behind them, but feeling as if they came

3

out of the air, or out of the ground. "The blues served as an outlet for
Black humanity and the expression of it," Victoria said at Yale. "The
blues allowed Blacks to sing about what they were unable to speak of
for fear of lynching. The blues allowed Blacks to sing from beyond the
veil superimposed onto them by a white supremacist, and often socio-
pathic, society. The blues allowed Blacks to step from behind the ste-
reotypes that Whites categorized 'The Negro' as, and allowed for the
full spectrum of experience that was their inner life—that theirs was
indeed a human experience. That they, too, could respond fully (and
'articulately') to the world around them. Ironically, this veil only managed to fool Whites who stood on the other side—unable to even entertain the idea that there was more to the simple, simpering Negro
than playing nanny, running elevators, and cleaning hotel rooms."

 4 ▪ Ben Miller Band, *Any Way, Shape or Form* (New West) Get hot or
go home, runs the old country-music warning; this Joplin, Missouri,
three-piece—Miller, vocals, guitar, banjo; Scott Leeper, washtub bass;
Doug Dicharry, drums, horns, mandolin, spoons, electric washboard—
aren't going home. They sound more like a train than a jug band,
even if Miller's Appalachian moan pulls back on the curves, only to
accelerate as if the train has turned into Robert Mitchum's Ford in
Thunder Road. The ancient rollin'-and-tumblin' syncopation is the engine in "Hurry Up and Wait"; the closest thing to "Burning Buildings" is the Avengers' "Car Crash"; "The Cuckoo," with "Darlin' Cory"
pieces thrown in, is as hard as the song gets. And they fool around.
They'll spend more than four minutes on a dumb-sounding joke song
that feels as if it can't be less than ten—and make you wonder if you're
missing something.

 **5 ▪ Vanessa Grigoriadas, "Justin Bieber: A Case Study in Growing Up
Cossetted and Feral," *New York* (June 30)** Grigoriadas was merciless a
few years ago on Britney Spears in *Rolling Stone*—merciless toward the
culture closing in on Spears, not her. Her vision is even darker here:
"Just a few years ago, Miley Cyrus wore a purity ring. She was worth
billions of dollars to Disney, a check in the form of four seasons of *Hannah Montana*, 10 million albums, $225 million worth of movie tickets,
a best-selling memoir, and 10 million *Hannah Montana* books. Now
she's put on her own costume—the butch femme, the funky porn star,
the whitest girl alive to lay claim to southern 'bounce' culture—
topping twerking by puffing on joints; hot-dog-riding; front-wedgie-

creating; *faux*–Clinton–and–Abe Lincoln–fellating; and grinding Madonna and kissing Katy Perry, though that's probably best understood as the latter two stars sucking her youthful blood."

6 ■ **Esmé Patterson, *Woman to Woman* (Xtra Mile)** Patterson, from Denver, had the idea of a set of answer records: what would the women in "Jolene," "Eleanor Rigby," "Caroline, No," or "Alison" say if they had the chance? What the idea turned into, especially on the floating, feather-light "A Dream," Patterson's comeback to Lead Belly's "Goodnight, Irene," is doo-wop torch songs. With a kiss-off.

7 & 8 ■ **Swans, *To Be Kind* (Young God) and Michael C. Ford, *Look Each Other in the Ears* (Hen House Studios)** Or, two versions of the Doors. Swans has been the guitarist Michael Gira's project since 1979, and the more than two hours of music he's now brought to bear is his *Winged Victory of Samothrace*, one great heroic arc. It calls up the most stately and heedless passages in the Doors' "The End" and "When the Music's Over," most inescapably on the 34-minute "Bring the Sun/Toussaint L'Overture," but also on the merely 12 minutes and 39 seconds of "Just a Little Boy (For Chester Burnett)"—and while I realize this sounds like a joke, a parody, for that matter a Doors parody, that's the point. Gira has taken on the embrace of excess and the idea of ruin that were at the heart of Jim Morrison's work, his best and his worst, without backing away from any of it—his *Winged Victory* is also his Headless Horseman—and you can imagine Morrison, now, in this band. But you can also imagine him as the kind of callow, seen-it-all-before beat poet Michael C. Ford plays on his album—a sharp, cutting, funny poetry-and-jazz number made with John Densmore, Ray Manzarek, and Robby Krieger, all of whom, along with Morrison, Ford knew and sometimes performed with around Los Angeles in the midsixties, before the Doors even were a band. The likes of "For Openers (Lost Jazz Bars in Four-Time)" or "A Simple Ode (To Frank O'Hara)" might have been a comedown from the bombast of Morrison's poetry—*Give Ford another year, let him hear "The Crystal Ship," and he'd be writing an ode to me!*—but it's better, and, by now, Morrison might even agree. To be nice.

9 ■ **Billy Sedlmayr, *Charmed Life* (Fell City)** Once Sedlmayr was everywhere in the Tucson punk scene; then for long years he was nowhere. This is his first solo album: a *True Detective* soundtrack after the fact. The case blows up with "Grapes in My Garden."

10 ■ *The Riot Grrrl Collection*, edited by Lisa Darms (Feminist Press) and Pussy Riot, *Pussy Riot! A Punk Prayer for Freedom, Letters from Prison, Songs, Poems, and Courtroom Statements, Plus Tributes to the Punk Band That Shook the World* (Feminist Press) "Written all in one house for once. Where I sleep in my closet, glue my trash to the walls," Cindy Crabb typed in the mid-nineties in number six of her fanzine *Doris*. "I haven't left San Francisco in six months it seems. I tried to leave once but it only lasted a day. I ended up taking my vacation in Stevenson alley." "Cynicism's in fashion," Masha Alyokhina of Pussy Riot writes in her poem "In Light of Current Events." "Ironic smiles and dull melancholy. / Know this: if you don't do it, possibly, no one will." In two books, people twenty years and nearly 250 years apart from each other speak the same language: that is, with newsletters, manifestoes, cartoons, screeds, rants, and confessions flying across the country then, and court statements, manifestoes, poems, songs, and prison letters flying around the world now, what looms up in the background is another revolutionary movement: the Committees of Correspondence.

December 26, 2014

1 ■ Sleater-Kinney, *No Cities to Love* (Sub Pop) Guitarists and singers Corin Tucker and Carrie Brownstein formed Sleater-Kinney in Olympia, Washington, in 1994; drummer Janet Weiss joined in 1996. Nine years after their last album and eight years since they last played a show, they sound as fresh and surprising—as unlikely, and as unsatisfied—as they did with *Call the Doctor*, *Dig Me Out*, or *All Hands on the Bad One*. The blast of fury that begins with the first seconds of the first song picks up force through "Price Tag," "Fangless" (*Yeah*, you say after the doubled voices are cut off with a note that feels like a slap, *right*), and "Surface Envy." A cloud of anger and hopelessness hangs over the music, even as whispers appear amid shouts, a stutter-step beat breaks the heedlessness of the opening numbers, echoes of the Shangri-Las and Patti Smith emerge in the singing—as you realize that "Hey Darling" could actually be something the band has never had, a radio song. You begin to hear the drumming as the most precise, knowing, furious, unforgiving voice of all. And then you hear Brownstein's and Tucker's quiet, reflective last notes coming off of Tucker's enraged deep-breaths at the end of "Bury Our Friends," and the fact of death Tucker has been railing against takes the song away from her—*Yell all you want, sister,* Death says, *I was here before you got here and I'll be here when you're gone.* But that's not the end of the record. That is "Fade," which starts where Nirvana left off, the counterpoint guitars and the high, trilling singing all but promising that this part of the Sleater-Kinney story is only at its start.

2 ▪ New Pornographers at Hammerstein Ballroom (New York, November 17) Every time I see them I break into a smile and it never leaves. Especially in their most painful moments—when Neko Case draws back for the line "That is the custom," the feeling of faith and idealism is overwhelming, and overwhelming because as the phrase is turned you understand how completely faith and idealism can disappear—their music is a celebration of life. Its complexity recalls the Gang of Four, but with seven or eight people on stage they can seem less like a band than a tribe, which is why when Dan Bejar deigns to stroll out and favor the crowd and the rest of the group with a tune, the gesture rings hollow, despite how good he is (he knows). The melodies are nimble, and they don't seem to start with any one person. All sounds swirl—even a guitar solo feels as if it's coming from the group. "You guys are so wonderful," someone shouted from the audience. "Thank you."

3 ▪ Spencer Day, "Why Don't You Do Right" and the New Standards, "Fever," at "Downtown Sings Peggy Lee: A Book Launch Celebration," Joe's Pub (New York, November 10) For James Gavin's *Is That All There Is? The Strange Life of Peggy Lee* (Atria), Spencer Day, all scarves hung on an elegantly Praying Mantis frame, wove his way through one of Lee's signature tunes, less singing the song than breathing it: it had no beginning, it had no end, it merely floated off into the air as he left the stage. Pianist Chan Poling of the New Standards, a trio from Minneapolis—with Steve Roehm on vibes and bassist John Munson—attacked "Fever" as if it were a wild animal, which had to be tracked, circled, and finally trapped, all with a demeanor of calm and menace, all good will burnt off like a bad tattoo. Both singers made you want to read the book.

4 ▪ Edvard Munch Room, Nasjonalmuseet, Oslo (July 18) There's a small crowd in front of one of Munch's versions of his *Madonna* (1894–95). There's no one in front of *The Day After*. In a city where you see women on the street so blond they've gone to some dimension of color beyond white, *Madonna* is the dark-haired sex demon, her arms behind her head and back, head lolling to the side, a line of red under the left breast, as if someone—she herself?—has tried to cut it off. It's the sexiest image in the world. It's all power, command, and most threateningly knowledge, the face of someone who has seen all around life, existence, and history.

In *The Day After*, a Bohemian dream painted around the same time, a woman lies on her back on a bed, bottles on a table at the side. Her dark hair tumbles off the bed. One knee is bent and raised; she's unconscious or she doesn't care. Her white blouse is open—there's a streak of red down the middle, and below her breasts a smear of blood, or a symbolic scarlet letter. They're the same woman, certainly, sacred and profane, mythical and real, and all that, but the sense of the link, or the identity of the two, is at once stronger and more prosaic. Each is dreaming of the other. Each is the fantasy of the other. Each is living out the life the other most wants.

A few days later we were checking into a dismal hotel in Bergen. The front desk was a tiny stand in a narrow corridor, with, on the left wall, a huge and gross remake of Norway's most famous painting, Munch's *The Scream*. Waiting for someone to show up, wondering if there was a buzzer or a bell or if you should just shout, you looked at the picture and said to yourself, yes, that's exactly right.

5–7 ▪ Viv Albertine, *Clothes Clothes Clothes Music Music Music Boys Boys Boys* (Thomas Dunne Books); *The Vermillion Border* (Cadiz, 2012); Mark Paytress, "Viv Albertine," *Mojo* (August) Albertine's blazing, rueful memoir about her time in the Slits in late-seventies London, her marriage, her years in the wilderness in a lovely house, her rediscovery of her own punk guitarist's fingers, is summed up by her last exchange with interviewer Mark Paytress. He mentions her writing that "because I grew up with music that was trying to change the world that's what I still expect from it" and that the singer she'd most like to sound like is Karen Carpenter, then offers a meliorative cliché: "Perhaps love and music work best as revolution in the head?" Albertine, who turned sixty this month, comes back as a Slit, when she and the other women in the band used to go up to strangers and tell them that the way they dressed or sang or talked was holding women back: "Except those love songs aren't a revolution; they keep you down, like bundles of sweets with poison inside, I've been utterly brainwashed. I can't undo that conditioning. All those love songs are a curse. When I hear them, I think, Please don't let that keep going into girls' heads." The solo album Albertine made two years ago is of a piece with those words, and her book. She makes the sound of a real person living a real life, and with an irreducible element of art, of fashioning, of fiction, always figuring in the songs. "I Want More," "Confessions of a MILF," "Don't Believe," "Little Girl in a Box"—these pieces aren't autobiography, they're experience translated into the sardonic. Until the last number, "Still England," a chirpy rundown of heroes from Emmeline Pankhurst to Sally Potter—scores of them—that's the flipside of the chapter near the end of *Clothes Clothes Clothes* titled "Lives Well Lived": Albertine's obituaries for old comrades Malcolm McLaren, Steve New, Ari Up, and Poly Styrene.

8 ▪ Mark Ruffalo and Keira Knightley in *Begin Again*, written and directed by John Carney (Weinstein Company) In his best romantic roles—*In the Cut, Life Without Me, The Kids Are Alright*—Mark Ruffalo carries a unique authority, maybe because when he walks into a situation he makes you believe he doesn't want it, wouldn't know what to do with it if he did. It works in *Begin Again*, where his character has lost whatever authority he had; all he can do is act big, with the fear coming through like a sunbeam full of dust. Keira Knightley's hopeful singer-songwriter is talking to his fallen record company hot shot. "I just think that an A & R man telling people how they should dress, or come across, is total *bullshit*," she says. "People don't want that, they want *authenticity*." "OK, babe," Ruffalo says, that *babe* meant to take away whatever authority she might have. "Authenticity. Give me the name of *one artist* who you think passes your authenticity test." Knightley thinks for her answer, gets it, lifts her head in a smug, that's-all-she-wrote toss: "Dylan." "Dylan," Ruffalo says, letting you know he's heard it a thousand times. "That is the most cultivated artist that you could have thought of. Look at his hair, his sunglasses, he changes his look every decade—" Knightley's face goes blank, then lights up: "*Randy Newman.*" "I fucking love Randy Newman," Ruffalo says, sick of the game he's playing, happy to lose. "You got me on that."

9 ■ **Edward Weston, *Nude* (about 1918), in "Truth and Beauty: Pictorialist Photography," Museum of Fine Arts, Boston (December 5)** Made, the wall card said, "when Weston's social circle was growing more bohemian": with hooded eyes glowing in the shadows cast by her tangled hair, the model looks at the photographer so piercingly you can imagine him bursting into flames. It could be Weston's attempt to translate Munch's Madonna into silver. But it also looks frighteningly like Barbara Stanwyck, and though it couldn't be—Stanwyck was in New York when Weston was, but she was only eleven in 1918—the picture foreshadows everything she would bring to the movies no one else did.

10 ■ **Bob Dylan at the Beacon Theater, New York (December 3)** There were many centers of gravity, where songs took on a new depth, where you could hear them as unfinished stories—of a piece with what Dylan did on November 23, when, before a show in Philadelphia, he played a four-song set for a single audience member (Swedish TV stunt, don't ask), and the highlight was a slow, ruminative version of Fats Domino's "Blueberry Hill" so full of death it would have sounded just right on *Time Out of Mind*. At the Beacon, the first crack in the ice that can form around familiar songs came with "Workingman's Blues," the melody pulled out, the pace ground down—all a look back, to when the word *workingman* had some dignity. Here the "sing a little bit of these workingman's blues" hit home, because now that's all anyone can expect: nothing. "Pay in Blood" came off like a Clint Eastwood spaghetti western. "Tangled Up in Blue" was a novel, seeming longer than any time before, truly tangled, turning into the rambling yarn of "New Danville Girl." Dylan stretched lines out. "*Soooooon* to be divorced" took pleasure in pure music-making—and it was the first hint of the expansive, four-lane-highway voice he was holding in reserve. "Lovesick" had a harsh, south-of-the-border feel, a sense of the nighttime opening of *Touch of Evil*. "Highwater" was almost a comedy by comparison—because it really is funny. But it was the comedy of a survivor sneering at those who didn't make it: this song will never hit bottom. There was the violin-led chamber music of the great "Forgetful Heart"—its roots in Arthur Smith's 1938 "Adieu False Heart" came to the surface as never before. There was "Scarlet Town," a mystery about time and place that's a thing in itself, with "the streets have names that you can't pronounce"—and the guy who's telling you this was born there.

The killer was "Long and Wasted Years." It was presented as such, with Dylan strutting back and forth, setting the stage for something big. And it was big—the music, but mostly the voice. It was bigger verse by verse, huge, then enormous, then too big for the hall, not a crack in tone, a voice that wore the lives it had lived like old clothes, a voice with a hint of snake oil—the carny barker of the gods, the medicine-show pitchman whose stuff really does cure all ills, but can also strike you dead, because it can tell the saved from the damned. It was fun, it was transporting, with the feel of a Davy Crockett or Abe Lincoln tall-tale teller in there too—I wear a bear for a hat, I comb my hair with a wagon wheel, I bring the house down.

So it made sense to encore with a supper-club version of "Blowin' in the Wind." The nice, bland setting gave the old warhorse a sting, a bite, it usually hides in its own falsely innocent righteousness. The song itself was always bland, but "Too many people have died" hit home out in this supper club, because you're not supposed to talk about that sort of thing in a place like that.

Thanks to Howard Hampton, Jasmine Hagans, and Robert Christgau.

January 19, 2015

1 ■ **Rhiannon Giddens, *Tomorrow Is My Turn* (Nonesuch)** In the Carolina Chocolate Drops, Giddens's voice is the one you wait for, and when you watch Giddens as part of the so-called New Basement Tapes band in Sam Jones's documentary *Lost Songs*—with Marcus Mumford, Elvis Costello, Jim James, and Taylor Goldsmith, she's searching for music for a cache of recently discovered 1967 Bob Dylan lyrics—you realize her talent is bottomless. Throwing out rehearsal lines for "Lost on the River"—on the album of the same name, the only performance

to redeem the song-fixing concept—the soulfulness is almost too elegant to bear; the suspense in the movie comes from the looming possibility that as the group runs through one false start or misbegotten arrangement after another, the song will really be lost.

On her first solo album, Giddens opens at the top, with Geeshie Wiley's 1930 "Last Kind Words Blues." Over the last twenty years the song has become a talisman of the way that some blues can never be solved. You can't know where they came from, what the singer meant to say, what the song says, only where the song leaves you: stranded, alone, wanting nothing as much as to hear it one more time. With a smeared sound, Colin Linden's rhythm guitar sets time in motion; Giddens sings from a step behind him, and the song itself is a step behind her, as if to say there's no way to sing this song that's not too fast. Everything you say could be a lie; every hiding word in Wiley's original could be something else. Does she say "rich man" or "Richmond"? "Blessèd" or "precious"? Does Wiley promise to see her lover when she crosses the deep blue sea, or does she say she won't? "The Mississippi river, you know it's deep and wide," Wiley says, but does she follow with the strange "I can stand right here / See my baby from the other side," or the much stranger "See my face"? What Giddens does with this line is beyond uncanny: she sings both words at once.

After that, the record flags. Covers of Odetta's "Waterboy," the Kingston Trio's "Round About the Mountain," Nina Simone's "Tomorrow Is My Turn," and the traditional "Black Is the Color" are at once frozen in homage and overwrought, and you're thrown straight into a 1960s overpriced nightclub, and whoever Giddens is that isn't someone else disappears. She sounds more at home with Patsy Cline's "She's Got You" and Dolly Parton's "Don't Let It Trouble Your Mind," but she doesn't bring anything to the songs they didn't. It's not until the end—with the songster Libby Cotton's "Shake Sugaree," the ancient Appalachian air "O Love Is Teasin,'" and Giddens's own "Angel City"—that the swing goes through the air again, and you want to know more.

2 ■ Lo-Fang, "You're the One That I Want," Chanel No. 5 commercial, directed by Baz Luhrmann (Regal Theaters) A mesmerizingly unrecognizable lounge version of the Olivia Newton-John/John Travolta hit, almost breathing life into a playlet about infinite wealth so soulless the model Giselle Bündchen comes across more like a variously upholstered piece of furniture than anything resembling a person.

3 ▪ "Picasso & the Camera," curated by John Richardson, Gagosian Gallery, New York (December 16, closed January 3) With small photos mounted on a board, taken in Picasso's studio around 1908, you can feel the beginning of the century, a new time about to seize its own voice, to assert the priority of its own eye. The war hasn't happened yet; it's not the ruling fact. What is is Cubism, and the conviction that Picasso and Braque and whoever can follow their lines are going where no one has been before. It's a manifesto implicit in Picasso's smile, and the smiles on the faces in the mockups and sketches behind him that will become *Demoiselles d'Avignon: What you can imagine, you can see. What you can see, you can paint. What you can paint, you can build. And if you can build it, you can live in it.* In photos from after the war, there's a sense of depression, of constriction. No matter how great the Olga paintings can be, there's no larger world present; it's all painterly. There's no hint of utopia, no claim of freedom: the world is not going to be remade. You can live wherever you like, and defeat will move right in with you.

4 ▪ Barry Day, *The World of Raymond Chandler—In His Own Words* (Vintage) A portrait of the mystery writer, his detective, and the Los Angeles he created as surely as Samuel Goldwyn or William Mulholland, drawn from Chandler's books, stories, letters, and essays—with Day, who has produced eleven books on Noël Coward, as a guest at a dinner party to which he was not invited, constantly interrupting (quotations are littered with ellipses) and offering supercilious comments to make it clear that whatever people are talking about is not really worth his time. Unreadable.

5 ▪ *The World Made Straight*, directed by David Burris, written by Shane Danielsen (Bifrost Pictures) "What are we listening to?" says Haley Joel Osment's layabout to Noah Wyle's Leonard, a disgraced former high-school teacher now dealing dope out of his trailer. "'Appalachian Spring' by Copland," Wyle says. "Never heard of it," Osment says. "Used to open for Skynyrd," Wyle says. Set in the early 1970s in Madison County, North Carolina, where at the time the oldest, most unchanging American folk sounds were still making themselves felt, it's a no-way-out story carried most of all by the folk singer Steve Earle, who underplays his role as the local Mr. Big so convincingly you get the feeling he tired of his life long ago and keeps going simply because no one else in the place can fill his shoes.

6 ▪ Bruce Conner, note posted by Thomas Gladysz, Louise Brooks Society blog (November 18, 2012) The silent-film actress Louise Brooks (1906–85) left Kansas for Los Angeles in 1922; when her career faded away she opened a dance studio in Wichita. The artist and filmmaker Bruce Conner (1933–2008) left Wichita for San Francisco in 1957. One day in 1997 he left a note at a local Louise Brooks exhibition: "I wanted to take dancing lessons from Louise Brooks when she moved back to Wichita in the 1940's. My parents wouldn't let me. They spoke to each other about her 'scandalous' relationship to her young male students."

Which if nothing else demands a double feature: Conner's 1966 music short *Breakaway*, with Toni Basil dancing her clothes off with such lightning cuts you barely notice, and Brooks's 1929 *Pandora's Box*. Conner would be smiling; Brooks would probably be complaining he didn't cast *her*.

7 ▪ *Syl Johnson: Any Way the Wind Blows*, directed by Rob Hatch-Miller (SylJohnsonmovie.com) Still in production,* but an interview moment from a documentary about a mostly forgotten soul singer from the 1970s, on a digital second career, his records sampled by everyone from Wu-Tang Clan to Kid Rock to Jay-Z and Kanye West, often with no credit and no money. "They sampled you?" says Hatch-Miller, speaking of En Vogue's "Free Your Mind." "No, they didn't sample me," Johnson says. "They stole my music. And my sound and my style. You call it a sample if you want to, that's easy. Sample. That's like somebody steals the tire off your car and you say, 'Well, they sampled my car.' What'd they do? They took the tire. So they sampled it."

---

* Rob Hatch-Miller provided this update in 2021: "The Syl film has unfortunately been stuck in distribution limbo for years now, primarily due to the fact that EMI and Al Green were never willing to give us anything close to an indie documentary rate for the composition 'Take Me to the River,' which is used in the film several times since it was the biggest hit Syl ever had. We had the rights to the song for festival use, but we've never been able to find a distributor for the film that was willing to pay an advance large enough to cover anything close to that one substantial license fee we still owe. All the bigger distributors like Netflix passed on the film, and the smaller distributors that did show interest were unwilling to put much money toward releasing it. It's frustrating, Syl's family has been trying to help us find a distributor or an investor/donor to help get us over that final hump but so far no luck. The film leaked onto some pirate sites and YouTube for a while, but we've tried our best to flag any copyright violations and keep it offline while we hold out hope that someday the film will have a proper commercial release through a streaming service and/or video on-demand platforms."

8 ▪ **White Lung,** *Deep Fantasy* **(Domino)** From Vancouver, Mish Way sings and Kenneth William plays guitar so fast you'd think the disease the band named itself for—asbestosis—is chasing them. The feeling—which catches winds still blowing from the 1970s with Wire and the Avengers, the 1980s with Sonic Youth, Fucked Up today—is heedless and terrified, until halfway through a song the singer finds her feet in the story she's telling. The storm seems to pause; you can hear the pulse of drummer Anne-Marie Vassiliou before Williams pulls Way off her feet again. But what makes the drama this band creates truly unsettling is the suppression in the sound. It's so muffled everything sounds far away—Way could be singing from the bottom of a cave—or on the verge of being forgotten. Maybe that's where the panic comes from—and the thrill.

9 & 10 ▪ *Selma,* **directed by Ava DuVernay (Paramount) and John Legend and Common, "Glory" (ARTium/Def Jam)** Here the wonderfully bug-eyed Stephen Root—moving over from his role as the blind radio man in *O Brother, Where Art Thou?*—is an aide to George Wallace when the Alabama governor asks if there's some way Selma Sheriff Jim Clark can be convinced to back off: "Look, George, I'm tellin' you, if the Lord Jesus and Elvis Presley come visitin' and they said 'Jim, now, we need you to treat them niggers nice,' Jim Clark would beat the shit out a the pair of 'em and throw 'em in jail." "I don't write white racist very well," DuVernay has said about why she kept screenwriter Paul Webb's "zinger"—which in a way points toward the reappearance of Jesus, if not Elvis, at the very end of the film, with Common, in the film playing the activist James Bevel as a man whose face and carriage are so powerful he doesn't need lines, now speaking over John Legend's singing as the credits roll over their "Glory."

The song sets the finale of the film far in the future, so that when Common's "That's why Rosa sat on the bus / That's why we walk through Ferguson with our hands up" arrives in the song it hits like lightning. There's something tremendously modest about the passion Common and Legend bring to the music—their tone says they're just tiny actors in a story they are privileged to be part of. It was a stance carried forward in Common's acceptance speech for Best Original Song at the Golden Globes, because you knew that if he and Legend win at the Oscars, he'll never be permitted to speak for so long, and so interestingly, and so eloquently: "As I got to know people of the civil rights movement, I realized: I am the hopeful black woman who was denied her right to vote; I am the caring white supporter, killed on the front lines of freedom; I am the unarmed black kid who maybe needed a hand but was instead given a bullet; I am the two fallen police officers murdered in the line of duty."

February 25, 2015

1 ▪ D'Angelo, *Black Messiah* (RCA) With whirling cries, moans, shouts, fadeaways, then more moans, more cries—the sound of lost souls finding themselves—the first track, "Ain't That Easy," opens a door to the secret room behind Sly and the Family Stone's "Thank You for Talkin' to Me Africa" on their 1971 *There's a Riot Goin' On*. The song at once proves that no one has caught up with that music, and that it's fallen to D'Angelo to make the follow-up album—a notion perhaps confirmed here with the "Side A"/"Side B" configuration of the then standard twelve LP tracks, each keyed with the sound of a needle dropping into the opening groove. It's a promise immediately fulfilled with "1000 Deaths," where a social context *Riot* sketched in shadows explodes all over the place: a funk beat builds over a preacher calling down the fight between Jesus and the Devil, crowds gather, speakers try to tell them what to think, voices are distorted beyond comprehension, then something like a chorus emerges, the hands-up raised arms on the album cover come to life, leaving the listener stranded between then and now, uncertain if the words make any difference. There is no center here, no fixed point around which the songs revolve—each one calls up its own time and place, and then takes its place in some greater song. You begin to drift into the pleasure of the music, its delight in a blinking stroll down the street, everything in a half-light, the ordinary miraculous.

2 ▪ Paula Rabinowitz, *American Pulp: How Paperbacks Brought Modernism to Main Street* (Princeton) In this unfailingly fascinating study, one image stood out, in its way far more vulgar than the lurid covers for the likes of Fletcher Flora's *Leave Her to Hell!* ("She went too far—too often"), Martha Gellhorn's *Liana*, or Irving Schulman's

The Amboy Dukes: the jacket for the 1948 Bantam edition of John Hersey's *Hiroshima.* Against an orange sky, a couple, both dressed exactly like middle-class or professional Americans, walks down the road, a woman with long, light-brown hair hanging her head, a brown-haired man looking back at standing buildings and an undamaged American car. It's blackface in reverse, whiting out inconvenient dark people, not to mention reconstructing a vaporized city while keeping the specter of doom hovering in the title, and the result is a complete absurdity: *The shocking true story of Americans caught in a firestorm meant to save them!*

3 ■ **Murder Vibes,** *Murder Vibes* **(murdervibes.com)** From Seattle, with computer beats by Jordan Evans, vocals and guitar by Peter Hanks, and play-it-all-day-long irresistible once you're sucked into its miasma. Remember Alphaville, the moody German synth band who got their "Forever Young" into every high-school graduation in the land by the end of the eighties? This is the Alphaville they'll be playing at funerals where nobody comes.

4 ■ *The Newsroom,* **"What Kind of Day Has It Been?" (HBO, December 14, 2014)** The last episode, set around the funeral for network president Charlie Skinner (Sam Waterson), but serried with flashbacks: "Name that tune," says Skinner as Jeff Daniels's anchor Will McEvoy walks into his office and Skinner snaps off his desktop boombox. It's Tom T. Hall's "That's How I Got to Memphis." Skinner's grandson has a band: "So, I was at their house last weekend, wandered out to the garage, saw Beau teaching 'That's How I Got to Memphis' to his friend, so I asked him, 'Why's a kid from New Rochelle singing about Memphis?' He said, 'Memphis is a stand-in for wherever you are right now. It really means, that's how I got here.'"

Later, after the service, Daniels talks with Jared Prokop's Beau, picks up a guitar, and begins the song. Beau, who looks uncannily like a sixteen-year-old Ricky Nelson, comes in on stand-up bass; John Gallagher Jr.'s reporter Jim Hall picks up a guitar too. They walk through the song like a road they've walked over and over without ever failing to find something new along the way. It may be corny. It may be a restaging of the Howard Hawks scene where the cast becomes a family through a song. It's a tough, beaten piece of fatalism: a great song.

5 ▪ **One Republic, "Counting Stars" (Mosley/Interscope)** This has been all over the radio for more than a year, and every time I hear it the plug-in moral catchphrases ("Everything that kills me makes me feel alive") sound more earned, the desire in Ryan Tedder's voice more real. It's the whiplash in the rhythm—the song never leaves you in the same spot long enough to register it.

6 ▪ **Bob Dylan, *Shadows in the Night* (Columbia)** Dylan approaches Sinatra the way he slipped into the old blues and folk songs of *Good as I Been to You* and *World Gone Wrong* more than twenty years ago: like someone putting on clothes older than that that still fit. It's the Sinatra of *The Manchurian Candidate* and *No One Cares*, with the singer in his trench coat and fedora sitting at a bar looking at his drink while the party swirls on all around him; it's the Dylan of "You Belong to Me" on the soundtrack of *Natural Born Killers*, fingers rubbing a magic lamp, but not hard enough to release the genie, because then the song would be over. But hard enough to turn Sinatra's 1963 movie theme "Stay with Me," written for Otto Preminger's *The Cardinal* by Jerome Moross and Carolyn Leigh, back into Stephen Foster's "Hard Times."

7 ▪ **Mannequin Pussy, *Gypsy Pervert* (mannequinpussy.bandcamp .com LP or cassette)** It may be under twenty minutes but there are ten albums here. Singer and guitarist Marisita Dabeast, drummer Drew Adler and second guitarist Athanasios Paul like music, and they have the damning punk spirit the Kills lost just like that.

8 ▪ **Harvey Kubernik, *Turn Up the Radio! Rock, Pop, and Roll in Los Angeles, 1956–1972* (Santa Monica Press)** A golden-age coffee table book, and memorable for all sorts of left-field comment, as with the writer Daniel Weizmann on Phil Spector: "Phil was born on Christmas Day in 1940. But I see him as the first truly post-Holocaust American Jew. He refused to grovel and play the Borscht Belt guy, the entertainment guy. Yes, he had one foot in that old world grandiosity. His music was for the new utopian, free-spirited teenagers, but it also contained the secret mania of having grown up with the shadow of genocide and the bomb. He meant business. In a way, he is the link between Lenny Bruce and Bob Dylan."

9 ▪ **Rolling Stones, "Gimmie Shelter," as used in preview for *The Gambler* (Regal Union Square Theater, New York, December 17)** As the song helicoptered over desperate characters, you could imagine none of them had ever heard it before: every note had grown new tentacles, which wrapped around themselves as the song played. Maybe the producers somehow got their hands on the real, occult version of the song, hidden for forty-five years—or maybe the displacement of the sound was right there in something the old-timey fiddler Tommy Jarrell once said: "Ain't nobody mastered the fiddle. There's notes in that fiddle ain't nobody found." But it didn't seem to be a new mix—there was nothing like this in the online version of the trailer. It had to be the sound system in the theater—so ten days later I went back to see how the song worked in the movie. It wasn't in the movie.

10 ▪ ***Better Call Saul,* Episode 1, directed by Vince Gilligan (AMC, February 8)** The show—Albuquerque lawyer with a haircut he hasn't heard went into a museum before he asked for it who makes ambulance chasing sound like white shoe—is fine. But the black-and-white lead-in with a middle-aged man working in a Cinnabon—who's either got an eye for a hunk who's got an eye for him, or who's hiding under a false name and has just been clocked—is the best film noir since Ellen Barkin's black-and-white lead-ins to *Theme Time Radio Hour.*

March 27, 2015

1 ▪ **Sonny Til and the Orioles, *Live in Chicago 1951* (Uptown)** The vocal quintet from Baltimore are three years into their career and still scoring hits; their biggest, "Crying in the Chapel," is two years ahead of them. With "It's Too Soon to Know," from 1948, they brought doubt, contingency, jeopardy—the sense of possibility and extinction that was the common dream of the immediate postwar period—onto the radio. This night there are small, even trivial songs, and a lovely close—"What Are You Doing New Year's Eve?" and the graceful "So Long"—but "It's Too Soon to Know" remains the well from which every element in their sound that made them different, that made them new, will always be drawn.

"Does she love me?" is the opening line. Sonny Til hangs the first two words over the song, refusing to let it begin. You can believe, in the moment, that it will stop right there and they'll walk off the stage, knowing there can never be an answer.

Often when a group plays a hit they speed it up, to compensate for its familiarity; Til slows it down, drastically, so that the listener hangs onto the music. It's scary—how are these singers going to get out of the song? The soul in the performance deepens. Til holds the word "die," but not its note, for ten seconds—it sounds easier than it is—but it doesn't feel like a trick. People around a table in the club laugh, maybe at something one of them said, maybe at the melodrama. Til follows by holding the note on "to"—"I can't wait," another Oriole says as Til begins to float across the ceiling of the song—for sixteen seconds. "I think you got this one by yourself," the second voice says. A woman laughs. There isn't a trace of melisma. He is stopping time, and you don't want it to move on.

2 ▪ Sleater-Kinney, First Avenue, Minneapolis (Valentine's Day) "They have more expensive haircuts," said a friend as we pushed our way up near the stage. Carrie Brownstein was half-blonde ("I'm going back to brown," she said in San Francisco three weeks later), and she did most of the talking (no *Hello, Minneapolis!* but a tribute to David Carr, who came from there) and most of the moving, but Corin Tucker, off to the side, was the visual rock, and the source of the most piercing noise. Every third song was like a rocket—it took off, there was a rush, and then you could feel it escape its own gravity the way a missile drops its fuel tanks. For their first shows since 2006, Brownstein, Tucker, and drummer Janet Weiss (with unintroduced visitor Katie Harkin in the shadows, moving from guitar to keyboards to tambourine—"I like to lurk," she said later) played songs mostly from the new *No Cities to Love* and the 2005 *The Woods*, their last album before it—when they shot out "Call the Doctor," from 1996, the song gave the shock the band delivered when they first arrived, the chant so mean you felt like pulling out your phone to do what they said.

3 ▪ *House of Cards*, Season 3, Episode 3 (Netflix) At a White House state dinner for the Russian president—named Viktor Petrov but wearing Vladimir Putin's saturnine face—Nadya Tolokonnikova and Masha Alyokhina of Pussy Riot, playing themselves and looking as if they just stepped out of the pages of *Elle*, are among the guests. When Petrov speaks, they stand and denounce him—and anyone who saw the two women beaten for speaking out, merely on a street, during the Crimea Olympics can believe they'd do exactly that. Petrov offers a conciliatory, above-it-all toast: *Whatever our differences, we are united in our love of our country*, etc. Tolokonnikova and Alyokhina turn their glasses upside down and dump their champagne on the table and walk out.

You can see people dismissing the two of them as sellouts to glamour, turning their backs on their comrades in Russia to hobnob with Kevin Spacey and Robin Wright, living it up in New York, appearing in a high-profile TV show in gorgeous dresses after a $600 afternoon at the hairdresser's. But from bright colors to eye shadow, glamour was never not part of Pussy Riot, or its Ukrainian-French-Tunisian cousin Femen. As Masha Gessen's *Words Will Break Cement: The Passion of Pussy Riot* makes clear, the group was always more of an agitprop video collective than the "punk rock band" they were named in the media. In that sense their few minutes in *House of Cards* is simply one more video—and that it was directed by Tucker Gates, not Pussy Riot, doesn't keep it from being something you want to watch again and again.

4 ▪ Bruce Jenkins is a sportswriter for the *San Francisco Chronicle* and the author of *Goodbye: In Search of Gordon Jenkins*. As he is the son of Frank Sinatra's finest producer, I asked him what he thought of Bob Dylan's *Shadows in the Night*. He wrote back: "I left my canvassing tools behind. I didn't want to know what any music critic felt about Dylan's project, or hear any bitter resentment over such a radical departure from the Sinatra mood. I listened to this album strictly from the perspective of being Gordon Jenkins' son—and I have to tell you, I found it quite sweet and tender.

"My father always said that he and Sinatra made 'September of My Years' at exactly the right time (1965) of their lives: mid-fifties, harboring untold memories of lost love and heartbreak, but still absolutely in their prime. I'm so glad to hear Dylan, in his interviews, speak to this. At his peak, he was far too contemporary to pay much attention to Sinatra. He wrote the smartest lyrics of his generation (and of many others, I might add) and spoke to the people right then and there. It seems that as a lover of words, though, he stashed certain lyrics in the back of his mind, deeply meaningful passages from songs he knew would stand up over time.

"He dug the melodies, too. And it was such a good idea to abandon any reliance upon strings, horns, or even the piano. That's been done. Dylan went into the studio with a wonderful pedal steel player, Donny Herron, who carried the instrumentals along with two guitarists, a bass player, and a percussionist. The result is a decidedly fresh interpretation of some classic material, and if Dylan's voice sounds a little raw, hey, the man's been belting 'em out for decades. My father used to get up and leave the room if some half-baked singer appeared on television, and Dylan's work might have driven him crazy after two or three bars. For me—and this is so crucial—the feeling is there, and if a Sinatra-Jenkins record strikes the image of a well-worn fellow pondering his fate in some lonesome tavern, Dylan resurrects it to perfection.

"I wonder if any of the old-school aficionados noticed a glowing tribute to my father's work at the end of Dylan's version of 'Where Are You.' Herron replicates the ending exactly: same key, the same four notes repeated, and then the finishing chord. How fine to hear just a touch of the old man in there, before drifting back into Dylan's special world."

5 ▪ **Walter Mosley, *Rose Gold* (Doubleday)** As Easy Rawlins mysteries go, this missing-rich-girl number, set in 1967, seems tired of its plot almost before it begins. But the subject of the Easy Rawlins novels has always been an investigation—an interrogation—of racism in postwar Southern California, and it's that strain of the book that gives it life. Rawlins puts flesh on Ralph Ellison's *Invisible Man*: as a detective, he says in a blues cadence that itself leaves almost no traces in the prose, white people "don't see me comin', don't know when I'm there, and couldn't tell you when I left." "Are you going to answer my questions?" an FBI agent asks Rawlins. "I am not," he says. "The freedom I had to refuse," he says to himself, "had its own history. Millions of people had died, and there were those who were still dying for my freedom to say no." That and much more comes to bear in a paragraph near the end of the book, when Rawlins goes to see an Indian named Redbird. Rawlins calls him "The-ha," "the last of the Taaqtam": when he's with him, Rawlins says, "I had the feeling I'd left white, European, and English America behind." "Redbird was a country unto himself, an independent nation that would fight to the death for the sanctity of its sovereignty," Rawlins says, taking the long view, then circling back to the present like a man planting stakes in the ground. "He would have let me walk away if he wasn't in a war to save the daughter of a woman, a vestige of his prior colonization, who had to be appeased for an obscure article in some ancient treaty, written in a dead language."

6 & 7 ▪ Parsonsfield, "Moonshiner" and Zoe Muth & the Lost High Rollers, "Country Blues," from *Signature Sounds 20th Anniversary Collection—Rarities from the Second Decade* (Signature Sounds) Parsonsfield is from Connecticut—in an age of artisanal bird feeders and terroir gin, you think they don't have moonshine stills in Connecticut? Their version of this ancient mountain standard couldn't be more ghostly, delicate, and thrilling—they hold the song back from itself, as if they're half afraid of it, and then, with a drumstick coming down hard, they dive all the way in. When you hear them sing the ancient lines "Then I'll go to some barroom / And drink with my friends / Where the women can't follow / And see what I spend," there's nothing old about the lines at all; they could be walking into the corner bar. The Texas singer Zoe Muth brings a light, slightly bent tone to the wastrel's tale "Country Blues." The Virginian Dock Boggs recorded the definitive version in 1927; Muth takes the song west, and back in time, giving the song to cowboys in Wyoming in 1892, just before the start of the Johnson County War. As her band sets a light, quick pulse, she skips across the tune, letting the melody shape her words, or the whole sense of being in the world, or out of it, that the song wants its singer to describe. She goes into her grave in the last verse, but you can see her rising out of it as if she's just getting out of bed.

8 ▪ Tommy Lee Jones, "Weevily Wheat," in *The Homesman,* directed by Tommy Lee Jones (EuropaCorp) At the end of this bitter western— "Nebraska Death Trip," as one person watching put it—Tommy Lee Jones, who seems to be physically disintegrating when we meet him, tries to put the whole terrible story behind him. In the dark, he steps onto a barge on the Missouri River and begins to sing a song Laura Ingalls Wilder quotes in *On the Banks of Plum Creek.* He's drunk, he's firing his pistol back at Iowa, he's going back to Nebraska to die, he's dancing a jig, and the scene, almost frozen in the half-light, is familiar. Jones has precisely restaged one of the great western paintings,

George Caleb Bingham's 1846 *The Jolly Flatboatmen,* and produced the sense of satisfaction you can get when the people in a picture lodged deep in your memory get up and walk.

9 ▪ Petula Clark, "La Nuit N'en Finit Plus," in *Two Days, One Night,* written and directed by Jean-Pierre and Luc Dardennes (Les Films du Fleuve) A young Belgian woman and her husband—Marion Cotillard and Fabrizio Rongione—are driving. She's desperately trying to round up co-workers to forgo a bonus so she can keep her job. The Petula Clark record—a 1964 rewrite of Jackie DeShannon's aching "Needles and Pins," a song so painful it makes Clark sound like Chrissie Hynde and even its elegant rhythm feels made out of doom—comes on the radio. Rongione turns it off. "Stop protecting me," Cotillard says. "I'm not protecting you," he says as he turns it back on. "You are. You thought the song was too depressing for me." "Well, it's not exactly—" She turns it up, and laughs at him with her eyes. These people weren't born when this song was made, but it's their music like the air they breathe.*

10 ▪ Bobby Donnie, *Bobbie Donny Sings the Bobby Donnie Songs* (Ehse) The Baltimore Sound, coming on seventy years later, and as unfixed as it ever was. There are primitive drums, played by songwriter Stephanie Barber, and crude guitar, played by Joan Sullivan, as there were when Corin Tucker and Tracy Sawyer formed Heavens to Betsy in Olympia, Washington, in 1991, and traded off on their two instruments. The first song here, "Birthday," echoes Heavens to Betsy's harrowing 1992 "Baby's Gone," but without the harrow: nobody dies, but the same feelings, of confusion, guilt, defiance, are there. The songs crack, bend, come apart, crawl back together. The singing is flat, sometimes toneless, and some people will find the music an unbearable sick joke; it could also be the Slits' first rehearsal in 1976. That "Birthday" and "Baby's Gone" sound so close to each other is likely not influence but accident, or coding—a song the form generates in search of itself.

---

* "Thank you for reminding me of this moment," a friend said. "'Who'd have thought,' I remember thinking at the time, 'that Pet Clark could cover a song more memorably than the Ramones?'"

April 29, 2015

1 ▪ War on Women, *War on Women* (Bridge Nine) Shawna Potter is in the lead of this Baltimore band; with guitarists Nancy Hornbug and Brooks Harlan, bassist Sue Werner, and drummer Evan Tanner, she makes the war real and the counterattack irresistible. A harsh wash of blithering riot grrrl noise—in different songs you can hear echoes of Sonic Youth, Sleater-Kinney, the Gits, Blondie on "Rip Her to Shreds"—pushes Potter back, and measure by measure, song by song, she crawls forward, screams out what she needs to say, and is pushed back again. "Roe v. World" reads like a programmatic lesson plan—it starts with a recording of a prissy, bored-sounding teacher offering just that, and then it's a ferocious version of the Gang of Four's "Paralyzed," or an answer record to the Sex Pistols' "Bodies." "I had an abortion! I had an abortion! I HAD AN ABORTION!"—Potter is giving a speech against a Led Zeppelin hammer of lesser gods. She's wilder with every repetition, not toward derangement but maybe a demonstration of how hard it is to be heard when people don't want to hear what you have to say. Or how you say it.

2 ▪ Wailers, "Redemption Song" (Island, 1980) I walked into 1010 Washington Wine & Spirits in Minneapolis; this was on the sound system, but you can't shop to it. You can't daydream. You can't have a conversation. You have to stop and listen, then contemplate how small and incomplete you are, how you've failed to leave anything in the world with a hint of the weight of this song.

3 ▪ Karl Ove Knausgaard, *My Struggle: Book Four,* translated from the Norwegian by Don Bartlett (Archipelago) It's 1985: the character named Karl Ove Knausgaard is sixteen and wants to be a rock critic: "In the evening I browsed through my old music magazines and studied the record reviews and articles. There were three kinds of writer, I concluded. There were the witty, smart, often malicious writers like Kjetil Rolness, Torgrim Eggen, Finn Bjelke, and Herman Willis. There were the serious, ponderous types like Øivind Hånes, Jan Arne Handorff, Arvid Skancke-Knutsen, and Ivar Orvedal. And then there were the knowledgeable, clearheaded writers who went straight to the point, like Tore Olsen, Tom Skjeklesæther, Geir Rakvaag, Gerd Johansen, and Willy B.

"It was as though I knew them all. I really liked Jan Arne Handorff. I understood virtually nothing of what he wrote but sensed his passion, somewhere deep in the wilderness of all those foreign-sounding words, while every second reader's letter accused him of being incomprehensible, although he didn't seem to care, he steered a straight line, further and further into the impenetrable night. . . . I had it in me. I just had to let it out."

So he pushes. He focuses. He gets a gig, digs down, writes "draft after draft, scrunched up the rejects and threw them into the growing heap on the floor," and turns in his review of Tuxedo Moon's *Holy Wars*, which appears on the page in full, the dullest record review ever written: "The band explores uncharted territory and discovers new musical paths . . ." You can't get to the end of the sentence without falling asleep. If Knausgaard is reprinting his own real review in this autobiographical novel, he's brave; if he made it up for the book, he's a genius.

4 ▪ **Scott Blackwood, *See How Small* (Little, Brown)** A novel that comes out of the still-unsolved 1991 murders of four young women in an Austin, Texas, ice cream parlor—fuzzy, floating characters, whether the shades of the dead girls, their families, a reporter, one of the guilty, all of whom seem most of all to want to talk to each other. It's a fractured dream of blocked gestures—when someone extends an arm to touch somebody else, it's not the person reached for who dissolves, but the hand of the person reaching. The crime bores holes in the mind of everyone who tries to think about it; Blackwood writes from those holes as if they were his office.

5 ▪ **Jim Linderman, *The Birth of Rock and Roll* (Dust-to-Digital)** There's a lot to look at in this big, expansive book of found photographs from across the first sixty or so years of the twentieth century—almost all snapshots of people singing, playing, dancing in churches, nightspots, community halls, and most of all parlors and living rooms. There's a lot to look at because the pictures are alive with the fact that you are encountering singular individuals who passed through the world and left some proof of their physical presence, shadows on paper. *Who are these people?* the pictures make you ask. Where did they come from, where did they go, what did they want? What happened to the seven-or-eight-year-old couple—a black boy in a suit and tie and a white girl in a party dress, a certain command in the boy's face, a hint in the corner of the girl's left eye that no one will ever know how happy she is to be right here, right now—after the real world stepped in? What became of the two African-American women, maybe from the 1930s, one with long straight hair, and a fancy pistol on her belt, and a face that says nothing can surprise her, the other more demure, dressed like a flapper, with a face that says she can't wait to be surprised?* There's a band, maybe from 1957, singer, saxophonist, guitarist, drummer, white guys in the crudest, heaviest, most horrible blackface you've ever seen, as if they're playing a lynching—what would they have to say if they could see themselves now?

6 & 7 ■ **Vexx, *Vexx* (M'Lady's, 2014) and *Give and Take* (Katorga Works 7")** An Olympia, Washington, punk combo—singer Maryjane Dunphe, guitarist Mike Liebman, bassist Ian Corrigan, drummer Corey Rose Evans—that's been listening to a lot of Avengers. As Vexx now uses it, the sound—more than that, the unthinking physical flight—of the best American punk band of the 1970s carries no dates with it into the present day. It feels like a language anyone might discover when she's trying to understand what she wants to say and how to say it.

Vexx doesn't come across like the best of anything: they come across like a band that you might find in any town in the country, telling you what's going on. The one-minute-twenty-one-second race of "Don't Talk About It," from *Vexx*, might seem like ordinary 1980s hardcore out of the box, but it's so extreme that all received riffs and voices are spun off by its own centrifugal force within thirty seconds, and before a minute is up you don't know where the band could possibly be headed. People don't put this much of themselves into a piece of music just to show they can; to find out if they can, that's another question. The four numbers on the *Give and Take* EP have more weight than the eight on *Vexx*, less apparent need for the musicians to convince themselves they mean what they say, less need to write regular songs. All the action is just off the beat, in Maryjane Dunphe's readiness to leap away from it. She's mapping a zone of freedom. What she can't

---

* If you look more carefully than I did, one woman, one man.

yet do is what the Avengers' Penelope Houston did from her first recorded note: put not just will, desire, and nerve into her music, but personality. You don't yet hear a whole person, looking you dead in the face, every shift in tone or pace a dare, but you lean forward, because that moment where the mask of style comes off is almost present.

8 ▪ Leah Garchik, "Public Eavesdropping," *San Francisco Chronicle* (May 17) People at a table in a restaurant: What's new? "I was waiting to talk to the pharmacist at Walgreens," says one man, "and the on-hold Muzak was 'I Wanna Be Sedated' by the Ramones."

9 ▪ Re "Six PEN Members Decline Gala After Award for Charlie Hebdo" (*New York Times*, April 27) The novelist Teju Cole sent out a letter asking various writers to join him and others who disassociated themselves from an event affirming solidarity with the remains of the Paris journal, which made perfect sense: those cartoons of Muhammad were really gross, and how can one speak for "a Muslim population in France that is already embattled, marginalized, impoverished, and victimized," as Deborah Isenberg put it in a supporting letter, if one's hands aren't clean, especially in the face of work "not merely tasteless and reckless but brainlessly reckless as well"? "Those who want to misquote or misunderstand will still do so," Cole said—as if the implication that the pure intentions of himself and those he spoke for could not possibly be questioned by people of good faith were not more offensive than anything the reckless fools at *Charlie Hebdo* ever published.

10 ▪ Stephanie Barber, *Night Moves* (Publishing Genius Press) "YouTube Comments" is the second to last song on *War on Women* ("These lyrics are laughable!" Shawna Potter quotes more than once). This book, from the songwriter and singer in the Baltimore band Bobby Donnie, is entirely made up of YouTube comments on the Bob Seger song, seventy-five labyrinthine pages, where predictable and repeating paeans to lost youth ("evokes memories of days gone by") and lyrics quoted as if everyone reading hasn't just heard them go back and forth with the blank ("Gina will never know the truth"), the not-so-blank ("uncle touchy puzzle basement"), the passionate ("How can one song bring up such a range of emotions?"), and days-gone-by without gooey self-regard ("got me knocked up in 84"). There are subplots involving *That '70s Show, How I Met Your Mother,* and the "Dislikes" count, which in the course of the book, presumably compiled chronologically, declines steadily from 88 to 75. That's not much of a shift, but a real drama builds up—either it's completely random, or you're actually hearing people's minds changed.

Thanks to Doug Kroll and Leah Garchik.

June 3, 2015

1 ▪ Steve Gunn and Black Twig Pickers, *Seasonal Hire* (Thrill Jockey) Gunn is from Brooklyn by way of Pennsylvania, the Black Twig Pickers from West Virginia and Virginia, and led by Isak Howell's harmonica they start out searching for the perfect drone. This is old-timey music half-buried in the ground, with a foot of grunge thrown over it, and after four songs and seventeen minutes, with fiddler and banjo player Sally Ann Morgan's singing more expressive than guitarist Gunn's but also more abstract, you figure you know what the band can do. Then comes the title track, and after three minutes, with Mike Gangloff's jaw harp the most distinctive sound, the piece is only barely under way, and you realize these people are bent on different territory. At four minutes a theme is still taking shape, but now the shadings are coming from Gunn's guitar. Howell's banjo moves up. Appalachian fatalism yields to raga tones that refuse to acknowledge time. At nine minutes or so it all seems to be winding down, and then there's a shift to a harsher, more atonal music, and the balance tips back to the mountains. The dead—the likes of Clarence Ashley and Roscoe Holcomb—are adding their instruments, everything slows down, everyone is resisting even the idea of an ending, until the dead depart and the sound begins to empty out, Gangloff's fiddle now completely in possession of the drama, until after more than sixteen minutes Gunn's simple, steady count on his guitar finishes it off. Though there's not a word spoken or sung, you might think of the Doors' "The End"; you might think of the Rolling Stones stumbling into "Goin' Home."

2 ▪ Beth Ditto from the "Rock and Romantic Collection 2011," in "The Fashion World of Jean-Paul Gaultier—From the Sidewalk to the Catwalk" (Grand Palais, Paris, through August 3) In a video, the singer from

Gossip comes down the runway in a reflecting flapper dress, bouncing from her toes to her neck with every step. With her severely cut bangs and her shimmering girth, she looks like the love child of Louise Brooks and Fatty Arbuckle. "He was a wonderful dancer," Brooks once said of Arbuckle. "It was like floating in the arms of a huge donut." In a photograph with Ditto, Gaultier, in a Gossip T-shirt, is grinning as if it felt just like that.

3 ▪ Verbs, *Cover Story* (Verbs) Covers of not-completely-out-front numbers from the mid-sixties to the early seventies—the Turtles' "You Showed Me," Los Bravos' "Black Is Black," the Kinks' "Till the End of the Day," the Brotherhood of Man's "United We Stand"—but that's not the feeling at all. With Meegan Voss at the mike and Steve Jordan overdubbing himself, they sound more like they're making the demos the people who made the hits were working from, and dumbing down— Voss putting heart into every line, hoping someone will notice, and let her make her own record. The biggest thrill comes with the Dave Clark Five's "Glad All Over," in the original probably the worst disc here. In Voss and Jordan's hands it explodes over big rhythmic breaks, with the ethos of David Chase's film *Not Fade Away* all over it: people making music to discover what they sound like, and finding they sound like nobody else.

4–8 ▪ Francis Picabia, *The Brunette and the Blonde, Seated Nude, Portrait of a Couple (The Cherry Tree), Spring,* and *Women with Bulldog* (1941–43), in "Keys to a Passion" (Fondation Louis Vuitton, Paris) The old dadaist was waiting out the war on the Riviera, and if, as the catalogue notes say, this wall of lurid paintings, assembled here from five different museums, collections, and a gallery, were based on 1930s girlie magazines, today you see what they so blazingly anticipate: postwar paperback covers on the order of *Women in Prison* and *Forbidden Passion* and *Life* magazine ads for cars and leisure wear. The pictures, with everything smacking of high art wiped away until only the get-it-done-and-move-on sensibility of an anonymous illustrator remains, almost seem to vibrate with everything they want.

9 ▪ New Order, "Temptation" (Factory, 1982) The 8:43 version, where singer Bernard Sumner now sounds exactly like Benedict Cumberbatch looks in *The Imitation Game*: stoic, blank, and ordinary, his face telling you what he's doing is the only thing in the world that matters and he's on the verge of shattering, with only a certain pattern—in the movie, a code, in the music, an electronic drum track as compelling as anything ever played with hands—holding him together.

10 ■ **Nine Antico, *Autel California* (L'Association)** By the author of a graphic novel about Bettie Page and Linda Lovelace, one about the adventures of fan and groupie Surfer Girl, whose story starts out with Elvis and closes with Jim Morrison singing "The End" just for her, even though she still hasn't lost her virginity (Antico promises a sequel). The title means "California Religion," and the book, in French, translates itself visually, with a certain tinge of regret, of disloyalty to old heroes as time moves on, never very far away. Best moment: in a Los Angeles classroom, students are reading their papers. As a ponytailed not-yet Surfer Girl writes

D
ELVIS
N
N
I
S

with a heart in her notebook, Dennis Wilson gets up and reads "409." And then Brian Wilson gets up and reads "Dans Ma Chambre."

June 24, 2015

1 ■ **Rihanna, "American Oxygen," on *Saturday Night Live* (NBC, May 16)** Over the last year countless panels, online threads, and editorials have asked, as if to the tune of the Kingston Trio's "Where Have All the Flowers Gone," *Where have all the protest songs gone?* Here. No, it's not "Masters of War," but this was powerful from the start and soul-shaking by the end. The official video for the song has Rihanna in a white T-shirt teasing out from under a leather jacket as a video of modern-world imagery—war, assassination, the Beatles, a bum on the street, a march in the street, flags, the Statue of Liberty, a rodeo, everything familiar—unspools behind her. This night, wearing an outfit

somewhere between guerrilla chic and a funeral suit, Rihanna sang in front of a wrap-around, three-screen version of the same parade, and it built like the ending of Abel Gance's silent-color-triptych finale of his 1927 *Napoleon:* it all but tore you apart with conflicting emotions. Made by Uprising Creative, directed by Darren Craig, Jonathan Craven, and Jeff Nicholas, the tableau was hard to read, because there was so much loaded into it. Familiar images—iconic to the point of cliché, such as Martin Luther King in front of the Lincoln Memorial—were carried off by those you didn't know, or almost knew but couldn't quite place. It was obvious and then it wasn't; it moved too fast to think about, and the ground under your feet began to shift.

There was a harsh disassociation between Rihanna in front, pushing out repeating lines as if coming up for air—"Breathe in, breathe out"—bringing Eric Garner and a hundred other people this spring with their heads shoved into the ground, against a wall, choked, pepper-sprayed, beaten, shot full of holes, humiliated, the names piling up until they're scrambled—and the pictures dancing behind her. It was as if there was an argument going on, between common memory and what she had to say. Words from the song seemed to float before her eyes, as if they, like the fractured history behind her, were coming to her in pieces. "This is the new America"—a chant, mournful, shocked, then flat, accepting—is frightening with so many faces and dead bodies and oblivious citizens tumbling over the words, and "We are the new America," the line that follows, is in some ways even more frightening, because it's a call less to arms than to a cauldron. It doesn't explain anything, it doesn't define a right side and a wrong side, it doesn't presume you agree with it—because an idea like agreement is not part of its language. As a protest song it doesn't presume to put ideas into people's heads; what it puts there are echoes. Rihanna opens her mouth, moves in front of a screen, and it's 3 a.m. and you're dreaming three dreams at once.

2 & 3 ▪ Öyvind Fahlström, *Mao Hope March* (1966) and Antonio Manuel, *Repressão outra vez—eis o saldo* (Repression Again—This Is the Consequence, 1968), in "International Pop," Walker Art Center (Minneapolis, through August 29) The key to this swirling show was *international*—yes, the predictable Warhols, Lichtensteins, Rauschenbergs, Rosenquists were there, even a collage from Bruce Conner. But the real action was all over the place, from everywhere. It didn't necessarily announce itself. Fahlström (1928–76) was a Swedish artist born in Brazil; the monitor with his video, high on a wall, was easy to pass by. On a New York street, various people are parading with posters of a smiling Chairman Mao, others with Bob Hope looking quizzical, or maybe a little confused. The New York radio man Bob Fass is interviewing people on the street, asking them if they're happy, if they know who the faces on the posters are, and the scratchy audio keeps bouncing off the posters. "You know, it really stops you, you know," says one passerby, after arguing with Fass over whether he's happy ("Are you a happy man?" "Certainly! Do I look happy, huh?" "Why?" "Because I live the type of life I do." "What type of life is that?" "The type that you don't"). "It makes you sort of stop and wonder," the first man says: "What is he running for? Because if you notice that most of these actors are going into politics now, like Ronald Reagan, for instance." "Whose pictures are they?" says Fass. "Bob Hope and I'm not sure of the other person, but it's, I think it's Mao Tse-Tung." "Is there some kind of connection?" "I hope not. The only thing I can think of is that they're inferring that Bob Hope is a communist, but . . . I wish I knew!" It's four and a half minutes, and you can't look away.

Antonio Manuel was born in Brazil in 1947. Before he was twenty he created a visionary installation that led to the police shutdown of an exhibition by young Brazilian artists meant to travel to Paris. In the Walker, again you might walk right by it: what appear to be five large black posters hung in a row. All black—but each has a white cord dangling several feet in front of it. It's a museum, you figure don't touch, but you do, you pull the string, and the black face pulls up to reveal black and red silkscreens of pages from the São Paulo paper *Última Hora* showing clashes between students and police. They suck you right in, not so much for the images or the headlines ("A STUDENT DIED") as for the symbolism at play. Yes, the black coverings represent censorship, but they're far more suggestive than that: they also represent torture. When you lift the black canvas, you are lifting the mask off the face of a prisoner in a hood.

4 ▪ Bruce Jenkins, "Cleveland's pain continues, but Oakland shows title-worthiness," on the NBA finals (*San Francisco Chronicle*, June 18)
"From a Cleveland standpoint, Game 6's final moments were difficult to watch. The Cavs were surging and flailing in equal measure, and it

seemed very much over at the 1:50 mark, when Stephen Curry sailed in for an uncontested layup against a beaten-down defense, giving the Warriors a 98–85 lead. There was a timeout. And absurdity ensued.

"The Cavs' marketing people, utterly clueless in the NBA's ghastly tradition, busted out 'Hang on Sloopy,' a bubblegum-variety hit from the '60s, over the sound system: 'Sloopy lives in a very bad part of town / And everybody, yeah, tries to put my Sloopy down.' What was this, a sing-along? No major titles in this town since the 1964 Browns, but let's all get down with the McCoys? And bring your dancin' shoes?"

5–7 ▪ Kenneth Anger, *Rabbit's Moon* (1950/1970) and the Capris, "There's a Moon out Tonight" (Lost Nite, 1960) and on *Sound Stage* (PBS, 1982) In 1950 Anger shot a fifteen-minute film in Paris, which he didn't finish; in 1970 he added a soundtrack and began showing it. It opens with a mime all in white lying in a forest. Instantly the Capris come on: a Queens doo-wop group with one of the most distinctive records of the form. Leader Nick Santo strikes a pose with the opening of every line, but especially the first: "There's a—" he sings in a clear tenor, and then the rest of the Capris come in high, even squeaky, but sending the song into the air—"*moon out tonight . . .*" and the song goes on like that, until you can't tell which part you love and which part you hate, until the parts change places, until you're lost in the music, as Anger clearly was. The mime brings himself to his feet, he lifts his arms in supplication, he raises his head, and there it is, a blazing full moon in a blue night sky, and the moon lights his face. The film goes on, but it's all there in the first scene.

"There's a Moon Out Tonight" came out on Planet in 1958 and went nowhere; the Capris broke up. But two years later it was reissued by the collectors' label Lost Nite and the song went to No. 3 in the nation— which was why, more than twenty years after that, Santo was back, with new and old Capris, to sing it on a PBS doo-wop special, and the change is shocking. "There's a—" Santo sings, and the Capris come in, "*girl in my heart,*" but what Santo has invested in his two words makes a whole world.* His voice—his body, his sensibility, his memory, his sense of loss, his belief in the future—is rich, flowing, at once behind the story being told and ahead of it. The theme of the song is what "I never felt before," and as Santo slides back over every appear-

---

* "Glow," actually.

ance of the notion there is a calm so deep it's hard to grasp, that any-one could want what the singer wants with such certainty—certain not that he'll get it but that he deserves it. The *doo-wah*s behind him rise like northern lights—but only because of the glow Santo is giving the song. It wasn't there in 1958; it's not there in later TV appearances. It was a moment when the singer talked to the song, and the song replied with something it had never said before, and the singer gave it back.

8 ■ Mezzo (art) and J. M. Dupont (words), *Love in Vain: Robert John-son, 1911–1938* (Éditions Glénat, Grenoble) A graphic biography: noth-ing that imaginative as narrative, exploding out of mere story in the drawings, with a luridness that might have its roots in record company ads for 1920s–1930s blues 78s but shoots far past them, until the pages al-most seem to sweat out the alcohol and sex in the panels. There are only hints of invention—at the end, as the Rolling Stones play Johnson's "Love in Vain" at Altamont in 1969, a hound walks across the stage*— but the frames are so crowded, with faces, bodies, bottles, lights, instru-ments, dozens of them like tiny versions of a Thomas Hart Benton mural, it's impossible to take them in at once. You begin to study them, and every time you blink you see something that wasn't there before.

9 ■ Lightning Bolt, *Fantasy Empire* (Thrill Jockey) Drums, bass, wah-wah: speed and words shouted out of a pit first dug in the Providence, Rhode Island, noise music milieu nearly twenty years ago. Perfect, if your dreams haven't been bad enough lately—or, with the eleven min-utes and twenty-one seconds of "Snow White (& the Seven Dwarfs Fans)," long enough. Even if too much melody sneaks in, as if purists Brian Chippendale (drums, vocals) and Brian Gibson (bass) just couldn't help themselves.

10 ■ Molly Gallentine reports on Sinatra Idol Contest (Hoboken, NJ) "Across the Hudson river from New York City is a one-square-mile city, birthplace of two cultural mementos: baseball and Frank Sinatra. You won't find walking tours or statues commemorating the latter. Locals hint at the singer's contemptuous relationship with his less-than-glamorous birthplace—and a result, reminders of Sinatra's life in Hoboken are strangely absent. But on June 11, in a packed auditorium,

* Not exactly invention—it happened. Real life generates its own symbolism.

Hoboken reclaimed Frank and his music once again, inviting a special pack of Sinatra sound-alikes from around the country (and Canada) to battle for the title (as judged by Mayor Dawn Zimmer and Frank's born-and-raised second cousin, Dale Monaco). This year, the competition celebrated the centennial of Sinatra's birth and marked the beginning of a weekend full of Hoboken-wide pop-up performances by roughly forty impersonators. Most shied away from the term *impersonator*—a word that would imply there was something base, kitschy, or inauthentic about their performances. Rose Cafasso, a primped and perfect ninety-three-year-old bobby-soxer, listened to her son sing songs from her past while chatting about broccoli rabe and the secrets of a long life. For many of the performers—having survived alcoholism, freak lightning strikes, cancer, and failed relationships—Frank's music became an anthem during hard times. He may not have won the Idol competition, but Charles Stayduhar Jr.'s soulful rendition of 'That's Life' became the mantra for every performer who has picked themselves up to 'get back in the race.' Rose made for the perfect cheerleader."

July 27, 2015

1 ■ *Amy*, **directed by Asif Kapadia (Playmaker Films)** The signal scene in this relentlessly depressing movie comes when Amy Winehouse is standing in a cramped closet-like space, recording "Back to Black" with headphones on. As the shot opens we hear only her voice, isolated both in terms of sound and person—she is so completely there she could be the last person on earth, with no one left to hear her. Then the music, presumably as she's hearing it, rises on the soundtrack, while her voice continues over it—or, really, under it, all but buried under it. But as the song bends toward its last lines, the music vanishes, and again, but now more cruelly, it's just a single woman and her voice, letting the words out slowly, as if they're being pulled out of her: "Black . . . black . . . black," with three full seconds between each breath. "Oh," she says, surprised, "it's a bit upsetting at the end, isn't it?" Her commitment to craft, tradition, art—to her sense of a song as something at once part of her and outside of her, another

being daring her to live up to it, is unerasable, and so is the stark fact of what was thrown away.

2 ▪ "HOOT! = = Hard Sell: Songs We Hate," St. Alban's Parish Hall (Albany, California, June 28) At the Experience Music Project Pop Conference this last April, a roundtable based on a poll of conference participants asked to name the worst songs of all time fell flat: people rationally discussed whether, say, "Hotel California" or "We Are the World" had redeeming social, musical, satirical, or any other forms of value, but there was no *loathing.* That was not a problem at "HOOT!" Impresario Joe Christiano reports on a show I wish I'd been in town for: "This themed, participatory Bay Area songfest has dedicated evenings to Bob Dylan, California, money, cars, and twenty-five or so other subjects in its four-year history. Last month's installment drew dynamically conflicted interpretations from its performers, and rowdy, sympathetic sing-a-longs from an audience who reclaimed—with righteous validation—that lamentable contemporary reflex, 'haters gonna hate.' The evening began with 'The Sound of Music' played by Theresa Kelly and Lisa Whiteman (The Shut-Yer-Von-Trapps), and sounding, without a changed chord, like an outtake from the third Velvet Underground album. Next was Paul Anka's '(You're) Having My Baby,' sung straight by Greg Reznick (and a bewigged Sparky Grinstead), every line met with a horrified NOOOOOOO! from the shocked crowd, which had apparently suppressed all memory of the inexplicable hit.

"The seventies were particularly well-represented: 'Ben'; 'Candida'; 'Feelings'; 'Gypsies, Tramps, and Thieves'; 'Silly Love Songs'; and of course, 'I Am Woman,' sung by Joshua Raoul Brody, who transcended camp by replacing the song's hollow assertions with lines like 'I am woman/watch me work/for a stupid macho jerk/who's devoid of any semblance of feeling/But I'll work just as hard as he/at two-thirds the salary/'Til I bash my head against that ol' glass ceiling.' Amy Kessler's 'I Am, I Said,' dared all to defy the unintelligible '. . . not even the chair' lyric, and received the first standing ovation in HOOT! history. Noam Rosen closed the first set with Journey's 'Don't Stop Believin',' which, line for line, people know now as well as they once knew 'This Land Is Your Land.' The unprompted sing-a-long was abashedly tender, and made the song seem as if it had been written by everybody's dad. Wendy Fiering stopped time with an unironic reading of Neil Young's 'A Man Needs a Maid,' sung, with chilling resignation, from the maid's point of view. And then came 'Playground in My Mind,' re-imagined by Josh Senyak as a minor-key rant by Charles Manson: 'My name is Mike-*KILL*, I got a nic-*KILL*, I got a nic-*KILL*, shiny and new . . .' et cetera.

"The eighties and nineties were not forgotten: 'Sweet Dreams (Are Made of This)'; 'Jump'; 'Everybody Wants to Rule the World'; 'Wonderwall'; 'Achy Breaky Heart,' and what would have been the ne plus ultra of the evening had the venom for the song not been tempered by the accidental death of its composer days before: 'My Heart Will Go On,' aka 'Love Theme from *Titanic*.' The group performing the song—the Short Tucanos—was named after James Horner's ill-fated aircraft. How better to end such an evening than with 'Hallelujah,' a song ruined for most by the embrace of a multitude who wouldn't know Leonard Cohen from their partner's gynecologist? Neither redemptive nor redactive, the song was sung like a true hymn—involuntarily—and blessed a satisfying evening that recalled Christopher Hitchens's mighty line: 'For a lot of people, their first love is what they'll always remember. For me it's always been the first hate.'"

3 ▪ **Jessica Hopper, *The First Collection of Criticism by a Living Female Rock Critic* (featherproof)** From the editor of the blazing quarterly *Pitchfork Review*, forty-one pieces drawn from journals ranging from *Punk Planet* in 2003 to the *Village Voice* in 2014, and not an expected note or a cowardly opinion in any of them. The story snaking its way through the book is indie rock as a little Stalinist clubhouse with NO GIRLS ALLOWED on the door. Stay away, go somewhere else, and Hopper finds herself face to face with R. Kelly's pedophilia, which isn't different at all, or forcing herself through "An Oral History of Hole's *Live Through This*," where the band members talk about heroin as if they're looking out the window to see if they'll need a sweater if they're going out later, as if bassist Kristen Pfaff did live through it. Hopper carries you through every piece with an eye growing ever more jaded, ever more clear.

4 ▪ **_Stung_, directed by Benni Diez, written by Adam Aresty (Rat Pack/ XYZ)** A very gory slapstick mutant-wasp picture with first-class steals from the basement scenes in *Night of the Living Dead* and the parasitic twin in the "Ventriloquist's Dummy" episode of *Tales from the Crypt*—plus, at the very end, the least expected version of the young-people-have-sex-and-then-die scream-movie requirement I've ever seen. Or want to. I was really on their side.

5 ▪ Darius Rucker, "Wagon Wheel" (Capitol Nashville, 2013) at Roller Garden, St. Louis Park, Minnesota (May 30) Maybe everything feels good on a roller rink sound system, especially with eighteen birthday parties under way, but this—a fragment of a Bob Dylan song fleshed out by the Old Crow Medicine Show, a pallid hit for them, a better one for Rucker—made you hope the system would get stuck and play it all day long. It's in the warmth of the singing, the fiddles sawing away like trees blowing in the wind but with a circling rhythm nature doesn't make, the sense of a long trip that's never going to end. In *The Sellout,* Paul Beatty's new novel about blackface, whiteface, and black towns wiped off the map not by the Ku Klux Klan but by mapmakers, he has his hero call Hootie and the Blowfish "the whitest music I knew" (along with Madonna and the Clash), maybe not in spite of but because they had a black lead singer, one Darius Rucker, but there's no white in this record, and no black, just landscape, movement, tiredness, laziness, getting up, stepping out, blinded by the sun.

6 ▪ Hush Point, *Blues and Reds* (Sunnyside) Or, "The Birth of the Cool." There's no sense at all that the birth took place sixty-six years ago; there is insider trading over *Sketches of Spain.* By the end they're running out of gas, but "Live in Stockholm" and "Grounds for Divorce" are more than good song titles.

7 ▪ Kim Gordon, "Design Office: The City Is a Garden," installation at 303 Gallery (New York, June 4–July 25) There were artificial hedges placed all around the room, and, scattered like bodies on the floor—maybe covering smaller hedges—crushed paintings with unreadable words on them. The juxtaposition made you bend down, squint, try to make the markings signify: were they Occupy slogans, already erased by history? Look for more than a moment and you're not in a gallery: you're in the vandalized lobby of a hedge fund, and they'll have it cleaned up before you know it.

8 ▪ Andy Abramowitz, *Thank You, Good Night* (Touchstone) Long years after Tremble's one hit—number one, but it might never have happened at all—their leader Teddy Tremble puts the band together again. He has great new songs. The chemistry is there. Everything's rolling along, until this hard-working, determined guy, our first-person narrator, turns ugly. Why couldn't the band come back? "The Pet Shop Boys were still at it because the musical tastes of Eurofags hadn't evolved in the past quarter century. The few members of Lynyrd Skynyrd who hadn't ridden over themselves with their own motorcycles could still do 'Gimme Three Steps' to a crowded barbeque because somebody had to make music for dirtballs." Never mind that he means the Allman Brothers, not Lynyrd Skynyrd—it feels like a violation, the author breaking his character to put a few of his own thoughts on the page. The novel seems to lose its voice right here. And then you find out that you weren't really seeing who was there at all: a total asshole, weak, incompetent, sneering. Not that he can't still convincingly get off a good line, or would be out of place at "Songs We Hate." "He paused to sniffle. 'I know no one said it'd be easy. But no one said it'd be this hard.' 'Pathetic,' Alaina jeered. 'It is pathetic,' I agreed. 'That's Coldplay.'"

9 ■ Elevator Repair Service, *The Sound and the Fury*, Public Theater (New York, June 23) As seen on *Hee Haw*.

10 ■ Barack Obama, "Amazing Grace," TD Arena (Charleston, South Carolina, June 26) Cecily Marcus comments: "In a week when the news should have been full of black people talking about the nine black churchgoers who were murdered by a racist—saying their names, who they were, what their murders mean, how it feels—the focus was stolen by white people talking about white power and supremacy: debating and explaining the Confederate flag, laws, heritage, Southern pride.

"President Obama's eulogy for Reverend Clementa Pinckney was the end of an awful week, and it was devastating. Maybe for the first time in his presidency, President Obama could be a black man without apology, finally embracing a language that no other president has been able to claim. It was shocking to hear the president use 'we' and 'our' so fully when talking about African American life and history. It was shocking to hear phrases I didn't know—'hush harbors' to describe the history of black churches where people could pray in secret—as a common parlance that he shares with honor and great ease. President Obama had planted the phrases from 'Amazing Grace' at the beginning of his speech, but when at the end he sang the song, he didn't sing well. He sang unforgettably, charging the words 'was' and 'found'—'I once was lost but now I'm found'—with a sound that comes from belonging to a community that for seven years of his presidency he seemed to run from. In the act of singing, his voice shed all oratorical skills and rhetoric, his words carried instead by the cadence of millions of black voices who sang before. For a few moments, he wasn't just a historic figure. He was utterly human, and part of a deep tradition.

"It's a lie of history that good things come from bad. There is nothing good about nine black people being murdered, or about six African American churches burning in the seven days that followed. This is the country we have built. We have waited a long time to have a president who shows the country what that means and how it feels. I hope it's not another 200 years before we have another."

Thanks to Emily Marcus.

August 26, 2015

1 & 2 ▪ John Lydon, *Anger Is an Energy—My Life Uncensored* (Dey St.) and Public Image Ltd., "Big Blue Sky," from *What the World Needs Now* (PiL Official) Lydon's first autobiography—the 1994 *Rotten: No Irish, No Blacks, No Dogs*, with full cover credit as "with Keith and Kent Zimmerman"—had its moments, but it was constantly interrupted and padded with other people's words, and it wasn't a real book. This, despite an inside note of "with Andrew Perry," is a real book—full of blather, guff, and repetition, at least a hundred pages longer than it might have been, but singing, pounding, shouting, even whispering with such an irreducible intelligence you can be brought up short on any page. Lydon apologizes for nothing, praises himself for everything, claims infinite meaning for the Sex Pistols ("Here we were, capable of making really big significant social changes to many things—not just the wonderful world of music, but to society itself") and his work with Public Image Ltd. from its start in 1978 to now, and makes you believe him. The Sex Pistols, he writes, were "a runaway train of thought," and whole books on the group haven't said a fraction as much. Even the songs themselves may not be as suggestive as those five words. When he digs in, paying off on his book title, he'll boil decades of newspaper stories into a paragraph with a reach so great it can leave you breathless. On growing up in the Catholic Church: "Did I know there was sexual abuse going on there? Oh yeah, abso-fucking-lutely . . . everybody knew to run when the priest came a-visiting, and by no means ever get yourself involved in the choir, or any altar-boy nonsense, because that was direct contact number one, so I learned *not* to sing very successfully—deliberately—bum notes, because I knew that would be a really dangerous thing to be waltzing into. So the love of singing was kicked out of me because of bloody priests. Imagine the joy of eventually joining the Sex Pistols, and making the world a better place—in a very vengeful way."

There's no end to the delight in language in the book. Lydon's description of PiL guitarist Keith Levene—"he never had a good word to say about anybody. That thrilled me no end—I'd never known such a professional misery"—is, in its last line, both poetry and something no one else would ever say, about anything. And if his music criticism sometimes leaves nothing behind but a hole in the page ("I love the Kinks—love 'em!"), sometimes it's perfect, too. "Deep down inside, I think I wanted to sing like Robert Plant," Lydon says at one point. "I mean, I don't like his hairdo, but so what?"

What the World Needs Now may be closer to PiL's second album, the epic 1979 *Metal Box*, three 12-inch 45s in a film cannister ("A stunningly beautiful tapestry of high anxiety," Lydon describes it: "The idea of it was, it would numb you, absolutely flatten your resistance, just wear you out with its omnipresence. I think we got there") than the tremendous *This Is PiL*, from 2012, which is probably closer to Bob Dylan's *Tempest*, from the same year—a recovery of ambition marks them both. *What the World Needs Now* and *Metal Box* share the sense of a blasted, nearly empty landscape—pretty much what Viggo Mortensen found in *The Road*. The songs struggle toward a shape more distinct than atmosphere, until "Big Blue Sky," where, over more than eight minutes, the atmosphere is itself so distinct, so American-desert, that you can see the singer in the last shot of David Lynch's *Lost Highway*, with his thumb out.

3 ▪ **Ratatat, *Magnifique* (XL)** From Brooklyn, Mike Stroud plays melodica and guitar; Evan Mast plays bass; both deal in synthesizers and percussion. They're infinitely more confident than they were on their debut, *Ratatat*: that was eleven years ago, and now they don't even need words, even a human voice, though there are times where voices come in, but just to say goodbye. Because changes are so quick, subtle, and seemingly inevitable—could anything in "Abrasive" move from one place to another in any other way?—favorite songs change each time you play the record. These are dreamscapes, the kind that, opening a dance floor, shutting down for the night, running tourist ships to the moon, say *don't let me wake up*. The inside and outside sleeve art, by the band, is a hill made of hundreds of faces. Moment to moment you might recognize Bruce Springsteen, Catherine Deneuve, Jim Morrison, Jonathan Franzen, Henry Kissinger, until they turn into someone else; the only one I'm sure of is Roy Orbison.

4 ▪ *Ubu Roi*, Cheek by Jowl (Lincoln Center Festival, July 22–26, in the Gerald W. Lynch Theater in the John Jay College of Criminal Justice) John Rockwell reports on a performance I couldn't make: "I was never a big fan of Alfred Jarry's play: maybe absurdist, maybe pre-Dadaist or pre-Surrealist, but too bratty, too self-consciously provocative, a prejudice only reinforced when reading how Jarry had orchestrated the riot at the 1896 Paris premiere. Never a big fan of the band, either, but what do I know?

"The French-language staging of *Ubu Roi* at the Lincoln Center Festival July 22–26 was so brilliant that it almost changed my mind. About the play, that is. What the director Declan Donnellan did was recalibrate Jarry's ravings as the murderous fantasy of teenaged, not to say punkish, angst. The show opens in a modern apartment wherein the teenaged boy in question is sprawled on a couch, fooling with a video camera. His parents are blithely preparing a small dinner party. They murmur inaudibly in the most polite French. Suddenly the lights change, casting a bilious green glow, and mom and dad become Père and Mère Ubu, shouting and carrying on in their mad, bloody way. All the other parts in the play are enacted by three guests and the son. Periodically things snap back to the decorous dinner party, the detritus of chaos all around but with everyone oblivious to anything odd having happened.

"It's all weirdly, shockingly illuminating, like *The Discreet Charm of the Bourgeoisie*, only bloodier. A transformative experience, not just of my prejudiced opinion but, maybe, of the play itself."

5–8 ▪ Leonard Cohen, "Nevermind"; Lera Lynn, *The Avenues* (lera lynn.com); Jake La Botz, "The Rose"; New York Dolls, "Human Being"; Rick Springfield, "Jessie's Girl," on *True Detective* Season 2 (HBO)

Despite the fraying plot lines, this was far stronger than the first season: if the story was absurd, real life bled every time you looked into Colin Farrell's and Rachel McAdams's faces. Didn't you always want to see Farrell as human wreckage—wasn't it clear, watching, that that's where, for him, all his old pretty-boy leads were leading? Didn't you wonder if Rachel McAdams could carry self-loathing through a whole season without blinking—wasn't it scary to find out she could, that anyone could? All reviews aside, the real disaster of the season finale was her losing her haircut.

Throughout, music created the most memorable ambiance. "Nevermind," the theme song, was Leonard Cohen at his most pretentious and preening, and across his long and hallowed journey through the forests of narcissism he's set a high bar. Unlike the Handsome Family's "Far from Any Road," the theme from the first season, which could have been sung by Matthew McConaughey without anyone wondering why, here the show bucked the song right off its back: you forgot it as soon as someone began walking or talking. The real action was in a Farrell fever dream of an Elvis impersonator with a big frizzy hairdo uncoiling himself like Arnold Schwarzenegger in the first *Terminator* for "The Rose," or Farrell drinking and snorting himself back to life to "Human Being," not only the New York Dolls' best song but the only one that altogether burnt off their pose, or Rick Springfield, looking as if he'd break if he stood up quickly, so tanned and planed down by plastic surgery you couldn't imagine "Jessie's Girl," which is all moving quickly, coming out of his mouth.

Lera Lynn, a Nashville singer whose most recent album has enough death—"Standing on the Moon," "Comin' Down"—in it to keep you listening through its love songs, was the specter, the fate that met Farrell, Vince Vaughn, and Taylor Kitsch, even though they died and she didn't. As she sat on her stool in a bar that never seemed to have more than her and two or three other people in it, or as she walked out, carrying her guitar, at the end of the last episode, as if she couldn't stand another minute in the place, the bruises on her legs spread, her shoulders bent even farther toward the floor, and her voice pushed toward 2 a.m., when she'd get paid, enough money to buy another fix from the bartender and go home.

9 ▪ James Gavin, *Is That All There Is? The Strange Life of Peggy Lee* (Simon and Schuster) Gavin brings the music to life: "Why Don't You

Do Right," "Lover," "Fever," and carloads of dreck. It doesn't matter that the story began in North Dakota—the carelessness of a Hollywood life takes over and never lets go, except when Lee commits herself to a song, to getting it right, as she does in the suspenseful pages Gavin devotes to his title song. It was Lee, not writers and producers Jerry Leiber and Mike Stoller, who wanted Randy Newman to arrange the number: she'd heard his first album, the dead-end American dream of "Love Story"—"We'll play checkers all day/Until we pass away"—and it took her back to home truths that had passed out of her own songs, and she put them back into "Is That All There Is?" as defiance, a refusal, as Gavin makes you believe, of the Weimar nihilism Jerry Leiber was after all along.

10 ▪ "Folk City: New York and the Folk Music Revival," Museum of the City of New York (through November 29) Housed appropriately in the exquisite City Museum on Fifth Avenue between 104th and 105th streets—which features Stairwell B in the back, billed as "THE MOST EXCITING STAIRWELL IN NEW YORK," and it probably is—the exhibit is skimpy, with infinite missed chances. There's stuff, and blown-up photos—you're pointed toward a showcase of holograph Dylan lyrics, all of which look very carefully written after the fact, maybe for sale purposes. They bear no resemblance at all to the smeared and crossed-out typed originals displayed in the past at the Morgan Library and elsewhere. Most interesting are a series of song clips, which reveal the utter confusion of the show, which can't decide if it's about politics, music, the brotherhood of man, or just being good.

There's Lead Belly's "Goodnight, Irene," first in a recording he made for the Library of Congress in 1934—though here it seems like a vocal dubbed over footage of him performing something else, which makes no sense: there's evocative footage on YouTube of him performing it in a New York apartment for well-dressed, mostly black people who seem like friends. Then the 1950 hit version by the Weavers, with Pete Seeger wrapping himself in a nightclub-grin, who are dead fish; Mississippi John Hurt with a down-home Pete Seeger and the folk singer Hedy West nodding along in approval, with Hurt looking uncomfortable and out of place—the song doesn't fit his style, and he'd never sing it if he weren't being used to construct a canon. Then the folk singers Arlo Guthrie and Steve Goodman, who have nothing to give the song, with Hoyt Axton, who brings his single verse dignity and sorrow, but he's just a commercial sellout, unlike the legacy Guthrie and the sainted Goodman, so who cares? There's Eric Clapton at some bizarre 1982 Christmas special, a bad-haircut version of *American Bandstand*: all the people dancing and singing along in swaying lines look like actors.

I once heard a woman tell of visiting the Morrison household in Belfast in the late 1940s, with George Morrison showing her his collection of blues and jazz 78s, while little George Ivan skittered around the floor shouting "Play 'Irene'! Play 'Irene'!" Here we see Van Morrison with Jerry Lee Lewis, both dragging music from their bones, stone-faced, silently saying that there are things in the song that still can't be said out loud. We see Jack White dive into the tune as if it were a lake, and then a big onstage singalong with Pete Seeger late in life surrounded by what seems like a hundred happy people—a terrible anti-climax, but it's Pete Seeger, and it's his song, isn't it?

A following set of performances of Lead Belly's "Midnight Special," with Seeger and the Greenbriar Boys, Bobby Darin, and Don McLean with the Persuasions, is more interesting, if less perverse: it makes you think it's not a very good song. Except for Paul McCartney, nobody can keep time.

September 28, 2015

1 ▪ Carrie Brownstein, *Hunger Makes Me a Modern Girl—A Memoir* (Riverhead Books) No one familiar with Brownstein from her work in Sleater-Kinney, as a singer, guitarist, songwriter from 1994 to now, her mordant NPR music commentaries, her writing and acting in *Portlandia*—is likely to be surprised by certain qualities of this book. For a memoir by a forty-one-year-old it is short, under 250 pages, without self-indulgence of any kind. It is modest. Like *A Freewheelin' Time*, the late Suze Rotolo's memoir of her life with and without Bob Dylan in Greenwich Village, it is devoid of sensationalism, scandal, or any violations of the writer's privacy, which is to say the reader's, too. Brownstein opens with her childhood in the Seattle suburbs, and the collapse of her family, which is rendered in terms of what it did to pets, who give voice to what people can't: a dog "turned back into a stray in her own home on account of the rest of us surrendering to emptiness, drifting away from anything we could call familiar, her skin itching and inflamed, covered with sores and bites, like tattoos, like skywriting, screaming with redness, as if to say *Please, please pet me!* But we didn't." When the nineties punk scene emerges in Olympia, Washington, in Brownstein's imagination, before she arrived, "it was Paris or Berlin in the '20s, it was the Bloomsbury group, it was the cradle of civilization." She went. As a student there at Evergreen College, and in the cauldron of bands appearing out of nowhere everywhere, Brownstein found "a community in dialogue with itself. . . . We operated as if in a constant seminar. Everything was mutable and vulnerable to critique." She also found the opposite of Paris or Berlin: "The claustrophobia of small-town dynamics makes for new rules in terms of greetings and salutations; privacy and alone time were often only achieved by looking down as you walked along the streets."

So you can feel what Brownstein is saying by the way she says it: thoughtful, everything put in doubt, a level, sober tone, so that the slightest gesture toward a smile—"They were like really loud librarians" she says of first seeing her future bandmate Corin Tucker's group Heavens to Betsy—may go off like a little bomb, or make no sound at all. As someone supposedly writing about herself, Brownstein is also a music critic, of her own band, a social critic, of her own milieu, and a literary critic, of her own self as she constructed it. She sees from the inside and the outside at the same time. With Tucker's initial attempt to coordinate with Brownstein's tuning, "her guitar happened to be in C sharp. . . . It's one and a half steps below standard tuning, which creates a sourness, a darkness that you have to overcome if you're going to create something at all harmonious and palatable. So even when we're getting toward a little bit of catchiness or pop sheen, there's an underlying bitterness to it"—and that is the twenty-year history of Sleater-Kinney as precisely as Brownstein's following chapters on albums, tours, the demise of the band, and after nearly ten years, a new start at the beginning of 2015. By the close of the book, what the person writing most wants to tell you about herself has a life behind it, a life ahead of it, and the clarity that a "strange world where you lived and examined all at once, questioned everything" can give you: "I can listen to soft songs, but I can't play them."

2 ▪ Ride service advertisements on Manhattan subway entrances (September 16) The sole copy on this ad from yet another app-based ride service boldly proclaims "$10 rides anywhere south of 110th St."

In other words, anywhere south of Harlem. Isn't that, you know, discrimination? Racist? Illegal? Or is it that now that there's gentrification in Harlem, we can call it post-racial and forget about it?

3 ▪ *Straight Outta Compton,* directed by F. Gary Gray (Universal) It's no wonder this was the number one movie in the country this summer: it's a tremendous picture. As the story of N.W.A it's part *Django Unchained,* part *Selma,* far more itself. Over two hours and twenty-seven minutes it's completely sustained, because the story expands, and not in predictable ways. There's a naturalism in the acting by the three principals—Corey Hawkins as Dr. Dre, O'Shea Jackson Jr. as Ice Cube, and Jason Mitchell as Eazy-E—that deepens as the picture moves forward. The actors grow into their roles, or maybe it's that the characters grow into themselves. Only Paul Giamatti, as the manager Jerry Heller, breaks the spell: he's so self-evidently a pro he takes you out of the story.

The story is thrilling, funny, suspenseful, and terrifying, though less for R. Marcos Taylor's label boss Suge Knight, a glance away from murder every time he appears on the screen, than for the moments when L.A. cops see young black men standing on a street—in front of a house, on the sidewalk outside an office—and immediately pull over and force them all onto their stomachs. You're not just in Los Angeles in the 1980s, you're anywhere in the USA now, and you know now more than you might have known then that one false move and any one of them could be dead.

4 ▪ "You Know I'm No Good," curated by Renny Pritikin, Contemporary Jewish Museum, San Francisco (through November 1) The main exhibit is "Amy Winehouse—A Family Portrait," a gallery-filling scrapbook comprising a family tree, a video of fifteen-year-old Amy leading a student chorus, LPs and DVDs and videos from Winehouse's own collection, most strikingly a few gorgeous, tiny stage dresses. But in an artist's alcove in the back, something else is going on. There are color drawings by Rachel Harrison of Winehouse as an artist's muse, Picasso's for one (for her face, or her aura of someone definitely out of reach?), and large cartoon works by James Jägel, including *New Ways of Thinking,* which is Winehouse as the comic-strip Nancy with a big thumb's up. But most of the space is taken by the Bay Area artist Jennie Ottinger's series *Mouth to Mouth: Pieces from an Animation of*

Cultural Appropriation, inspired by Daphne Brooks's "'This Voice Which Is Not One': Amy Winehouse Sings the Ballad of Sonic Blue(s)-face Culture," a 2010 essay from the journal *Women & Performance.*

You hear Winehouse's "You Know I'm No Good" layered over audiences clapping for Nina Simone, Ella Fitzgerald, Billie Holiday, who appear on the walls along with images of Winehouse, the Ronettes, the Supremes, other girl groups, gospel singers—and what immediately strikes you are the mouths. These are all cut-out figures, and the mouths are further cut out from the faces, then pushed out an inch or so from the cheeks and chins (eyes, hair, arms, and legs too may be cut out and distended). All over the walls there are countless black mouths floating, disconnected from any faces, as if the sign of hundreds of years of white-on-black ventriloquism, with a dozen or more white legs, cut off at the knee, and feet, too. All of the figures appear passive, or polite, in the way they stand, in the quiet expressions on their faces, but there's violence everywhere.

Most unnerving is a section where a doubled Winehouse—standing and singing, seated with her legs splayed out to one side—is pictured in front of eight much smaller black women, in groups of two, three, four. Winehouse's right arm tattoo of her grandmother as a young woman in short shorts is visible, along with Winehouse's bouffant. An arm cut off from her body is holding a mike. And there's a line cut right through her head, from the back of the head through the mouth—to suggest a strap-on black mouth, still an inch or two out from Winehouse's mouth, to say it could never reach the face, become part of it, be anything more than a pathetic mask.

It's a powerful argument, and a disturbing image absolutely complete in itself, a closed circle. But the violence on the walls is not foreign to the violence in Winehouse's music—to the faint sounds you could hear of "You Know I'm No Good," "Back to Black," "Tears Dry on Their Own." There was a woman coming apart as you listened—and not just Winehouse. The other singers on the walls—Florence Ballard of the Supremes, Ronnie Spector of the Ronettes, so many more, exploited, used, discarded. I see a picture where no woman on the wall owns her own mouth, where no woman is really in possession of her own voice. Ottinger may have meant to show a white woman taking the voices of black women; she may have produced a tableau of women talking to each other, or trying to draw sounds and speech from their throats, and failing to make a sound.

From an adjoining comments wall: "A strange collection of ephemera. Certainly talented, certainly died too young, but totally lacking in anything truly sublime. Perhaps the fault of the exhibit, perhaps my fault, but seems to be a glorification of self-centeredness. Dieing young is easy to do."

5 ▪ Jeffrey Foucault, "Slow Talker," on *Salt as Wolves* (Blueblade) From a Massachusetts singer, a country plea, a blues reach for facts beyond sound, the sense of immediate doom that only a slide guitar can make in its hesitations, its sense of suspension, that seem to hold everything a step behind where it ought to be. This is scary in the bend of the first note from Bo Ramsey's milky, softly picked guitar. The way notes continue to break away from each other in the relentless syncopation of the piece leaves you stranded. Yes, this should have been the theme music for the second *True Detective*, but it doesn't matter. Listen once, twice, three times—the beat is so elusive it keeps pulling you back— and you'll hear the whole third season.

6 ▪ Wyndham Baird, "Fair and Tender Ladies," 5th Annual Washington Square Folk Festival (New York, September 13) From Brooklyn, Baird plays all over the map—the Cadillacs' 1955 doo-wop masterpiece "Speedo" with a country accent, the Nu Grape Twins' weird 1926 nursery rhyme cum commercial jingle cum gospel sermon "I Got Your Ice Cold Nu Grape," alongside Jackson Lynch of the old-timey string band Downhill Strugglers, Bob Dylan's "Desolation Row." But among various chestnuts, this touched what the late Mike Seeger called the true vine. Affect seemed to vanish, the crowd disappeared. "You'd make me believe, from the fall of your arm," he sang in a slow, droning voice, a woman thinking of her false lover, "That the sun rose in the west." It was a deep dive into the loneliness and abandonment of the song. Baird drifted away from the ends of lines—not, it felt, because he didn't want to sing them but because he didn't want to hear them.

7 ▪ *Time Out of Mind*, written and directed by Oren Moverman, music supervisor Stephanie Diaz-Matos (IFC) Aside from the moment when Richard Gere, as the confused and homeless George, sits down at an antique piano in a café and plays a harsh and twisting sophisticated blues ("Time Out of Mind," Gere's own composition) the music here, like the street noise and constant ambient noise of conversations (in the theater, you look around to see who's talking), has the texture of weather. In a shelter, a second or two of the Handsome Family's "Far from Any Road" wafts in like a slight change in the air pressure. The Velvet Underground's "Candy Says" is heard in a bar, but it feels less like anyone is playing it than that it's been in the room, like a smell in the walls, since the place opened, or even before.

8 ▪ *Sleeping with Other People*, written and directed by Leslye Headland (IFC) In a college dorm, Jason Sudeikis is trying to talk Alison Brie out of a crush she has on a creepy floormate. *It's like telling an Australian aborigine he's going to hear the greatest music ever made,* he says, *and then playing him Blues Traveler instead of the Beatles. You're dooming him to a life of mediocrity, and that's what's going to happen to you.* Which turns out to be convincingly true, even if it is the high point of the movie.

9 ▪ "From Bauhaus to Buenos Aires: Grete Stern and Horacio Coppola," Museum of Modern Art, New York (through October 4, 2015) Stern (1904–99) started working in collage photography in Germany and continued in Argentina when she and the Argentine photographer Coppola (1906–2012), after 1935 her husband, left Europe in the face of the Nazi takeover. Stern's most immediately striking work is her Sueños (Dreams) project, from 1948, where for the Buenos Aires magazine *Idilio* she collaborated on the "El psicoanálisis le ayudará" ("Psychoanalysis will help you") column—then as now, Buenos Aires had as rich a psychoanalytic community as could be found anywhere in the world. Readers would send in their dreams; analysts would interpret them; Stern would illustrate them. Seemingly influenced by Salvador Dalí's dream sequences in Alfred Hitchcock's 1945 *Spellbound,* her collages are blazingly sexual, funny, sometimes obvious, usually not. A hand holds a paintbrush, with a woman's feathery head of hair where the brush ought to be; people in theater boxes attend a concert where a woman plays a piano made of giant typewriter keys.

Stern's most subtle and insinuating work—images that are likely to stay with you longer—were advertisements made in the early 1930s with Stern's partner Ellen Auerbach in their design studio ringl + pit, especially two for the nerve potion Heliocentrin. Both are done in black, white, and yellow, both show women, and both, for anyone raised on the advertising of the last seventy years or so, glow with a grasp for the new, for a spirit of artistic freedom that can speak as loudly in an ad as on a stage, on a wall, on a page.

In one, a plainly depressed woman rests her head on a pillow, her eyes showing bitterness, hatred, and a wish for revenge; it's clear nothing out of a bottle is going to change anything. A second ad shows a thin woman with very short hair, in a low-cut formal dress, looking away from the camera, to her left, unsmiling, but not necessarily unhappy. She's not pretty, but she is beautiful, in a way that envelopes her in modernity—in the idea of the modern as a faith, a religion—and what you can see in her eyes, in the way her face holds her features, is someone thinking. About the party where her picture is being taken. About her dress. About her face. About what's happening in the streets outside the mansion or the hotel where the party is taking place. About why she was born, and how long she's going to live: how long she ought to live, how long she wants to live, and where, and why—thinking about everything.

10 ▪ Jon Stewart's *Daily Show* finale (Comedy Central, August 6) Forget the satire, the greetings, the tributes. On this night when the GOP presidential debate offered a glimpse of an American future that may actually come to pass, let's go straight to the tears: Bruce Springsteen and the E Street Band's closing "Land of Hope and Dreams." As a push into a future more full of freedom than the original "This Train," which starts out naming all the people it won't carry, this train has room for everyone. It breaks my heart every time, but never more so than this night. It pulled no punches, starting with "You don't know where you're going, but you know you won't be back"—nothing could have been easier than to say, with a wave to the host, "You know that you'll be back." "This train—carries souls departed," the heart of the song ends—and it ended. A few bars of "Born to Run" made a dance party finale, but this song hung in the air, over the future that had been prophesied just a click away, just a click away.

November 8, 2015

1 & 2 ▪ Lana Del Rey, *Honeymoon* (Interscope) and Jon Caramanica, "Lana Del Rey: She'd Be Sad, If She Cared (Which She Doesn't)," *New York Times* (September 17) When Lana Del Rey appeared on *Saturday*

Night Live in 2012 to sing "Video Games," in effect her national debut, she really did look like a debutante: long gown which didn't exactly fit, an air of nerves. It struck me as the exact opposite of the normal *SNL* musical spot: uncertain, unfinished, and most of all not obvious—the most radical music on the show in ages. It brought forth a storm of derision, so unrelenting that not long after the show parodied its own former guest in the person of Kristen Wiig in a floppy long-hair wig, embarrassing prom dress, and wan face.

You might realize, listening to Lana Del Rey's new, most fully realized album, comparable in its way to Amy Winehouse's *Back to Black*, that her songs slip when even a hint of the specific breaks the spell. In "Art Deco," the words "You're so art deco" take you away from the pure, liquid syllables of the opening lines, away from the way the song can feel like a cloud passing in front of the moon. There's no way to pin this music down—and at its best Lana Del Rey's music never wholly comes across right away. It reveals itself over time. Play the album, come back two weeks later, play it again, and you might find yourself listening to a different record.

There are hints of a rock 'n' roll frame of reference—or something like a penumbra—all through this music: "Hotel California" in the words and Duane Eddy in the opening notes for "God Knows I Tried," the Kinks' "Celluloid Heroes" in "Terrence Loves You," even Connie Francis in "Music to Watch Boys To." None of it matters. The strongest songs impose their own gravity, and nothing escapes it: they create self-enclosed, imaginary landscapes, where winds blow through whatever might be taking shape as a theme.

Tunes don't progress in any conventional manner. They sway, until you can almost see the movies they're scoring. Lana Del Rey floats on her own voice: a song calling up a café in Budapest in 1937 feels as if it's coming out of a radio at least as old, but there are no sound effects. The effect is all in the phrasing, the hesitation, the commitment to the situation that's being created. Most complete is "Religion," with more than ten instruments credited, none of which seem to be there, all of them erased like the filler lyrics by a distant, gorgeous beckoning toward the specter painted by Arnold Böcklin as *Isle of the Dead*. The creaminess of the voice can hide but not negate the acrid, suicidal loathing that drives this song, or "The Blackest Day," or the title song, where you know that even if there's a wedding, the marriage will never make it to a honeymoon. When Del Rey ends with a song that isn't hers—covering the Animals' "Don't Let Me Be Misunderstood"—it's no message. This singer is enough of an artist not to care whether you understand her or not, or to claim there's anything to understand. It's a chance to sing in a different rhythm, to focus the song on a word, opening up "good," letting it breathe, letting it tell the whole story. The organ close by Rick Novels, Lana Del Rey's co-writer, is lovely.

Jon Caramanica, who holds the hip-hop and country fiefdoms in the *New York Times*, is the sort of arts pundit described in Paul Beatty's novel *Slumberland*: a "master spy who used his cover as a pop-culture critic to prop up dictatorial movements like 'trip-hop,' 'jungle,' 'Dogme 95,' and 'graffiti art' instead of puppet third-world governments." All music is reductively slotted into ever more finely sliced genres, as if Caramanica not only recognizes but owns them, and judged according to how it follows (for hip-hop) or breaks (for country) the rules, as discerned or invented by the writer, of its branded style. Individual performers are presented either as actual people, and their songs treated as personal messages from artist to audience, or as personas, with the music of each personified personage judged according to how effectively, given, in Carmanica's schema, the performer's always transparent intent, the persona is ironically or flatly constructed or deconstructed. Caramanica is the critic as cop—Vice Squad or Red Squad, depending.

"She's been angry, and then bored of being angry, but now she's just bored," he wrote in a review of *Honeymoon*, stretching the sneer he's tried to impose on Lana Del Rey since the release of her *Born to Die*. (Oh, the effrontery, using a name she wasn't given!) He went on, alternating left-handed admiration for her elaboration of her being ("her boredom is entrancing") with barely disguised contempt, until he reaches the point where he can compose a closing paragraph so perfectly self-referential it seems less meant to make the writer's point than flatter him: "And so after four years in the limelight, here lounges Ms. Del Rey, immune to the gravitational pull of the discourse about her. Once a careful invention, she is now glassy-eyed and glassy-voiced, too cool to care. The result is something like a dog that, when its leash is tugged, simply lies on the ground and shuts its eyes: basking in the sun, feeding off its warmth, never giving an inch."

A male writer calling a female singer a dog somehow got past the *Times*' copy editors—or maybe, given how effectively Lana Del Rey offends people, they cheered. But the writer gave himself away with that "immune to the discourse about her," which is to say her real sin is not paying enough attention to the police reports. No one's getting away with that, especially when the cop owns the discourse, too.

3 ▪ Remy Francois, "House of the Rising Sun," Sixth Avenue and Herald Square subway station (New York, October 15) A loud, abrasive, supremely confident scattershot electric guitar seemed to shuffle the tiles on the walls. A poker-faced man with a crown on his head was pushing the song's strong melody into abstraction, but the melody would not give itself up; he set off sparks of high notes he erased with a slash. You realized the song would never wear out, not with a musician like this proving that the old folk song, the tenth cut on Bob Dylan's first album, the Animals' worldwide rock 'n' roll hit, had only begun to break out the stories it could tell. A lot of people gave him money.

4 ▪ Gee Gee Kettel, "Sultans of Swing," rue de Buci and rue Mazarine (Paris, October 11) A man who's busked around the world since 1980 on a street corner: there was something unyielding in the curl he found in the tune, his steel-body National Resonator turning it into a modal drone—and it sounded better, more alluring, more unsettling, at a distance, in the cold air, than close up.

5 ▪ John Seabrook, *The Song Machine: Inside the Hit Factory* (Norton) Seabrook is a fine business reporter, and his detailed, bustling portraits of the hit-making of Kelly Clarkson, K-pop idols, the Backstreet Boys, 'N Sync, Rihanna, Katy Perry, Lou Pearlman, Clive Davis, Dr. Luke, and such Swedish technicians as Max Martin are always fascinating. He makes a convincing case that the pop past is as irrelevant as the future, and that hits depend on absolute predictability: of what a song will do once it has presented itself, and of how anyone listening will react. All of which passes by as a kind of roller coaster seen through a thick glass—until Seabrook begins to adopt the language of the people he's writing about ("a listening party that included Ty Ty fucking Smith, Jay-Z's homeboy"), gets caught up in the hype surrounding him (Alanis Morrisette's *Jagged Little Pill* is an "epoch-making hit"—really, what epoch, in the soul of the land or the music business, did it make?), and an inescapable *Invasion of the Body Snatchers–Brave New World–1984–They Live* cloud begins to hover over every story. IGNORANCE IS STRENGTH, WAR IS PEACE, FREEDOM IS SLAVERY—or, rather, slavery is freedom, at least in the sense that by giving up your ideas, your desires, and your personality, you can have endless hits and enormous amounts of money. Seabrook may be drawing this picture in spite of himself.

6 ▪ Jakob Dylan and Cat Power, "You Showed Me," from _Echo in the Canyon_ (Pitchfork) Aren't tribute albums terrible? Who knows about this one, featuring the likes of Beck, Fiona Apple, and a refugee from Edward Sharpe's hideous onstage hippie commune the Magnetic Zeros taking on mid-'60s L.A. so-called canyon music—it won't be out till next year. "You Showed Me" was an unreleased Byrds song covered in 1969 by the Turtles. Their version, inexplicably, or not really, a top ten hit, was so forgettable you couldn't remember it while you were listening to it. It was a tinny pop song: the Byrds played it fast, as if to cover up their own embarrassment (they were going to be a serious band, not some dumb teeny-bopper hit machine, but they were short on songs for demos). Cat Power teases out the foreboding in the corny, cramped melody, until the tune begins to open up, to stretch out, and you can take pleasure in the way she treats words as a chance to almost fall asleep.

7 ▪ _Van Morrison Live on Cyprus Avenue,_ Belfast, Northern Ireland (BBC Radio Ulster, August 31) A live broadcast as Morrison returned to boyhood haunts to mark his seventieth birthday, spending two hours explaining that, yes, everything really does slow down when you turn that corner, everything sounds like everything else, and where was I? Highlights: "Whatever Happened to P. J. Proby," featuring the long-lost Proby himself, a Texas rocker who never had a hit in the U.S. but tore up the U.K. in the years before the Beatles, who sounds three hundred years old (he's seventy-six); "Sometimes We Cry," for the way the lines "I'm not going to fake it / Like Johnny Ray" still stick out. I don't know why Morrison thinks Johnny Ray was faking it, but he sounds as if he knows exactly what he means, and if you don't, he really doesn't have time to go into it.

8 ▪ Pere Ubu, _Elitism for the People_ (Fire) A four-LP box containing the Cleveland "avant-garage" band's first two albums, the formally avant-garde _The Modern Dance_ and the musical film noir _Dub Housing,_ both from 1978, a set of earlier singles that in 1975 or 1977 sounded like science fiction and today communicate like a news report, and a *Live at Max's Kansas City* 1977 set where real drama takes place. "Sentimental Journey" is stuttering, then desperate, because something isn't right, something isn't working—a fabulous acting out of a moment of complete panic.

9 ▪ Dilly Dally, "Desire," from *Sore* (Partisan) Watching the Toronto singer and guitarist Katie Monks with her not-quite-shoulder-length chopped blonde hair and the dark-haired guitarist Liz Ball bent over her instrument in the video for this chiming and corrugated song, it's hard not to think of Samuel Bayer's video for Nirvana's "Smells Like Team Spirit." There's the same visual focus on both truth-telling and craft, and the feeling that the two elements may have nothing to do with each other. The ground beneath your feel slips a little, then a little more. You stop thinking, as Monks seems to have stopped thinking. You begin to hear the music being made; Ball is only being more careful. This isn't typical. Some of the band's songs can feel contrived, tripping over their own smartness. But this song doesn't explain itself, doesn't reveal itself, and seems to have no limits.

10 ▪ *Time to Choose*, directed by Charles Ferguson, prerelease screening at the Ford Foundation (New York, September 22) Walking-in music for this alternatingly kill-me-now/future-is-bright documentary on what Laurent Fabius, host of the December world conference on climate change in Paris, calls "climate destruction" (gruesome footage of mountain-top removal, then wind farms so vast they look like they're on another planet): Motown. Walking-out music: Tears for Fears, "Everybody Wants to Rule the World."

December 18, 2015

The name of the set is an embarrassing cliché, especially for a production that allows you to follow the adventures of collective imaginations: the flickers that flare up like the Northern Lights in Bob Dylan's first albums made as rock 'n' roll—three albums that rewrote what those three words meant. There are many books in the nearly four hundred tracks on **Bob Dylan's *The Cutting Edge 1965–1966 Collectors Edition: The Bootleg Series*, Vol. 12 (Columbia)**—eighteen CDs comprising the complete recording sessions for *Bringing It All Back Home* (March 1965), *Highway 61 Revisited* (September 1965), and *Blonde on Blonde* (May 1966), plus a final disc of hotel room composing. There is the complete recording session, over two days, with different musicians, for "Like a Rolling Stone." There are the eleven versions of "Desolation Row." *Blonde on Blonde* especially looms up as a huge, spouting whale, cresting again and again with the thirteen takes of the discarded "She's Your Lover Now"; twenty-four takes of "One of Us Must Know (Sooner or Later)" plus the master take broken down into separate tracks for vocal, piano and drums, and guitar and bass (the sound, perhaps the only attempt to reinhabit the terrain opened up with "Like a Rolling Stone," is so rich you almost can't hear the whole song at once); the fifteen takes of "Stuck Inside of Mobile with the Memphis Blues Again" (but what was wrong with the title the song first carried, the simple, elegant "Memphis Blues Again"?); and the eighteen of "Just Like a Woman." But for glamour, uncertainty, doubt, and more than once a seeming completeness, a moment when the song, like a hare outrunning the people trying to catch it, is brought to ground, and then gets up and disappears again, there may be nothing to match what happens in the twenty-one takes—rehearsals, breakdowns, false starts, and, six times, to the end—of "Visions of Johanna," an epic of Bohemian gloom, convulsion, and silence, all caught in a measured tone of hipster disdain trying to escape from itself: "We sit here stranded, we all doing our best to deny it." It was recorded first in New York, on November 11, 1965, with Dylan on guitar and harmonica; Robbie Robertson, guitar; Garth Hudson, organ; Richard Manuel, piano and electric piano; Rick Danko, bass; and Bobby Gregg, drums, and in Nashville on February 14, 1966, with Dylan on acoustic guitar and harmonica; Robertson again on guitar; on two tracks, with Charlie McCoy on guitar; Wayne Moss, guitar; Al Kooper, organ; Joe South, bass; and Kenneth Buttrey, drums—the session that, in its fourth and last take, made the version that was released on *Blonde on Blonde*. To scramble these performances into a set of ten is the most patent absurdity this column has perpetrated in all of its thirty years.

1 & 2 ▪ New York, takes 3 & 4 The song was different from so many others: Dylan brought it in written, from first line to last, and except for the slightest slips the words never changed. Unlike almost any of Dylan's songs, "Visions of Johanna" scans on the page not as a footnote to a recording but as a thing in itself; it communicates in its own black-and-white. The lines are mean and balanced. The song is an explosion waiting to happen; the question is how close the musicians can take the song to the point of no return. Here, with three first tries, none of which gets past three minutes—well short of the more than seven minutes the song is written for—they start off fast, with a syncopation that everyone seems to be trying to keep up with, as if the pace is being set by some invisible whip. The band comes together instantly; what's striking is how plainly Dylan can't find the song. His singing slides from one wrong rhythm to another, mannerism to mannerism, reaching for words with a smeared melodrama. Dylan repeatedly stops the music, at one point calling for cowbell from Bobby Gregg, complaining that they're going too fast. At the end of the second take Dylan forces the pace down, singing word for word, the meaningless elisions he'd been trying out before abandoned, and something like realism is filling out the voice. You can hear these words ("Louise holds a handful of rain") and actually imagine that someone might say them. With the third take, lasting 2 minutes, 53 seconds, Dylan again tries to pull back: "It's not hard rock—the only thing is, that's hard, is Robbie." Hudson's organ comes in loud. "No, no, no," Dylan says, hitting on the key to the music: "This way: instead of *bomp bomp, dis baaaaahhhh. Dis BAAAAAHHHH.*" He's written the song, it's finished, but that means the song stands apart from him, with its own desires, its own brain. The song has more power to say how it needs to be sung than the singer has to tell the song what to do, and the singer is listening to the song, trying to learn its language, and here he catches the grammar. It's the first moment when he gets a purchase on the tune. He arrives again at "Louise holds a handful of rain, tempting you to defy it," and you realize that these are the lines on which the song turns, when suddenly everything is in jeopardy, nothing is for sure, the floorboards could drop right off your feet—not the "handful of rain," a play on the 1957 film about a junkie, *A Hatful of Rain*, a phrase already part of the common frame of reference, a borrowing so blatant it would feel fake if the singer didn't sound as if he were naming an idea, not something so factual as heroin, but the "you to defy it," everything invested in *defy*, so that the bomb of the song almost goes off right here. And then Dylan turns away from the line, defusing it. You can almost hear him physically turn away, to look out the window of the loft where the song is playing out to the loft across the way, to watch the lights flicker—and the story is free to go on. Then the singing sags, and the take is lost.

With charismatic guitar, the next, fourth take starts up, and within the fast tempo all sorts of slow, delicate negotiations are taking place. There's room in the song. No gestures are blocked. Dylan's singing is deliberate, still emotionally off but pushing forward as if the song will explain itself before it's made a fool of him. Then the musicians throw the engineer out of the locomotive and bet a runaway train will take them where they need to go. The music comes together in a single thrill—a waft of harmonica from Dylan has more singularity, more personality, than any words he sings. The band begins to crash down on the ends of words, doubling down, and the shock in the sound seems to break Dylan free. "The ghost of electricity breathes in the bones of her face"—as the song goes on, as it finishes months later in Nashville, it will be the famous "howls in the bones of her face," but isn't the word Dylan uses now less a poetic effect, more disturbing, an image you can't fix, that won't hold still for its close-up, that carries through to the end of the song? As sound, it's a first step: now the tension is doubled again, Dylan's singing achieves its true shape, and he's gone. From this point on the most indelible moments won't come with the lines that would, with *Blonde on Blonde*, burn the song into any listener's mind, but when, three times, Dylan comes off a line with a long, long "AAAAAWWWWWWWWWW," not as if words can't say what he wants to say, but as if he's shocked at what he's just said. It's "Hound Dog" with all the kidding pulled out of it like a tooth.

3 ▪ New York, take 5 Compared to what has just happened, this is monolithic, all values boiled down to momentum. But halfway through, odd things begin to happen. Again, the song seems to slow down inside of its own rush. "Inside the museum"—and, in a displacement that feels like a suspension, you really are in a museum. It's specific. It's the Museum of Modern Art in New York, and you're looking at the jelly-faced women, the demoiselles of Avignon. It makes perfect sense one of them can't find her knees; you can't either. Then you turn your head and you're in the Louvre. You come up with a good line for the Mona Lisa, but she's not really giving anything up. This is a dream inside a maelstrom, and the maelstrom comes back. When it ends you can't see the musicians merely going back to another take—as it happens, after an attempt that ends after less than two minutes, a deadly slow nine minutes during which nothing connects. You see them passing out from exhaustion and being carted off to the hospital.

4 ▪ Nashville, take 4 As it appeared on *Blonde on Blonde*. The pattern of notes on the harmonica open the song as if they've always been there, as if this is the full voice of the song, passing by from beginning to end in seconds; from beginning to end the performance feels less made than fated. The drums begin late, absolutely on the pulse of the song but rickety, offhand, as if the drummer walked into the studio and said, "Oh, right. This one."

5–7 ▪ Nashville, takes 1–3 A false start at just over half a minute, a breakdown at 2 minutes, 45 seconds, another false start at just under half a minute, but a single drama: a folk song.

8 ▪ New York, take 13 A breakdown at 1 minute, 13 seconds, but there's a lift in the music that hints at an undiscovered song. The guitarist and the organist walk around the singer, each circle they make wider than the next, but the harmonica says it all. The singing is stiff and false, with words missed and even mispronounced; it's a botch. But almost imperceptibly the ground has been cleared.

9 ▪ New York, take 14 From the first half second, the song lifts off the ground and stays there. The sound is so gorgeous you can barely register the words the singer is singing, but the singer is now less a person with a text than pure body, a body subsumed wholly into the voice, which is clear, forceful, determined to get the story told.

10 ▪ New York, takes 9–12 Two minutes, 17 seconds, slotted as a single track. After the nine minutes in which the song seemed to have wandered off to die, a new approach: the song taken even more slowly, but without any pretense that it has anywhere to go or anything to prove. There's a hint of country music; then of a western ballad. Takes 4 and 5 had been so inflamed—this is elegiac, its motive regret. The next take barely sets the stage: you can see people putting props down here and there, with the feeling that one false move would break not only the mood but the song. "No, no, no," Dylan says, then again, and then the song is edging away from the Sons of the Pioneers toward something richer, fuller, closer to *My Darling Clementine*—the movie, not the song.

January 26, 2016

1 ▪ **Colin Donnell, "House of the Rising Sun," on *The Affair* (Showtime, December 20)** For the finale of the second season, Donnell's Scotty Lockhart, just out of a three-month stint in rehab, starts drinking at his brother Cole's wedding. He gets up with the band to say he didn't really get the happy couple a gift, but he does have this song: "It's an old one, but, man, it's a hell of a song. And nobody really knows what it's about but—to me, it's about *family*." In a creepy David Lynch setting with dim red light, he launches himself into the most vengeful, self-loathing, threatening, shamed, they-will-pay rendition of the old folk song imaginable, stretching into hysteria at the end of the verses, and yes, he's right: you don't know what it's about, just that he's turned a wedding into a wake.

2 ▪ **Waco Brothers, *Going Down in History* (Bloodshot)** The apostate honky-tonk band from Chicago with alternating suicide notes and cynical breast-beating: "The day after the music died/We can't take all the credit, but we tried." But their fervor, the sense of what's been lost, is as hard as you can find anywhere—"We Know It" could have been called "Going Down in Flames"—and the suicide notes can be stirring. Dean Schlabowske brings off a cover of the Small Faces' "All or Nothing," which could have been pure corn, because you can hear him standing back from every line before committing himself to it.

3 ▪ **Sleater-Kinney, Irving Plaza (New York, December 14)** "Jumpers" (2005) made an arc that minute by minute seemed to push toward a receding horizon like a black rainbow. But the highlight might have been when Corin Tucker came back for a six-and-a-half-minute encore of the B-52s' "Rock Lobster" (1979) led by Fred Armisen, Tucker wearing a metallic Cindy Wilson pink wig that came off about two thirds of the way in, while she was lobstering on the floor. With Armisen gone they closed the night with "Dig Me Out" (1997), as desperate as it ever was. The walking-out music was the Spaniels' "Goodnight Sweetheart, Goodnight" (1954).

4 ■ Gimme Shelter Realtors "Proof that home ownership isn't just for squares": listing for 616 Page Street, San Francisco, $1,500,000. Special feature: occupied by the Manson Family in 1967. Who in the fall of 1969 might have been the inspiration for the song.

5 ■ *Steel Hammer*, Julia Wolfe, composer, Anne Bogart, director, text by Kia Corthron, Will Power, Carl Hancock Rux, and Regina Taylor, score commissioned by Bang on a Can, Brooklyn Academy of Music (December 2) Which would be more remarkable—that John Henry's race with a steam drill actually happened, and was then lost to history, the legend remaining but the facts gone, or that, one day, someone simply made it all up? Here John Henry is going to prison and he and Polly Ann are breaking up. They'll never see each other again. *Make sure the children remember me,* he says. *Oh, I'll tell them stories,* she says, with a hint of I've-had-enough-of-you sarcasm in her voice. *I'll tell them what a great steel driver you were. I'll tell them you beat a steam drill!*

6 ■ *Hamilton*, book, music, and lyrics by Lin-Manuel Miranda, directed by Thomas Kail, Richard Rodgers Theatre (New York) "Go, man, go"—it's a shout out of the hubbub, and, watching, you might find yourself experiencing a sense of double consciousness. In your first mind, the intelligence, speed, and glee of the voices, and the magnetism of the actors, especially Daveed Diggs doubling as Jefferson and Lafayette, is so complete you forget that most of the actors are black or Hispanic, that their language is hip-hop. This is how they had to talk, you can think: this is what the whole revolutionary crew should have said. And then you realize that if the same play were put on in its time, or even fifty years later—let's say a blackface minstrel show with black actors blacking up, as African Americans did after the Civil War—most of these people would have been slaves. So the hammer comes down. This is the absolutely marginalized fantasizing their way into the history that excluded them. And still does.

7 ■ Philippe Margotin and Jean-Michel Guesdon, *Bob Dylan: All the Songs—The Story Behind Every Track* (Black Dog & Leventhal) One element of philistinism is the denial of the imagination, which is also the denial of thinking, which is also a denial of style. Any song, poem, film, painting—any representation, including the most abstract—must be seen literally, tied to an actual happenstance. No creative occasion can simply *occur*. No image, no pile of words, can leap out of an artist and appear as if according to its own will, then to be shaped by the artist and made into something that wasn't there before. I opened this book at random, to the section on the Basement Tapes tune "Goin' to Acapulco." Each number is broken into "Genesis and Lyrics" and "Production"; this began with "In this song, Bob Dylan may have only wanted to sing about a trip to Mexico" (Acapulco is a city in Mexico) "and an unexpected encounter with a mysterious Rose Marie." There follows speculation that one line with a commonplace expression might refer to the Book of Revelation, and also that the song mentions the Taj Mahal, and that "some Dylan scholars see a link to the 1957 novel *Candy*, which tells the story of an eighteen-year-old girl who has many sexual experiences and undertakes a journey to India" (the Taj Mahal is in India). But there may be more: "Or did Dylan just want to refer to Elvis Presley's film *Fun in Acapulco*?" (The page features a poster for the movie.) I leafed through the thing; that's the book in one. Unless you have $50 you need to get rid of and like carrying around an 11″ by 8″ 703-page book that weighs five pounds, read Michael Gray's *Song and Dance Man* instead.

8 ▪ *Anomalisa,* **directed by Duke Johnson and Charlie Kaufman (Paramount)** "I think Charlie Kaufman wants to punish us" said the person next to me: in this animated film hailed as a work of beauty, humanism, and compassion, with critics swooning over Jennifer Jason Leigh's precious recital of "Girls Just Want to Have Fun," a motivational speaker with a hit how-to book encounters two women in his Cincinnati hotel who've driven all the way from Akron to hear him, takes them down to the bar and gets them drunk, peels off the one he sizes up as most vulnerable, takes her to his room to have sex with her, tells her he loves her and that he's going to leave his family, and—after she starts to get on his nerves—goes home and forgets all about her.

9 ▪ *Ork Records: New York, New York* **(Numero)** Started 1975. Forty-nine numbers including first singles by Television ("Little Johnny Jewel") and Richard Hell—the unusually double-parentheticalled "(I

Could Live with You) (In) Another World" b/w "(I Belong to the) Blank Generation." Added to those are tracks by Alex Chilton, Chris Stamey, Lester Bangs, the Feelies, and Lenny Kaye's 1965 Link Cromwell single "Crazy Like a Fox" b/w "Shock Me," as well as a superbly designed book with interviews with Terry Ork and others and extensive commentary by Ken Shipley and Rob Sevier. A comment from Ork's contemporary Michael Zilkha, who with Michel Esteban founded Ze Records in New York in 1978: "When you start a label you can only sign bands that no one bigger wants. If your resources are limited, all you can offer is commitment and belief that your taste is prophetic. My first signing was James White & The Blacks, a band that didn't yet exist: White's Contortions slowed down to a disco beat. This alternate identity strategy, pioneered by Parliament/Funkadelic, enabled the Contortions to put out music and still hold out for a major label deal. I planned to meld a disco beat to a nihilistic attitude, and the marriage actually worked. Once *Off White* was recorded the Contortions signed too. Chris Blackwell financed my label, Ze Records, in return for European distribution rights for Island. I had suggested he sign Talking Heads when they were a trio, so he took a gamble. Terry Ork took a more traditional but difficult path. He paid for, pressed and distributed his early records himself. Then, predictably, once his artists had the opportunity they left him for larger labels. Too few producers ask themselves, 'Does this record really need to be made?' The first three tracks here unquestionably did. There may be more definitive recordings elsewhere of Television's 'Little Johnny Jewel,' the Feelies 'Fa Ce-La,' and Richard Hell's 'Blank Generation,' but it's magic hearing these urgent originals in succession: there's an energy and sincerity that perfectly reflects the druggy schizoid ambitions of the early CBGBs scene. Bands want to make it, even if they are too cool to admit it.

"Like so many labels of love, Ork Records didn't focus on the money. But it also failed to build an identity because it was a singles-centric operation and it was mostly hopeless at getting its products released with any impact. By the time Ork rebooted with proper distribution it was too late for the label. Their key artists had left, and the new ones got lost in the shuffle. I wasn't much better at business. I forgot to pick up my Waitresses option when they were in the top forty and Kid Creole bought themselves out of their contract once they hit. Being a middleman/farm team was untenable financially, and it was hurtful emotionally that my artists then viewed me as a tax, devaluing the contribution

I had made advising and editing them so carefully. However because of that effort Ze did have an identity. We had developed a repertory company, and we put out coherent albums that told a larger story. When that magic was gone I quit. Continuing Ze would have been a business rather than a mission, without the joy and excitement. *Ork Records New York, New York* conveys that sense of mission. With its deluxe slip case and its informative annotated and photograph-filled 180 page booklet, it is endearingly out of sync with the squalor and disarray in which its recordings were conceived and produced."

10 ▪ David Bowie, 1947–2016 He wore his heart up his sleeve, but it was almost always there. In Alexander Trocchi's phrase, he was an astronaut of inner space. Maybe now he'll tell us if there's life on Mars.

With thanks to Brett Lyman. And deep thanks to Bill Tipper, Nick Curley, and Jim Mustich, who gave this column a good home. Starting in February it will appear at pitchfork.com.

Pitchfork

2016·2017

February 17, 2016

1 ▪ The Platters, "Smoke Gets in Your Eyes" in *45 Years,* directed by Andrew Haigh (The Bureau) Sometimes you can listen to a song all your life without hearing it. That's what happens to Charlotte Rampling. When we first see her in the film, she's thinking about the forty-fifth anniversary party she and her husband, played by Tom Courtenay, are planning. Almost idly, she's humming the Platters' huge 1958 hit. It was already an old song, then; here, the orchestration of their version— its quiet, calm statement of the theme, then the music taking on body and heat—produced a romantic sweep that locked it into her heart when she was a girl and it's never left it. Yes, the song was a warning from its first verse—the smoke that gets in your eyes is the blindness of love, and love is sure to fail—but the passion of the Platters frontman Tony Williams's singing left the fire burning, the smoke giving off the most luscious warmth, and everything else fell away.

Later we see Rampling putting together a playlist for the party— "And the Platters, of course," she says after naming half a dozen other songs, almost an afterthought, because it goes without saying it would have to be there. But by now, over the course of a few days, her marriage has begun to come apart; watching, you can feel her pulling away as inexorably as Williams climbs the steps of the melody. She can feel it, but she doesn't know it, not yet.

At the party, with all of their friends gathered—barely anyone too young to have heard the Platters on the radio in their time is even glimpsed on the screen through the whole course of the film—there's a sense that Rampling and Courtenay might get through it and come out the other side. Then the Platters sing, and the lines she has always ignored, which she's never really heard—because when you love a song, the words say what they say to you, not what any songwriter might have meant you to hear, you rewrite the song according to what you want it to say, the feeling it produces in you may cut absolutely against any literal reading of the words, what you keep is the promise in the music, not the judgment of its moral lesson—rise up out of the stupendous finale of the record. Each word of the last line is like a star exploding, and each one slams her in the face: "When that lovely flame dies/Smoke/Gets/In/Your/Eyes," the last word hanging in the air as the music swirls around her. Dancing with her husband, Rampling slams her hand down and out of his in the most violent ending to a movie about love you'll ever want to see. For forty-five years, the song saved the marriage; now it saves her. Will she ever listen to it again?

2 ▪ Eleanor Friedberger, *New View* (Frenchkiss) With her brother Matt in the Fiery Furnaces and on her own solo albums, Friedberger's singing has always created a world of nervousness, anxiety, a sardonic sense of fate, of life as a joke she wishes she didn't get. As music, that meant someone walking down the street with someone behind her and instantly turning to face the other person: *Who do you think you're kidding?* It meant wild humor, rampant noise, songs breaking out in all directions just when you were settling into what seemed to be a steady beat. On *New View* the songs—"Open Season," "Because I Asked You," "Two Versions of Tomorrow," "A Long Walk"—can seem like throwaways. Everything is in a minor mode. No one is making trouble. But the record takes time to open up. The situations in the songs don't yield to laughter; they are impervious to tears. You can put on your usual act and no one pays attention. So the people in the songs begin to draw on reserves of patience, bitterness, and desire—for an end to small talk, for a moment when nothing needs to be said, for an admission that can't be taken back—that they didn't know were there. Friedberger's songs used to answer their own questions, even if all it took was a grin. These don't.

3 ▪ Cole Coffee, Oakland, California (January 20) "I'm really enjoying this Republican game show," said regular Matthew Shoemaker, standing in line. "You know how Ted Cruz looks like Joe McCarthy? If you listen closely, he sounds just like Truman Capote."

4 ▪ *Winter on Fire: Ukraine's Fight for Freedom,* directed by Evgeny Afineevsky (Netflix) "Having to decide who was already dead, that was the hardest thing."—Dr. Katya Koriyka, on the last days of the Maidan Square insurrection in 2014.

5 ▪ Sarah Vowell, *Lafayette in the Somewhat United States* (River-head), publisher's disclaimer On the copyright page: "While the author has made every effort to provide accurate telephone numbers, Internet addresses, and other contact information at the time of publication, neither the publisher nor the author assumes any responsibility for errors, or for changes that occur after publication." I asked Vowell what this meant. She had no idea. I asked literary agents. They didn't have a clue.

6 ▪ "The Final Countdown," Geico commercial featuring "the band Europe" (Martin Agencyo) The bottom. Not a dive bar that advertises "Europe—'The Final Countdown,'" since they know you might remember the song (1986, #1 all over Europe, #8 in the U.S.) even if you don't remember who did it. Not a car dealership opening. Not a 1990 Sweet Sixteen party. A bottom beyond any band's imagining: a grimy lunchroom where the band has to be introduced as "the band" since the band Europe has so completely vanished into obscurity people might think someone's announcing the place. The band is firing off pyrotechnics and bending over and shooting back up as if they're still playing stadiums, and the already-tired lower-level employees can't be bothered to pay attention to anything but the microwave counting down until the burrito is hot. Nobody makes the connection between the machine and the song. Lead singer Joey Tempest hasn't changed his stage clothes for thirty years even if the real countdown is imprinted on his face and he's emoting as if he's describing the end of the world.

7 ▪ Tacocat, Bottom of the Hill, San Francisco (December 9, 2015) Doug Kroll, former proprietor of Rather Ripped, Berkeley's original punk record store, reports on a night I would have made if I hadn't been 3,000 miles away: "A highlight of the '50s TV show 'American Bandstand' was when a couple of kids were asked to rate a song an act had just lip-synced; the better the song was to dance to, the higher the score. But to really understand Tacocat's performance you'd need a rating system that goes beyond the dance question. Take Tacocat's 'Crimson Wave,' a surf anthem about having your period, which closed the show. Under the new rating system, we could hope for a comment from Sally: 'I give it a 98 because you can dance to it, and it makes me less ashamed about having my period,' and from Billy: 'I give it a 95 because you can dance to it, and it made me realize that I have periods too.' (This being a show in San Francisco, when the Seattle band introduced the song by asking those on their period to raise their hands, both girls and guys raised them high.) 'Men Explain Things to Me,' from Tacocat's upcoming album, *Lost Time*, features a chorus that spotlights a litany of known male transgressions, 'Explain it to me,' or 'Tell me to calm down,' each phrase repeated three times, followed by a pointed pause before singer Emily Nokes delivers a weary 'again.' Figure a Sally rating of 96, because she can dance to it and it speaks to why she gave up on men years ago, and figure Billy for a 78 because although he can dance to it, he really doesn't understand what this has to do with him. This would be a great Hillary Clinton campaign song. It would definitely get out a big chunk of the woman's vote. I'll bet Tacocat would play it at the inauguration. I'd go."

8 ▪ "Jimmie Rodgers . . . He used to sing 'Hoo da lay dee,' you know what I mean?" Howlin' Wolf interviewed by Chris Strachwitz, San Francisco, 1967 (arhoolie.org) In 1931 the Father of Country Music visited the Carter Family. "Yea hey, howdy folks, yodel-ay hee he," he sang as he drove up to their house on the novelty record Victor put out. About the same time he met Howlin' Wolf. "That was my friend," the blues singer said one afternoon in a San Francisco music club, remembering Mississippi more than thirty years before. "On some of those plantations, he had some friends. While he'd been down there, he'd just taken up with me. It seemed like I had good, sound sense. I was a good boy. When I'd sit down, he'd be out there on the porch playing to the white people. When he'd get through playing, he said, 'You seem like you're innocent.' 'Yes,' I'd say. 'I am.' He'd sit down and yodel to me." "You two were making history," someone says—why can't there be a record of *this*? "Yeah," Howlin' Wolf says: suddenly you hear Jimmie Rodgers in "Smokestack Lightning," and you hear Howlin' Wolf in "Waiting for a Train." "He'd sit down and yodel to me and then I'd get out in the field and yodel. I wouldn't yodel just like him. I brought mine down more different. You know."

9 ▪ Jarett Kobek, *I Hate the Internet* (We Heard You Like It Books) Forget the kneejerk title. This book has nothing in common with Sunday think pieces about how personal technology may be eroding our ability to communicate in a meaningful way, or the dystopia of Dave Eggers's *The Circle*, where every *Invasion of the Body Snatchers* horror is telegraphed in the first ten pages. This is a relentless, cruel, hilariously inflamed satire of a loop of economic mystification and the reemergence of the credibility of the notion of Original Sin in the technological utopia of the present-day Bay Area and the world being remade in its image. The book is an adventure of the translation of the given into a reality almost too blunt to credit: *"governance,* an organizing principle used by societies to determine which individuals were granted homes on high ground and which individuals were forcibly executed." Commonplace takedowns are shot into the sky with eruptions of fury: "The many forms and shapes of The One True God"—already defined in terms of "In God We Trust" appearing "on each piece of paper of American money"—"did not come close to describing the actual God. The actual God was wonderful and useless. The actual God was nothing more and nothing less than the sound of Etta James singing 'I'd Rather Go Blind.'" Kobek is most lucid deconstructing the meaning of fame as a symbolic acting out of political economics in the relationship between Beyoncé, Rihanna, and their fans, and most painful, in a manner you might find yourself impossible to dig out from under your skin, in a few brief pages on the transmission of supposedly deleted sex photos to everyone in the town of Truth or Consequences, New Mexico: "Ellen was twenty-two years old and her life was over."

My favorite moment may be on the parable of racism in a story concerning how and why the first side of Son House's 1930 78 "My Black Mama," about sex, was, in generations to come, ignored, while the second side, about death, was, in small part due to people like me, celebrated all over the world, but almost anyone reading this book will be telling everyone they know about something else.

10 ▪ Blythe Danner, "Cry Me a River" in *I'll See You in My Dreams,* directed by Brett Haley (Bleecker Street) At 73 Danner has lost nothing of the script girl Trouty she played in *Hearts of the West* forty years ago. The name she carried like a badge summed up her whole personality: You couldn't push her over with a bulldozer. Here her pool boy brings her to a karaoke bar; she used to be in a band. As opposed to the half-dozen formal-gown costume changes Julie London went through when she sang the original "Cry Me a River" in *The Girl Can't Help It* in 1956—up against Gene Vincent, Eddie Cochran, the Platters, and Little Richard, she didn't flinch—Danner wears a film-noir trench coat, curling the lines of the song like smoke from an invisible film-noir cigarette.

Thanks to Tom Luddy and Reenee Gregg.

March 24, 2016

1 ∎ **Rihanna, *Anti* (Wesbury Road/Roc Nation)** It's been out for two months, celebrated, analyzed, and it's at the top of the charts, but the music on this album isn't likely to reveal itself quickly. There are dramas here that don't fit the critically constructed pop mind, where all that matters is how a given release will affect a given career, which is to say balancing the long-term bottom line against the short one. There is no pop category, let alone any infinitely gene-sliced genre name, to contain the lead in Rihanna's voice in "Needed Me." Part of it is the conviction in the way she shoves out "Fuck your white horse and a carriage"—a verbal match for the look on Kim Hunter's face in *A Streetcar Named Desire* as she walks back down the stairs after Marlon Brando has beaten her up. It's a line that opens up into a dozen directions at once, seven words that in the months and years to come may be under the breath of countless people, just as once men and women of all sorts went through the day muttering "Don't push me /'Cause I'm close to the edge." The songs have echoes in them. To be heard they need airplay and memory.

2 ∎ **Tacocat, *Lost Time* (Hardly Art)** Emily Nokes again delivers a sting inside every laugh ("You can bring a boombox," she trills in "Night Swimming," "but you can't play R.E.M."). Sometimes you can't tell the sting from the laugh: in "Leisure Bees," where people work like bees in a hive, the low croon over "What won't be on your tombstone?" repeated four times, coming out of a bright, clattering beat, is no fun at all. Hilarious songs from "Dana Katherine Scully" to "Men Explain Things to Me" rest on a conviction that essentials of life—a sense of purpose, a belief in yourself, trust in your friends, work worth doing, free time that actually feels free—are not only missing but out of reach. While all that is present in the words Nokes sings, it's more alive in

her tone: she could be singing in French and you'd come away feeling the same. The music is most undeniable when it's the least simple, though it always seems simple: all through "Talk," the least obvious, most unsettling song here, textures shift, the tone darkens, and the song and the singer seem to be hiding from each other, not wanting to hear what the other is saying. The music has force, handclaps drive the sound forward, and the person in the song is quietly, resolutely, very consciously losing her mind. By the end she seems to have found it, but who knows?

3 ▪ Interview with John McGraw (MSNBC, March 14) "I do find him refreshing," Keith Richards told Hugo Lindgren of *Billboard* last year. "He's cut through a lot of crap, and eventually . . . well, can you imagine a President Trump? The worst nightmare. But we can't say that. Because it could happen. This is one of the wonders of this country. Who would have thought Ronald Reagan could be president?" It was one of Richards's nine lives earlier—twenty-six years earlier—when, at the close of the Rolling Stones' 1989 American tour, as the promoter Michael Cohl said in a 2015 speech for *Pollstar*, Richards pulled a knife, laid it on a table, and threatened to cancel the band's pay-per-view show in Atlantic City if Trump, whose casino was sponsoring the event, didn't get out of the hall: "One of us is leaving the building, either him or us."

And now, just after slamming an unlooking Rakeem Jones in the face at a Donald Trump rally in Fayetteville, North Carolina, on March 10, a proud and beaming John McGraw, the pony-tailed white gun-rights American to a T, is telling the mike in his face "Next time we see him we might have to kill him" as the London Bach Choir's opening passages of the Rolling Stones' "You Can't Always Get What You Want," a staple at Trump events, hung in the air in the distant background. It made no sense: Trump's message is precisely that if he gets to run the show you can always get what you want. Maybe it was payback for that long-ago insult. But I'd seen the McGraw clip a dozen times in the previous few days, without feeling, as I did now, that I was about to throw up, because before I'd never noticed the music. Maybe it was the smashing contradiction of the ugliness of one voice against the beauty of the others. Maybe it was the elegy for a precious, disappearing idealism that bleeds all through the song in the very process of its replacement by an idealism of a different kind. Maybe it was the new line McGraw and Trump had now crafted into the music: "You can't always get what you want/But if you try sometimes, you might find/You get what you need"—or deserve.

4 ▪ Barney Hoskyns, _Small Town Talk—Bob Dylan, the Band, Van Morrison, Janis Joplin, Jimi Hendrix & Friends in the Wild Years of Woodstock_ (Da Capo) Substitute "Heroin" for "Wild" and you have the real subtitle. The most depressing music book I've ever read.

5 ▪ The Americans, "The Right Stuff," from _I'll Be Yours_ (theamericansmusic.com) From the first rolling guitar notes, carrying sadness and defiance like dust, this sweeps me up: I want to know everything about where that feeling came from, and where it's going. You're not surprised when the singer comes in, telling you about how the right stuff is what he doesn't have, how the place he bet his life on is blowing him out, and as the song careens toward its end he sings louder, the band pushes harder, and what he's lost seems to cost more with every measure. The Americans are four guys from Los Angeles: this is a tale, somehow steeped in the past, a story that retraces the history of the once ever-advancing, then ever-retreating frontier every time it's told, that lives up to their name.

6 ▪ David Phinney, Abstract California Red Wine, 2013 (Orin Swift Cellars, Napa) It's a mouth-filling, coolly satisfying wine, but I bought it for the label: an overwhelmingly complex collage of images that shot out from the swarm around them for their familiarity and their violation of familiarity—the loyalist soldier falling back with his rifle still in his outstretched arm from the Spanish Civil War, a pensive Elvis with the "Nowhere" and "Boredom" busses from Jamie Reid's sleeve for the Sex Pistols' "Pretty Vacant" tattooed on his forehead—until you're caught, trying to see every picture at once, to read each one, yes, Beckett Lenin Bobby Kennedy dying on the floor of the Ambassador Hotel Tilda Swinton King Mob graffiti Patti Smith naked in a Mapplethorpe photo with someone else's head Lenin again Hemingway the Adverts a Marlboro Man a Situationist poster from 1966 and scores more that someone else could identify and you can't. You could spend years and never quite get to the end of it.

"When you're tired, had a glass of wine, creativity comes out," said the collagist Phinney, who owns the winery and makes the wine. "After

I put my kids to bed I'd spend four or five hours a night working on it. It was much more difficult than I expected. It's a puzzle." He collected the images over three years; the piece took three weeks to come together. A passion for Hemingway led to a fascination with the Spanish Civil War. As a poli sci major he wrote a lot of papers about communism: "I was a young, idealistic kid." And "a skateboard rat, a huge punk fan," and a fashion maven: "I wanted to be just gay enough to understand the female mind." None of which accounts for the internal gravity of the label—the way it holds together, forming some indecipherable whole. The way it's a version of the twentieth century, shouting at itself.

7 ▪ Heron Oblivion, *Heron Oblivion* (Sub Pop) A San Francisco foursome that posits the wah-wah pedal as the answer to all questions. There are a few moments when you can almost believe it.

8 ▪ Eric Alterman, "Interview with Steve Earle," *Nation* (March 19) Earle on the Mississippi blues singer Robert Johnson and Earle's album *Terraplane*, named for Johnson's "Terraplane Blues," from his first recording session in 1936: "As far as we know, and it's the beginning of recording so there wouldn't be recordings that predated it, but there is tradition and people have done the research and I've done the research. There aren't earlier versions of those Robert Johnson songs that anybody knows about, so as far as we know, the entire genre of the blues as we know it, every bit of it, is based on one Robert Johnson song or another . . . There's not one single thing that's not really based on a Robert Johnson song. I mean the whole 12-bar, 16-bar modern blues thing—it's all based on Robert Johnson."

It's as if Earle is channeling Donald Trump: *I've done the research!* Robert Johnson was born in 1911; at that time, the blues guitarist Elvie Thomas, who would not record until 1930, had been playing and singing early, shared blues songs for nearly a decade. So had countless others. Blind Lemon Jefferson was recording hit blues records in 1926, and Blind Willie Johnson a year after that. Older Mississippi bluesmen, some of whom shamed Robert Johnson as an incompetent when he first tried to play with them—Charley Patton, Son House, Willie Brown, Tommy Johnson, Skip James—were writing the story of the blues on 78s from 1928 to 1931. As Bob Dylan would take phrases and constructions from Johnson, many of Johnson's songs were derived from records by House, James, Kokomo Arnold, the Mississippi Sheiks, and more, transformed by Johnson's sense of language and his rhythmic daring. That was how blues artists made blues.

There is in fact no way to extract meaning from what Earle said. Alterman was taken aback; he tried to throw Earle a lifeline. "Who else would you say contributed fundamentally to the genre?" he asked, and Earle doubled down: "Nobody wrote any songs, everybody just repackaged Robert Johnson songs and used verses from Robert Johnson songs and took one verse from one Robert Johnson song and one verse from another Robert Johnson song . . ." Did he think this would help sell his record?

9 ■ **Bruce Springsteen, Oracle Arena (Oakland, March 13)** It was a big, loud, smiling show, where the almost German severity of "Point Blank," where a girl grows up to be a junkie hustling on the street, fell right into Jerry Lee Lewis sweeping his fingers across the keys, which is to say "Cadillac Ranch." In a novel, the lines "She asked if I remembered the letters I wrote, when our love was young and bold / She said last night she read those letters, and they made her feel 100 years old" would keep you from turning the page, but the key to the way they hang in the poisoned air of "Stolen Car" is in the way Springsteen doesn't sing to their literary quality, but instead repeats them to himself as if he can't believe he didn't even notice when his life ended.

The highlight of the show came with a request from the crowd: the early tune "Growin' Up." It was from a young man named Steven Strauss, pressed up against the stage with his parents at his side, wearing an unmistakable black and white checked shirt. "I sing (hopefully not too loudly for those standing around me), all the words," he wrote of a show in Albany on February 8 in the Springsteen magazine *Backstreets*. "I dance to all of the songs, I jump up and down, I cry, I fistpump, I air guitar, I do things that no one has figured out how to describe in words yet." Springsteen pulled him onto the stage to sing the song with him, and he was *great*.

10 ■ **Rickie Lee Jones, "Dark Was the Night, Cold Was the Ground,"** *from God Don't Never Change: The Songs of Blind Willie Johnson* **(Alligator)** Aren't tribute albums terrible? Yes, and even when devoted to one of the great artists of the twentieth century. On a set stuffed with two tracks from Tom Waits, who given that his shiver-me-rotting-

timbers act was Blind Willie Johnson from the start is doubly redundant, and two from tribute-album queen Lucinda Williams, whose
mush-mouthed soulfulness is so affected she makes Taylor Swift sound
like Etta James, plus mediocre work from the Cowboy Junkies, Luther
Dickinson, Maria McKee, the Blind Boys of Alabama, and Derek
Trucks and Susan Tedeschi, Jones's closing number is a door to another
world.

When the Texas gospel blues singer recorded this song in Dallas in
1927, he used no words: He hummed and he moaned, as if when you
spoke to the night and listened to the ground, only a language before
language could say what you had to say. But the tune came from a hym-
nal: "I looked up some lyrics I found from the last century, or the one
before," Jones said before beginning the song in New York last year.
With Fairport Convention's wordless "'The Lord Is in This Place . . .
How Dreadful Is This Place'" and Bob Dylan's "Sign on the Cross"
swirling around her—and Jones's performance makes it plain that
Dylan's song was based precisely on Johnson's—she seems unflinch-
ing in the face of eternity, with the sense that no word she speaks, no
sound she makes, will be less true a thousand years from now than it
was a thousand years ago. She trusts the chords to carry her out of her
own petty present. With bare notes abstracted from any melody on her
guitar, she seems absolutely alone, and when Lee Thornburg's horns
and other voices come up around her, you feel relief for her, comfort,
even if the voices you're hearing, that she's now leaving the song to,
are the voices of the dead.

Thanks to Steve Weinstein, Barbara Carr, Steve Perry, Jon Pont, and Doug Kroll.

April 25, 2016

1 ▪ **My friend Jo Anne Fordham writes in from Jackson, Mississippi
(April 6)** "At 15, I saw Mick Jagger at Altamont. I was leaving as city
kids lit evening fires in dry grass almost always visited by high winds.
As soon as I saw Jagger's face, I knew I was far tougher. Not so, Merle.
Never. RIP."

2 ▪ **Ensemble Mik Nawooj,** *The Future of Hip Hop* **(miknawooj.com)**
This Bay Area orchestra—guided by pianist JooWan Kim, with MCs
Do D.A.T. and Sandman, operatic soprano Anne Hepburn Smith, cellist Lewis Patzner, violinist Mia Bella D'Augelli, flautist Bethanne
Walker, clarinetist James Pytko, stand-up electric bassist Eugene The-
riault, and drummer Lyman Alexander II, with Christopher Nicholas
on choruses—play with an elegant severity, which can break up into a
back and forth between Do D.A.T. and Sandman that makes you forget the band until they throw the music back to the players like a second baseman completing a double play to first. Behind a music stand,
Smith opens her mouth and as high, clear, swirling sounds come out,
she makes you realize how much room there is in hip-hop—sonic
room, conceptual room—that it's a language that after more than forty
years remains in flux. The textures swimming through the sound are
like the world's fastest ping-pong game: they can make you dizzy, trying to hear and see everything at once, and you do. They make the
Kronos Quartet, perhaps as much a model as Prince's "When Doves
Cry" band or the Roots, feel like they're afraid of their own voice. No
one seems capable of hitting a predictable note.

3 ▪ **PJ Harvey,** *The Hope Six Demolition Project* **(Island)** This album
may be about the collapse of the world, soulless capitalism, imperial-
ism, and speaking truth to power—songs, or maybe more fully song
titles, include "The Ministry of Social Affairs," "River Anacostia," and
"Near the Memorials to Vietnam and Lincoln"—but clunky choruses
and sing-songy rhythms make it plain that good intentions are not
music. An attempt to ground ethereal singing—it all but screams not
merely good but pure intentions—in a darker, slowly chanted "Wade
in the Water" feels cheap. This album says everything it means to say
in the profoundly discordant saxophone Harvey plays in "Ministry of
Defence"—the sound she makes, huge plates of metal bending and
scraping against each other, doesn't last long, but the break it makes
in the music echoes through the songs that follow, most often an echo
of where they fall short. And when you go back to it, to try to feel how
the sound was made, how it works, you can feel it: the collapse of
the world.

4 ▪ **William Bell,** *This Is Where I Live* **(Stax)** Starting with "You Don't
Miss Your Water" in 1961, Bell had many hits on the R&B charts with

Stax into the '70s. This feels like the album he should have made in 1967 but wasn't ready for: with every smoothly delivered lesson about satisfaction and pain, you sense how hard each one was to learn, and how finding the right words—the right tone of voice to make what you have to say mean anything—is much harder. With the most delicate, modest, contemplative soul guitar: in 1967 it would have been Curtis Mayfield, but it's producer John Leventhal, who does the same for Rosanne Cash. Can't Leventhal have Cash and Bell make their next album together?

5 ▪ **Rolling Stones, "Midnight Rambler," from** *Sticky Fingers* **expanded edition (Rolling Stones, 1971/2015)** A 1971 performance at the Round-house in London. On most of the American tour during the fall of 1969, and on *Let It Bleed*, released just one day before the Altamont finale, the song couldn't take its shape. As the band played it they hollowed it out. It was there in full on *Get Yer Ya-Yas Out!* recorded at the end of the tour in New York—but not compared to this, two years later, where near the end Mick Taylor and Keith Richards find a rhythm in the song they've never heard before and begin to drive the music for its own sake, taking it right over a cliff. It's what Richards described as the height of music-making in his *Life*: "If you're working with the right chord, you can hear this other chord going on behind it, which actually you're not playing. It's there. It defies logic."

6 & 7 ▪ **Rolling Stones, "You Can't Always Get What You Want" (1969) and Paul Krugman, "Learning from Obama,"** *New York Times* **(April 1)** Or, updating the Trump rally staple and why President Obama's approval ratings have shot up over the spring: "Voters have lately been given a taste of what really bad leaders look like," Krugman wrote. "I'd like to think that the public is starting to realize how successful the Obama administration has been in addressing America's problems. . . . Those caught up in the enthusiasms of 2008 feel let down by the prosaic reality of governing in a deeply polarized political system"—even if, Krugman details, ten million jobs have been created, Obamacare is working at a higher level and at a lower cost than predicted by the Congressional Budget Office, significant financial reforms are in place, and major climate protections have been imposed through executive action. "Assuming Democrats hold the presidency, Mr. Obama will emerge as a hugely consequential president—more than Reagan,"

Krugman finished up: "The lesson of the Obama years, in other words, is that success doesn't have to be complete to be very real. You say you want a revolution? Well, you can't always get what you want—but if you try sometime, you just might find, you get what you need."

8 ▪ Shangri-Las, "Leader of the Pack" (Red Bird, 1964) Another shot on the Trump rally soundtrack—against the objections of Shangri-Las lead singer Mary Weiss. But really, Trump ought to know the song. He was eighteen in New York when the New York group hit the top of the charts. Doesn't he realize the leader of the pack dies?

9 ▪ Rock & Roll Hall of Fame Inductions, Barclays Center, Brooklyn (April 8) For the record: Ice Cube, the day before, in an interview in the *New York Times* with Joe Coscarelli. Coscarelli: "Gene Simmons, of Kiss, said a few years ago that rappers didn't belong in the Hall of Fame, because they don't play guitar or sing." Ice Cube: "Rock 'n' roll is not an instrument and it's not singing. Rock 'n' roll is a spirit. N.W.A is probably more rock 'n' roll than a lot of the people that he thinks belong there over hip-hop. We had the same spirit as punk rock, the same as the blues." Steve Miller, acceptance speech: "At the University of Wisconsin, I was a member of the Student Non-Violent Coordinating Committee. I was a Freedom Rider, and a war protestor." "I encourage you," he said at the end of his eloquent eight-minute address, "to keep expanding your vision. To be more inclusive of women. And to be more transparent in your dealing with the public. And to do much more to provide music in our schools."

Women: the Shangri-Las have never been nominated, let alone inducted. But maybe that's why Donald Trump doesn't really know "Leader of the Pack"—they're losers, and he doesn't truck with scum.

10 ▪ Lonnie Mack, born July 18, 1941, Dearborn County, Indiana–April 21, 2016. Prince, born June 7, 1958, Minneapolis, Minnesota–April 21, 2016 Two guitarists from the Midwest. Who could toll their own bells.

Thanks to Daniel Wolff.

May 24, 2016

1 ■ **Best News of the Month: Nico Lang, "Beyoncé speaks for herself: Stop demanding an artist be all things to all of her fans—Her decision to play N.C. instead of protesting HB2 sparked the latest round of calls for Bey to fit many molds" (Salon, May 8)** Lang: "Beyoncé simply works in mysterious ways, like God herself."

2 ■ **Parquet Courts, *Human Performance* (Rough Trade)** There's nothing spectacular about the music here. Sometimes it seems functional—support for words. And then a guitar part—a riff, a single chord—can spin your head, bursting out from the side of a vocal as if it's from a different song, even a different band. (The spaghetti western guitar in "Berlin Got Blurry" is perfect.) The singing—Andrew Savage most of the time, the weaker Austin Brown—is Lou Reed non-singing at its best, without any Lou Reed drawl: colorless. It can be almost unbearably flat. But it's never dull. It's not hollow. A sense of blocked desire is always present: the singer's need to say how the world looks to him cut with the belief that while the need is what keeps him human, it's pointless. No one's listening, and even he's tired of thinking the same thoughts every night. Especially on the six-and-a-half minutes of "One Man No City," the vortex of the album, the result is a drama of dissent and dislocation that deepens with every play.

3 ■ **Commonwealth/McCann Detroit, Corvette advertisement (*New York Times*, April 22)** As it happened, I was standing in line to board a flight to Minneapolis when Minnesota Public Radio called, saying they had a report that Prince had died, it wasn't confirmed, but was there anything I could say in case it was true. *He had so much left to do*, was all I could think of. Over the next days, in a city where, really, there was only one social fact—from the I-35W Bridge lit up in purple that we could just see from our apartment window, Prince's glyph replacing the name of a store on a sign down the street, the overwhelming absence of a world figure who never left town—an ad taken out by Corvette, contrived in an instant, appearing the very next morning, a full page in the *New York Times*, was the plainest statement, and the most honest. There was a tall column, except for two lines of type and the bottom eighth of the image a bottomless black, like the top third of David's *The Death of Marat* (what, you think advertising designers weren't art history majors?). The lines of type were

Baby, that was much too fast.
1958–2016

and at the bottom was the top half of a red roadster, pictured from behind, looking like a never-used prototype for a Bugatti. The whole thing was so stark that that it was the top of a Corvette barely registered at all. This was far less any kind of ad than the most severe tombstone imaginable. It was a fan's note, in fan's language: unsentimental, heartbreaking, and funny.

Then came the deluge. Prince had done everything possible to keep videos and unreleased tracks offline; now they were everywhere, his vaults along with private and commercial archives emptying, a ghost ship drifting through the ether. "Does this mean that because he died intestate his lawyers stopped enforcing his copyright claims for fear of not getting paid?" wrote Jeffrey St. Clair of *Counterpunch*. There was a slowly coiling "Little Red Corvette" from a performance at Montreux ("film noir," said the friend who sent it). There was the nine-minute piece based on the slave song "Sometimes I Feel Like a Motherless Child" it would take a John Henry to tunnel through. And a live mashup of Tommy James's "Crimson and Clover" and the Troggs' "Wild Thing," tunes Prince would have heard on KDWB before he was a teenager—a fan's note.

4 ▪ Nicolette Rohr, "She Loves You YEAH YEAH YEAH: The '60s Soundscape of Beatlemania," Experience Music Project Pop Conference (Seattle, April 15) Fans' screams drowned out the music, Rohr said, but you could listen for the music in the screams: "What does it mean to scream? What do screams voice? I'm happy, I'm sad, I'm excited, I'm scared, I don't know what I am. Or as some have surmised, I feel trapped, I need to scream. I *can* scream. I feel free."

5 ▪ Brad Dukes, *Reflections: An Oral History of Twin Peaks* (short/ Tall press) Until Dukes comes to the 1990 episode where Laura Palmer's killer is revealed—when he murders Sheryl Lee's Maddy Ferguson, Laura Palmer's cousin, in a mirror version of the murder that began the show—this is pure Hollywood, everyone falling all over themselves to praise everyone else, not a hitch, a moment of rancor, jealousy, even difficulty. But in the chapter "Back to Missoula," with, in one day over twelve hours, David Lynch shooting three different death scenes with three different killers—the developer Ben Horne, played by Richard Beymer, Laura Palmer's father, played by Ray Wise, and "Bob," played by Frank Silva—and Sheryl Lee dying over and over again, the story explodes on the page just as it did on the screen. "She gave everything she had, she gave more, she gave more than she could afford to give, and she spent years coming back," says Grace Zabriskie, who played Laura Palmer's mother. "The performance itself tells the story. No one walks away from work like that unscathed." Lee is listed as part of the cast for the *Twin Peaks: The Return* series scheduled on Showtime for 2017.

6 ▪ Rich Cohen, *The Sun & the Moon & the Rolling Stones* (Spiegel & Grau) When he was twenty-six, Cohen covered the Rolling Stones' 1994 American tour for *Rolling Stone*. Today he collaborates with Mick Jagger as a co-creator of *Vinyl*. That he can tell the Stones' story in just over 300 pages—while cutting forward when it's called for, ending the tale with "The Last Great Record," *Some Girls* in 1978 ("*Steel Wheels* was old even when it was new")—is uncanny. Even more so is the way he brings the entire cast of characters down to earth. His familiarity with Jagger, Keith Richards, Charlie Watts, and more allows for a realism the group has always deflected. He writes as someone who thinks he missed the party, but isn't sure he'd like who he'd be if he hadn't. "Why was this music important?" he asks, calling up a time when people "believed the next album would clarify everything." "Can rock save your soul? Is it a religion? If so, why did it go the way of Zoroastrianism?" He can catch the way a record can seem to remake the world ("The song fanned out like a poker hand, all face cards," he says of hearing Muddy Waters's "Mannish Boy" in a café in Amsterdam), and, with the story of how Brian Jones was so paranoid about Bob Dylan he thought both "Like a Rolling Stone" and "Ballad of a Thin Man" were about him, how songs make a world you can't escape.

Cohen likes to fix the meanings of songs, as if songs have single meanings ("'Parachute Woman' which is about groupies, or record promoters, or possibly both"—as opposed to, as a review of *Beggars Banquet* I've never forgotten put it, Mick Jagger merging himself with the map of the USA, a notion that doesn't close the song but opens it). But he can see through petty claims of influence and ownership, as with Ry Cooder's insistence that Keith Richards stole open G tuning from him to write "Honky Tonk Women" ("The songs don't come from tuning; tuning is a net woven to capture the song that was there from the beginning"). At Altamont in 1969, as the Stones played "Under My Thumb," the fan Meredith Hunter drew a gun after being attacked by Hells Angels and was murdered by them; Cohen is absurdly credulous about self-serving claims by the likes of Angels chief Sonny Barger that Hunter fired the gun ("According to Barger, he fired once. Others say he fired twice") when, as has been made clear from the *Rolling Stone* Altamont cover story on January 21, 1970, a deeply researched account that defined the event,* to Joel Selvin's forthcoming book *Altamont*, no shots were ever fired. But Cohen can also look into the eyes of his story without blinking: of those left behind, whether Marianne Faithfull or Andrew Loog Oldham or Brian Jones or a hundred others, he writes, "When you're out, you're out. Of energy, confidence, everything. They got so much from the association—a sense of importance, belonging, borrowed celebrity. More than they realized till it was over. They spend the rest of their lives telling the stories." Cohen can perhaps see himself in those lines, but he's already done the job.

7 ■ **Blackball, "Bone to Pick," from *Blackball* EP (Sorry State)** Pure rage, against nothing so vague as the machine, and even better in a fifteen-minute YouTube set from Slim's in Raleigh, North Carolina, last year. There is no room in their sound not to take it seriously: Ericka Kingston's voice feels like she reamed out her throat with a trowel, in order to speak more precisely.

8 ■ **Sandy Denny, *I've Always Kept a Unicorn: The Acoustic Sandy Denny* (Island)** Demos, outtakes, live performances, broadcasts, from 1967 to 1977—Denny, the most ethereal, faraway voice in all of anything that could ever have been called folk rock, died in 1978 at thirty-one. Listening, you can't credit that she would have lived much longer, or wanted to. Death is everywhere in these performances, hovering over "Fotheringay" at the start and crawling through "I'm a

---

* I worked on the story but the editor, police reporter, and principal writer was managing editor John Burks (1937–2021).

Dreamer" at the end, and not just because you know how the story came out.

9 ■ *My Golden Days,* **directed by Arnaud Desplechin, written by Desplechin and Julie Peyr (Why Not Productions/France 2 Cinema)** A teenage romance. A lifetime later, two of the boys involved with the same girl run into each other, and in a few brief moments, happening in sequence but with such frightening emotion they seem broken off from each other, Mathieu Amalric lets you understand how some events in a life can never be resolved; how, as you move through a lifetime, memories dragging it down can make certain you can never live it.

10 ■ **Nige Tassell, "Never mind the bus pass; punks look back at their wildest days" (*Guardian,* May 7)** As modestly moving as a newspaper piece can be, with Steve Ignorant, lead singer of the Essex band Crass, now a lifeboat man; Lesley Woods, fearlessly acrid lead singer of the Birmingham quartet Au Pairs, now a barrister; Terry Chimes (aka Tory Crimes), drummer for the Clash, now a chiropractor; Manchester fan David O'Brien, now a vicar; Jordan, Sex Pistols stylist, now a veterinary nurse; and Ausaf Abbas, bassist in the South London combo Alien Kulture ("Our name came from Margaret Thatcher, who'd made an infamous comment about how Britain was in danger of being swamped by an alien culture"), now a banker, all testifying to how punk never left them. "The experience of challenging and changing the establishment was good for everyone at the time," Chimes says. "Whatever you do after that you bring that with you: the sense that things don't have to be the way they are." "Punk showed me you could be whatever you wanted to be, and that's the way I've lived my life," Jordan says. "I haven't changed." She remembers "the trouble I got in at school" for her red and pink Mohawk. "A lot of my old teachers still live locally and bring their animals in," she says. "Now these teachers say, 'Oh, I always loved how you looked.' A bit of history has been rewritten." "I'm sure my 20-year-old self would look at me and shout, 'Sellout!'" says Abbas. "But I don't feel like a sellout. I'm just older and wiser. I'm 55 now. I'm old, fat and bald. When I tell people I was in a punk band, most just laugh and think I'm joking. But I'm very proud of what we did. In our own way, we helped Asian kids stand up and be counted for the first time in this country. Why wouldn't you be proud of that?" And though she does, posing in her courtroom wig and cloak, Lesley Woods doesn't have to say a word.

June 16, 2016

1 ▪ **Christian Marclay, "Six New Animations" (Fraenkel Gallery, San Francisco, through June 28; also at Les Recontres de la Photographie, Arles, France, July 4–September 25)** Marclay, a visual artist who for years worked with musical themes, had a blockbuster in 2010 with his twenty-four-hour video *The Clock*, a compendium of movie clips where each one showed what time it was in the scene, which was, as you watched in a museum theater, precisely the time your own watch would have told: if it was 2:43 p.m. for you, the woman on the screen fleeing a stalker was passing below a clock that read 2:43 p.m. Marclay's new work is back down to the scale of the reconstructed album covers and broken LPs he started with. He took his camera out on the streets of his East London neighborhood and photographed what he found on the ground, edited the pictures into sequences, and then speeded them up. The result, a series of short loops that move so quickly you can't tell when they end or begin, is something like a video flip-book of litter, or maybe what's left after the end of the world.

Cigarettes comes across as if discarded butts are not only the detritus but the mind of civilization. As the tiny white nubs rush by, you feel each one as a thing in itself; as the texture and color of the sidewalk or the pavement changes in tiny fractions of a second, as each cigarette seems to light the next, you feel the totality. It's sickening, it's irresistible; it's a critique of capitalism, a comment on addiction, and several million people trying to figure out what to do tonight. There is *Bottle Caps*, *Straws*, *Chewing Gum*, and *Cotton Buds*—for cleaning crystal meth pipes. The most evocative, the most like a diffusion of modern art into real life, into time and money, Malevich into functional objects, is *Lids and Straws*, a one-minute loop of Starbucks plastic. You just stare at it, as the litter reassembles itself into a statement about balance, affinity, replication, equality—or none of that, merely things insisting that functionality *is* art, and beautiful, too. "After *The Clock*," Marclay said at the gallery one afternoon, looking at *Lids and Straws*, "people were always asking, 'What's the new *Clock* going to be?' Well, here it is. These are all drugs—caffeine, sugar, cigarettes—the stimulants we need to live in the city." A visitor asked Marclay why, unlike so much of his earlier work, there was no musical element. "There's rhythm," Marclay said. "So it's very abstract," the visitor said.

"It's not abstract," Marclay said. "This is everyday life. This is the life beneath our feet."

2 ▪ Jon Bon Jovi, "Turn Back Time," DirecTV commercial (Grey Group) Really, this will live forever: what sounds like a very good Bon Jovi song, but is in fact a number dreamed up for the ad, strummed and sung soulfully by an impossibly handsome blond-gray Jon Bon Jovi, standing behind a couch where a husband and wife sit in front of their TV bereft that they missed their favorite show. But now DirecTV can give them the irresistibly rhythmic POWER TO TURN BACK TIME! and watch it, while Jon reserves for himself the power to completely upend their lives, first disappearing their irritating second child as if he'd never been born and in a second installment bringing back the guy the wife had a thing for before her husband came into the picture—all while Jon offers the smallest, most devious smile, promising us that he's just getting started. It could be the best new series of the year.

3 ▪ *The Lobster,* directed by Yorgos Lanthimos, written by Lanthimos and Efthymis Filippou (Element Pictures/A24) Funny before Rachel Weisz shows up, not afterward, with Olivia Colman as the boss of a facility that calls up the boarding school in *Never Let Me Go* and Léa Seydoux as a puritanical cult leader, this movie doubles down on *Invasion of the Body Snatchers* so relentlessly that when it was over I wasn't sure I still had a personality.

4 ▪ Don DeLillo, *Zero K* (Scribner) Speaking of *Invasion of the Body Snatchers*—somewhere in the general vicinity of Uzbekistan, DeLillo sets a compound where billionaires go to bet on living forever. The tone is that of Todd Haynes's movie *Safe*: measured, calm, with hysteria in every reassuring word. It's scary, but not so much as a scene where the narrator sees a woman standing on a New York street, "arms bent above her head, fingers not quite touching," a "fixed point in the nonstop swarm," a prophet of some kind, but without words or signs to say what's coming, and absolutely nothing passing between the two of them: "I watched her, knowing that I could not invent a single detail of the life that pulsed behind those eyes."

5 ▪ Thalia Zedek Band, "Afloat," from *Eve* (Thrill Jockey) Through Live Skull, through Come, Zedek's guitar always bore weight—you could feel the whole twentieth-century catastrophe bearing down on it. That weight is still there, as through a long instrumental introduction—enveloping, full of confidence, elegiac—you find yourself at a funeral for someone you've never met. With Hilken Mancini coming in as a second vocal behind Zedek's lead, there's a sense of looking back, from a long time ago—or a sense of someone imagining looking back, because that means they didn't go down in the flood the song describes. Lyric clichés float on the song—"the rains come down," "rivers rise," "higher ground"—until a line makes its way out that is not a cliché: "What we left behind, someone else will find." This could play next to Geeshie Wiley's "Last Kind Words Blues"—the exit is that final.

6 & 7 ▪ **Jonathan Weisman, "The Nazi Tweets of 'Trump God Emperor'" (*New York Times*, May 26) and Yamiche Alcindor, "Die-Hard Bernie Sanders Backers See F.B.I. as Answer to Their Prayers" (*New York Times*, May 27)** Weisman tweeted "an essay by Robert Kagan on the emergence of fascism in the United States," and the result, keyed by Weisman's last name, was an avalanche: "Trump God Emperor sent me the Nazi iconography of the shiftless, hooknosed Jew. I was served an image of the gates of Auschwitz, the famous words 'Arbeit Macht Frei' replaced without irony with 'Machen Amerika Great.'" That was just the start. "'I found the Menorah you were looking for,'" another Trump celebrant tweeted: "it was a candelabrum made of the number six million." "I am not the first Jewish journalist to experience the onslaught," Weisman wrote. "Julia Ioffe was served up on social media in concentration camp garb and worse after Trump supporters took umbrage with her profile of Melania Trump in GQ magazine. The would-be first lady later told an interviewer that Ms. Ioffe had provoked it. The anti-Semitic hate hurled at the conservative commentator Bethany Mandel prompted her to buy a gun." But in its way, Yamiche Alcindor's straight report on a Bernie Sanders rally was just as bad. "Victor Vizcarra, 48, of Los Angeles, said he would much prefer Mr. Trump to Mrs. Clinton," Alcindor wrote. "Though he said he disagreed with some of Mr. Trump's policies, he added that he had watched 'The Apprentice' and expected that a Trump presidency would be more exciting than a 'boring' Clinton administration.

"'A dark side of me wants to see what happens if Trump is in,' said Mr. Vizcarra, who works in information technology," Alcindor went on. "'There is going to be some kind of change, and even if it's like a Nazi-type change, people are so drama-filled. They want to see stuff like that happen. It's like reality TV. You don't want to just see everybody be happy with each other. You want to see someone fighting somebody.'"

In between these two news stories are two broader stories that go to the heart of contemporary life. As the radical sociologist Georges Bataille wrote in "The Notion of Expenditure" in 1933, any society can find itself drawn irrevocably to actions "with no end beyond themselves," to a game of life in which one gambles not to win but to lose, to create "catastrophes that, while conforming to well-defined needs, provoke tumultuous depressions, crises of dread and, in the final analysis, a certain orgiastic state." That is, the other side of fascism is nihilism, and citizens like Victor Vizcarra speak for a deep desire, shared by millions, not to change America but to blow it up, to be rid forever of the oppressions of liberty, justice, equality, fairness, and democracy—and that includes self-described so-called progressives who would never admit that anyone like Victor Vizcarra could speak for them. And the other side of *that* story is the incomprehension on the part of so many professional rationalists as to what politics is: an argument about the good.

Fascists and nihilists don't care about contradictions—all they want is someone to smash people not like them. Liberal commentators tut-tutting over the not-rich voting-against-their-own-interests could not be more obtuse in their blinkered idea of what politics is about and what it's for: one's own interest isn't merely a matter of who will put more dollars in your pocket. It's a decision about what kind of country you want to live in, and how you can be permitted to define yourself. People aren't stupid, and their votes aren't bought. *Independence Day: Resurgence* opens this month; you can see America destroyed before it gets saved. Those who want a more gratifying ending, that orgiastic state, can stay home, save their money, turn on the news, and root.

8 ▪ Small Glories, *Wondrous Traveler* (MFM) From Winnipeg: Cara Luft plays banjo, JD Edwards plays guitar, and in moments they find the darkening chord change the best bluegrass—from the Stanley Brothers to Be Good Tanyas—has always hidden in the sweet slide of the rhythm, the tiny shift where the person telling the story suddenly understands it.

9 ▪ Laura Oldfield Ford, *Hermes Chthonius* (soundcloud.com/laura -oldfield-ford/hermes-chthonius) and as part of the exhibition "Chthonic Reverb" (Grand Union Gallery, Birmingham, U.K., June 17–August 5) Ford, born in West Yorkshire in 1973, who from 2005 to 2009 published the zine *Savage Messiah,* a street walking excavation of the ruins of present-day London—it was collected in 2011 by Verso—has never accepted stable time. The past is always present, but it isn't history: it's a promise just over the horizon, or a hand in a horror movie pulling you down. In this thirty-six-minute soundwork, she's traversing Birmingham, looking for "the psychic contours of a city," speaking quietly into a tape recorder, traffic humming around her, sometimes the noise of crowds or small groups of people, pop songs occasionally mixed in, and you are following the trail of a woman who seems to remember 1974 as if she were her own aunt, the one the rest of the family never talked about, so that when she says 2016 it barely feels real. "You keep finding the embers," she says, with previous allusions to IRA bombings and urban riots as a rolling backdrop: "Places you must have seen from car windows 23 years ago."

There is the building that once housed the Birmingham Press Club: "They used to have the upstairs, a litany of names, they've all been here, Bernard Ingham, Margaret Thatcher, Enoch Powell, Barbara Cartland, Earl Spencer, Cliff Richard—it's all too much," she says of the specter of bland power, of seeing herself on the same stairs, in their footsteps. "This is where it was all concocted"—a conspiracy of government officials, pop stars, romance novelists—"in those rooms upstairs."

She looks at graffiti on a pub: "A refusal to accept what England has become, they hover above the walls as a negative ambiance," a gateway "into those undercurrents of excess, violence, destruction for its own sake. You've tuned into the undercurrent that speaks of refusal, a hatred of doing the right thing." It's a civil war of the dead, people turning into specters as she passes them, as she does to them. At the very end you hear Rod Stewart, with "You Wear It Well," from 1972, the sound rickety and distant, as if you're listening not to a record but to the woman you've been listening to remembering what it was to hear him sing it at a show she attended before she was born, and it's never sounded more true.

10 ▪ Marlene Marder, 1954–2016 The first single by Kleenex, a punk band from Zurich, appeared in 1978; their second album, and their

last, after Kimberly-Clark complained and they changed their name
to Liliput, came out in 1983. Across those mere five years their music
was made of glee and dread, playground chants back-flipping into songs
about rape; there was nothing like it before and there's been nothing
like it since. Marlene Marder was the guitarist: she could go from the
primitive to the grand and back again without turning her head. She
died of cancer in Zurich on May 15; just a month before, *She Shreds*
magazine, celebrating its tenth anniversary, reprised an interview with
Marder from its second issue, from just four years ago, and its ending
says as much about why good punk records, regardless of when they
were made, always sound like the first word, never the last. "What is
your favorite setup now?" asked Kana Harris. "It is still my Fender Strat
with Marshall MS-4," Marder said. "You've also been an activist for
environmental protection, going to college for it and working for the
World Wildlife Fund," Harris said. "Do you feel your music is inspired
by activism?" "I guess our music was inspired by that time, maybe activism, too, art and DIY," said Marder. "We didn't think much in such
terms, we just played. We never ever had the idea that our music would
last this long." "What did you learn from playing in a band that you
were able to take with you into this career?" Harris asked finally. "I
learned that everything is possible," Marder said. She would have said
it plainly, as if it were never in doubt; that's the woman I knew.

July 21, 2016

1 ▪ **Adrian Daub and Charles Kronengold, *The James Bond Songs—
Pop Anthems of Late Capitalism* (Oxford)** Daub and Kronengold are
Stanford professors who have written the most scintillatingly analytical book on music I've read since Robert Cantwell's *When We Were
Good: The Folk Revival*, and that came out in 1996. They avoid jar-
gon, often to hilarious effect ("These lyrics are," they write of "For Your
Eyes Only," "to use a technical term, a huge fucking mess"); they write
about music with casual rock-critic mastery ("From Russia With Love"
is "a characterless ballad whose most notable instrumental touch was
a modified piano that stood in for a Hungarian cimbalom that [taking
liberties from the zither you hear in *The Third Man*] was supposed to

somehow signify Russia"). They have fun, and you do too (on the New Romantics' takeover of the Bond song in the 1980s, with Duran Duran's "A View to a Kill" and a-ha's "The Living Daylights": "Let Mick Jagger or Sid Vicious sound like ancient deities rebirthed into the late twentieth century; Le Bon's and Harket's voices were those of the wunderkind money-manager caught by the boss at Le Cirque with the company credit card"). But what makes the book sing is Daub and Kronengold's rare sense of songs thinking, as creations that acquire their own agency, and their acute ability to put flesh on the bones of the late-capitalist shibboleth, which in other hands is meant to imply that capitalism is on its way out, and in theirs is a far more defeated, cynical argument that capitalism has swallowed the world.

Adele's "Skyfall," they write, "is terrified of being just another song in a series. Instead of being another entry in James Bond's dream-diary, it wants to be the psychoanalysis of that diary"—which, nearly two hundred pages later, at the very end of the book, doubles down to the song completely escaping its singer, as if by its own volition, or its own, encoded destiny: Adele was "trying to figure out what made a Bond-song a Bond-song. If Adele and her songwriter Paul Epworth had hopes that they'd mastered the quintessence of the Bond-song, they were surely disappointed. Their song is not the summa of the Bond-song. It is a Bond-song. It was everywhere for a while, and it is nowhere now. In a few years' time, another song will take its place. Adele may not be okay with that, but some part of her song always knew." And this analytical progression marches through the book in step with the way the late-capitalist theme grows from funny story to horror.

For Gladys Knight's "License to Kill," Daub and Kronengold write, composer Narada Michael Walden came up with perhaps the first truly modern Bond song—that is, a song actually in tune with the sound of its time, in this case "drum machine-driven soul"—but "Walden actually got punished for the one Bond-sound touch he included. 'License to Kill' alludes to the opening of 'Goldfinger'"—in Daub and Kronengold's story, composer John Barry's permanent Bond-song template—"borrowing the I-bVI chord-oscillation and a bit of the rhythm; Knight ad-libs magnificently over Walden's new arrangement. John Barry's people came after him with papers, demanding co-songwriting credit. We know how Walden *should've* responded: 'Seriously, guys—hearing Gladys Knight ad-lib over your bullshit chords should be payment enough, you cheap tax-dodging fucks.' But alas, he signed. How very late-capitalism . . . paying a professional to perform affective labor and then threatening to sue him for performing it too well; refusing to hear the difference between homage and plagiarism; treating everything under the sun as fungible IP; the franchise's left hand reaching an out-of-court settlement with its right hand"—as Burt Lancaster's embodiment of pure capitalist lust, the make-'em-and-break-'em Broadway columnist J. J. Hunsecker, says in *The Sweet Smell of Success*, "my right hand hasn't seen my left hand in 30 years." But that will turn into something that isn't funny at all. "The late Bond-song" is, like late-capitalism, a matter of increasingly empty repetition: "We've sped up and perfected the circulation of capital, people and goods, but the newness this world brings us is just another iOS and even faster delivery for shit you don't need." Which is not the Sex Pistols' prophecy of no-future, but its structural, ideological guarantee: "Deep down we think: this is all there is, and it's so solid. Another world, good or bad, seems impossible. That steadies us, but it pains us too." And here it could be the Bond song itself talking: "We've been so good to the market . . . but it hasn't led to anything new and different, just more of the same."

"We inhabit the world we inhabit," Daub and Kronengold say finally, as the next Bond song plays over the horizon of the book, "not because we think it's the right one, let alone because it's the good one— we inhabit it because there isn't another world, because we've learned to distrust all those who'd seen such a world." This book is the best answer there is to all those who say you can make too much of a song— it's proof that even writers as determined as Daub and Kronengold can't come close to exhausting a song, the world it came from, and the world it makes.

2 ▪ **Har Mar Superstar, *Best Summer Ever* (Cult)** Imagine Paul Giamatti in his jockey underpants singing soul in the '80s manner of ABC's *The Lexicon of Love* and the Communards' "Don't Leave Me This Way"—that same elastic rhythm, synthesizers swimming through the heart-on-my-sleeve vocals so easily you can watch the heart beat: you can't turn away. "Youth Without Love" is a great title and Mr. Har Mar—Sean Tillmann of St. Paul—runs with it. At first "Haircut" is a suspenseful romantic ballad the Shangri-Las could have done; then it's a crazed name-of-the-dance number ("Hey! Everybody! Do the Crew-Cut! Do the Jheri Curl! Do that Comb-over!"); then somehow

it's a ballad again, and as convincing as it was the first time around, as if the shouts in the middle, with an audience clapping and talking, just dropped in to see what condition its condition was in. I've only just begun to hear this record.

3 ▪ Julie Ruin, *Hit Reset* (Hardly Art) Kathleen Hanna, now on the cover of *Bust* and by next year maybe *Vogue*, deserves the tony attention, but the first thrill here comes when she's ten seconds into the first track, the title song, and you realize there's not going to be a single step toward acceptability. Her singing is still flat, still girly, twenty-five years after Bikini Kill's *Revolution Girl Style Now!* still carrying the feeling of someone finding her voice and the courage to use it. It doesn't matter that "Rather Not" is an irresistible pop song that could have been made in L.A. in 1963 by the Honeys and produced by Brian Wilson. Regardless of how dark the territory her lyrics might inhabit, there's an aura of fun, release, and glee all over the record.

4 ▪ Tomi Lunsford, "Go to People," on *Come on Blue* (Speedbank) From a Nashville singer, on an album where her steps sometimes seem hobbled, a tune that could have been written by Guy Clark: with Pete Finney on pedal steel as if he's less playing the song than overhearing it, a where-are-all-my-friends lament that's sultry, delicate, sly, even sinister.

5 & 6 ▪ Stefan Zweifel, "Dada Zürich Planétaire," dada100 symposium, Kaufleuten, Zurich (July 8) and Barack Obama, address at Dallas Memorial, Morton H. Meyerson Symphony Center (July 12) Speeches as music: Zweifel delivered a forty-minute address of finely woven themes without a pause, a hesitation, seemingly without drawing a breath, his tone never varying. It was as mesmerizing as Th' Faith Healers' thirty-two-minute "Everything, All at Once, Forever"—the complete lyric. Using almost exactly as much time as Zweifel, Obama played it differently. The pauses in his talk were so long that, if you were listening, not watching, you could wonder if the broadcast had stopped. They weren't dramatic; they didn't feel like effects. You caught the feeling—no matter how contrived—of someone not struggling for the right words, but thinking through each sentence or clause to the heart of the events he was facing, events that cut so deeply they could not be summed up, which is to say dismissed. Obama suspended not his words but the event of seven murders in the air, and then, as was said of Jonathan Edwards delivering a sermon at Enfield, Connecticut, in 1741, while his eyes were fixed on the bell rope at the back of the church, "looked it off," as if the collective event—Alton Sterling, dead in Baton Rouge, Philando Castile, dead in Falcon Heights, Minnesota, Brent Thompson, Lorne Ahrens, Michael J. Smith, Michael Krol, and Patrick Zamarripa, dead in Dallas—was too much to look at. His clipped speech at the end of sentences, sometimes irritating, sometimes seeming to communicate impatience or lack of involvement, here had the effect of taking any gaze off of him, and directing the locus of gravity onto what he was talking about, with the sense that what had happened over three days resisted words, and that words resisted, too, as if they knew they would fall short. Obama put all of that into a rhythm that even he will never match.

7 ▪ Temescal Farmers' Market, Oakland (July 10) I would have thought "Practice Random Acts of Kindness and Senseless Acts of Beauty" was the all-time winner in the Pompous Words of Self-Congratulation sweepstakes, until I saw this logo on a canvas shopping bag: "I WAS CALLED FROM ANOTHER WORLD TO WORK WITH PEOPLE."

8 ▪ "Beat Generation," Centre Pompidou, Paris (through October 3) The big show is comprehensive about who, when, and where, and sometimes startling. In an early typescript of "Howl" that Allen Ginsberg sent to Jack Kerouac, with "starving hysterical naked" originally "starving mystical naked," and "negro streets at dawn searching for an angry fix" originally "angry streets at dawn searching for a negro fix," you get a sense of the dimension of the poem that's pure wordplay. But with many vitrines of publications, the art on the walls, films and film clips running everywhere, even phones where you can dial up John Giorno's "Dial a Poem," what was most conspicuous was absence. Except for a Jess collage here, the pulp cover of William Burroughs's *Junkie* blown up poster-size there, what's missing is drugs, sex, and homosexuality. As in, say, "who let themselves be fucked in the ass by saintly motorcyclists, and screamed with joy."

9 ▪ Mekons, "Fear and Beer (Hymn for Brexit)" (Bloodshot) A statement of defeat and exile as hard as "King Arthur," their scared tale of being cast out of their own country, their own skin, by Thatcherism, now with people gathered in a pub, huddling together as if for warmth: the song is lovely, comforting, their own requiem.

10 ▪ Dada-sour, Cabaret Voltaire bar, Zurich (July 7) For the centennial of the nightclub where dada was born, bartender Vincent Clifford contrived a drink so seductive you feel like you could sit behind it all night long: gin, lemon juice, thyme syrup, and a spray of absinthe.

August 19, 2016

1 ▪ Michelle Leon, *I Live Inside—Memoirs of a Babe in Toyland* (Minnesota Historical Society) Guitarist and lead singer Kat Bjelland was a heroin addict; drummer Lori Barbero was organized, frugal, and drove the van; bassist Michelle Leon was a nice Jewish girl from a professional family who gave up college for another life, though she never gave up Minnesota nice. When Babes in Toyland took shape in Minneapolis in 1987 they were as sulfurous as any punk band the form, the idea, has ever produced—compared to them the Seattle bands of the time were the Dave Clark Five. You can hear that on their first album, *Spanking Machine*, which came out in 1990; you can hear it even more on a YouTube video of their April 14, 1988, show at the Cabooze Bar in Minneapolis—eight-and-a-half minutes in, Leon sings the unrecorded "Milk Pond" with a pleased smile on her face, as if she's gotten away with something. She left the group in 1992, having, you get the feeling, lived a hundred lives as part of it, none of them finished, which may be why there isn't an obvious sentence in the book. Over a little more than two hundred pages, Leon's short, self-contained chapters, often less than a page, are the opposite of diary entries: considered, honed, until every word has its own reason for being where it is.

There are triumphs and misery, but no self-praise, no self-pity. Humor is deadpan. After an accident in Arizona the band buys a new van: "a brown two-tone Ford Econoline with real backseats from a car rental place in Phoenix. The seller tells us the vehicle was owned by a woman who was kidnapped and is currently missing. He gives us a good deal." The British rock writer Everett True "asks a riveting question: 'What's it like to be girls in a band?' Lori kids that we get our periods at the same time." Along with the day-to-day facts of life for an unknown band playing any out-of-town show they can get—sleeping on floors, not eating, making just enough to make it to the next town, common experiences never put down with more simple, direct conviction—you are brought into the sense of impersonation that comes with even hometown fame. This is "Everyone," the whole chapter: "People recognize me out at shows, or shopping for groceries, at the movies, in line at the post office. Everyone acts extra friendly, buying drinks and introducing themselves. I am not sure who is for real, if someone is really interested or just wanting in on the scene. All the attention gives me a false sense of self-worth, illusive and distorted, with the ability to vanish like melting snow. I define myself through the gaze of strangers and I have never felt so phony. I have never felt so whole. I am disconnected, capable of caring very little, especially about those who are the closest to me. I am losing myself but it doesn't matter. Boys think I'm foxy and want to make out. Girls want to be my friend; they also try to make out with me. Everyone thinks I'm really great."

The deepest moment in the book, one that any good novelist would recognize in an instant as the crux of the story, comes out of the most ordinary incident, when Leon and Bjelland take Barbero's no to mean no when it means yes—*We're going to the music store, do you want us to get you anything?*—and the comradeship between the three women begins to unravel—*You* knew *I needed new sticks!* "I look right at her and she looks right back at me, the fire of anger in our eyes. So begins resentment that lasts for weeks." "I want to be warm and kind and open to everyone, like Lori," Leon says a page later, maybe a month later, maybe two, after watching Barbero in a club, "so charming to strangers that all of her goodness gets used up, and there is nothing left but her husk, and then she is such a total fucking bitch to me and Kat. Take a deep breath. We all have our struggles. *But I still hate her!* Let it go. *But I asked if she wanted anything at the music store and she said no!* Let it go." It's not really a surprise, after this, that the life Leon lives after the band is no less rich, not an incident predictable, not an ending preordained.

2 ■ **Lake Bell as Chloe in *The Secret Life of Pets* (Universal)** As someone whose own movie, *In a World . . .* is about the movie-trailer voice-over business, this is casting: in the distant purr of an overweight blue cat, the perfect bored hipster.

3 ▪ **David Reid, *The Brazen Age—New York City and the American Empire: Politics, Art, and Bohemia* (Pantheon)** There is no depth in this five hundred–page account of the immediate postwar period, centered on 1948, one of the most fascinating years in American history. But there is one immediately striking photo among the images you can find anywhere else, revealing contours of bohemia Reid's text doesn't touch: six people at a table in the San Remo Café in Greenwich Village, one unidentified man looking at the camera, two women seen from behind, and, as captioned, the actor Montgomery Clift (*Red River*, *A Place in the Sun*, name-dropped by Reid once), the actor Kevin McCarthy (*Invasion of the Body Snatchers*, a beat critique if there ever was one, not mentioned), and Jack Kerouac. What were they talking about? Casting *On the Road*? Clift as Sal Paradise, McCarthy as Dean Moriarty? Except it's not Jack Kerouac.

4 & 5 ▪ **Ted Hearne, composer, *But I Voted for Shirley Chisholm*, and Libby Larsen, composer, *Ferlinghetti*, Aspen Music Festival (August 13)** Hearne was born in 1982; ten years before that, Shirley Chisholm, congresswoman from Brooklyn, was the first African American from the Democratic or Republican party to run for president, and fifteen years after that, in 1987, Biz Markie, in "Nobody Beats the Biz," gave Chisholm a rap wave she must have treasured until her death in 2005: "Reagan is the pres but I voted for Shirley Chisholm." Like many hip-hop artists before him, Hearne started with that sample, and then, with the sound of ear-splitting feedback from Seohee Min's violin and God knows what else, the twelve-member Aspen Contemporary Ensemble jerked the piece to clanging life. With the original Chisholm shout subsumed into a call-and-response of city sounds—honking horns, pneumatic drills, or gunshots—and the stuttering rhythms of the group, with drummer Hannah Weaver acting it all out in the back, you couldn't tell if you were listening to Markie or Andrew Heath's trumpet and Harry Gonzalez's trombone. It was only steps away from the Lovin' Spoonful's 1966 "Summer in the City," but those steps were slippery enough to let the music turn jittery, almost to the point of breaking—until it slipped away into an idyll that called up Miles Davis's 1960 *Sketches of Spain*. It was only seven minutes, and so fast on its own switchbacks you wanted to hear it again, right away.

Larsen was born in 1950; she read Ferlinghetti's 1958 beat-poetry best-seller in high school, and went back to compose to it just two years ago. There are six short pieces, keyed to Ferlinghetti lines that never resonated that strongly in the first place ("Crazy to be alive in such a strange world") and don't now. The players were riveting to watch: the straight man, James Dunham, viola, looked to be six-foot-six ("a pyramid," said one person in the audience) and never cracked a smile or a frown; the exuberant Juan Gabriel Olivares, clarinet, a head or two shorter, was all Stan Laurel to Dunham's Oliver Hardy; and Tengku Irfan, piano, who compared to the others looked like a wind-up toy brought in when the scheduled pianist took a powder. The compositions were coy satires on the American scene, and the performances became less substantial one after the other, until ". . . fifty-one clowns in back all wearing nothing but Stars & Stripes," which despite its characteristically condescending title immediately took off, with all sorts of patriotic airs floating through sounds that were pushing toward an abstract reworking of Jimi Hendrix's Woodstock deconstruction of the national anthem. They made it right to the blazing heart of the history Hendrix made all those years ago, and you couldn't tell if you were in a country that had ceased to be or remained to be made. Irfan had earlier used an elbow on the keys; now he stood up from his piano bench like Jerry Lee Lewis and pounded across any shaped melody, any definite beat. When the three bowed, you knew he'd been somewhere.

6 ■ **Felice Brothers, *Life in the Dark* (Yep Roc)** The casual, sliding rhythms in Ian Felice's voice don't wear out because they're filled with regret. That feeling doubles back on itself, leading to the band's startlingly empathetic rewrites of such traditional ballads—you could say traditional murders—as "Stagger Lee" (Lee "Stag" Shelton shoots Billy Lyons in St. Louis, 1895) and "Frankie and Albert" (Frankie Baker shoots Albert Britt in St. Louis, 1899). As the Felice Brothers tell the tales in "Dream On" and "Frankie's Gun!" they're taking place in the present and the singer is in the songs, thinking it all over. That's what regret is all about: what could have happened if just one thing had been just slightly different, if you woke up an hour later, if you hadn't taken what someone said for what it probably didn't mean anyway. And now you can never take it back.

You can hear that small drama almost anywhere on this album, and especially in the first lines of "Aerosol Ball," the first song here: they're so quietly absurd, with accordion and fiddle swaying in the background ("The rain in Maine/Is made of novocaine/In the Florida Keys/It's made of antifreeze"), you want the song to keep going until it covers the other forty-eight. You don't even have to notice when the tune turns into thirdhand social critique by way of a put-down of "the doll of St. Paul." "Her dreams her thoughts are made by Microsoft," Ian Felice sings, without changing his tone, and lines seem just as made up on the spot as the ones he started with. The more the band try to be serious, the more they daydream, conjuring up melodies and phrases, unable to stick to the script, letting their music play itself.

7 ▪ Andy Bienen writes in on the first night of the Democratic convention (email, July 25) "It was strange on the 51st anniversary of Newport to hear all that self-righteous booing. Superficial differences aside, the Sanders crowd seemed cut from the same sanctimonious cloth as those who booed Dylan in '65 and '66. It seemed possible that some of the older delegates could even have been at Newport booing then as they were booing now."

8 ▪ Laurie Penny, "I'm with the Banned," on the Republican convention (medium.com, July 21) Reading Penny, who writes for the *Guardian* and the *New Statesman* and on her own blog, is not like reading any American political writer, no matter how passionate (Timothy Egan), funny (Gail Collins), inflamed (Matt Taibbi), or apocalyptic (Jonathan Chait). She's faster, tougher, and she writes as if words were made for her. Her clever writing ("America is a nation eaten by its own myth") is never merely clever; ideas ("The entire idea of America is about believing impossible things. Nobody said those things had to be benign") explode out of it. Here she's at "the gayest neo-fascist rally" at the Republican convention, starring the troll Milo Yiannopoulos, just banned from Twitter for his racist abuse of Leslie Jones, and reveling in it. Beyond the photos of naked men in Trump hats that cover the walls of the venue is the VIP room, where Penny meets Geert Wilders, head of the Dutch Party for Freedom: "the most obviously disturbed member of the neo-right suicide squad in attendance. He cannot finish a sentence. His voice drifts, and he trails away, already out of the room. There is a dustbin fire behind the blank eyes of his human suit." "Milo Yiannopoulos is the ideological analogue of Kim Kardashian's rear end," Penny has already written, and as she goes on that sentence sounds all through her report, translating everything she sees: "Wilders is a less polished, wholly charmless rendition of the neo-right demagogue character creation sheet that gave us Donald Trump and Boris Johnson. These people do not have personalities, they have haircuts."

9 ▪ **DJ Shadow, *The Mountain Will Fall* (Mass Appeal)** For the great sampler of bits and pieces of dislocation in modern life—finding yourself in the wrong place at the wrong time, and realizing you were born there—the textures can seem meretricious, accepting, as if there's really nothing left to argue against. But as the record summons a movie-music sense of phony peace of mind in its last ten minutes or so, all of that begins to break down. By the end, yes—you don't know where you are.

10 ▪ **A friend writes in (August 4)** "Last night we were at the WH for Obama's birthday party. I finally met Paul McCartney, which had been a dream of mine. I tried to act cool about it but secretly I was like one of the Beatlemania girls at Shea screaming on the inside."

Thanks to Barry Gifford, Emily Marcus, and Paula Bernstein.

September 27, 2016

1 ▪ **Fantastic Negrito *The Last Days of Oakland* (Blackball Universe)** He could be inventing blues for the first time. With a guitar that has a pick-up that catches people talking as they pass the street corner where he's playing—talking in time. In a city where the huge old Sears building is the new world headquarters of Uber.

2 ▪ **"FRENCH COURT TO RULE ON BURKINI BANS" (*Financial Times*, August 25)** Story: "Demonstrators held a protest outside the French embassy in London on Thursday against the banning of so-called burkini swimsuits on beaches in more than a dozen coastal towns in France.

"The State Council, France's highest administrative court, is due to publish an initial ruling on a claim by human rights groups that the ban contravenes civil liberties.

"The burkini, labelled as a provocative political symbol by critics, was barred in the wake of recent Islamist terrorist killings in France. Photos showed armed police ordering a Muslim woman to remove her burkini in Nice this week.

"Prime Minister Manuel Valls defended the ban, saying the burkini symbolised women's enslavement."

The photo with the report showed Muslim and non-Muslim women holding multicolored, well-made posters on clean white paper— ISLAMOPHOBIA IS NOT FREEDOM, WEAR WHAT YOU WANT, and MISTER! HANDS OFF MY SISTER. In the background was a rough piece of cardboard with black lettering that by comparison looked like a scribble: WE ARE BURKINI KILL + WE WANT REVOLUTION GRRRL STYLE NOW! OH ISLAMOPHOBIA UP YOURS!!!

With its references to Bikini Kill and its 1991 cassette, its first release, and X-Ray Spex's 1977 "Oh Bondage Up Yours"—Poly Styrene's clarion call, and her band's first single—that placard was a pure punk *no*, pure because it was doubled: that crude sign was a critique of the burkini ban, but it was also a critique of the demonstration.

The next day the French high court overturned the ban.

Corin Tucker, who not so long ago played both a suburban mom and Poly Styrene in a video for her band's single "Neskowin": "Who knew twenty-five years later those words would take on a totally new meaning?"

3 ▪ Cyndi Lauper, "Money Changes Everything (Live in Romania 2001)" (YouTube) A great performance, and her best haircut ever.

4 ▪ James Parker, "Donald Trump, Sex Pistol" (*Atlantic*, October) A piece that makes its point without showing off, though many lines are so good they feel as if they're shot out of a cannon. As on Trump's "followers—about whom one should not generalize, except to say that most of them would rather be waterboarded than sit through an episode of *Wait Wait . . . Don't Tell Me!*"

5 ▪ *The Night Of*, Episode 6: "Samson and Delilah" (HBO, August 14, Kier Lehman, music supervisor) An afternoon scene in a bar, with attorneys John Stone and Chandra Kapoor discussing the hopeless murder trial they've taken on. Kapoor is unraveling—she just broke up with her boyfriend, she's panicking over the opening statement she can't write. As Stone stops her from ordering a fourth drink, you hear a song playing deep in the background on the bar sound system, maybe a radio, all broken up, impossible to place, and for a moment it can take you right out of the scene. It turned out to be "I'm Just an Ordinary Man" by Benny Latimore (Atlantic, 1969): a soul singer with a strong voice that he seems to want to hide, to take down, so each breath comes out crying. There's so much yearning and regret in every syllable it's hard to take—and as the song deepens the characters' misery, you can believe neither Stone nor Kapoor is hearing a word, and feeling every note.

6 ■ Eric Clapton, *Sessions for Robert J* (Reprise DVD and CD, 2004) Aren't tribute albums terrible? Yes, especially when they're drowning in respect, as with Clapton's notoriously dull 2004 *Me and Mr. Johnson*, an offering to the 1930s Mississippi specter who had been an inspiration and nemesis since Clapton was a teenager. But in this little noticed follow-up—with a film made of band rehearsals for the tour that followed—a sense of freedom only builds. "If I Had Possession over Judgment Day" might jump out first, its rolling-and-tumbling riff syncopating it right out of the room, then "Stones in My Passway," then the ineffable "From Four Until Late," then anything else. It's as if Clapton finally heard Johnson speaking plain: "I'm *dead*, man. All my records have disappeared and no one can hear me. You tell the story."

7 ■ *Full Frontal with Samantha Bee* (TBS, September 19) On Jimmy Fallon's buddy act with Donald Trump on *The Tonight Show* four days before: "There were no cutaway shots to the Roots."

8 ■ "I Feel Loved in #MyCalvins," featuring Frank Ocean (Carrer de Pelai, Barcelona, September 17) On a huge billboard entirely dominating a triangle intersection. Ocean, with a slightly confrontational cast in his eyes, wearing a white T-shirt, is clasped by a small woman—she comes up to his neck. She's a secondhand Christina Aguilera dressed in a white gown, a white fur, full length white gloves—her eyes closed, her head tilted down against Ocean's chest, as if to say, I know it's a shame for a white woman like me to love a black man like him—but I can't help myself. You're supposed to feel a sense of violation, and a sense of racism itself put to shame. In a city where interracial couples are as common as well-dressed and seriously tattooed older women, the message could hardly fall more flat, or seem more cynical.

9 ■ Vivien Goldman, "Private Armies," from *Resolutionary* (Staubgold) From 1979 to 1982 the music journalist made dub music in London and Paris. None of it is ordinary, but nothing really touches this six-minute cultural travelogue, one of her first tracks, about how you can no longer walk down your own, suddenly racialized street. With Vicky Aspinall of the Raincoats on violin, Keith Levene of PiL on bass and guitar, John Lydon producing, and Goldman singing in a voice that can't quite believe what it's describing, snakes slither through the rhythms, then turn into rhythms; you can see the notes bend.

10 ■ *The Color Line: Les artistes africains-américains et la ségréga-tion, 1916–1962* (Frémaux & Associés) For decades, Frémaux has com-piled three-CD concept anthologies, and this, linked to an exhibition opening at the Musée de Quai Branly in Paris on October 4, is as am-bitious as any. It begins by running the unmistakably white blackface vaudeville star Harry C. Browne's "Oh! Susanna" ("Killed five hundred nigger") straight into Marcus Garvey's 1921 speed-rapped sermon "Ethiopia Shall Stretch Forth Her Hands unto God," with women screaming with excitement around him; it heads toward its end with Louis Armstrong's 1958 version of "Nobody Knows the Trouble I've Seen" providing no preparation at all for Bo Diddley's terrifyingly un-characteristic "The Great Grandfather," a rewrite from the following year of the 1840s blackface minstrel song "Old Dan Tucker" ("He wore the same suit all his life") that seems to suck the whole of slavery and its aftermath into a two-and-a-half-minute moan. The sixty tracks here aren't a history lesson, they are history—a history that isn't remotely over, especially given the looming possibility of a president whose father may well have been a proud member of the Ku Klux Klan.

Thanks to John Stewart and Richard Price.

October 17, 2016

1 ■ *Last Week Tonight with John Oliver* (HBO, October 9) This is the best show on television. The most screamingly funny moments come when true outrage is brought down to earth with references to third-rate bands or bad movies that somehow make the outrage more real (on this night, in the central segment on Guantánamo, an analogy of Vanilla Ice stealing a song from Queen, with interview footage of

Mr. Ice, who looks like a robot made out of Swiss cheese going green around the edges, explaining that the bass lines are different, and then singing them, trying to make his sound different from theirs, and failing). There might be a running subtext on media idiocy almost too gross to credit (here, on the mind-boggling odiousness of Billy Bush). A main story might run twenty minutes and say more than a three-page takeout in the *New York Times*, let alone any story on any other television or radio outlet.

This night the subject was President Obama's failure to close Guantánamo Bay. There is a history of the place, international condemnation of the atrocities we've perpetrated there.

There's a shot of the prison library; it's explained that the most popular books are *Harry Potter* titles.

"And before you think that those library books provided an escape," Oliver says, "just listen to Shaker Aamer, who was released last October, after being held without charge for nearly fourteen years." Oliver goes off, and we are looking at a deeply self-possessed forty-nine-year-old Saudi citizen and British resident with a beard and long hair pulled back.

"You know," he says, "they got, they got an island in *Harry Potter*, it says, Azkaban—where there's no happiness. They just—*suck* all your feelings out of you. And—and you don't have no feeling anymore."

Oliver returns: "No amount of sugar-coating can cover up the reality of what we have done at Guantánamo Bay. Because in the early years, interrogation techniques included physical beatings, short-shackling, a very painful technique in which a prisoner's arms and legs are shackled together, for long periods, and hours, and sometimes days, of repeated loud music, which is horrendous, although sometimes, that last technique backfired, because that same *Harry Potter*–loving inmate grew up loving American rock music, and would annoy the guards by singing along. And just listen to him describe the one song that gave him the most consolation."

There's a cut back to Aamer. He smiles. "I'm sure everybody would laugh when they hear this, 'cause I used to sing it a lot. Because the words, I thought, the words affect me, the words make me feel like, *Yeah, it's me again.* Which is Whitesnake, 'Here I Go Again.'"

In the theater where the show is being taped and Aamer is shown on a monitor, the audience laughs. And in a terribly serious tone, Aamer says, "The words go," and from the heart of a standard power ballad, he recites the last lines of the chorus. The singer walks the only road he's ever known. Alone. A "street of dreams"—and it's unclear if that's the road he's on, or the road that, someday, he might reach.

"And it's true," Aamer says, "because it's just dreams, dreams that I'll be home one day, dreams that I'll be free. Dreams that Guantánamo will be closed."

Oliver comes back: "You know you are miserable when you are finding solace in a fucking Whitesnake song." Yes, they are possibly the most degrading band in the history of popular music—perfect, really, to score the Donald Trump sex tape—Oliver had opened the show with it, of course. But it wasn't a cheap way for Oliver to take the sting off—in other words, to sugarcoat what he'd just shown. That's the way Oliver works: kill you, jerk you back to life with a gobsmacked joke, and then go right back to the story—and because he moves so fast, almost always leaving you a half-step behind, the joke takes nothing away from what you've just seen. Somehow, the show left Aamer with even more dignity than he would have had if Oliver had played him straight. You can go back to him on YouTube over and over again, like a song you can't get out of your head.

2 ▪ Bob Dylan, "Masters of War" at Desert Trip (Indio, California, October 8) More than in any other performance of this song I've ever heard, the young-man perspective was completely erased, and in its place was the fading image, the Rayogram, more than the presence— as if the physical fact of presence had been elided—of an old man who has seen everything and is unwilling to accept anything, someone who has become more and more certain of his right and power to judge as time goes on, the world does not change, and the critique he made of it so many years before suffers no cracks or rust, only scars, like notches on a gun. As the crimes the song speaks of expand in the telling, you hear the judgment pronounced, and you all but hear it received.

3 ▪ *White Girl*, written and directed by Elizabeth Wood (FilmRise) At the end, Morgan Saylor's Leah sits down for her first class of her sophomore year at her college in New York. "How was your summer," someone asks. Well—

4 ▪ **Kaleo, "Way Down We Go" (Elektra)** I heard this on the radio just after the shattering ending of "Smells Like Teen Spirit," and it was as if the second song had grown out of the first. There are hints of Chris Isaak, Robert Johnson, Marvin Gaye, Flipper, and most of all the steely cadence, the two feet planted and nothing moving them, of Rihanna's "Stay" in this severe and elegant soul ballad. I had no idea what it was, but I guessed at the title and found it on YouTube. I wasn't expecting an Icelandic band fronted by one Jökull Júlíusson. As Chuck Berry put it, it goes to show you never can tell.

5 ▪ **Colson Whitehead, from Acknowledgments, *The Underground Railroad* (Doubleday)** "The first one hundred pages were fueled by early Misfits ('Where Eagles Dare [fast version],' 'Horror Business,' 'Hybrid Moments') and Blanck Mass ('Dead Format'). David Bowie is in every book, and I always put on *Purple Rain* and *Daydream Nation* when I write the final pages, so thanks to him and Prince and Sonic Youth."

6 ▪ **The Handsome Family, *Unseen* (Milk & Scissors)** Over the last few years, their albums got somewhat obvious. This is not. And it's gorgeous.

7 ▪ **Randy Newman, "Putin" (Nonesuch)** This is the perfect conceptual bookend to pair with Newman's 2007 "A Few Words in Defense of Our Country," a quiet, despairing song about the wreckage and ruin of the George W. Bush administration and those before it—a song that takes comfort in the belief that while "the leaders we have" are "the worst that we've had," there *were* worse. Newman names the Roman Caesars, the divines of the Spanish Inquisition, Hitler and Stalin and King Leopold of Belgium—but he doesn't sound very convinced. It was a truly miserable thing to listen to.

"Putin," Newman's intervention in this year's election—an answer record to Vladimir Putin's own—couldn't be more different. Kurt Weill and Bertolt Brecht must be jumping up and down in their graves in happiness: this is so German, so 1920s, so after-hours-Berlin with everyone doped to the gills and shouting along. Newman is Putin: the song takes flight with its chorus, the Putin Girls, pumping him up, erasing his doubts, jabbing him in the side to get him going. The weight of history presses down on him—*can* he become the master of the world?

Then he thinks back to the glorious past. "Who won Napoleon?" he yells and the girls answer: "We did!" "Who won World War II?" "The Americans!" comes the answer, but he knows they're just boosting him up. Then fear takes over again: "Lenin couldn't do it! I don't know, Stalin couldn't do it! If they couldn't do it, why you think I can?" Because who *else* is going to do it?

In Randy Newman's best music he leaves you wondering where you stand, what you think, what you believe, how the world works. This is a postcard that may take years to truly be delivered.

8 ▪ William Stout, *Legends of the Blues*, with an introduction by Ed Leimbacher (Abrams ComicArts, 2013) "Dedicated to Willie Dixon & Robert Crumb," this set of cartoon and text portraits of more than ninety musicians—including people R. Crumb, who once published a collection of blues trading cards, would never touch, like Johnny Otis, Chuck Berry, and Screamin' Jay Hawkins—is distinguished by the softness of Stout's lines, which resolve themselves into warmth and empathy. You open the book (I found it on a remainder shelf) at random and see—hear—a musician you think you know as someone new: Blind Willie Johnson in the middle of the night in a graveyard, a spare tree hanging over his head like a hand. But best of all is what Stout does with cigarettes. The ash burns right through a thin cloud of white smoke, making an eye that's looking right at you.

9 & 10, ▪ Little Walter, "Blue and Lonesome" (Chess, 1959) and Rolling Stones, "Blue and Lonesome" from *Blue & Lonesome* (Interscope, December 2) "I'm blue and lonesome," Walter Jacobs declares in his thick, measured voice. He takes a deep breath—and then from the absolute depths of that act the word "as" in "as a man can be" emerges, slowly, drawn out, like a sea monster, and the record has begun. The audacity of tackling a work on this level—a work where the harmonica break, a hurricane, sums up the career of Little Walter, whose "Hate to See You Go" and "Just Your Fool" are also included on this album of blues covers, as "Blue and Lonesome" itself could sum up the blues— is pretty shocking. How in the world would you do it? When I heard the Rolling Stones were taking it on, it seemed the only way to approach this song was on your knees: do it as a simple, quiet folk song, or go down in the flood. We'll see.

November 10, 2016
SPECIAL ELECTION EDITION!

1 ▪ **Ramones programming on the Current, 89.3 FM (Minneapolis, November 7)** "'Twenty-twenty-twenty-four hours to go'"—"Yes," said a friend, "I wanna be sedated."

2 ▪ **A friend (U.S., November 9)** "It's like someone you love dying."

3 ▪ **Jean-Martin Büttner, a journalist at *Tages-Anzeiger* (Zurich, November 9)** "What would Jarry say?"

4 ▪ **Garrison Keillor, "Trump voters will not like what happens next" (*Washington Post*, November 9)** "Don't be cruel. Elvis said it, and it's true. We all experienced cruelty back in our playground days—boys who beat up on the timid, girls who made fun of the homely and naïve—and most of us, to our shame, went along with it, afraid to defend the victims lest we become one of them."

5 ▪ **Kirsty Wark, sign-off, *Newsnight* (BBC Two, November 3)** "You might have seen the demand by Conservative MP Andrew Rosindell that BBC One should play 'God Save the Queen'"—well, actually he called for "our national anthem"—"at the end of the day's programming to mark our departure from the EU. Well, we're not BBC One and it's not quite the end of the day, but we're incredibly happy to oblige. Good night." Rosindell likely didn't have a coruscating performance video of the Sex Pistols' version in mind, which is what he got.

6 ▪ **A friend (U.S., November 9)** "It occurred to me this morning that in a sense the only subject I ever had as a politics writer was the approach of this day. But for the longest time I couldn't really believe it would come. Nothing more American than the faith that chickens will always go somewhere else to roost."

7 ▪ **Dakota Fanning as Merry in *American Pastoral*, directed by Ewan McGregor (Lionsgate)** In a film set half a century ago, a face for our time: almost too convincing to watch as a teenager inflamed at Lyndon Johnson and the Vietnam War, and as a young woman as the willing casualty of her own war against ours.

8 ▪ Joshua Clover (November 9) "And in the cafe in Madison on this difficult day—on comes 'Like a Rolling Stone,' live version. 'The historical shudder,' as Benjamin writes somewhere." But memory digs up its own connections without leaving you a clue, leaving you caught in your own crossed signals, wondering why you thought what you thought. "The great reminiscences, the historical shudder," Benjamin wrote in *The Arcades Project*—"these are a trumpery which [the flaneur] leaves to tourists."

9 ▪ Hope for the Future Department: Michael Barbaro, "What Drives Donald Trump? Fear of Losing Status, Tapes Say" (*New York Times*, October 25) Based on hours of Michael D'Antonio's 2014 interview tapes, a cheap, glib piece of amateur psychoanalysis, with one notable moment: as Trump talks about Peggy Lee's 1969 "Is That All There Is?" perhaps the only occasion on record where the president-elect has expressed genuine empathy for another person. "It's a great song because I've had these tremendous successes and then I'm off to the next one. Because, it's like, 'Oh, is that all there is?'" Trump says. "That's a great song actually, that's a very interesting song, especially sung by her, because she had such a troubled life."

10 ▪ Joerg Haentzchel, a journalist at *Süddeutsche Zeitung* (Munich, November 9) "Tonight I'll watch *The Manchurian Candidate* again." But you can watch it in your head, as images from the film float through real, ordinary life. The affinities are natural, obvious, coded in our history, written in our imaginations—we can't help seeing this story. Soon enough there will be a new Oval Office portrait, the new president framed by the old Lincoln faces, to match both a central scene from the movie—Angela Lansbury calmly bullying Laurence Harvey, as Lincoln, in the form of a desk lamp, with a stovepipe hat for a shade, looks on—and Pete Souza's official White House photograph of Barack Obama sitting at his desk in the Oval Office, Obama looking bitter, to his left a bust of Lincoln with the head facing down, to his right, on the wall, a framed painting of Lincoln in a broad blue suit. And that next portrait could be more than an inevitable presidential symmetry.

The Manchurian Candidate is a 1962 movie about a right-wing U.S. presidential candidate created by China and the Soviet Union as their front. Donald Trump has said that in his capacity as president-elect he would meet with Vladimir Putin before taking office. Constitutionally, and legally, he would have no legitimate position to do so: for a private citizen to negotiate on behalf of the United States with Russia would be treasonous. And why the urgency?

Presume that Trump is carrying hundreds of millions, or even a billion or more in debt to private Russian financial entities. At that level, in Russia, there is no difference between private holdings and the state. Presume that Trump wants to clear that debt before taking office, and that in exchange for that, he would offer Putin a free hand in all surrounding countries—not to mention Syria, or anywhere else. That would of course leave Putin as Trump's blackmailer, but as with Trump's Atlantic City casino, the debt in question would now be the responsibility of the United States, not Trump.

The United States has elected a white supremacist, a classic anti-Semite, and a man for whom women are commodities to be bought and sold. It may have also elected a Russian agent.

December 20, 2016

1 ▪ **For the record: Bob Dylan, Nobel Prize acceptance speech as read by Azita Raji, U.S. Ambassador to Sweden (Stockholm, December 10)** "I was out on the road when I received this surprising news, and it took me more than a few minutes to properly process it. I began to think about William Shakespeare, the great literary figure. I would reckon he thought of himself as a dramatist. The thought that he was writing literature couldn't have entered his head. His words were written for the stage. Meant to be spoken not read. When he was writing *Hamlet,* I'm sure he was thinking about a lot of different things: 'Who're the right actors for these roles?' 'How should this be staged?' 'Do I really want to set this in Denmark?' His creative vision and ambitions were no doubt at the forefront of his mind, but there were also more mundane matters to consider and deal with. 'Is the financing in place?' 'Are there enough good seats for my patrons?' 'Where am I going to get a

human skull?' I would bet that the farthest thing from Shakespeare's mind was the question 'Is this *literature?*'"

The line about the skull is the one that jerks your head, but the lines about money and tickets are what make this stick.

2 ▪ Fantastic Negrito, Bill Graham Civic Auditorium (San Francisco, November 12) Joshua Clover reports: "Fantastic Negrito's *The Last Days of Oakland* begins with its title phrase: the first voice, as another intones 'The Black Panthers.' 'It's the end of something.' 'Crack cocaine.' 'And the beginning of something . . .' The interlude, like much of the album, is a seduction scene between the abstract and concrete. The album cover shows a black figure with guitar and bird mask astride the street signs at San Pablo Avenue and 32nd Street. Local residents will know this as 'Triangle Park,' a concrete catchment of misery where those closed out of the town's renewal trade in all the famous informal economies. It's always last days in Triangle Park.

"Last month, with a four-piece band, Fantastic Negrito opened the San Francisco stop on Temple of the Dog's reunion tour, across the bay. He was twice as alive, and not just in that way that opening acts often are. He's just lit up. The audience seemed puzzled. Something was happening, but they didn't know what it was. The show was for them, because they had tickets. But the album is not, and that left things a little unsettled. Negrito offered nary a feel-bad power ballad, grunge's calling card. Or maybe one, reaching back to Lead Belly or some older Appalachian version of 'In the Pines.' That was only a taste of the bad feelings, despite Negrito's rocker leaps and funk outfit. He got deep inside an off-kilter blues that carried him across the stage. 'Most of my fear is sitting right here with you for the rest of my life,' he sang, and you could believe it. Neither is he likely to sit in his current sound. Something like Led Zeppelin's debut, Negrito is too weird and wired to stay in the blues channel, though he is unlikely to head off toward hobbits. He is headed somewhere, that's for sure.

"Near the end of the show, he enjoined the audience to form collectives and pool their money for the coming hard times. But he must have been talking to somebody else. In the Bay Area back in the '90s, modern rock boasted the wealthiest demographic of all formats. They were in the house along with their cousins from a fast-gentrifying Oakland, new playground for tech bros and the developers who love them. They are not the 'Working Poor' (as *Last Days*' second track, and a single on the Fat Elvis label, is called) much less those who can't even get in the door.

"'Penned up in the ghettos of America, surrounded by all his factories and all the physical components of his economic system, we have been made into "the wretched of the earth," relegated to the position of spectators.' That's Huey Newton, from the last last days of Oakland. There aren't even factories anymore; the sharing economy is not shared with Triangle Park. When Newton was waiting to be inducted to prison in 1968, he listened over and over to 'Ballad of a Thin Man,' rattling off his notes while working on the Panther newspaper. One gets the sense that, were such a moment to come around again with him intact, this time he might listen to Fantastic Negrito. We can hope."

3 ▪ Bob Dylan, *The 1966 Live Recordings* (Columbia/Legacy) Out of this compact, unpretentious 36-CD set, on No. 14, Liverpool, May 14, just after Dylan and the Hawks—Rick Danko, Garth Hudson, Richard Manuel, Robbie Robertson, and drummer Mickey Jones in place of Levon Helm, who had quit—have finished "One Too Many Mornings" and are about to slide into "Ballad of a Thin Man," a moment unheard on bootlegs or recorded in histories. Dylan's tone that of an aside addressed to the musicians around him, his words plainly addressed to the crowd, an anthropologist documenting his research, sighting the balcony: "There's a fellow up there looking for the savior. The savior's backstage—we have a picture of him."

4 ▪ Robbie Robertson, *Testimony* (Universal) A companion album to his autobiography, up to 1976, of the same name ("We had to be constantly on alert," he writes of backing Dylan in Liverpool in 1966 to storms of boos and curses. "I adjusted the strap on my Telecaster so I could release it with a quick thumb movement and use the guitar as a weapon"), and the revelation is what an interesting singer he is. In the Band, his voice never had the fullness or the subtlety of Helm, Danko, or Manuel, but in its cramped way, zig-zagging through a lyric, it was just as true, more vulnerable, and more personal. Here, after the horribly overproduced title song, from Robertson's first solo album—Gil Evans's horn section, U2, Nile Rogers, Ivan Neville, Bernard Edwards, all to *hide* his voice—there are, with the Band, the fragile, alluring "Out of the Blue" and "Twilight," and on his own, the dreamy storytelling of "Soap Box Preacher" and the shimmering "Unbound." But why did he leave the photo of his blond, charismatic, mobbed-up Toronto uncle Natie Klegerman and local muscle Tony Volpe out of his book?

5 ▪ *It's All One Case: The Illustrated Ross Macdonald Archives,* by Paul Nelson and Kevin Avery, with Jeff Wong (Fantagraphics) Based on nearly forty hours of interviews the critic Paul Nelson (1936–2006) conducted in 1976 with Kenneth Millar (1915–83), aka Ross Macdonald, the author of the Lew Archer detective novels, and illustrated principally with every iteration of every cover of every book published in any country by Millar under whatever pseudonym, the book is entrancing and frustrating: enormous territory is covered, modesty and decency emerge as compelling values, but too often you can feel Nelson's real questions remaining unspoken and you can almost always feel Millar holding back. What he doesn't hold back: how from at least *The Galton Case* in 1959 through *The Zebra-Striped Hearse* (1962), *The Far Side of the Dollar* (1965), *Black Money* (1966), and *The Instant Enemy* (1968), he was rewriting *The Great Gatsby* over and over again ("It opens doors in all directions, into the past and the future. And they're still open"), and how, from the start, with *The Moving Target* in 1949, he was leading Lew Archer into a life Nick Carraway should have lived.

6 ▪ Levon Helm and Rick Danko, *The Living Room Tapes,* Starry Night Club (Portland, January 28, 1983) A YouTube album, complete with cover. After Robbie Robertson left the Band following the Last Waltz in 1976, the rest of the group scrambled into solo projects. Here, from just before Helm, Danko, Manuel, and Hudson, broke and fading, went on the road again under their old name, letting it go only after Danko's death in 1999, is an almost perfect night from two of them, with sound that makes you feel as if you're sitting in: sixteen songs, played on acoustic guitars, harmonica, and mandolin, from Levon's leads on "The Girl I Left Behind" and "Milk Cow Boogie" to a thrillingly intricate rhythm inside of "Rag Mama Rag" to a cover of Kenny Rogers's "Blaze of Glory" to Danko taking "It Makes No Difference" to places you can imagine it never got to before, and never reached again. It's careful, delicate, and afraid—the singing a harrowing warble. "Without your love, I have nothing at all"—a trite pop song sentiment, and here Danko makes the nothing open up beneath his feet, and you are caught in his gravity. It's the deepest thing I've been able to stand for six weeks.

7 ▪ **Rolling Stones, *Blue & Lonesome* (Interscope)** Aren't tribute albums terrible? Yes, and this homage to '50s and '60s Chicago blues, the sort of album young groups used to make forty or fifty years ago, doesn't touch *The Paul Butterfield Blues Band* (1965) or Fleetwood Mac's *Mr. Wonderful* (1968). The rhythm section is mechanical; Keith Richards's clumsy, uninspired playing doesn't create a moment of excitement. Everything good here comes from Mick Jagger—and his harmonica, rolling waves over the songs, is more convincing than his voice, and more soulful, too.

8 ▪ **Jonathan Lethem, *A Gambler's Anatomy* (Doubleday)** "His gaze was an object closer than it appeared."

9 ▪ **Shovels & Rope, "The Last Hawk," from *Little Seeds* (New West)** Next year, with luck, Garth Hudson will turn eighty; this song, from the Charleston, South Carolina, duo Cary Ann Hearst and Michael Trent, is written as his last word, or suicide note. It's testimony from a man who has seen all around his life, who is almost forgotten, who is now going out into the woods, where no one will find him: "This is my last stop / I'm gonna take a long walk / 'Fore I take my boots off." The premise is corny and the realization is so full of passion, so painful and proud, you want to believe every word as much as you don't.

10 ▪ ***Hell or High Water,* directed by David Mackenzie (Lionsgate)** It's both *Bonnie and Clyde* and *The Last Picture Show* nearly half a century later, with Jeff Bridges bridging the gap—in his mid-sixties when he made this, he looks it, but as soon as his Texas Ranger Marcus Hamilton retires he looks ten years older. What makes the film more than its plot asked for is the landscape, the colorless, anonymous towns and strips, with the geography still seeming too big, too open, too empty, too dead.

There's an original soundtrack by Nick Cave and Warren Ellis, but the real music is in the old-timey modern folk and country songs that punctuate the film: opening with Townes Van Zandt's "Dollar Bill Blues," which has never sounded better, Ben Foster's older-brother bank robber singing "Streets of Laredo" under his breath as the last chase begins, and closing with Chris Stapleton's "Outlaw State of Mind," a fracking earthquake that covers at least as much of the American map as Chuck Berry's "Promised Land."

In this West Texas territory, except for two Indians—a Ranger and a gambler—everyone on the screen is white. "This is all Trump country," said a person watching, and Stapleton's fatalistic drawl catches why and how: "From East Kentucky down to Alabam' . . . From West Virginia to the Rio Grande," and he doesn't really have to so much as inhale to put that across—it's coded in the song. But not the kicker, taking this ballad out of the South, claiming the country: "Yeah there's people all across the land / From New York out to old San Fran' / Just don't give a damn all the time." That elected Trump: not people voting for "change," not people voting for "someone who'll stand up for me," but just enough people voting to see the whole show blown up and blown away.

January 18, 2017

1 & 2 ▪ **Mats Gustafsson and Christian Marclay, *In Hindsight* (Vinyl Factory) and Okkyung Lee and Christian Marclay, *Amalgam* (Northern Spy)** Marclay's work has been so powerfully visual over the last few years—his twenty-four-hour film *The Clock*, the comic-book-inspired *Actions* aka *Onomatopoeia* paintings, his sidewalk animations videos— that you can forget he started out as a turntablist in New York art-punk clubs in the early 1980s, sometimes running eight records at a time. These live recordings from two shows at Café Oto in London with the saxophonist Mats Gustafsson (2013) and the cellist Okkyung Lee (2014) are proof Marclay hasn't lost a step. He's invented new moves, because he has to.

Gustafsson's sound is so big and harsh it feels as if he's shoved Marclay off the stage; with the music chasing the STOMP FOOM FWHAM ZWEE NOOOOHS BLECH words of the *Actions* paintings (collaged on the sonically blank back side of the *In Hindsight* 12″), it can take a while to realize that the echo in the music is Marclay scratching his way into the saxophone. With Lee, the excitement again comes when you can't tell the musicians apart—when Lee separates her own tone at the end of a movement, the pleasure is like the absolutely satisfied relief you feel when a solo ends and the singer takes back the song. What could be a voice could also be a needle drag, a sample, or even the cello itself; you don't want to decide. This is less of a tour de force than the show with Gustafsson, and far richer: much longer, meandering, teasing out holes and hollows in the cave the musicians seem to be building inside the club they're playing. On side two, as Lee makes an almost industrial noise—now it's she who's scratching, Marclay keeping her time—you could be listening to the Rolling Stones' "Goin' Home": the momentum is that unstoppable, that free. The music seems to have dropped from a low sky, as if Marclay and Lee caught it and ran, got lost, slowed down, and stopped.

3 ▪ *Passengers*, directed by Morten Tyldum (Columbia) On a 5,000-passenger spaceship on a 120-year voyage to colonize a planet (Earth having become, among other things, "overpriced"), Chris Pratt wakes up in his hibernation pod. He doesn't think much about why no one else is waking up, follows computer directions to his cabin, changes into regular clothes, and in the bathroom the piped-in music is playing "Like a Rolling Stone." It sounds tinny and small, with the band inaudible; it sounds like a folk song, a 78 from the 1920s or the '30s, with the vocal never sounding more hillbilly, but the muscular rhythmic lifts in the melody are still there, and they still give that complete and subtle thrill. Pratt isn't really listening, but he catches that; possessed by a spirit of confidence, even bravado, with an unstressed but unmistakable change in the way he carries himself, he steps out of the door and into the plot.

4 ▪ *Arrival*, directed by Denis Villeneuve (Paramount) The alien ships descend around the globe, apparently at random: the best explanation anyone can come up with is that wherever they landed, Sheena Easton once had a hit.

5 ▪ A. O. Scott and Manohla Dargis, "Big Statements from Smaller Films," *New York Times* (January 8) One of the *Times'* faux critical conversations, which usually seem like a lazy alternative to actually composing something (he writes a statement, emails it, she writes a statement, emails it back)—but with the piece focusing mostly on race, racism, and "unexamined assumptions," in this case not at all. If *Moonlight* and *The Birth of a Nation* and *Barbershop: The Next Cut* are films about race, Scott asks, why aren't *Manchester by the Sea* and *La La Land* and *Sully*—and by the way, why does *La La Land* feature "a white pianist as the savior of jazz and a black musician as its corrupter"? Nothing about Elvis's birthday, though.

6 ▪ Sleater-Kinney, *Live in Paris* (Sub Pop) "Start Together," "Jumpers," "Dig Me Out," and especially "Turn It On" seem to leap off the stage, but it's the last number, the light, breezy "Modern Girl," that makes it all stick. When Carrie Brownstein exhales the line that keeps coming up like someone coming up for air—*My whole life*—you can hear a whole life. You can hear tiredness, regret, dissatisfaction: a thin sigh of wanting more. Next, in a fan's world, *Covers Live*—this band has always been a jukebox. Start with "Rockin' in the Free World," go to "White Rabbit," "Tommy Gun," "The Promised Land," "Fortunate Son," "More Than a Feeling" (from their first recording session, in 1994), end with "Faith," which along with "Rebel Rebel" closed their San Francisco show on New Year's Eve—or whatever funeral they cover next, because they're fans before they're anything else.

7 ▪ Brokeback, *Illinois River Valley Blues* (Thrill Jockey) Tortoise bassist Doug McCombs has always been more relaxed, more unconcerned, with his instrumental Brokeback side project (vocals by Amalea Tshilds are noted, but the credit ought to read "texture"), and Tortoise is a pretty relaxed and unconcerned band. This starts slowly and it ends that way, a fantasy soundtrack for *Once Upon a Time in the West*, a western Quentin Tarantino hasn't made yet, or one of the forthcoming episodes of *Twin Peaks*, or even a Tarnation album without Paula Frazer. It's music as weather when there really isn't anything else to talk about. It's impossible to pick one song over another; if it's "Cairo Levee" today it'll be "Spanish Venus" tomorrow. If you're certain McCombs has found what he's looking for with "Andalusia, IL," with "Night Falls on Chillicothe" you hope he never will.

8 ▪ Pete Wells, "Making Way for the Tried and True at Cut by Wolfgang Puck," *New York Times* (December 20) On entering: "It's how you'd imagine a sexy downtown bar if you'd never been downtown, gone to a bar or had sex."

9 ▪ Why Jack White Has So Much Money (College Football Playoff National Championship, Alabama vs. Clemson, ESPN, January 9) Because a snatch of a martial-anthem trumpets-and-tubas version of

"Seven Nation Army" is used between every pause, between plays, at timeouts, with what sounds like an instant of the real thing to introduce every commentary, to signal every commercial. In the course of a single game, hundreds of times.

10 ▪ **Bob Dylan, "Once Upon a Time," in *Tony Bennett Celebrates 90: The Best Is Yet to Come* (NBC, December 20)** After Lady Gaga, Elton John, Stevie Wonder, k.d. lang, and nearly countless more, it was the last performance before Bennett's solo finale: a no-happy-ending song recorded by Bennett in 1962. There were notes Dylan couldn't hit—as the song was written, but not as he thought it through, felt it out, sang it. He used the mike stand as a kind of mast, or harpoon: shifting it from one side to the other, moving it higher or lower, he dramatized all the unknown directions a song beginning *Once upon a time* might take. He made the song interesting, unsettled—"He made it about America," said one person watching.

February 21, 2017

1 ▪ **Fleetwoods, "Unchained Melody" in *Things to Come* (*L'Avenir*), written and directed by Mia Hansen-Løve (Arte France Cinéma)** At the very end, after Isabelle Huppert's philosophy professor has been abandoned by her husband for another woman, dropped by her publisher, and left stranded by her mother's death, this song comes on, less to bless than to seal a scene of bourgeois family life—and, so modestly put across by the Fleetwoods' Gretchen Christopher and Barbara Ellis, whose precise singing is a kind of signal to let you feel how much the song is taking them out of themselves, into a preternatural clarity that makes the sound of the recording feel so deep that you can get the sense that the song is not merely bigger than the singers but bigger than life. Was it a trick of the sound designer, a remix that brought out something that was never there before? I know the Fleetwoods—it was as if I'd never heard this, from 1959, what one could have taken as a filler track on their first album, a standard with nothing more to say. Here it's a cloud, with the voices of the two women in the group floating over the tired, all but instantly clichéd words of the song, so that the

song is abstracted from itself—and so fully that you might not even recognize this most familiar of familiar songs, and though it sounds like
the Fleetwoods, it seems impossible that it is.*

2 ■ Lithics, *Borrowed Floors* (Water Wing) When I first heard this
ten-song LP I thought it was a throwback of truly alarming scholasti-
cism: I was sure I was listening to a retrieval of a 1979 Leeds band in
the Gang of Four/Delta 5 circle that for no good reason—because there
wasn't a moment that wasn't hard and brittle at the same time—no one
ever noticed until someone dug these tapes out of a basement. All the
signs were there: strict and angular rhythms, all instruments but the
bass lead dropping out as if someone had turned off the power and then
flicked it back on, a harsh, flat, determined lead singer who communi-
cated resistance to both her band members and whoever might be
listening.

It was so odd I kept going back to it, and very quickly any sense of
the past dropped away. These are four young people from Portland—
though you can imagine that it's in keeping with the anarchist ano-
nymity of the Leeds contingent that, while there are pictures of four
people here, there are no band members' names here or on their Bandcamp site—who are interested in tension. They make it, they drama-
tize it, they play with it, they don't question it. That gives their songs
a sense of contingency, accident, catch-it-while-you-can: even when the
singer seems to dive into a freer pulse, as on "Thing in Your Eye" (put
that in the punk-title hall of fame), you might be wondering—you can

* Mia Hansen-Løve wrote in response (May 20): "I will tell you the story of the Fleetwood
song in *L'Avenir*.

"One day, one year before the shooting, the sound designer who has been working on all
of my films, and knows me quite well, sent me an email from Berlin, where he was working
with some artists, an email with this song. He tells me an artist had him listen to it (I don't
remember why) and this song reminds him terribly of the melancholy of my films. I listen to
the song . . . The song makes me cry. And it stays with me. There is a simplicity, a softness, a
purity in it, that overwhelms me. Somehow I see a connexion between the song and the mood
of my next film. A few months later I know that even if there are going to be only 4 songs in
L'Avenir, this one has to be in it. And then, it becomes even more than just one song, it becomes THE song of the film for me—the reason why it ends up being at the very end. It could
be a lullaby—for the baby—but also a love song, for the man who is not there yet, the love
that's she's waiting for—even if she didn't admit it before, the song tells it now—that love is
essential. Not only love for the baby.

"It's the way I see it, it's this ambiguity that the song has for me that moves me so much."

feel the group wondering—how long it can last, and when the singer goes back to bits and pieces on the next song, "Human Doctor" (something, apparently, you can no longer take for granted), it's thrilling, because you're learning their language and you really don't want them to stop speaking it.

In the musically open spaces of their dynamics as a band they create an atmosphere of tremendous emotional density: though the album barely covers twenty minutes it seems to last twice as long.

3 ▪ On a Women's March (January 21) From the time of the first protest marches in which I ever took part—there were those in 1964 and 1965 that were peaceful, and for the next years those that weren't peaceful, or safe—seeing babies and little children wearing political hats or T-shirts, professing an allegiance they couldn't possibly understand, always bothered me. It wasn't an affirmation of a collective good. It was a denial that the child had a self and an affirmation that the child could be used as a prop. A picture that circulated on social media last month shows something different: a small person bundled against the cold, on his or her father's shoulders, holding up his or her own statement, in his or her own language, as a public citizen, in the street, for everyone to see, a piece of cardboard with shapes and scribbles in different color crayons, saying, "I'm here."

4 ▪ Cecily Marcus writes in (January 21) "On a cold, grey, wet, miserable day, the first day, the day I should have been in St. Paul or Oakland or Washington, D.C., or Berlin, I was at the butcher shop in Minneapolis. In a place owned and operated by people like me—white people in their 40s—I hear quiet, deliberate guitar chords going down the scale. I tell my 6-year-old that this is a good song. Sleater Kinney's 'Modern Girl,' the darkest picture of a sunny day ever. Two good songs, with Bikini Kill's 'Rebel Girl' coming right after: I tell the only woman working there that I never hear this kind of music in public, not even on the radio. She tells me that she thought that the men working with her—for her?—needed to hear it today. On a day when what you hear and what you say in public feels more important than ever, this was a small, momentary sigh of relief. And then it was gone."

5 ▪ Charles Lloyd and the Marvels with Lucinda Williams, "Masters of War," on *I Long to See You* (Blue Note) From the jazz saxophonist

Lloyd, riffs that wouldn't disturb a car commercial. From Williams, a performance in which sententiousness is made into the master of all values.

6 ▪ **From an academic conference at Yale** We're used to Donald Trump punctuating his pronouncements with a quick "OK?" as if to simultaneously block any disagreement and reassure himself that he's right. There's a match in the habit of self-consciously hip younger academics presenting papers at a conference, reflexively hitting "right" at the end of declarative sentences, but in a manner that makes you hear a comma, not a question mark: a way of certifying the assumption that everyone present shares a certain set of opinions and terms of discourse. *Right*—it's not an aggressive pronouncement but a congratulation of both the speaker and the audience for the truth that they already agree and that no fundamental preconceptions will be challenged. In other words, they and Trump are speaking the same language.

7 ▪ **Lindsey Lee Johnson, *The Most Dangerous Place on Earth* (Random House)** In this novel set in a high school in Mill Valley, a moment to remember: "You fucked one teacher. That doesn't make you an adult."

8 ▪ **Frame of reference in undergraduate class at Berkeley (January 19)** About eighty students, mostly freshmen and sophomores: asked if they knew who Bob Dylan was, almost everyone raised a hand. With *The Great Gatsby* still a staple of high-school English (a linchpin in *The Most Dangerous Place on Earth*, as it happens), the same for F. Scott Fitzgerald, and close to that for F.D.R. Robert Johnson, very few hands—more for James Dean, but still less than a third of the class. Only a handful knew the John Henry song or story, but well over two-thirds said yes to Tupac Shakur and more to Amy Winehouse. More people than not had seen *The Godfather*, and perhaps as a sign that the ground for the apocalypse has not been laid as firmly as some might hope, almost no one had heard of Ayn Rand.

9 ▪ **Levon & the Hawks, *Live at Crang Plaza in Ontario 1964* (YouTube)** "When Rick Danko and Richard Manuel sang 'Bring It on Home to Me,'" Robbie Robertson writes in *Testimony*, "the sun came out," and even through the awful, foggy sound, you can hear that happen.

10 ▪ Y Pants, *Y Pants* (Water Wing 12″ 45) Barbara Ess, Verge Piersol, and Gail Vachon fooled around with toy-store instruments in the downtown arts milieu in New York in the late 1970s and early '80s, and they never sounded like they weren't having a wonderful time. If their best record is still a snakepit version of Lesley Gore's "That's the Way Boys Are"—it could be women out of some girls-in-prison pulp screaming about rape by their guards—everything they did felt just a step away from ordinary life and nothing they did was something you could see coming. The six numbers here—from 1980 sessions not included on the 1982 Neutral album *Beat It Down*—catch their whole narrow, quivering range. In "Favorite Sweater" the mere fact of Pierson singing about something everyone has and nobody thinks very much about is pleasurable, and when Vachon and Ess come in behind her the fact that they all believe something momentous depends on it is even more so. When Mick Jagger sang "Off the Hook" on the Rolling Stones' second album, when they were just beginning to write songs, he was irritated, then he was bored. When Y Pants cover it fifteen years later they do what anyone would do: they go through every good and bad reason someone's not answering, from having forgotten to hang up the phone when phones still hung up to being dead.

With thanks to Emily Marcus.

March 27, 2017

1 ▪ Alison Krauss, *Windy City* (Capitol) This album didn't have a producer, it had a stylist.

2 ▪ Steve Jones with Ben Thompson, *Lonely Boy: Tales from a Sex Pistol* (Da Capo) "He never learned to read or write so well, but he could play a guitar"—and end up knowing where he's been and what it meant. Jones on Johnny Rotten rejecting the band's admittance to the Rock & Roll Hall of Fame in 2006: "He sent them a letter at the last minute refusing to appear and calling the whole ceremony 'urine in wine.' . . . Left to our own devices, the rest of us would probably have done the show, but in the long run what he did was best for the Pistols as an idea."

3 ▪ Paul Ryan, tweet (February 21) and Rubella Ballet, "Money Talks" (Ubiquitous, 1985) Ryan: "Freedom is the ability to buy what you want to fit what you need." Rubella Ballet: "In this corrupt society / The rich pay to be free." But given the government we chose, with the country to be remade through tax cuts to the wealthy, the effective repeal of the corporate income tax, elimination of regulations inhibiting profit, the abrogation of prohibitions against bribery and self-dealing, and the removal of estate taxes—insignificant in terms of macroeconomics, but symbolically, in terms of how America defines itself, enormously significant—the reality is not quite as either the Speaker of the House or a Thatcher-era London punk band defines it. The reality is that the rich will be paid to be free—to represent freedom, as an ever-receding but infinitely alluring possibility, to everyone else.

4–7 ▪ Van Morrison, *The Complete Them, 1964–1967* (Legacy/Exile/ Sony); *It's Too Late to Stop Now . . .*, Vols. II, III, and IV and DVD (Legacy/ Exile/Sony, 1973/2016); *Keep Me Singing* (Caroline/Exile, 2016); at SFJazz (October 18, 2016) The sixty-nine tracks on the Them set, so much of it conceived and worked out live in Belfast with Morrison fronting a hurricane band, all of it recorded in London, with Jimmy Page's hands tangled in the sound, remain unparalleled in their ferocity and lyricism: at their most unique, as with "Mystic Eyes" or their cover of Bob Dylan's "It's All Over Now, Baby Blue," both at once. In 1973, as the leader of Marin County band Caledonia Soul Orchestra, he combined performances from the Troubadour in Los Angeles, the Santa Monica Civic, and the Rainbow Theater in London for a 1974 double live album, and to listen now to all three shows, with unpredictable song choices ("Since I Fell for You," "I Paid the Price," "Sweet Thing," "Take Your Hand Out of My Pocket") dancing around "Gloria," "Caravan," and "Cyprus Avenue" (but not "Madame George," which I saw him play once at the Avalon Ballroom in San Francisco in 1969 and never again), is to fail utterly to place one above another: you'll change your mind every time you listen. Which means it's a risk to put your past on the market with your present.

Keep Me Singing is so tepid not even a version of Bobby "Blue" Bland's 1963 "Share Your Love with Me," a profound song which brought so much out of Richard Manuel on the Band's *Moondog Matinee* ten years later, seems to demand anything from Morrison, and the most notable new song, "Too Late," catches your ear because, you realize sooner or later, it's using the same melody as "Share Your Love."

And the story on stage is not necessarily different. As Joel Selvin reports on a recent show in San Francisco: "SFJazz is the bright, shiny 600-seat auditorium dedicated to jazz performance, funded by wealthy technocrats, who have turned to jazz instead of the opera or symphony for their cultural philanthropic impulses. Many notable figures in the jazz world such as Herbie Hancock or Chick Corea have worked the room, but Morrison, the first major rock performer to appear at the cozy, intimate showroom with pristine sound and generous sight lines, was able to command $250 tickets for this prestige booking. If he certainly looked the part in stingy brim fedora, shades and pin-striped suit, he didn't deviate from his typical concert program one bit because he was playing a jazz room.

"For an hour and a half, Morrison ambled through a procession of largely recent material backed by a lean, pared down four-piece band and backup vocalist. He brought his daughter, Shana Morrison, out to duet on 'That Old Black Magic' and invited boogie-woogie pianist Mitch Woods, who had recently recorded with Morrison in New Orleans doing duets with Taj Mahal, to play a couple of songs. Otherwise, the show was a standard indifferent Morrison affair.

"He can be such a frustrating performer. He never really stepped on the gas until late in the set when he bellowed 'Step right up' from 'Ballerina,' from *Astral Weeks*, his chest pumped out, his head tilted skyward. He closed the set and returned for the briefest of perfunctory encores—a chorus of 'Gloria'—leaving the stage while his band played extensive solos for an additional 10 minutes."

But between 1980 and 1996 Morrison put out fifteen albums without one that stuck, and a year later released *The Healing Game*, music of menace and sadness a younger man likely wouldn't have understood, let alone made. You can never write him off, which is why Selvin was there for one more lousy show and I'll always buy anything he does.

8 ▪ Lana Del Rey, "Love" (Polydor/Interscope) Michael Robbins writes in: "What gets me is the way she rhymes 'all dressed up' with 'in particular,' which wouldn't work on paper. It's all in her vocalization. Singers often understand intuitively things about sound that many poets never learn."

9 ▪ Rhiannon Giddens, *Freedom Highway* (Nonesuch) The album is named for a Staple Singers song from 1965. Listening especially to Giddens's own slavery songs—"At the Purchaser's Option," the title taken from a newspaper ad that can make you sick to read; "Julie," which, knit to the bones of the traditional murder ballad "Pretty Polly" for its rhythm, continues the tale to a finale that could end a novel Toni Morrison hasn't written; and "Come Love Come," a story that compared to the first two feels dutiful, with programmatic words that nevertheless dissolve into the sweep of the singing—and then watching the Nazi and White Power signs from the Civil Rights era in *I Am Not Your Negro* or the separate-but-equal legalized contempt in *Hidden Figures*, it's hard not to wonder how much of that country may be coming back. That makes this record, in the moment, almost unbearably difficult to listen to, and just as difficult to stay away from. It may be too measured in its weighing of the emotion proper to this word or that pause; it may be too careful, too precise, to stand up to the country it's claiming. But if it fades, if it's forgotten, sometime in the future someone will find it at a yard sale, in an online search for something else, and be shocked that anyone ever spoke so clearly.

10 ▪ Chuck Berry, "The Things I Used to Do" (YouTube) It was 1965. He was two years out of federal prison, where he'd been sent in 1962 for a racially targeted Mann Act conviction, now appearing in a Belgian television studio surrounded by a large circle of young teenagers, the girls in dresses, the boys in coats and ties, who look as if they've been dragged there on a field trip. There's a pick-up band of local musicians: a white-haired pianist, a goateed bass fiddle player, a drummer, and a rhythm guitarist, all of whom seem nervous and full of pride over the chance to play with this man. The pianist hits the first of a series of trilling high notes he will follow throughout the performance and Chuck Berry, lithe, taking small, catlike movements, impossibly handsome, with a large, loose pompadour, bends slightly into a crouch for Guitar Slim's already classic 1953 tragic New Orleans blues.

He tracked the song, looking not at the bored students, not exactly at the moving camera in the center of the circle, but to the woman in the song, who he knows is "out with your other man." He looks her straight in the eye, not with anger, scorn, or pain, but with something just short of a wink, saying that he knows she knows he's done the same.

Not the curl of a note or a word is rushed. A flurry in the rhythm rises up and disappears. Guitar Slim had a harsh, angular tone on his guitar, creating a sense of drama he couldn't quite sustain. With a quieter, more specific feeling in every musical or verbal phrase, Berry seemed to slow the song down from the inside. He let the listener all the way into the song, and then, when it ended, left the musicians, the woman in the song, you watching now, days after his death, maybe even himself, wanting more.

The column of April 19, 2017, was accidentally omitted. It can be found at greilmarcus.net. It was the last installment of this column in Pitchfork. *Beginning in May the column appeared in the* Village Voice.

Village Voice

2017·2018

May 17, 2017

1 ▪ **Filthy Friends, "Any Kind of Crowd" b/w "Editions of You" (Kill Rock Stars 45)** With guitarists Corin Tucker of Sleater-Kinney, Peter Buck of R.E.M., and the always airborne Kurt Bloch of the Fastbacks in front, both the A-side original and a Roxy Music number taken away from Bryan Ferry come across as pure fun. What's new is a certain deepening in Tucker's tone. From the start, she's had the most ambitious voice in pop music. Now, with the burden of the singer saving her own life and maybe yours lifted, you hear the sound of ambition realized.

2 ▪ **Jacob Jordan and Jeff Martin, "Musician Col. Bruce Hampton collapses at 70th birthday concert and dies" (Associated Press, May 2)** "ATLANTA—When Col. Bruce Hampton slowly fell to his knees during the finale of his star-studded birthday concert, fans and musicians alike thought it was another one of his quirky performance acts.

"Fourteen-year-old guitar phenom Brandon 'Taz' Niederauer tore into a blistering solo as the 70-year-old man lay motionless just feet away, his arm draped over a speaker"—and John Popper and Warren Haynes and John Bell kept on playing "Turn on Your Lovelight," which has *always* wanted to be played all night. "It made me want to teach a course in jam band CPR," said a friend of a friend. "OK, so, like, you see somebody who's not moving or breathing, the first thing you're going to need is an electric guitar . . ."

3 ▪ **Ellyn and Robbie, *Skywriting with Glitter* (ellynandrobbie.com)** An L.A. poet who makes sarcasm feel like love and an L.A. keyboardist and singer who makes the music the poet thinks she can't. There's not a moment you can anticipate; everything is a surprise.

4 ▪ **Particle Kid, *Particle Kid* (Hen House Studios)** One minute into the first song on this album—"Forever is my best friend," Micah Nelson sang—I thought I was back in 1971, experiencing the Platonic form of lame: James Taylor's little brother Livingston on the radio, singing "Get Out of Bed."

5 ▪ **Ayron Jones, *Audio Paint Job* (Sunyata)** From Seattle: He says he plays rock 'n' roll. Like he knows it'll confuse the people who are sure he has to call it something else.

6 ▪ **Taiwan Housing Project, "Maintenance of an Application," from *Three Song Record* (M'Lady EP, 2016), and *Veblen Death Mask* (Kill Rock Stars LP)** From Philadelphia: Kilynn Lunsford sets an almost always set-myself-on-fire lead in front of a Captain Beefheart saxophone and feedback that's all bad weather when it isn't thoughtful—asking itself what it's for, or trying to translate the cold humor of a housing project submitting an application in the form of a song. The band is weakest when it finds itself trapped in conventional structures, strongest when they don't hear them. This is the kind of stuff you have to listen to until you decide you love it or hate it, or at least until you can hear if it's really Mr. Theory of the Leisure Class they're talking about.

7 ▪ ***In Their Lives: Great Writers on Great Beatles Songs,* edited by Andrew Blauner (Blue Rider)** It's not a shock that Gerald Early, in a quiet voice, dives deepest. Here, music on TV teenage dance shows "altered its authenticity," and the authentic was not music unfettered by capitalist imperatives but AM radio: "White youth music was for me exotic but also the sound of the mainstream. To know this music, to appreciate it, gave me, in some strange way, total access to my culture, to my society—in effect, total access to my own life."

8 ▪ **Emma Silvers and Sarah Hotchkiss, "A Broken Record," KQED .org, reviewing "The Summer of Love Experience: Art, Fashion, and Rock & Roll" at the de Young Museum (San Francisco, through August 20):** "We are not convinced that any of this summer's grand retelling is necessary."

9 ▪ **Bob Dylan and the Band, "As I Went Out One Morning," Maple Leaf Gardens, Toronto, January 10, 1974 (dailymotion.com)** Apparently the only time he's ever performed the song. It's like a fragment of an old tale with all context gone, a song that doesn't explain itself, so that its tone becomes its subject: regret.

10 ▪ Historian John Shaw (*This Land That I Love*, on Irving Berlin and Woody Guthrie) writes in "Had Andrew Jackson been a little bit later you wouldn't have had anybody put the bomp in the bomp ba bomp ba bomp. He saw what was happening with regard to the bomp, he said there's no reason for this. People don't realize, you know, the bomp, if you think about it, why? People don't ask that question, but why did anybody put the bomp in the bomp ba bomp ba bomp, why couldn't that one have been worked out?"

Thanks to Andrew Hamlin, Steve Perry, and Steve Weinstein.

June 14, 2017

1 ▪ "1927 Il Ritorno in Italia," Museo Salvatore Ferragamo (Florence, through May 2, 2018) The shoe designer sailed back after twelve years in Hollywood, a return marked by the makeover of his museum as a steamship, with a gallery of photographs of then-famous women from the twenties and thirties, each framed by a porthole, and almost all in clothes or hair or expressions that fix them in the foreign country of the past. But around a corner is Ines Donati, identified not, as with the rest, as "Actress," "Writer," or even "Mussolini's wife," but "Fascist Militant," daring you to deny that she is absolutely present.

Born in 1900, she embraced violence as a teenager. She joined the Blackshirts; she was one of the few women in the 1922 March on Rome that put Mussolini in power. Framed by a short pageboy, her barely smiling face had vengeance waiting behind the eyes. Though she was dead of tuberculosis by 1924, there is a lot of the twentieth century in that face.

2 ▪ Chris Stapleton, *From a Room: Volume 1* (Mercury) Stapleton has overwhelming physical presence, and on his 2015 debut, *Traveller*, the most authoritative music was of a piece. Here he's thrown that formal authority away. This is a folk album. Without a big sound he might have been exposed as all mannerisms; that's what too many singers marketed as country are selling. Instead he feels smaller, ordinary, and more convincing than ever.

3 ▪ *The Randy Newman Songbook,* Vol. 3 (Nonesuch) One too many.

4 ▪ Gina Arnold, "The Arms of America," foolsrushinredux.blogspot .com (May 15) On the opening of the *Joshua Tree* tour in Seattle: "U2's stock in trade is how moral they are, it is the bedrock of their bullshit."

5 ▪ In France after the presidential election We asked friends who their candidates were. Most said Macron both in the first round, in April, and the second, against Le Pen, in May. One first backed the leftist Mélenchon, another "The Shepherd" La Salle from the Pyrenees, and one the conservative who collapsed in scandal and still came close to making the runoff. "I'm gay, I'm Catholic, and I have money," said a bartender. "I voted for Fillon."

6 ▪ "Walker Evans," at the Centre Pompidou, Paris (through August 14) The most expansive and imaginative Evans exhibition I've ever seen, with as much or more conceptual space devoted to the 1938–41 hidden-camera New York subway photos as the iconic but cliché-resistant 1936 FSA work on Alabama tenant farmers. "I would photograph anything that attracted me," Evans (1903–75) says in a 1969 interview film by Sedat Parkay. He was against beauty, a kind of permanent happy ending: "Out of anger, I did the opposite." "To a rather rebellious individual," he went on, with the Show-Me poker face of his native Missouri, there "was outright communism, which was a trap. I didn't want to be told what to do by the Communist Party any more than I wanted to be told what to do by an advertising executive making propaganda for soap." For all that, one day in Alabama, when the destitute family he was living with was gone, he rearranged everything in their house—furniture, decorations, plates—to get the pictures he wanted, to find the source of the attraction.

7 & 8 ▪ Sophie Abramowitz, "'Run Him Right Out of the Country': The 1949 VD Radio Project," Mo Pop Conference, Seattle (April 21) and Red Foley, "Ballad of the Man of Steel" (wnyc.org) On a panel where everyone was from the University of Virginia, Abramowitz gave a coolly gleeful presentation on a government effort against venereal disease, the highlight of which was an excerpt from Foley's fourteen-minute radio play. It's the John Henry story, with the John Henry melody— except it's the story of Joe Pullman, because John Henry is black, and Red Foley is a white country singer and the government has hired him to tell a white country story. Warned against liquor and women, Joe stays pure until a rival spikes his nightly forty-gallon shot of lime juice (if there's an original contribution to the John Henry saga here, lime juice is it) and hires one Rosie to do him in, and the melody turns to "St. James Infirmary" before it goes back to "John Henry" and Joe dies of syphilis. So remember, boys—remember that the devil is always waiting, and that in America, just as any white man can put on blackface, any black hero can be made white.

9 ▪ **Daveed Diggs and William Hutson of clipping. at the University of California at Berkeley (April 13)** And whiteface can be washed off until all that's left is a mask anyone can use. For a class on "America Song by Song," programmer Hutson and rapper Diggs of the futurist hip-hop combo described how on their murkily alluring album *Splendor and Misery* they took "our fake John Henry" back—with what Diggs called "rap work songs" and Hutson "field recordings from inside a spaceship." "In my mind," Diggs said, "it's been passed down for so long"— and they were not about to let the story end.

10 ▪ **Rob Sheffield, *Dreaming the Beatles* (Dey Street)** Why neither the Beatles nor anyone else has ever owned their songs. Usually hilarious, always surprising; that Sheffield quotes lyrics only to reveal a musical effect opens up tune after tune. High: on John naming Elvis in his litany of apostasies in "God" ("That's where he has doubts mid-syllable and tries to gulp it back"). Low: doesn't know "I'm Looking Through You" with the vocal channel turned off is the music of the spheres.

Thanks to Sophie Abramowitz and Kathleen Moran.

July 19, 2017

T Bone Burnett, Robert Redford, Jack White Present American Epic is a project of many parts. There's (1–3) the three-episode, three-hour documentary, directed by Bernard MacMahon, on the emergence of recorded vernacular music in the USA in the 1920s and 1930s (BBC Arena/PBS), a (4) single-CD *The Soundtrack* (Sony Legacy), a (5) book by MacMahon and producer Allison McGourty, with Elijah Wald (Touchstone), and the (6) two-hour film *The Sessions*, where contemporary musicians are seen recording on a (7) reconstructed 1928 Western Electric machine. There is (8) a magnificent 100-track compendium, paralleling Harry Smith's 1952 *Anthology of American Folk Music* but expanding on it, with a remastering I can only call profound. Performances you might think you knew sound as if you've never heard them before—never *apprehended* them.

There are (9) seven redundant individual artist and genre best-of LPs from White's Third Man label, and the (10) startling three-LP *The Sessions* (Third Man), drawn from highlights and outtakes from the record-machine film. (*The Sessions* and the best-ofs are also available digitally from Sony; the documentary and *Sessions* film are streaming through PBS.)

There are many dead spots and more highlights. The documentary, organized around occasionally eloquent and sometimes stultifyingly empty commentary by descendants of the now deceased people we're being told about, is dragged down by clichés that are embarrassing to quote ("Though poor in material goods, the mountain folk were rich in tradition") and a flat narration by Redford, which incorporates the time-honored PBS *American Masters* trick of making unlikely stories seem obvious. There is also the thrilling discovery of a picture of a radiant Ma Rainey as a young woman ("from an extraordinary photo album compiled by a Chicago-based African-American twenties/thirties concert promoter," Bernard MacMahon said when I asked about the source), a bone-chilling 1968 Son House performance of "Death Letter Blues" so relentless it's hard to listen to, and a revelatory search for Elder J. E. Burch—the overwhelming power of whose "My Heart Keeps Singing" throws a weakness of the entire filmic approach into relief. We learn about his life, his Triumph church, its message of uplift, and its connection to the civil rights movement, but the music is not simply biography and sociology. It's also the singularity of a man who led a congregation that, on one day in 1927, caught a spirit so rich as to shame the poverty of ordinary life. Why is it so great? Among its other voices the film needs critics, people who if they can't answer the question can at least raise it.

The book is a making-of account that often rescues material from interviews that can be muffled in the film, as with the Columbia record man Frank Walker, speaking to Mike Seeger in 1962 of the auditions he held throughout the South in the twenties: "You got everything you thought they were capable of doing well and would be salable, and that was it—you forgot about them, said goodbye, and they went back home. They had made a phonograph record, and that was the next thing to being president of the United States in their mind." Those lines can echo through the *Sessions* film and LPs. The Western Electric machine—one more fruit of Jack White's obsessive love for artifacts that represent the first successful effort to solve a question of recording technology—runs by pulleys that allow for no more than three minutes for any live take; you get it or lose it. Producing nearly every number, White and Burnett capture performances so good you can hardly listen without thinking of how close each recording is to not existing at all.

Willie Nelson, so encrusted in shtick for so long, emerges as if out of a lake for a duet with Merle Haggard on Haggard's "The Only Man Wilder Than Me." Bettye LaVette's "Nobody's Dirty Business," made with the absurdly handsome Zac Sokolow of the Americans keeping company on guitar, is so snaky you can almost hear Frank Stokes, who recorded the song in 1928, singing softly behind her. The star is Nas, riding Lillie Mae Rische's fiddle as he high-steps his way through the Memphis Jug Band's 1928 "On the Road Again" as if he's telling the story for the first time. "As long as there was English, and black people," he says on film, "there was rap."

The moment that seals the project comes at the close of the third episode of MacMahon's documentary. We see Mississippi John Hurt, who recorded in 1928 and then, as Walker put it, was forgotten—who, in Hurt's own words, waited thirty-five years for Dick Spottswood and Tom Hoskins to locate him in Avalon, Mississippi, in 1963 and bring him to the Newport Folk Festival that same year. Now it's 1964, Hurt is again at Newport—and all but alone among all the musicians Mac-Mahon has been seeking, he speaks for himself. He's being interviewed about folk music. "You didn't think of it as folk music at the time, did you?" the interviewer asks, referring to Hurt's first recordings. "Well," Hurt says, "I didn't know what folk music was—I began to kind of learn what they meant by folk music . . . I think it means songs that . . . what I call, died out. Went back and renew 'em. That right?" It's somewhere backstage; in a confluence almost too stupendous to believe, as John Hurt speaks, you can hear Bob Dylan singing "Mr. Tambourine Man."

"John Hurt was the inspiration for *American Epic*," MacMahon said when I asked if this was real. He described going through Newport footage: "I was reviewing a reel and saw his beautiful face and thought, 'Wow, this looks like an interview.' When we projected the film with sound and he started talking, I heard the unmistakable harmonica playing in the background. He must have been behind the main stage. The hairs on the back of my neck stood up, and then John says, 'The Bible says the old men teach the younger ones. I'm glad I've got something they want.' I knew then I had the end of my film."

August 8, 2017

1 ▪ Dan Rather on the White House, *All In with Chris Hayes* (MSNBC, July 11): "They've been slipping and sliding, peeping and hiding, and now the game is closing in on them."

2 ▪ Brad Paisley, "Song for All Your Sides," Nationwide Insurance commercial (Oglivy) This has been bothering me for months. Why is the country superstar so convincing as a front-porch troubadour who just got off his tractor, now idly picking up a guitar, contemplating the meaning of life, gazing off into the distance, and singing "Nation-wide/Is on your side" as if the thought has just occurred to him, the answer to any question you might ever want to ask, with a slight deepening on *your* to make it seem as if he knows you? Because it's so close in style, melody, and ethos to country songs you've been hearing your whole life whether you wanted to or not?

3 ▪ Lana Del Rey, *Lust for Life* (Interscope) This is the deepest vortex she's conjured up. If she seems to float above whatever world she's mapping, it's because she quietly gets it across that there's nothing on land that won't disappear at the touch.

The same is true for the sense of time that governs the songs. Everything is already in the past. It's more than the circles of pop echoes—"Don't Worry Baby," "Leader of the Pack," "A Change Is Gonna Come," "Stairway to Heaven," "I Fall to Pieces," "Tiny Dancer," "Tomorrow Never Knows," and a hundred others I haven't caught yet. It's not the Weltschmerz that artists have been trafficking in for more than two hundred years. It's harder to get a fix on. "Now you're the future," she croons to "You kids" in the first lines of "Love," and it's a sick joke: *I was the future once too, and look how fucked I am now.*

It's too gorgeous not to be alluring. When the Weeknd weaves in and out of Del Rey's singing on "Lust for Life," he's not a second vocal, he's the first singer's second mind. A$AP Rocky is real-life ballast in "Groupie Love," which makes the drift that rules the song unbearably morbid. Again and again, there's a sense of no-way-out, with an undertone that Poe would have recognized: Who says you have to leave? It all comes to a verge with "In My Feelings," where the voice dives down into the churning black emptiness again and again, then surfacing each time. As her tone goes higher, escape seems like a physical reflex, the descent something between an idea and desire.

This album would have been understood in Germany in the eighteenth century, France in the nineteenth, in Berlin cabarets and after Long Island parties in the 1920s, playing in a dead TV in the future of *The Terminator*, in the ruins of America after the record has been banned.

4 ▪ Susanna Mälkki, conductor, *The Rite of Spring*, San Francisco Symphony (June 11) Lucy Gray reports: "At last I know why people rioted when they first heard *The Rite of Spring*. Once a cellist, in the opening solo Mälkki implored with plucking fingers to the high-pitched bassoonist that his instrument confess an anguished loneliness, but soon her stiff torso was cutting through the air, chopping like a sharp blade at the wind and then string sections, until together they hardened into one shrill, hideous plea. She put her mark on the sound of the drum, which was pounded until I thought the skin would break, until I heard the earth quake. This was spring; this is irreconcilable birth; blood must be drawn."

5 ▪ *Lindsey Buckingham/Christine McVie* (Atlantic) Where does talent go when it goes away?

6 ▪ Neon, "Neon" b/w "Nazi Schatzi" (Static Age/Water Wing) Four women in a Zurich punk band in 1978: singer Astrid Spirig went on to Liliput, but her first group never recorded. Rescued from a cassette of a TV appearance, this is their first single. It sounds fresh.

7 ▪ *Twin Peaks: The Return*, Episode 2 (Showtime) "James is still cool," says Mädchen Amick's Shelly as James Marshall's James Hurley walks into the Bang Bang Bar, smiling as if he's mildly surprised to find himself in the place. Why is it so affecting to see him? He was always the most decent person in town—is that why it's a shock he's still alive? Or, as Robert Fiore writes in, "Have you ever noticed that the *Twin Peaks* theme is basically 'Telstar' played really slowly?" Or that the device of almost every episode ending with an interesting indie band on the Bang Bang stage, which gives the show the only grounding it has—last Sunday with Marshall's silencing version of David Lynch and Angelo Badalamenti's "Just You" in a disturbing little-girl voice—is a tribute to the way Ricky Nelson and his band closed out so many episodes of *The Adventures of Ozzie and Harriet*?

8 ▪ **Heisenburger Burger Lab, 5054 Gorriti, Palermo Viejo, Buenos Aires** Where if you look at your order too long it comes out well-done? "The only city in the world where everyone would get it," said a passerby.

9 ▪ **Dion, *Kickin' Child—The Lost Album 1965* (Norton)** Columbia recordings mostly produced by Tom Wilson, who that same year put his name on Bob Dylan's *Bringing It All Back Home*, "Like a Rolling Stone," and Simon and Garfunkel's "The Sound of Silence." With all the celebration that's surrounded this release—as if Dion would not, to this day, go on to any number of disparate, invaluable albums—you can be forgiven for expecting something more than a mediocre 1965 folk-rock record.

10 ▪ **Stevie Nicks in "Beautiful People Beautiful Problems," Lana Del Rey, *Lust for Life* (Interscope)** Her voice is thick, reflective, and unstylized; it could be anyone.

Thanks to Steve Perry and Cecily Marcus.

September 13, 2017

1 ▪ **This item has been omitted.**

2 ▪ **Billy Joel, Madison Square Garden (New York, August 21)** For his encore, nine days after Nazis marched and killed in Charlottesville and the president of the United States demurred, Joel appeared with yellow stars on the front and back of his jacket. The signifier gave him a fierce, humbled dignity, which his face and his weighted, burdened posture said was less his own than that which those who wore the Jüden badge before him were stripped of.

3 ▪ Dorothea Lange, *Crossroads General Store, Gordonton, NC, July 1939*, from "Dorothea Lange: Politics of Seeing" (Oakland Museum, May 13–August 27) The first thing you saw as you entered this exhibition of the work of the Depression-era WPA photographer was not what Lange is best known for: such images as the iconic 1936 *Migrant Mother* or the 1941 scenes of Japanese Americans tagged and lined up on Oakland streets for deportation to concentration camps—pictures of suffering, distress, displacement, or oppression. It was an in-your-face blowup of a clapboard store covered with metal tobacco and cola signs, with the smiling white owner leaning his elbow against the door jamb and five smiling young black men seated on the porch, four facing the camera and one, who could almost pass for Robert Johnson, turned to his right, looking at you more slyly. It was a picture of people at home in their own place and their own skin. Is that because the younger men know how handsome they are, how good they're going to look in the frame?

4 ▪ Randy Newman, *Dark Matter* (Nonesuch) "Political Science" over and over, and musically inert—the staples holding these pastiches together are all too obvious, and the little skits on Putin and evangelicals seem dutiful. "I'm done," he says at one point, and it carries more attitude than anything else here, a dare: *Like you care.*

5 ▪ Elvis Presley, "When It Rains It Pours" Takes 1, 2–4, 5/M, 6–8, from *A Boy from Tupelo—The Complete 1953–1955 Recordings* (RCA Legacy) He's in the Sun studio in Memphis in early November 1955, laughing about Carl Perkins, who though not credited seems to be all over the music. He roars into every take as if it's the first time, leaving everyone else behind, the sound of his voice like the feeling in a body as it pitches headfirst down a twisty slide, so loose his bones seem detached from each other.

6 ▪ Tom Toles, political cartoon, *Washington Post* (August 2) Toles's Trump is a squashed muffin with yellow frosting on top and the mouth of a blow-up sex doll in the middle. "Take off her helmet and bang her head," he says as a cop guides Lady Liberty into a police car. "She died of head trauma," says the cop in the dialogue Toles runs on the bottom of his pictures. "That's too bad," says the president. "I was just joking." That's all fine. It's quick and sharp. But the drawing is really about the woman, huge and green, dominating the center of the frame, her lowered head, her whole body, communicating defeat, surrender, humiliation, and shame.

7 ▪ Allen Ginsberg's tape of Bob Dylan and the Hawks, Masonic Memorial Auditorium (San Francisco, December 11, 1965, on YouTube) The performance is savage, physical, like a riot where the tension only builds and is never released. *What's wrong with those booing idiots on the East Coast?* I'd thought at a show in Berkeley the week before. *What took him so long?* Now I can hear what they were afraid of.

8 & 9 ▪ Full City Expresso, Thames 1535, and Jarana Records, Soria 5125, Palermo Soho, Buenos Aires The neighborhood is crumbling sidewalks, bright colored murals, countless small shops, cafés, bars, Beatles and Stones iconography everywhere. In Full City, where there are dot portraits of Robert Johnson, a young Elvis, a naked Kate Moss, and the Argentine bandleader Charly Garcia over the bar, there sometimes seems to be no music from later than 1966 (the Who's "I'm a Boy," all of *Revolver*, so full of thought, doubt, *play*), and almost no one in the place born when the music was recorded. The aura is the same in the all-vinyl Jarana, where two back walls are covered with photo collages by the Buenos Aires street artist Santiago Spirito, aka Cabaio. The ruling image is the face of the Mississippi bluesman Son House, here as he was after his rediscovery in 1964, unsatisfied, his hands folded at his chin, surrounded by repeating motifs from panel to panel—Chuck Willis, Iggy Pop, Nina Simone, a short-haired sixties U.K. teen idol who might be Georgie Fame—thus proving that pop history is a Möbius strip with all of us falling off the curves at any moment.

10 ▪ William Faulkner, describing Mississippi in May/June 1929, from *Sanctuary* (1931) "The sunny air was filled with competitive radios and phonographs in the doors of drug- and music-stores. Before these doors a throng stood all day, listening. The pieces which moved them were ballads simple in melody and theme, of bereavement and retribution, and repentance metallically sung, blurred, emphasized by static or needle—disembodied voices blaring from imitation wood cabinets or pebble-grain horn-mouths above the rapt faces."

Thanks to Justin Desmangles.

October 13, 2017

1 ▪ **Dean Torrence, *Surf City: The Jan & Dean Story* (SelectBooks)** His career in rock 'n' roll spans sixty years. At seventy-seven, he writes as if he's still twenty-four. Not as good as "Dead Man's Curve" (but what is?), as much fun as "New Girl in School." More next month.

2 ▪ **Nuclear-armed rock criticism, from Mark Landler, "President Trump Inside and Outside the Lines at the U.N.," *New York Times* (September 21)** "'Rocket Man is on a suicide mission,' he declared Tuesday, very deliberately from the rostrum of the General Assembly, about the North Korean dictator, Kim Jong-un. North Korea one-upped Mr. Trump on his reference to a 1970s Elton John lyric by labeling the president the 'Madman Across the Water.'"

3 ▪ **Patty Schemel, *Hit So Hard: A Memoir* (Da Capo)** For Courtney Love's Hole, Schemel was the junkie drummer in a junkie band. She doesn't pull punches. On prostitution to pay for heroin: "If what happens in Vegas, stays in Vegas, I was Vegas."

4 ▪ **Loudon Wainwright III, *Liner Notes: On Parents & Children, Exes & Excess, Death & Decay, & a Few of My Other Favorite Things* (Blue Rider)** Weightless musings. Regrets, he's had a few, but you won't care. Each chapter ends with lyrics from one of his songs, which on the page don't sound like songs at all.

5 ▪ **Mr. Wrong, *Babes in Boyland* (Water Wing)** With a wave to the 1990s Minneapolis trio Babes in Toyland, which re-formed in 2014 after nearly twenty years in the wilderness, and far more in common with the late-1970s Zurich quartet Kleenex, this combo from Portland,

Oregon—drummer Ursula Koelling, guitarist Lindsey Moffett, and bassist Leona Nichts—starts off with the playground chant of "I DON'T WANNA I DON'T WANNA," leaps into the all-German "Baby Stimmen," throws voices back and forth like a basketball team in "Troll," and pulls out all the stops for its last song, "Asshole." There's a lead screech that keeps you in the song, waiting to hear it again, but at the end all three pound down on the *chop chop chop* bassline, which suddenly is as much words as sound: "Are you cool enough for Mr. Wrong? No!" These people are having a very good time.

6 ▪ Filthy Friends, The Independent, San Francisco (August 29) As were Filthy Friends. Their best number was the hovering "Love in a Time of Resistance," not on their album *Invitation;* the best song there is "The Arrival," which Josh Kantor played on the organ at Fenway Park as the Orioles beat the Red Sox 16–3 four days before. "Feels strange to have so much fun in such troubled times," Corin Tucker said from the stage—saying, it felt, what everyone was thinking.

7 ▪ Brad Paisley with Peyton Manning, "The Jingle Is Almost There," Nationwide commercial (Oglivy Agency) Where the singer pretends that maybe selling his style to an insurance company wasn't such a good idea. He and his producer go over the matter in great detail on "Behind the Scenes of the Jingle Sessions," as if "Nationwide / Is on your side" is Paisley's *Basement Tapes.*

8 ▪ *Twin Peaks: The Return*, Episode 18 (Showtime, September 3) In this series, people live parallel lives: two, three, or more, sometimes simultaneously, that can begin before they were born and continue after they die. These other lives are forms of energy, generated by the last flash of thought before death, by the fantasies we entertain for ourselves or that others harbor about us, and by certain cultural eidolons—a song, perhaps, like the Platters' "My Prayer," or an image of a place that may not have ever existed, but which seems right, a place where parallel lives go to find out where the next turn might be, like an old gas station.

On such a stage, with a story taken up twenty-five years after it was presumed to be over, a key element is how people from then look now: how they've changed, how they've aged, or how they haven't. In every case it's displacing and confusing, alluring and factual. The phenomenon undermines both the surface reality of the story and the subterranean weirdness of the weird effects: it's its own special effect.

Peggy Lipton's diner owner and Miguel Ferrer's FBI agent haven't changed at all. As Audrey Horne, Sherilyn Fenn's middle-aged features are unbalanced as if by some inner rot. Dana Ashbrook's Bobby Briggs has white hair and a who-me expression but he's still the same useless jerk he was before, even if now he's a cop for a force that seems to have forgotten he's a murderer. Kyle MacLachlan's Agent Cooper, Mädchen Amick's Shelly, and half a dozen more are older in a nice, orderly, acceptable way. There is even Catherine E. Coulson's Log Lady—Coulson was dying of cancer when her scenes were shot, and that's exactly what is happening to the Log Lady, with the faint wisps of hair on her head like a memory of it.* But it's not surprising that the revelation is Sheryl Lee's Laura Palmer. In the second-to-last episode, in a cut-in from the indelible 1992 film *Twin Peaks: Fire Walk With Me*, we see Lee at twenty-five, playing a high-school senior, her eyes opening in anguish and terror with the depths of an actress from the silent era. In the final episode, Cooper, awakened from his life as a zombie Nevada insurance agent, freed from his murderer doppelgänger, once more from the FBI, tracks Laura Palmer down in Odessa, Texas. She opens the door to her house. Sheryl Lee is fifty; she looks every day of it and maybe ten years' more. Now Laura Palmer's face is squared and puffy, dented, remade, you can see in an instant, by a life of heroin, street prostitution, beatings by the men she's lived with—you can imagine anything you want, including that the dead man in a chair in her living room, shot through the forehead, blood on the wall behind his head, whom Cooper seems to see and forget in the same look, is his fantasy, or hers.

She doesn't recognize the name Laura Palmer, but she freezes when Cooper says the names of her mother and father. She leaves with him for Twin Peaks because she has nothing better to do. Her whole being radiates jeopardy and soul: you are now watching a real person being taken to a place that isn't real. Which will win, her reality principle or the principle that there is no fixed reality that governs the show? The scream that ends the story is not an answer. It's merely an acknowledgment that the pieces can't be made to fit. And it too is from the silents.

---

* Ferrer too died before the series aired. Peggy Lipton died in 2019.

9 ▪ **Jay-Z, "Bam" and "4.44,"** *Saturday Night Live* **(NBC, September 30)** Looking like himself, and with the emotional range of a light switch.

10 ▪ **Josh Charles in "CSI: Crime Scene Idiot," on** *Last Week Tonight* **(HBO, October 1)** Following a segment on the evidentiary standards for forensic medicine—"'a reasonable degree of scientific certainty,'" which in English means precisely nothing—the best sitcom I've ever seen.

November 20, 2017

1 ▪ **Eminem, "The Storm," on** *BET Hip Hop Awards* **(BET, October 10)** The video of this solo attack on Donald Trump and his supporters, shot in a parking structure with nine other rappers looking on from the shadows, is more frightening to me than anything Donald Trump has said in the last year or that anyone else has said about him. Maybe it's because Eminem isn't afraid to sound as if he's searching for words, not playing with them.

2 ▪ **Bob Dylan and Mavis Staples, Xcel Energy Center, St. Paul, Minnesota (October 25)** Overheard in Row 7: "Have you guys seen Bob Dylan before?" "No, but we never miss Mavis."

3 ▪ **Hanif Abdurraqib,** *They Can't Kill Us Until They Kill Us: Essays* **(Two Dollar Radio)** This first collection by a pop critic from Columbus, Ohio, is funny, painful, precise, desperate, and loving throughout. Abdurraqib's most ambitious piece might be on Kendrick Lamar's "Alright" and the difference between what white people and black people tend to say when someone asks them how they're doing. I hear that question every hour I'm out of the house and it's as if Abdurraqib put a little loudness button under it. Not a day has sounded the same since I read him.

4 ▪ **Dean Torrence,** *Surf City: The Jan & Dean Story* **(SelectBooks)** There are so many memorable passages in this book—hilarious, bitter, pleasurable simply for the phrasemaking—that I may feature one per column for the next year. This month it's 1963 and Brian Wilson has brought our boys "Surf City," but Dean is a surfer and Brian isn't and Brian doesn't know that, say, "I bought a '33 panel truck and we call it a woody" is not going to work because a panel truck is not a woody and anyway they didn't make them in 1933 so they change that to "I bought a '34 wagon," and "ain't got a heater or a radio" is wrong because you have to have a radio and "if this woody is missing anything, it should be the back seat and the rear window because that's where the surf boards go. Plus, window rhymes with 'go' in the next line." If anyone asks you where culture comes from, this is the answer.

5 ▪ Bruce Springsteen, *Springsteen on Broadway,* Walter Kerr Theatre, New York (October 18) Cecily Marcus writes in: "In *20th Century Women,* Annette Bening's Dorothea is talking to us, sometime after her death, about how her younger charges have no idea that in 1979, when the movie is set, 'this is the end of punk. They don't know that Reagan's coming. . . . It's impossible to imagine HIV and AIDS, what will happen with skateboard tricks, the internet.'

"Since we elected Donald Trump, the legacy of the 1980s that Bening's inscrutable, unusual, utterly California mother describes has never been clearer. At *Springsteen on Broadway,* the best moments have their roots in the Bible: 'Promised Land,' sung in the dark with no guitar, no piano, no nothing, and 'Land of Hopes and Dreams,' which may not be of the Bible but has always sounded like Noah's ark. The sad truth of the show is that everything that Bruce Springsteen has done, brought to life, stood up for—or everything we have done over thousands of years of human civilization—has led to this."

6 ▪ Joe Hagan, *Sticky Fingers: The Life and Times of Jann Wenner and Rolling Stone Magazine* (Knopf) That Hagan names as inspirations *The Lives of John Lennon,* Albert Goldman's attempt to destroy John Lennon, and *Positively 4th Street,* David Hadju's attempt to discredit Bob Dylan, means that his book is one more proof that a biography grounded in its author's contemptuous distaste for his or her subject is not a good idea. There's a huge amount of information here, but if what Hagan did with what I told him is remotely typical then it can't be trusted.

When I became the first Records editor at *Rolling Stone* in 1969, I told Jann that the section would have to be like an independent republic: I would print what I decided to print. He could suggest that I cover certain records, he could read every review and object, but the only way he could overrule my decisions would be to fire me. This always held.

At one point, I assigned Langdon Winner Paul McCartney's first solo album, which had arrived with a self-interview—for the press kit, not the public—dismissing the Beatles as a whole and denigrating the others as not really worth his time. Langdon's review didn't mention this; Jann said it had to; I said no. We went back and forth for twenty minutes and got nowhere. Jann said he had other things to do and that when he'd finished we should go out to dinner and talk more. We did; we argued for three straight hours, and finally he convinced me. I went to Langdon's house and we spent three more hours arguing until I convinced him. He rewrote the review. Both he and I considered it an example of why *Rolling Stone* was a great magazine and why Jann was a great editor.

In *Sticky Fingers*, that story is not there. There is mention of a dispute, and the implication that Jann either forced Langdon to insert negative comments into his piece or that Jann rewrote the review himself.

Hagan's book has already had such an effect that one review said that it was proof that as the creator of *Rolling Stone* "Wenner was the wrong man for the job"—as opposed, presumably, to all those other people who would have done it if Jann hadn't pushed his way in front of them. The book is vile.

7 ▪ Van Morrison, *Roll with the Punches* (Exile) His own strong songs and R&B standards, and a tremendous rebound from his last few albums. He may go farther down "Lonely Avenue" than even Ray Charles did. He makes Sam Cooke's "Bring It on Home to Me" feel like it has a hundred years ahead of it.

8 & 9 ▪ Maria Alyokhina, *Riot Days* (Metropolitan Books) and Nadya Tolokonnikova, on *The Last Word with Lawrence O'Donnell* (MSNBC, November 3) Alyokhina's book is a retrospective present-tense journal from Pussy Riot's anti-Putin performance in the Cathedral of Christ the Savior in Moscow in 2012, to their Alice in Wonderland trial, to Alyokhina's two years of prison and resistance (Tolokonnikova's two years are closely followed in Masha Gessen's *Words Will Break Cement: The Passion of Pussy Riot*). In an invisible translation, Alyokhina is all punches: short, direct sentences driven by thought, rage, a sense of history, and a kind of disbelief in the official reality and philosophical chaos of an unfree country. It is easy to read and hard to read: hard to get one inch away from the gravity of Alyokhina's voice. "The door closes. I sit on the bench. I need to understand what has happened. I need to understand. The turn my life has taken. My life in prison. I have to remember things in the proper order. I need order."

Both Alyokhina and Tolokonnikova see protest as a form of life based in the thrill of proving your own reality—in concert with others, if possible, or if necessary alone, as it was for Alyokhina in prison. "I believe that the main problem right now about political action is that people treat it as *duty*, that they have to do as a part-time thing," Tolokonnikova said to O'Donnell. "I believe that if politics will become an important and joyful part of your life, then things maybe change." O'Donnell offered Tolokonnikova a gift of his new book—the title of which, in a strikingly nonpromotional gesture, he neither mentioned nor displayed—coming out November 7: the same day, he noted, as her birthday. "This is about the protests of the 1960s and the activism of the 1960s, which you say inspired you," O'Donnell said. "I think 1968 is my favorite year in history," Tolokonnikova said, noting that her birthday fell as well on "the date of the Russian Revolution," an idea she left hanging in the air.

10 ▪ Robert Plant, "Dance with You Tonight," from *Carry Fire* (Nonesuch) "I offered up the secret places/Reveal the magic of the land/All bound by blood and lipstick traces," he sings in one of the best songs ever written, right up there with Old Weird America Pale Ale. I'm not as cool as Lawrence O'Donnell.

January 11, 2018

1 ▪ Tokyo Fish Market, Berkeley (January 4) A Japanese-American woman in a motorized wheelchair pulled up to the fresh-fish aisle. It was clear she wasn't going to be able to reach the Take-a-Number dispenser; a man offered to pull a slip for her. "No," she said. "I don't like numbers. I was in a concentration camp." She looked as if she'd be happy to wait there all day. "They'll notice me," she said.

2 ▪ **Bob Dylan, *Trouble No More: The Bootleg Series*, Vol. 13/1979–1981 (Columbia Legacy)** Reviewers have stood in line to praise this testament to the years when the singer performed as a born-again Christian. In its fullest version, it's eight CDs (concerts, rehearsals, alternate takes from *Slow Train Coming, Saved,* and *Shot of Love*), plus a DVD of concert footage and scenes of Michael Shannon reading sermons written by Luc Sante. The denunciations, warnings, prophecies, damnations, and entreaties Dylan offered from the stage between songs in those years were funnier, more inventive, scarier, and more horrible than the music, and while they were collected in 1990 as *Saved! The Gospel Speeches* in a watch-pocket book—and put across with acerbic heart by Christian Bale in Todd Haynes's 2007 film *I'm Not There*—there's none of them here. But no matter. This set documents as deep a creative dive as any in the singer's career, one writer after another has said. The band is as good as any he's ever played with—maybe better. And the choir line—in different combinations, Carolyn Dennis, Mona Lisa Young, Regina Peebles, Regina McCrary, Helena Springs, Madelyn Quebec, Mary Elizabeth Bridges, Gwen Evans, Clydie King, Jo Ann Harris—oh, the way they lift these songs up to . . . people have barely been able to restrain themselves from adding the word, and some haven't. But they reach up and touch the Hem of His Garment on cue, their ecstasy so automatic that if the quest for God is real to you—and even if God isn't—it can make you sick. Dylan's singing on a 1980 version of the hallowed "Every Grain of Sand," aka "You'll Never Walk Alone," is the worst from him I've ever heard. Michael Shannon has played the sinner as avenging angel for years, but the role never takes on shadings. While there are interesting attempts to make "Slow Train" a more interesting song, and live versions of "Pressing On" that capture at least some of its beauty—though not, again, as much as Christian Bale did, with John Doe's voice coming out of his mouth—as a friend said, there's more piety in the few minutes of Van Morrison's recent cover of Rosetta Tharpe's 1946 "How Far from God" than in the hours of bullying collected here.

3 ▪ **Bob Dylan, "Louie, Louie" (YouTube)** Uploaded just weeks ago (as of the first week of January only a few thousand people had seen it), from 1985, a rehearsal with Tom Petty and the Heartbreakers for the first Farm Aid show. It's raucous, precise, determined, and somehow cruel, with Dylan singing words that can't have been in the song before, though it might take months of listening to string three of them together. The backing singers—as from the revival shows, Carolyn Dennis and Madelyn Quebec, with Peggi Blu and Queen Esther Marrow—seem charmed by the song, and if the pleasure Blu takes in getting the Louie-Lou-*Ay* syllables exactly right doesn't make you smile you've got a heart of stone. To say that it's better than anything on *Trouble No More* is sort of a cheap shot. But it is.

4 ▪ G-Eazy, *The Beautiful and Damned* (RCA) Swift.

5 & 6 ▪ Neil Young + Promise of the Real, *The Visitor* (Reprise) and Eminem, *Revival* (Interscope) Two musicians try to get inside Trump's country—and get out alive. Young struggles to create the sense that all that much is at stake—countering MAGA with a first cut called "Already Great" is a wan gesture, and the song is barely a wave.

It's stunning the contempt Eminem has brought forth from so many critics policing their critical neighborhoods—the continual citing of his age seems to be an argument that he has no so-called street cred because he's not dead yet. With eighteen full-length numbers and two slips, the album is too long. He does seem to run out of gas two-thirds of the way through—or the listener does. He may have lost a few miles off his fastball: the cutting snap that has always made his delivery so distinctive seems soft, which makes him sound distracted. But that may be style, not form. The most powerful pieces here—"Walk on Water," with a lovely, altogether down-to-earth echo from Beyoncé, and "Like Home," a twisting, intimidated, blindman-with-a-pistol attack on the man who as president of the United States, the song says, humiliates the country's own citizens—create an atmosphere of uncertainty, displacement, the desperation and defiance of someone trying to regrow a tongue that's been cut out. Taking the choruses on "Like Home," Alicia Keys pulls back, but her vehemence as she traces lines about nostalgia as the engine of patriotism—"There's no place like home," and there's no place harder to hang on to—is different from Eminem's in tone, not in kind.

So much of the discourse against Trump and his clear vision of the country he means to create says little more than NOKD. As a pure demographic, not a person, Marshall Mathers is a pure Trumper. He knows it, and that's why he sounds like Charles M. Blow and Masha Gessen, not the likes of E. J. Dionne or Frank Bruni. He can see himself as an enemy of the state, in a country where, in point of constitutional fact, there is no state, and no such thing as a crime against it—even if in the United States today the Constitution is just another set of regulations.

7 ▪ Wolf Parade, *Cry Cry Cry* (Sub Pop) Spencer Krug has a full, rounded voice that calls to mind Jim Morrison, Marian Gold of Alphaville, David Eugene Edwards of the fire-and-brimstone band 16 Horsepower. Without changing his tone, he can go anywhere: embrace, despair, a demand for freedom, a call to arms. From British Columbia, the group looks over the border and wonders if it sees its own country's future—or if the future is in the past. Seek out "Valley Boy"—what the guitarist Dan Boeckner does in the break is like someone discovering fire.

8 ▪ Lana Del Rey, *Lust for Life* (Interscope) The question has been raised as to whether Del Rey's singing here draws more from Lauren Bacall's Vivian Rutledge in *The Big Sleep* (from 1946) or Claire Trevor's Velma in *Murder, My Sweet* (from 1944). With "Change," in the way Del Rey's rides her own magic carpet, it's Vivian. With the scraping "In My Feelings" ("Shot herself clean through the heart—twice," says a cop in *Farewell, My Lovely*, which *Murder, My Sweet*, was made from), it's Velma. But she's saying things they never did.

9 & 10 ▪ Bob Dylan and Mavis Staples, Xcel Center, St. Paul (October 25) He was so strong, the highlight was "Thunder on the Mountain," which is a nothing song. She sang "Freedom Highway": "March for freedom highway / March each and every day / The whole world is wondering / What's wrong with the U.S.A." Once that last line referenced Emmett Till; now it didn't have to. Then, with the band vamping behind her, in a kind of call-and-response with herself, she gave a speech about how her father had written the song in 1965 for the march from Selma to Montgomery: "I was *there*, and I'm still here. I'm a living witness. I'm a soldier." She summoned the presence to fill the hall with history that was made and history that was being unmade. It was very overdone, very showbiz, and it was true. Even if you couldn't get out from under what an act it was, it was impossible not to be humbled, at least if you were listening. Fans at Dylan shows are the rudest anywhere. They never shut up. They're in the presence of a legend. Anybody else is trash, and he might as well be dead.

Thanks to Steve Perry, Joe Levy, and Jon Bernstein.

February 21, 2018

1 ▪ Henry Holt & Co. announces Lucinda Williams memoir (February 12) "I have a lot to say and a big story to tell," Williams is quoted in a press release. "I want everyone to know what's behind the songs and to know more about me than what people previously thought they knew." Her whole career has been an act of condescension toward the stupidity of the world, and she just can't keep it out of her voice.

2 ▪ Elizabeth Flock, "Modern Love" (*New York Times,* February 4) She's been living with an architect for three years. They're going to build a cabin in the woods, travel the world, have lots of kids, except he's always tired and won't talk. "Around this time, a man I had worked with began sending me links to music, the kind of folk-blues songs that got inside you and unsettled parts better left untouched. . . . At night, I listened to the songs he sent me, or the music of old punk bands I used to love, with lyrics that asked me questions about freedom whose answers I didn't like." It's the most acute music writing I've read in years. I asked Flock for her playlist: "Folk-blues songs: Hurray for the Riff Raff, 'Junebug Waltz,' 'Blue Ridge Mountain,' 'Hungry Ghost.' Punk albums: Pixies, *Doolittle* and "Gigantic" from *Surfer Rosa*; Dead Kennedys, *Fresh Fruit for Rotting Vegetables*; Ramones, *Ramones*—and newer: Downtown Boys, *Full Communism*."

3 ▪ Chris Collingsworth, commentary, Super Bowl LII (NBC, February 4) "This game has been as good as Justin Timberlake!" he shouted seconds before Philadelphia went ahead of New England with 2:21 left in the fourth quarter, on a touchdown Collingsworth immediately disavowed, though for some inexplicable reason the call was upheld. The game actually was good.

4 ▪ Franklin Foer, "The Plot Against America: Decades before he ran the Trump campaign, Paul Manafort's pursuit of foreign cash and shady deals laid the groundwork for the corruption of Washington," *Atlantic* (January 28) In 1939, in the spy thriller *The Mask of Dimitrios*, Eric Ambler wrote about a klepto-capitalist conspiracy that traveled under such names as Pan-Eurasian Petroleum and the Eurasian Credit Trust. If he were alive today, he could have written this.

5 ■ Bettye LaVette, "Things Have Changed" (Verve) Bob Dylan won an Oscar in 2001 for this tune for *Wonder Boys:* a good song in a good movie. It was always down, but never sounded so much like an exploration of nihilism as it does here. Under a huge bass, a soul singer who hit the charts before he did wonders what she doesn't want to do tomorrow, and with such determination she makes you want to come along for the ride, or at least watch from across the street. From her forthcoming all-Dylan album of the same name. I can't wait to hear what she does with "Ain't Talkin'."

6 ■ *Springsteen on Broadway*, Walter Kerr Theatre, New York (January 12) Along with a strange version of "Born in the U.S.A." that was somehow reminiscent of Paul Robeson, the great actor and oratorio singer of prewar years, the most striking moment in the show—as drama, timing, theatricality, personal history, musical history, and social history—came when Springsteen described encountering his future wife Patti Scialfa climbing onstage to sing the Exciters' "Tell Him" with a local band in a New Jersey bar. "The first words I ever heard her say were, 'I know/Something about love,'" he said. A line he followed with a sound lexicographically impossible to render, and vocally impossible probably for anyone else—something between "Hmmmm . . ." and "Oooo!"

That is storytelling. Though I felt cheated that Scialfa, onstage for all this, didn't then dive right into the song.

7 ■ Halsey, "Bad at Love," *Saturday Night Live* (NBC, January 13) I have nothing to say, but I can inflate my gestures to the point that maybe you won't notice, and anyway I have enough money to hire people who look like they would have something to say if they got the chance and have them stand around me as if I do.

8 ■ Advertisement for "Great Music by Nice People" from Party Damage Records, in *The Believer* (February–March) Inexplicably including nothing from the Telluride, Colorado, band Niceness.

9 ■ Kesha, "Praying," 60th Annual Grammy Awards (CBS, January 28) As self-deification goes, right up there with "We Are the World" and Lillian Hellman. Presumably running this kind of number as Ke$ha might have compromised its purity.

10 ■ *How to Be a Rock Critic: Based on the Writings of Lester Bangs,* written by Jessica Blank and Erik Jensen, directed by Blank, acted by Jensen, scenic design by Richard Hoover, sound design by David Robbins, Under the Radar Festival, Public Theater, Martinson Hall, New York (January 13) A marvelously fast and convincing one-man play, set in Bangs's disheveled New York apartment, which the late critic (1948–82) finds full of people to whom he proceeds to act out what he does and why. The structure is, interestingly, on a parallel with *Springsteen on Broadway*—riffing through Bangs's work as dialogue, instead of stopping to sing a song as Springsteen does to mark a point in his life, Jensen walks over to a phonograph, puts on a record, and talks over it. The music instantly confirms whatever case he's making: the sound that comes out is so rich it's as if you've never heard Otis Redding's "I've Been Loving You Too Long (To Stop Now)" or Van Morrison's "Cyprus Avenue" before.

Blank and Jensen get to the heart of the matter: the play is about Bangs's struggle to believe that music can not so much save his soul as allow him, through signal moments of music, to construct a soul in which he might want to live, and his struggle to believe that he can pass that truth on to other people. For Lester, all good music, or all real music, was soul music. It didn't matter if it was the nerd soul of White Witch or the heroic soul of Lou Reed, the doomed soul of Otis Rush or the intellectual soul of Charles Mingus. Because it was never absolute that what they had, could he write about it, would truly come to him, his work was full of longing, revelation, self-mockery, and pain. Jensen gets it all.

March 21, 2018

1 ■ **Bettye LaVette, *Things Have Changed* (Verve)** She started singing in Detroit in 1962 at sixteen; her career didn't really begin to come into focus until fifty years later. Her first single was a hit; the next forty years were snakebit. In *A Woman Like Me*, her 2012 autobiography written with David Ritz, LaVette describes what her future looked like to her in the 1970s: "I'd walk into a bar, order a drink, and watch a woman in her sixties singing in front of a makeshift band. She was fifty pounds overweight. Her makeup was running. Her clothes were frayed. I could hear that once upon a time her voice had been strong, but now her voice was shot. Her eyes were sad. While she sang, she worked the room, urging the patrons to stuff a dollar bill or two in her bra. Some did, but most didn't. At one point, a guy screamed, 'Let's turn on the jukebox. Anything is better than this bitch.' I wanted to slug the guy. I wanted to cry. I wanted to stop seeing myself in this woman."

That future that didn't come to pass is in the performances of Bob Dylan songs that make up this album—most of them obscurities from the 1980s on, "Emotionally Yours," "Seeing the Real You at Last," "What Was It You Wanted." What is not in them is whatever past the songs themselves might carry, even when they're "The Times They Are A-Changin'" or "It Ain't Me Babe." "I wasn't going to tributize him," LaVette said in an interview in *Bluegrass Situation* earlier this month. She had to make the songs "fit into my mouth," she said, "just as if they'd been written for me."

That's how they sound. After the first few tracks, with the unforced unpredictability of the arrangements, the quiet, determined way La-Vette enters the music, the open spaces of the band—with the guitarist Larry Campbell, who worked in Dylan's band for years, playing behind LaVette as if he never played the songs before—you realize you have no idea how any song is going to sound: what it will be.

She needed the songs to fit in her mouth: "The Times They Are A-Changin'" and "Ain't Talkin'"—one a programmatic manifesto that has always sounded to me as if it were written by a committee, the other a long, twisting parable of knowledge and revenge—feel like real talk, to the point that you don't even hear the lines rhyme.

She rewrites the songs by the way she sings them, but she also re-writes the words. Dylan's "Do you remember St. James Street/Where you blew Jackie P.'s mind?/You were so fine, Clark Gable would have fell at your feet/And laid his life on the line," in "Don't Fall Apart on Me Tonight" here comes out carrying the double first name LaVette was born with: "Do you remember 14th Street/When you blew Betty Jo's mind?/You were so fine"—as *fiiiiiiiine*, the word caressed as it's stretched over its own whole measure—"Tina Turner would have fell at your feet/And left Ike hanging on the line," which is the crack of a completely different whip.

I keep coming back to LaVette's closing track, "Going, Going, Gone." It was a hole in time on Dylan's *Planet Waves* in 1974; now there's an Ennio Morricone feeling in the opening phrases of Larry Campbell's steel guitar. *Once Upon a Time in the West* rises up in the background. But the music deepens, touching the small-label soul records made in the South in the sixties and seventies—George Perkins and the Silver Stars' "Cryin' in the Streets," Bill Brandon's "Rainbow Road," or LaVette's own "Let Me Down Easy," where despair was like the lead instrument. "Going, going, gone": LaVette takes the phrase, the idea, to such depths of defeat that the fat woman in her sixties in that nowhere bar is anything but the worst that might come, and as the song goes on, you can hear the singer die over and over again. And yet it's a perfect last track: it makes you begin again from the start.

2 ▪ Steve Eder and Ben Protess, "Hotel Carrying New Trump Brand Secures $6 Million Tax Break," *New York Times* (February 21) On the opening of the first of the planned nationwide Scion chain, in Cleveland, Mississippi. To take advantage of Robert Johnson tourism. For real: it's in the business model.*

3 ▪ "On the Radio," SFO Museum, San Francisco International Airport, Terminal 3, Departures Level 3 (through September 30) The United concourse features exhibits so alluring you avoid the moving sidewalk and walk to your gate as slowly as you can. Here, along with predictably stunning deco radios from the 1920s and '30s were much odder pieces: from Arvin Industries of Columbia, Indiana, a 1956 box with the speakers covered in an abstract design based on the cool-jazz cartoons that were running in movie theaters at the time; from Kong Wah Instrument Company in Hong Kong, a 1977 device in the shape of a peanut, with, on top, a bright red grin, Jimmy Carter.

4 ▪ *Double Lover*, directed by François Ozon, soundtrack by Philippe Rombli (Mandarin Films) In this movie about sex, schizophrenia, and psychoanalysis—so "freely adapted," as it says, from Joyce Carol Oates's *Lives of the Twins* that, as she says, "I did not really understand the ending"—the main musical theme often drifts in or out of Elvis Presley's "As Long as I Have You," from *King Creole* in 1958. Though there are hints of doo-wop in the structure of the song, and Jesse Belvin in

---

* No hotel ever opened, in Mississippi or anywhere else.

its texture, it feels much later—closer to "Always on My Mind." It's corny and powerful, but also menacing: "Can't Help Falling in Love" as a curse, the voice of someone watching over the characters as they dance toward self-destruction, knowing everything they don't. But the characters may be even more schizophrenic than they seem. If the heroine is moving into a new apartment in 2017, why is Linda Scott's 1959 "I've Told Every Little Star" playing in the background?

5 ■ **George Washington and Matthew Oshinsky, "George Washington's Ten Favorite Songs,"** *Paste* **(February 22)** Pissed that Alexander Hamilton is getting all the noise, and channeling the voice of Taran Killam's nineteenth-century movie critic Jebidiah Atkinson, the first president strikes back. Topping his chart: Magnetic Fields' "Washington, D.C." "Ever been to the great city of Hamilton? That's what I thought."

6 ■ **Tony Kushner and Sarah Vowell, "The Lincoln Legacy: The Man and His Presidency," Cal Performances, Berkeley (February 21)** It was a pleasure to listen to people who knew what they were talking about. "'Negroes like other people act upon motives,'" Kushner quoted from a letter Lincoln wrote during the Civil War. With the context he and Vowell had built, the heresy of someone in the 1860s so casually referring to black people *as* people went off like the bomb it was.

7 ■ **Denis Johnson,** *The Largess of the Sea Monster* **(Random House)** In 2009, Johnson published a crime novel called *Nobody Move*. It seemed forced and slumming. But "Doppelgänger, Poltergeist," the last story in this posthumous collection, where Jesse Garon Presley, Elvis's stillborn twin, if not Elvis himself, appears as the Maltese Falcon, might be what Johnson was aiming for all along. "You could see her mind wiggling right through her eyeballs"—that's from another story, but it's how you feel when you get to the end of this one.

8 ■ **Darling West,** *While I Was Asleep* **(Jansen)** American folk music from Norway, though it could be from Duluth. Inside the always curving modal lines in "Ballad of an Outlaw" and "Don't I Know You," there's a pop insistence that lets Mari Sandvaer get closer to "Always on My Mind"—Elvis's or the Pet Shop Boys', it doesn't matter—than to a traditional song like "John Riley," and closer to Aoife O'Donovan

on Crooked Still's 2006 *Shaken by a Low Sound* than perhaps anyone has since.

9 ▪ I'm With Her, "Ryland (Under the Apple Tree)" and "Crescent City," from *See You Around* (Rounder) Except, along with Sara Watkins and Sarah Jarosz, O'Donovan herself.

10 ▪ Bettye LaVette, "Most of the Time," from *Chimes of Freedom: The Songs of Bob Dylan* (Amnesty International, 2012) Her first recording of a Dylan song. Fit in her mouth? Here she lets the song strangle her.

Thanks to David Ritz, Joyce Carol Oates, and Julia Casey.

April 25, 2018

1 ▪ Viv Albertine, *To Throw Away Unopened* (Faber & Faber) An unsparing, unforgiving book where Albertine—guitarist for the Slits from 1976 to 1982 and solo pub performer more than thirty years later—unravels and reknits her life around the death of her mother in 2014. It's all caught in a single incident. One night not long ago, when Albertine is trying to get her songs across, a table of loudmouthed drunks up front refuse every polite request that they give her a chance, maybe go back to the bar. They couldn't care less: "Instead of the audience witnessing Viv-Albertine-the-ex-punk come back to shake them up, they saw a middle-aged woman being disrespected and ignored." So Albertine confronts the men: "It comes back to you, your punk attitude, when you need it." She picks up one man's beer and sweeps it across their faces. Then another: "A Guinness," she says, because Albertine's mind is pitched to the capture of the smallest details in any fraught moment.

In *Clothes Clothes Clothes Music Music Music Boys Boys Boys*, published in 2014 and likely the best book on punk anyone has written, the word always had quotes around it, as if Albertine wasn't convinced punk ever really happened at all; in this book the quotes are off.

2 ▪ "25 Songs That Tell Us Where Music Is Going," *New York Times Magazine* (March 11) By twenty-five writers, from the *Times*' Wesley

Morris, John Jeremiah Sullivan, and Jody Rosen to the critics Jessica Hopper and Hanif Abdurraqib. "If you want to know where music is going," writes editor Nitsuh Abebe, "ask an 11-year-old." So why didn't he?

3 ▪ **Gina Arnold writes in on Pussy Riot at the Rickshaw Stop (San Francisco, March 28)** "When members of Pussy Riot were arrested in 2012 in Moscow for performing a crude anti-Putin punk song atop an altar in a Russian Orthodox church, the overblown reaction of their government seemed positively quaint. Six years on, after Russian interference in the U.S. election, Pussy Riot's concerns have become ours. It's now impossible not to feel politically energized by the sound of the Russian language, particularly when caught shouting feminist slogans over poppy EDM in front of fun video art depicting police brutality and political corruption. At the very least, the sight of Nadya Tolokonnikova in a neon-pink ski mask yelling, 'Pussy is the new dick' to a bunch of bouncy hipsters is a reminder that we in America are still at liberty to goof on this stuff. But one wonders for how long."

4 ▪ **Jack White, *Boarding House Reach* (Third Man/Columbia)** Or playing darts without a target.

5 ▪ **Eels, *The Deconstruction* (E Works)** Cloying songs about personal misery. It all really happened! The insipidity of sentimentalizing your own life.

6 ▪ **Yo La Tengo, *There's a Riot Going On* (Matador)** It's true that the title track of Sly and the Family Stone's 1971 *There's a Riot Goin' On* was blank. That doesn't mean you can use the title for music to put people to sleep.

7 ▪ **Ad break on TruTV (March 17)** "This is your brain on TruTV," a guy in a hoodie says. He holds up a TruTV device and places a plastic model of a brain on it. He looks blankly at you through the screen. "What were you expecting?" he says. "A metaphor?" As if it wasn't in the budget.

8 ▪ ***Elvis Presley: The Searcher,* directed by Thom Zimny (HBO)** In Part 1, ending with Elvis in the Army, the use of music is imaginative—

"Blue Moon" unspools at almost its whole length, and it sounds more unearthly than ever. The documentary footage is fabulous. Some is unseen, and what's been seen is made fresh. It's a welcome relief to have soundtrack commentary but no talking heads. But only Bruce Springsteen looks for a social context, and with the banal dronings of Alan Light, Warren Zanes, Bill Ferris, and Tom Petty, there isn't the slightest deviation from the conventional, chiseled-in-stone narrative. Before long it's stupefying: any new idea would die in this intellectual desert.

Part 2 is better: the conventional wisdom is less oppressive because no one seems to care that much if you believe it or not. It begins with unbelievably wild footage of Elvis performing Lowell Fulson's "Reconsider Baby" in Hawaii in 1961—his last live performance until the 1968 comeback TV show—which confuses the "he died in the Army" story the film seems to want to tell. Even more striking is a snatch of interview with Colonel Parker—has anyone ever heard him?—who is so clearly a colonel from somewhere in Europe.

For good or ill, this film comes down to an interview near the close of the film, after a title has announced Elvis's death. The TV writer and producer Chris Bearde, who died last year, is talking about that '68 TV show. Every day, he says, he and Elvis and the director, Steve Binder, would gather in Binder's office. He recalls one day: "We had a little black-and-white TV in the corner. On the TV, Robert Kennedy has been assassinated. Elvis picks up a guitar, and he started playing. Talking a mile a minute. He said, 'I want you to understand me, because this is a moment in time'"—and Bearde's voice breaks, as if he's overcome by the memory, yes, but also acting out how, in the moment, Elvis's voice broke—"'when we'll,'" coming out *w'eeeel*, "'have to understand each other.'"

"We didn't know how to end it," Bearde had said of the TV show, and now that becomes the entry for the end of *The Searcher*. The last song of that night now becomes the last song of this film—and the last word: "If I Can Dream," the whole performance.

He's wearing an ice-cream suit that doesn't seem to fit. The song comes across like a building with all the nuts and bolts still visible. There's no groove, and the delivery is clumsy and hesitant. And all of that is overwhelmed by the passion Elvis is digging out of his heart, and his story, his whole life as he has lived up to his heroic singularity and failed to.

9 ▪ Bettye LaVette at Freight & Salvage (Berkeley, April 19) "He complains about *everything*," LaVette said about her affinity for Bob Dylan, whose songs she was singing this night. "Just like an old woman. And I'm an old woman. But when a black woman ages, she can do it in less than nine verses. So I'm finishing Bob Dylan's arguments." At their best, the songs were final and transformed works of art: With "Things Have Changed," presented as a classic blues, or "Ain't Talkin'" or "Going, Going, Gone," now a deep soul ballad you could swear had to have been written by Bert Berns, LaVette started at the emotional top of the songs and stayed there. Most unsettling was her at first unrecognizable "The Times They Are A-Changin'"—because the times have long since changed back, and the demand for a better country, so palpable when the song first appeared, can now be swept off the stage by a single presidential tweet. She had started the show with "Things Have Changed," but it played behind everything she sang.

10 ▪ Paul Robeson, "King Joe (Joe Louis Blues)" (Okeh) I'm teaching a course on the postwar period, where the reading includes the detective novelist Ross Macdonald's 1947 *Blue City*, about a veteran returning to his midwestern hometown, so I was reading Tom Nolan's 1999 Macdonald biography. At one point he mentions that in 1941, Macdonald loved to sing Paul Robeson's "King Joe" to his little daughter: "Lord, I know a secret, swore I'd never tell / Lord, I know a secret, swore I'd never tell," the novelist and now songwriter Richard Wright had written. "I know what makes old Joe who can punch and roll like hell." You can imagine: *Daddy, sing the hell song again!*

I'd never heard of it. Neither had anyone I asked. It's a shock—the august, six-feet-under voice of the great actor recording with the Count Basie band, singing across two sides of a 78, in and out of the irresistible, yawning swing of the music, like he wants a pop hit.

May 23, 2018

1 ▪ Jennifer Castle, *Angels of Death* (Paradise of Bachelors) You might bet against the notion of anyone other than Lana Del Rey calling an album *Angels of Death* and not drowning in her own pretentiousness.

With the Toronto singer Castle, you'd lose. The first song is last night's dream you can't remember; Castle remembers it for you, and as the songs roll on she stays on that path. The action is all in the interstices between the melody and the cadence, the voice and the instrumentation. The melody seems called up by the cadence, the instrumentation feels like a reflection of the voice, and you can find yourself listening for those tiny lifts, the suspensions in the songs replacing the songs themselves.

2 ▪ **"The King of the Delta Blues,"** *Timeless* **(NBC, Season 2, Episode 6, April 22)** In this time-travel series, the bad guys go back to 1936 to kill Robert Johnson "to prevent the birth of rock 'n' roll music and eventually the counterculture of the 1960s, the civil rights movement, the fall of Nixon, and the end of the Vietnam War." The good guys go back to stop them, presumably to allow the birth of rock 'n' roll and end the Vietnam War. Johnson, as played by Kamahl Naiqui, seems absolutely convinced.

3 ▪ **Jackie Fuchs, at "What Difference Does It Make? Music and Gender," MoPop Pop Conference 2018 (Seattle, April 26)** The former bassist Jackie Fox, on how being raped as a member of the Runaways led her to become an entertainment lawyer working with women in the music business: "It's a lot easier to stand up for someone else than to stand up for yourself." Harvard Law, she said of her alma mater, "turns out 600 lawyers a year: 'Next!' And there were so few female musicians in the Seventies—I wish I had known how much power I actually had."

4 ▪ **Les démons, window in the Nouveau Théâtre de Montreuil (Montreuil, France)** From floor to ceiling: silk-screened on the glass, Kevin McCarthy and Dana Wynter in 1956 near the end of *Invasion of the Body Snatchers*, evanescent pods over their heads, are running right at you, so physically present you want to reach into the glass and pull them over to the other side. And they're there forever.

5 ▪ **Jose Cuervo, "Last Days," directed by Ringan Ledwidge (CP+B)** In some southwestern bar, the radio announces the end of civilization. Some people flee; one man cues up Elvis's "It's Now or Never" on the jukebox. He begins to dance, a woman joins him, the roof blows off, and as the bartender pours a shot and then leans back, singing along with indescribable pleasure, you might wonder why the song never sounded as good as it does here.

6 ▪ Rachel Kushner, *The Mars Room* (Scribner) Kushner's celebrated last novel, *The Flamethrowers*, was so relentlessly brilliant I couldn't finish it. I got the point: Kushner is brilliant. This book, about a former sex worker and convicted murderer serving double life sentences in California, is quiet, deliberate, slow. Iron Maiden, Denis Johnson's *Jesus' Son*, "the wind of Elvis's empty soul," Richard Nixon playing piano at the Grand Ole Opry, the 1950s L.A. radio DJ Art Laboe (still taking prisoners' requests in the twenty-first century) flit through the story like someone flicking a switch on and off. Kushner doesn't know how to end the novel, which barely matters; by the time she starts faking the plot, the reader understands that the story doesn't need an ending, because the real story won't have one. One line I'm still turning over and over: "People are stupider and less demonic than some can admit."

7 ▪ "Images en Lutte: La culture visuelle de l'extrême gauche en France (1968–1974)," Palais des Beaux-Arts, Paris (February 21–May 20) Mostly May '68 posters, many made at the École des Beaux-Arts over a few weeks of hurry, excitement, and fear that the new world glimpsed as art students worked in concert could vanish overnight, and the posters looked like the analytic committee work they were. They didn't have the casual flair or scrabbling insistence of the utopian graffiti that covered the walls and hoardings of Paris at the same time, which the show ignored. But in the back, off to the side, was *La Datcha*, a painting, from just a year later, of five radical French philosophers. Credited to Gilles Aillaud, Eduardo Arroyo, Francis Biras, Lucio Fanti, Fabio Rieti, and Nicky Rieti, it too was a collective work, but there was no sense of a group effort; the six dissolved into one whom they didn't bother to name. They were having fun picturing a scene of absolute solemnity, in the style of a sort of socialist realist suburban pastoral. There was a very modern house, comfortable chairs, a gorgeous sunrise, all set up to catch a perfect May '68 fantasy, matching perhaps the most inspired graffiti: "Run, comrade, the old world is behind you!" There was a plaque attached to the frame with a subtitle: "*Louis Althusser hesitates to enter Claude Lévi-Strauss's dacha Tristes Miels,* *where, already reunited, are Jacques Lacan, Michel Foucault, and Roland Barthes, at the moment when the radio is announcing that workers and students have decided to joyously abandon their past."* They all look miserable, but your eye is drawn to Foucault, in the foreground, the only one not frozen in the tableau, who really does seem to be thinking it over, plotting how he's going to escape the curse of redundancy that, the painting says, the rest definitely will not.

8 ▪ **Mekons 77, *It Is Twice Blessed* (Slow Things)** Over the Mekons' forty-plus years, Jon Langford and Tom Greenhalgh have emerged as principal voices; in the beginning, in 1977, in the art student milieu of the University of Leeds, Mark White and Andy Corrigan were the singers, Greenhalgh and Kevin Lycett played guitar, Ros Allen, who would soon form Delta 5, played bass, and Langford played drums. They each do here what they did then, not with "Where Were You" or "Never Been in a Riot," from their very first singles, but with new songs that could have been written and played right alongside of them. The argument is that while the affirmation that clatter and hum trump all other values might not have carried the band through forty years, once every forty years, with the title of this album continuing that of the band's first, it's a punk rock grail.

9 ▪ **Michelle Goldberg, "A Grotesque Spectacle in Jerusalem," *New York Times* (May 14)** "The juxtaposition of images of dead and wounded Palestinians and Ivanka Trump smiling like a Zionist Marie Antoinette tell us a lot about America's relationship to Israel right now," Goldberg wrote—and her line about the Presidential Daughter tells us more about Trumpism than a thousand fulminating screeds, let alone the condescending sneers that continue to appear in the likes of the *New Yorker* (see, or don't, Ann Beattie's recent "Tasting Notes for a Teetotalling President"). What Goldberg wrote won't change anyone's mind. It won't change anything. But it adds to the record that people will have to sift through if the republic emerges from these times with any sense of what it was and what it was supposed to be.

10 ▪ **Philip Roth, 1933–2018** Which was his great subject. Before and after everything else, Roth was a patriot, and consumed by the complexities of loving one's sometimes hateful country. *American Pastoral, I Married a Communist* (to me, his best book), *The Human Stain, The*

Plot Against America, and *The Great American Novel* are proof of that. I'm sure he wanted to live to see Donald Trump gone. But his death saved him from a lot of torment, and deprives the rest of us of a voice unlike that of anyone else.

June 25, 2018

1 ▪ **Eleanor Friedberger, *Rebound* (Frenchkiss)** From a singer who in Fiery Furnaces could come across as someone backing you into a corner and talking a mile a minute while giving you the unsettling feeling she's thinking over every word as she says it, music that, with no sense of hurry, wraps each song around the next. Angelo Badalamenti synths from old Julee Cruise records carry the tunes as if teaching them how to swim. It's a report from a certain state of mind, one that's saying, *Time out.* And as one number fades into another, a bigger question: *And what if I said time out and froze everyone in the world in place and walked away? What would that sound like?*

2 ▪ **The Carters, "Apes**t" (YouTube/Tidal)** First impressions: There's a lot of nice art in the Louvre.
The smugness of the poses doesn't erase the thrill of the faster-than-sound words coming out of Beyoncé's mouth.

3 ▪ **Neil Young, *Roxy—Tonight's the Night Live* (Reprise)** His death record, and if on the original album the chant of the title song seemed almost too much to take, here the killers—and they can make you skip a breath—are "Roll Another Number" and the oh-so-casual fatal dope deal of "Tired Eyes." There's a lot of stage talk, particularly about the stripper Candy Barr. "We're doing OK in the seventies," Young says near the end of a show recorded in late September 1973. "We really are. History's coming back"—there's that displacement of someone historicizing a moment as it takes place—"everything's OK. Spiro says it's all right." The vice president resigned on October 10.

4 ▪ **Dana Milbank, "Finally, a president with the guts to stand up to Canada," *Washington Post* (June 11)** "They inflicted Nickelback on us.

We did nothing. They sent us Justin Bieber. We turned the other cheek. They were responsible for one abomination after another: Poutine. Dipthong vowels. Hawaiian pizza. Instant mashed potatoes. Ted Cruz. Still, we did not retaliate—until now."

5 ▪ Overheard, Minneapolis (June 8) Two young children idly singing "Nation-*wide . . .*" and you realized that this lilting, wistful insurance commercial, bathing the airwaves with Brad Paisley and Leslie Odom Jr. and Tori Kelly offering the tune as if it held more truth, more revelation, more of *themselves* than anything they ever recorded before, had already colonized the minds and corrupted the aesthetic sensibilities of the nation's youth, until the kids finished the line: ". . . is suicide."

6 ▪ A reader who goes by Uhuru Comix writes in (June 14) "Tonight, there was a surreal moment on *Jeopardy.* The category was Combat Rock, and the $800 clue was 'Pere Ubu: 30 Seconds Over _____.' None of the contestants knew the answer, of course, and Trebek had to say (in a tone that made it sound as though he thought the answer was obvious), 'What is Tokyo.' I think there must be an Ubu fan lurking among their writers. Either that, or the apocalypse is upon us."

7 ▪ Daniel Zakroczemski, illustration for Marc Stein, "Warriors and Cavs Star in N.B.A.'s Version of Groundhog Day," *New York Times* (May 31) "How can you root against LeBron?" a friend asked. "Because I've been a Warriors fan for more than forty years and I live in Oakland?" I said. "But it's like rooting against John Henry!" he said—and the next day, taking up more than half a page, was a blazing, Cubistlike painting by an artist whose work usually appears in the *Buffalo News* showing just that: an embattled but indomitable giant stopping the balls of four other muscled men as if they were just so many steam drills. And then John Henry broke his hand.

8 ▪ Allen Ruppersberg, "Intellectual Property: 1968–2018," Walker Art Center, Minneapolis (through July 28) Born in Cleveland in 1944, working out of Los Angeles, Ruppersberg practices ideas in action, and despite the time covered in this vast but uncrowded retrospective the feeling was that anything that might catch your eye could have been made either fifty years ago or the day before yesterday. Among dozens

of other works that could as easily be called phenomena as constructions, with a revisit to the 1969 *Al's Café* (where among the all-non-
food items on the menu the cheapest was a diner plate with a 45 of the
Kingsmen's version of "Louie Louie") and a room devoted to blowups
with cutouts of Uncle Scrooge's battle with the Maharajah of How-
duyustan over who can build the biggest statue of himself, my favorite
was the 1996 installation *Good Dreams, Bad Dreams—What Was
Sub-Literature*, with an announcement for "Lecture today at 4 PM,"
which unfortunately was idea, not action, because the piece really made
you want to know. There were real books in a vitrine, and rows of titles on the wall behind it: Was an 1891 cheap paper *Oliver Twist* sub-lit
because of its format, or its writing? What about a beautiful edition of
Evangeline? Classics Illustrated versions of *Adventures of Huckleberry
Finn* and *Typee*? You could probably put money on Jack Hanley's *Let's
Make Mary* as sub-literature, but what about Mickey Spillane's *Kiss
Me Deadly*, which may have been a lousy book, but was made into a
great movie? The titles were a riot of pure id and the actual books
were the mental attic of a whole country.

**9 ▪ *Here to Be Heard—The Story of the Slits,* directed by William E.
Badgley (Head Gear Films/Moviehouse Entertainment)** A documentary
about the punk band that began in London in 1976, dissolved in 1982,
put part of itself back together in 2005, and ended when singer Ari Up
died in 2010 at forty-eight. It's workmanlike, and because of the story
as it was captured then and the present-day testimony of bassist Tessa
Pollitt, drummer Palmolive, and guitarist Viv Albertine, stirring. There
are bits of revelation that capture the essence of both the band's mission to confront, attack, and destroy the marginalization of women in
culture and rock 'n' roll as such, as when Palmolive describes the Slits
on the Clash's White Riot U.K. tour in 1977: "Sometimes we were playing different songs. And we couldn't even tell! Sometimes we could
tell." There is the absolute primacy given to the clothes the Slits wore,
as public action, free speech, political demonstration, and pleasure (Albertine, on "feeling like myself for the first time in my life": "They
couldn't tell if we were male or female, or even human"), and the way
the end of the band felt like a death sentence. "I fell into the terrible
bath of heroin," Pollitt says; Albertine, who as a Slit was all screaming
blond hair and frilly white slips, "started dressing in brown clothes. I
let my hair go back to brown."

10 ▪ Nathan Lane, acceptance speech for Best Featured Actor in a Play, 72nd Annual Tony Awards (CBS, June 10) For his role as the tribune of McCarthyism, mob fixer, and AIDS death Roy Cohn in *Angels in America*—a role that took on far more resonance in this year's revival than it could have had when the play premiered in 1993, since in the 1970s Cohn was also a mentor to Donald Trump—Lane produced a real thrill in the way that, in under two minutes, he thanked twenty-two individuals and groups, often in detail, with nuance, without a crib sheet, without pauses or hesitations, until the end, when he thanked his husband. It felt like a kind of rounded farewell, not that he doesn't still have work to do. "Where's my Roy Cohn?" Donald Trump said in a moment of frustration not long ago, and you can just imagine what Lane would make of the chance to materialize in his face.

Thanks to Steve Perry and Bill Brown.

July 26, 2018

SPECIAL PROTEST EDITION!

1 ▪ Algiers, "Cleveland," from *The Underside of Power* (Matador) The band originated in Atlanta; on its second album everything is inflamed, and "Cleveland" opens in a storm of noise, one made up as much by distant voices as weather. Inside the storm is the late gospel singer James Cleveland, singing "Peace Be Still." He's like a mountain; he's one person the song is named for. His voice is big, commanding, and when Algiers's Franklin Fisher takes the song it's hard to tell where one voice leaves off and the other begins. There's no sense of one person passing some greater song to another. The voice is everything: huge, flailing, blocked, crashing through all barriers. It's like Paul Robeson who still has all his old Clash albums.

In this maelstrom—the pieces of it so loud and unstable there's no center—you might think of Tamir Rice, the twelve-year-old shot to death by a white police officer in a Cleveland park in 2014. His name isn't mentioned, but he's invoked by Fisher as he begins to sing: "I never saw your face / But I can tell you're there."

"We're coming back," insists the chorus. Two and a half minutes into the song, sounds of people crying, wailing, sounds of fear, of separation, of death, seem to have replaced whatever instruments or machines are making the fundamental noise, but in fact they have only joined it—and Fisher rides over the clamor like some kind of judge. "It's been the same evil power since in '63," he says cryptically. Names begin to flash up, as if they're being chiseled into the statue of the song. Some you might recognize, others you almost certainly won't, but every one is that of a black American whose death was written off as suicide or overdose, sometimes in jail, whether their families feared murder and a cover-up or not.

These are people, Algiers is saying, who need to be memorialized in a song this big, this good—so that after ten, twenty, a hundred years, when they and the song too have been completely forgotten, "Cleveland" will be found again. People will be attracted to it, to the terror in it, the refusal, the life. They won't know the referents in the words, and to be caught they won't need to, but they will want to know everything about the song, to understand why it's so powerful, so they will try to find out what it is, where it came from, and who the people whose names appear actually were. Who was Sandra Bland? Who was Andre Jones? Who was Roosevelt Pernell? People will, in their way, want to join this community of the dead, because a community of the dead can also be a community of the future.

2 ▪ Shannon McArdle, "Country Music," from *A Touch of Class* (Shandelion) If you'd read Michael Robbins's poem in the *New Yorker* in 2014, you might not have known that a modest, painfully nostalgic guitar solo was already running between the lines. McArdle, once of the Mendoza Line, erases Robbins's sardonic loser's digs (bless me, he says to Jesus, "I'll make us both famous") as if every thought in the song is one she's had a thousand times before.

3 & 4 ▪ Jim Dooley, *Red Set: A History of Gang of Four* (Repeater) and Cam Cobb, *What's Big and Purple and Lives in the Ocean? The Moby Grape Story* (Jawbone) The Dooley takes up 432 pages, features no less than three pictures of the author posing with his subjects, two of the shots so dark the figures could be almost anybody, and no index. It's interesting. The Cobb is an A+ production. Not only is there an index, the sixteen pages of well-printed black-and-white and color illustrations are balanced in an excellent design. It's also stupefying. Cobb imagines Moby Grape bassist Bob Mosley rising, along with the other members of the once-great, now-fallen band—the finest band to emerge from the San Francisco Sound, only to implode the night of the release party for its first album in 1967—to fly to New York for a reunion session four years later: four years that feel like forty. It's first-class: "He nods at the bartender. 'What'll it be?' the bartender asks. 'A beer.' 'What kind?' 'Any kind. I don't care.' The bartender removes a bottle, opens it, and pours the beer into a glass. 'Here,' he says, handing the glass to the man with blond hair. The traveler raises his glass. 'Thanks,' he says, before taking a gulp. There's a brief silence. 'I'm John Smith,' the bartender says, holding out his hand. 'Bob Mosley,' the traveler replies. 'Is this your first time heading to New York?' the bartender asks . . ."

5 ■ **Deaf Wish, *Lithium Zion* (Sub Pop)** From Melbourne, they have the courage of their convictions: that early Sonic Youth was *it*. The sound is compressed, claustrophobic, as if the studio had a ceiling that lowered as the songs were played.

6 ■ **Barbara Dane and the Chambers Brothers, "It Isn't Nice" (1966), from *Hot Jazz, Cool Blues & Hard-Hitting Songs* (Smithsonian Folkways)** I heard this on the radio a few months ago. I couldn't imagine what it was: some kind of doo-wop gospel protest song? I called the radio station. The DJ said it was Barbara Dane. I remembered her from anti-war rallies in Berkeley in the sixties: humorless, hortatory, giving speeches in songs. This turned out to have been written in 1964 by the Berkeley folk singer Malvina Reynolds, sparked by the Sheraton Palace Hotel sit-in that year—part of a wave of occupations attacking racist hiring practices that also targeted auto dealers and the Bank of America. The first lines of the song start right in the lobby, blocking doors, the police already there, everyone sitting on the floor, going limp, hauled off to jail: "There are nicer ways to do it/But the nice ways always fail"—Reynolds had been part of the action, which didn't fail.

The song is music before it's anything else. It opens with a lovely, evocative folk guitar figure by Willie Chambers, one of the four who began in Mississippi in the early fifties; by 1965 they were singing backup on an early version of Bob Dylan's "Tombstone Blues," and in 1968 would take over the new FM rock radio format with the furiously authoritative eleven-minute "Time Has Come Today." Dane is anonymous and forthright: she means to get it across that what she's advocating isn't obvious, that the argument the song is making is a choice. And then she begins to wail, not like a jazz or blues singer, not like a gospel singer, but like Dion in "Lovers Who Wander."* You can tell she isn't entirely comfortable with the style, and that's what gives her performance its pathos—this is another choice, another struggle. It moved me: the way it takes all of Dane's concentration to let go, to let her vowels fragment as she sings the word *mind* in "We don't mind," and she somehow also sings over it at the same time. More than half a century later, the performance can put you on the spot: wondering what the music is, wondering where you are in the song.

7 ▪ **Neko Case, *Hell-on* (Anti-)** When I last saw her with the New Pornographers she never seemed to get a purchase on a song, and she doesn't come close here.

8 ▪ **James Williamson, "Last Night a Record Changed My Life," *Mojo* (July)** The founding Stooges guitarist is a teenager, having trouble at home, and his West Point father hates rock 'n' roll, so his mother sends him to an Army psychiatrist, who hospitalizes him; when he shows another patient his switchblade he ends up in the psych ward. He asks his mother to bring him his Bob Dylan albums. "So here I am," he remembers, "and I laid that needle down on *The Times They Are A-Changin'* and you could just see the horror, and the unsettling effect that it had on the people in there, until eventually they wouldn't let me play it anymore! That sort of made it crystal clear to me about the impact of this guy, and how much that voice and that message would polarise people, and unify people in my age group."

9 ▪ **The Beat, *Here We Go Love* (Here We Go/Megaforce)** Dave Wakeling and Ranking Roger broke up the band in 1983; now they both lead their own versions. Here Wakeling still reaches for what he can't quite grasp, and ends up with more than most people even want. There's nothing here to match "Save It for Later," but a whole album of "Tenderness" is nothing to apologize for. With "The Love You Give" you hear the beat the group named itself for; "If Killing Worked" ("It would have worked by now"), a dance of flow and release, gives a spe-

---

* "Sam Cooke," Dane corrected in an e-mail.

cial pleasure as you wait for the horns you just know are coming in, almost right now.

10 ■ **Pussy Riot, "Policeman Enters the Game," World Cup Finals, Moscow (July 15)** With France leading Croatia 2–1, four members of the performance collective—three women, one man—ran onto the field. Each was dressed as a police officer: the late poet Dimitry Prigov's "heavenly policeman," the "carrier of the heavenly nationhood." They had issued a manifesto stating the reasons and the purposes of their action, and a list of demands, starting with "Let all political prisoners free" and ending with "Turn the earthly policeman"—who "imprisons people for 'reposts' and 'likes'" and "enters the game not caring about the rules" and "breaks our world apart"—"into the heavenly policeman." Veronika Nikulshina and Kylian Mbappe of France high-fived with both hands: "I think I brought luck to his team," Nikulshina said later.

A furious Croatian dragged Pyotr Verzilov off the field; his team lost 4–2. A video of the interrogation that followed—all four were sentenced to fifteen days in jail—featured the displacing drama of an unseen cop shouting at Verzilov and one of the women, who looked more like real police than he sounded, as he wished out loud "that it was 1937," when he could have taken them to the basement and had them shot. Someone will make up a World Cup trading card of Nikulshina and Mbappe touching hands and they'll both carry it in their wallets the rest of their lives, with the man who stood in front of tanks after the Tiananmen Square massacre on the back.

Thanks to Brian Schill.

August 22, 2018

1 ■ **Tropical Fuck Storm, *A Laughing Death in Meatspace* (TFS)** Whether it has come as the leader of the Drones, on his own, or now fronting the mass of nonsignifying words that make up his new band and its first album, Gareth Liddiard's music has always been about war. You can't prove that by parsing lyrics, which will tell you that the songs are about something else. It's a matter of tone of voice, of instruments

clashing until rhythm and melody feel like lies, of the fatigue of centuries: a stench that a million showers won't wash off, because as the
dead bodies of past wars fade, the dead bodies of future wars loom up
before you.

Compared to Tropical Fuck Storm—Liddiard lead singer and guitarist, Fiona Kitschin of the Drones bassist and singer, Erica Dunn guitarist, keyboards player, and singer, and Lauren Hammel drummer,
all from Melbourne—the Drones, whether on their mid-2000s albums
Wait Long by the River and the Bodies of Your Enemies Will Float By
and *Gala Mill* or at a show in Brooklyn where Liddiard seemed to be
carrying a hundred pounds of flu, as furious a band as I've ever seen,
can seem austere. The explosions in "Two Afternoons," "A Laughing
Death," and "Rubber Bullies" are glorious and frightening, so big they
don't feel quite real, but there's a story trying to climb out of the noise,
carried by Liddiard's weariness, his uncynical fatalism, but shaped by
the countervocals of Kitschin and Dunn. Liddiard is responding in-
stinctively to the war they are all describing; they are thinking about
it. Soon you may begin to hear him as the background singer, and the
women in the background as the leads. The balance shifts inside the
songs, back and forth, back and forth, and you can hear that this is
what history would sound like if it were being written in real time.

2 ▪ Telegraph Avenue between Haste and Dwight, Berkeley (July 26)
I was in Amoeba Records looking for an Otis Redding reissue. Jackie
Wilson's "That's Why (I Love You So)" was playing in the store. "You
ever see him?" a guy working there asked me. "Otis Redding?" "No,"
he said, pointing to the speaker above us. "Him." "My Empty Arms"
was playing now. "I never did," I said. "Mr. Excitement," he said. "I
heard he was a show." I crossed the street to Moe's Books, where Wilson was singing "To Be Loved." "Jackie Wilson in Amoeba, Jackie Wilson here," I said to the man at the counter. "What's going on?" "I
don't know," he said. "An anniversary? Of his collapse?" I looked it up:
Jackie Wilson was born on June 9, 1934; he suffered a heart attack onstage while singing "Lonely Teardrops"—"My heart is crying, crying . . ."—on September 29, 1975; he died after years of incapacitation
on January 21, 1984. It must have been that on July 26, God was simply
in the mood.

3 ▪ *SPF-18*, written and directed by Alex Israel (Netflix) In which the
celebrated Los Angeles painter takes five putatively good-looking young

people and has them hang out at Keanu Reeves's Malibu beach house while he's off on a shoot. Very likely the most vapid movie, TV movie, or for that matter sunscreen commercial ever made.

4 ■ Sasha Frere-Jones, "I Thought I Was Taking Medicine: Twelve years on benzodiazepines," popula.com (July 22) I've never read a piece on addiction, dependency, or attendant personality disorders with anything approaching Frere-Jones's gently hard-boiled tone—or so absent self-pity, special pleading, self-congratulation, or the mandated redemptive flourish.

5 ■ Steve Lowenthal, *Dance of Death: The Life of John Fahey, American Guitarist* (Chicago Review Press) At the start, in the late fifties, he was a collector, driving through the South, "knocking on doors, asking for old records" from the twenties and thirties. It was art: the music, but also the collecting. "Occasionally," Lowenthal writes, "Fahey destroyed extremely rare records he found but which he already had, just to make his own copy more valuable."

6 ■ David Lynch and Kristine McKenna, *Room to Dream* (Penguin Random House) As collected in her 2001 *Book of Changes*, in 1986, 1989, and 1992 McKenna, the unrivaled historian of the postwar Los Angeles avant-garde, published interviews with Lynch as heretical as they were hilarious: you couldn't anticipate a word. For this all-new autobiography–career survey she provides continuity while he talks into a tape recorder, and there doesn't seem to be a line you haven't heard before, even if there is.

7 ■ Joe Henry, "The Ghost in the Song: Songwriting as Discovery," Aspen Ideas Festival (June 29, aspenideas.org) A fifty-two-minute talk by the somewhat under-the-radar record producer (the shimmering post-Katrina *Our New Orleans*, the Carolina Chocolate Drops' perfect-pitch *Genuine Negro Jig*), performer, and composer on how to listen as the song you flatter yourself you're writing tells you what to do. As generous and revelatory a primer on creativity as anyone has not written—delivered conversationally, without drama, without notes.

8 ■ The Who, *Live at the Fillmore East 1968* (Geffen) The first piece I ever published was a 1968 review in *Rolling Stone* of an album called *Magic Bus: The Who on Tour*—a collection of B sides and throwaways disguised as the live album all Who fans were pining for. But I didn't know they'd already turned into Led Zeppelin, which didn't even exist yet. If you go for the vinyl edition you can hear more than thirty minutes of "My Generation" spread across both sides of a single LP. As instructions for a record I can't quite place once had it, PLAY LOUD AND LEAVE THE ROOM.

9 ■ Blindspotting, directed by Carlos López Estrada, written by Rafael Casal and Daveed Diggs (Lionsgate) There are countless details around the edges of the frame and in throwaway dialogue ("I hate suspense. Fuck Alfred Hitchcock. Fuck M. Night Shyamalan. He makes me nervous") that may come back over time with as much force as anything in the foreground, but in this great picture—with the impact of *Straight Outta Compton* and the inventiveness of Baz Luhrmann's *The Great Gatsby*—Daveed Diggs is the center of gravity. It's in the way he acts so fully, with such layers of depth and thought, altogether with his face: He makes it into a canvas where any emotional image may appear—terror, rage, shame, panic, determination, fury, control— only to be overpainted by another. It's in the way he slips into his role as a man with three days left on his probation, knowing a single slip by himself or for that matter anyone around him will put him back in jail, and so trying to navigate the changing streets of his West Oakland standing grounds as if he's actually, officially free, idly trying to put together rhymes as if there's some song out there they might someday fit into, all of them shooting blanks until a climactic scene when that song arrives like the cavalry coming over the hill with Diggs's character leading the charge.

Really, Diggs should run for president. "Nobody wants to be president," he wrote back at the suggestion. "That job sucks. That's how we end up with lunatics in office." Sure, but can't you just see the first commercial: "Hi. I'm not Thomas Jefferson. But I played him in *Hamilton*, and I'm here to tell you . . ."

10 ■ Aretha Franklin, 1942–2018 August 16: A friend writes in from Mississippi: "As I was nearing the Big Black River border between Warren and Hinds County, I saw the time and turned on NPR for the news. They said something about the weather, the live from somewhere standard intro, and then the first bars of 'Chain, Chain, Chain.'

"I turned off the radio."

I don't know how much more needs to be said. But when I heard of Aretha Franklin's death, two voices arrived at the same time. The first was of a businessman in his thirties, sitting at the bar of a London pub in 1967. "I Never Loved a Man (The Way I Love You)" was on the jukebox. He seized up. I was sitting next to him: I could physically feel his desire to say what he felt burning out of his body. Finally Aretha shouted the last two shouts of the song and he shouted too: "Did you hear that? Can you believe that?" I realized at that moment that a particular woman, living her own life, trying both to make a hit record and say what she felt, had drawn out of herself the ability to touch absolutely anyone on earth. She had become a world figure.

Despite a thirty-two-year-old Donald Fagen in "Hey Nineteen" singing "She don't remember the Queen of Soul"—and that was almost forty years ago—she was never anything less. I thought of that man in the pub when I first heard the Steely Dan song, knowing that somehow he'd given it the lie so long in advance. That's what happens when you put something new into the world, which is what Aretha Franklin did: time wraps its straight line from then to now into a circle.

Thanks to Jo Anne Fordham and Bob Scheffel.

rollingstone
.com
2018·2019

September 21, 2018

1 & 2 ▪ Lana Del Rey, "Mariners Apartment Complex" and "Venice Bitch" (Interscope) As a song from her announced 2019 set *Norman Fucking Rockwell* (the Rockwell estate not yet heard from), "Mariners Apartment Complex" can be heard as part of the 100-track album Del Rey seems to be working on. But at more than nine-and-a-half-minutes, "Venice Bitch" is something else. This might be the most expansive California beach record ever made, and not just for its length. As it unwinds, continuing Del Rey's claim on all of sixties pop music—you can hear the Beach Boys' "Surfer Girl," and inside of that their "In My Room," and you can sense Randy Newman's "Lucinda" lurking in the background, and, as she chants over and over near the end, the long, shifting version of Tommy James and the Shondells' "Crimson and Clover"—the whole of the coastline seems to come into view. There's no hurry. The ribbon will be there as long as you need it—the song might as well serve as a celebration of the reopening of the Big Sur section of Highway 1 this July, after being shut down for more than a year from a mudslide.

It opens like a love letter, prosaic, direct; then a little more than two minutes in it begins to swirl, and you could be listening to an affair that began years ago or has yet to start. As the song goes on it turns into a series of reveries, suspended by the gorgeously sustained sound of liquid guitar feedback: it's the feeling of a series of clouds passing. Turn your head, look up again, and the last one you saw, the one that looked like a face, is already gone.

3 ▪ Amy Winehouse, "Will You Still Love Me Tomorrow," from *Lioness: Hidden Treasures* (Universal Republic) The song was an epochal hit for the Shirelles in 1963; it was the kind of swooning, post-doo-wop music Winehouse turned to in the last years of her life, songs that seemed finished but that she heard as dialogues that were still going on. The girl in the Shirelles song was asking if her boyfriend would

183

still look at her the same way if she slept with him; with a question like that long in the past for any persona Winehouse might inhabit, she sang as if she were interrogating the world, or even herself.

Mark Ronson's arrangement is posthumous, and almost a wall against the singer: staccato horns, with unnecessary backing vocals, blatant, harsh, hitting notes of doom, as if to let you know the singer is already dead. What's unusual is the way Winehouse feels her way through the song—the way she gets out from under the detritus that wasn't there when she heard the music. It's a kind of war between the singer and the producer, who, out of love, wanted to sign the painting too. The voice escapes; no one has sung *this* song before.

4 ▪ Kitchen Sisters (Davia Nelson and Nikki Silva), "The Pack Horse Librarians of Eastern Kentucky," NPR (September 13) In this riveting seven-minute re-creation of a lost WPA program—women riding horses into Appalachian hollers at the bottom of the Great Depression with donated books and scrapbooks they made from used magazines (recipes, ballads, local histories, "dogs, Spain, Nazis, model airplanes")—you hear the voices of FDR and Eleanor Roosevelt, of scholars and descendants, but most of all you hear Mary Ruth Shuler Dieter, who is ninety-seven and sounds like she's already outlived time. There are bits of songs in the program, but she makes the music. It's her voice you wait for: "They were so happy to get a book. Tickled to death. We always sat under the big old chestnut tree. They didn't know how to read so I read it and read it again so they could understand it."

5 ▪ Jessica Hopper, *Night Moves* (University of Texas Press) A reconstructed journal of a woman in her early thirties living in the Chicago punk world from 2004 to 2008: though the entries jump around and there's no sense of time passing ("Living in a city of drunk jocks will keep you punk forever"), as the book goes on the humor is tougher, the point of view sharper, the writer's purchase on her city like a fist closing. Lines jump out of the this-then-that, all but making you jerk your head: "Whiffing hits of VCR cleaner from a little bottle"—did you read that or hallucinate it? An impatience begins to gather. A lame performer is one thing ("I would say his musical influence is the Capitol Steps. Lyrically, it was more like . . . Rufus Wainwright as a fourteen-year-old chess champion"). Seeing through the complex of gentrification and any Bohemian's insistence that the scene was over before you got there is a leap far beyond that, but the demeanor is the same. "His nostalgia for the 'Wicker Park of two years ago' was enough to turn my stomach," Hopper says bluntly, as if she's said enough, but this book is about writing, and the action is in the parenthesis that follows: "(Has Wicker Park even been Wicker Park since Algren left in '75? Since they stopped finding bodies in the alleys, circa 1999? Boo-fucking-hoo, the 'cool' shopping area is not very cool anymore!)" Except for the use of the scare quotes, which is a writer undercutting her own authority, that is as hard as can be.

6 ▪ Swearin', _Fall into the Sun_ (Merge) From Philadelphia, guitarists and singers Alison Crutchfield and Kyle Gilbride and drummer Jeff Bolt: what it sounds like when people hold nothing back.

7 ▪ Marti Noxon, showrunner, _Sharp Objects,_ Episode 7: "Falling" (HBO) In the swampy, sweaty milieu of the town, where the past is both formally and emotionally intercut with the present, the music undercuts the very idea of the present, laughing off its claims to know anything at all. Every episode opens with a needle coming down on an LP. The sheriff gets in his cruiser and it seems like the same Patsy Cline song is always playing. Amy Adams's alcoholic cutter newspaper reporter lives off Led Zeppelin instead of food. But on this penultimate episode, the lack of focus was acute. In a diner, Jody Reynolds warbling his 1958 death ballad "Endless Sleep" is just barely audible—any louder and it'd be a metaphor, not atmosphere, which in this show is already a metaphor. At a joint in Beantown—the Hispanic neighborhood—it's Fairport Convention and "Who Knows Where the Time Goes" from 1969: on the jukebox? Spotify playlist? Cook's choice? Or the playlist in Adams's character's head, because she knows Sandy Denny sang with Robert Plant on "The Battle of Evermore"? At the end, as the case breaks, the worthless husband puts on a record; you barely glimpse the Everly Brothers on the album cover. The show goes out on the slow, deliberate, mystified murder ballad "Rose Connolly," from their 1958 _Songs Our Daddy Taught Us_, though this daddy never taught anyone anything.

8 & 9 ▪ Cat Power, "Woman" and "Stay," from _Wanderer_ (Domino, October 5) Despite Lana Del Rey somewhere in the smoke of the background, "Woman" is nothing anyone hasn't heard before, from elsewhere. The same is true of Cat Power's version of Rihanna's "Stay," but in a different way: one song has moments of exquisite singing but ends up hammering against a wall, and the other is almost an apotheosis. "Stay" became and has remained so popular that it's now performed as if it's seeped the bloodstream of anyone who sings it, as if it describes their own memories. As a well of emotion, the song is pure gravity: I don't know if I've ever heard a version that wasn't almost shockingly soulful, and that includes videos by ten-year-olds. Cat Power catches that ordinariness, or maybe it's truer to say she follows it. She might be noodling around an old folk song, something she thought she knew from some Smithsonian Folkways reissue, like her "Moonshiner" from twenty years ago, and got more than she bargained for.

10 ▪ Marianne Faithfull, *Negative Capability* (BMG) A poor, forced album, casting back to her first hit, from 1964, looking back only three years to the Islamic State attack on the Eagles of Death Metal show at the Bataclan in Paris, where she lives. It could also be Lana Del Rey before she was born and after she's outlived a lot of the people who bought her records.

Thanks to Steve Perry and Davia Nelson.

October 25, 2018

SPECIAL ALL BOB DYLAN EDITION!

1 ▪ "Nobel Prize winner Bob Dylan plays River Spirit Casino Resort," *Tulsa World* **(October 13)** Though it does carry an echo of the Cheek to Cheek Lounge of Winter Park, Florida, where in 1986, after a show by a reconstituted version of the Band, pianist Richard Manuel went back to his motel and hanged himself, better this than the White House. I hope he wore his medal.

2 ▪ Bob Dylan, *More Blood, More Tracks: The Bootleg Series*, Vol. 14 (Columbia Legacy) The six-CD, eighty-seven-cut set—complete recordings in New York in September 1974, some with Eric Weissberg's Deliverance band, mostly solo or with bass accompaniment, and the five surviving numbers made in Minnesota three months later with local musicians—is the only way to go if you want to hear what the 1975 *Blood on the Tracks* almost was, and how it was saved from itself. Suspect aspects of an album that has been overpraised and over-fetishized for more than forty years are made clear. The fetishism is devoted to the New York sessions, which at one point resulted in a finished-album acetate that was circulated and then bootlegged. Especially once the Weissberg outfit was out of the room, with their eight consecutive takes on the stupid hoedown "You're Gonna Make Me Lonesome when You Go"—yeah, that's a real heartbreaker of a breakup song, especially if you can't remember the name of the person you're supposedly breaking up with—the New York performances are pure, real, acoustic, searching, pure, anguished, soulful, unencumbered, and pure. You can see right through them, to the person who's singing! It's like reading his autobiography! This is the truth!

It's also, with many exceptions—when a song that seems to be fading away is found, sometimes only for a moment—tiresome and monotonous. It's not the boredom of sitting in a studio listening to someone do a song over and over until it's right. It's the songs themselves that bring these qualities to the surface. Though there are lyric changes here and there—most noticeably the "Tangled Up in Blue" verse "He thought they were successful/She thought they were blessed/With objects and material things/But I never was impressed" which luckily didn't make the transition from New York to Minnesota—these numbers are very carefully crafted; in terms of their formal parts they're all but nailed down from the start. They're so crafted that a certain slickness curdles the most well-made of the tunes. Five of the ten songs on the *Blood on the Tracks* album (plus the sharp "Up to Me," left off but released much later on the *Biograph* compilation) work off tag lines: the coy device where the title of the song is also the last line of every verse. The song has to fit itself, and often it can't breathe. You might hear this most vividly in "Shelter from the Storm." Everything is in perfect balance. The lines "In a little hilltop village/They gambled for my clothes" seem almost biblical. But listen too closely, and it begins to sound far too contrived, and the emotion begins to feel phony. "'Come in,' she said, 'I'll give ya/Shelter from the storm'"—would any real person give that too down-home "ya" such a jocular lift? This is less bad singing than bad acting—and if you start to hear it this way, that "gambled for my clothes" feels much too self-consciously mythic, and of course it would have to be in a little hilltop village, instead of Eighth Avenue, where in 1974 people probably did gamble for their clothes. Maybe the true story in this set comes in those takes when you can hear Bob Dylan slide away from the songs, when you can hear him give up ownership of them, listen to them, and hear the songs tell him how they want to be played.

For me, the great drama comes with "Tangled Up in Blue." The first time Dylan tries it (Disc 3, Track 1), in New York, with only Tony Brown on bass at his side, it's in a drawl with words cut off, somehow the essence of hard-boiled. Musically it's a mess, it wears out, but as with any hard-boiled detective novel you want to know what happens next. Is that why the song is so appealing, one long, snaking, beckoning finger? That feeling is there from the start. Then after two takes of "You're a Big Girl Now," there's a confusion of attitudes, the perspectives of the "he" and the "I" almost not so much tangled as random, with the song not talking but organ from Paul Griffin loosening it up, trying to find room in it (Disc 3, Tracks 4–5). After five takes on other songs, they try it again (Disc 3, Track 11), looking for a jump. The song is falling short of itself. You can hear it; you can almost hear the musicians hearing it, but the charm of the song, the story it's throwing out in pieces that don't exactly match, with then and now and a farther then so scrambled that a swirling, all-encompassing present dissolves its riddles, is always there. On the last of the four days of New York sessions, fourteen songs in, Dylan and Brown go after it again, three times in a row (Disc 5, Tracks 1–3). The first time is a breakdown, but before they put the song back together a faraway, completely different melody rises out of the song, as if the singer is for a moment not telling a story but remembering it in a dream. It's stunning—a glimpse of another world in a closed book. And they try again, in the last moments of the last New York day (Disc 6, Tracks 2–3). First there's a wordless vocal, and then the voice is strong, confident, aggressive, coming down on "In the 13th cen-*tury*" as if the last syllables are an inside joke. And it's still a sketch.

In Minnesota, with guitarists Chris Weber and Kevin Odegard, keyboard player Greg Inhofer, mandolinist Peter Ostroushko, bassist Billy Peterson, and drummer Bill Berg, the music explodes—you can hear the songs getting what they wanted. In New York, "Idiot Wind" was an essay; here it's a tornado, leveling a whole town and then coming back to destroy anything it missed the first time around. "Lily, Rosemary and the Jack of Hearts," which in New York was a ballad, is now the big crowd-pleaser at the Virginia City opera house in 1878. And "Tangled Up in Blue," with the band playing hurdy-gurdy, carries the thrill you get at a show when the band hits the first note of the song you came to hear, a song you've heard hundreds of times, the thrill of hearing something that's become part of you, less part of your mind than your reflexes. It's as if the new musicians were there for all the previous attempts at the songs, carrying with them the frustration of not getting it into the take (Disc 6, Track 6) that will be the claim of these unknown, forgotten people on history, on time. With the song under way, Berg makes a tap, and you can feel the hesitation, not his, but the song's, and then a final determination, a wrangler saying, "All right, round 'em up, we've waited long enough."

The result is joyous. Dylan sounds like he's singing with whips. He tears through the story, tearing it up as he goes, dropping the pieces like Hansel's bread crumbs, circling back, plowing them under, leaving another trail. The performance builds up a momentum, never rushed but unstoppable, with Dylan singing and the band members playing as if they can't wait to get to the end, not to get it over with, but in an anticipation of how satisfying it will be when the song, finally, finishes itself. It's music where the fanfare comes at the end—the only song on *Blood on the Tracks* with a classic ending. The three hard breaths: two short, one long. An exhalation that says the last word as if it were the first.

Like all the master takes that eventually made up *Blood on the Tracks*, it sounds different from what you've heard before, even if you've heard the album those hundreds of times. As it was released in 1975, the record was washed with echo; here that's gone. You don't hear a fated work of art; you hear people trying to get something done.

3 ▪ Heaven's Door Tennessee Straight Bourbon Whiskey (Heaven's Door Spirits, Columbia, Tennessee) The striking bottle comes emblazoned with one of Dylan's ironworks designs, and despite the odd name—drink this and die?—what's inside lives up to it. It's rich, full, most of all smoky. You can't taste it all at once. It seems to change from sip to sip.

It reminded me of the bourbon my grandfather Isaac Gerstley made in Philadelphia before Prohibition—Rosskam Gerstley & Co. Old Saratoga.

With friends, we did a taste test, and no, Heaven's Door's three or four levels didn't match the ladder of sensations floating in the dark thimbles of Old Saratoga. But Heaven's Door, the label says, "is aged for a minimum of 6½ years." Old Saratoga has passed a hundred. What if Heaven's Door makes it that far, well after Bob Dylan and anyone else alive to try it now will be beyond knowing if it did or not?

4 ▪ Todd Alcott, "Mid Century Pulp Fiction Cover Project" (opencul ture.com) After reimagining songs by David Bowie, Elvis Costello, and others as cheesy paperbacks, most of Alcott's Dylan works don't tease anything out of the songs, they flatten them: his "A Hard Rain's A-Gonna Fall" is less about the song than a new cover for J. G. Ballard's *The Drowned World*. But he scores with a knockoff of the Now-a-Major-Motion-Picture 1940s and '50s covers capitalizing on movies made from such 1930s Erskine Caldwell Southern sex 'n' soil best-sellers as *Tobacco Road* and *God's Little Acre*: "Maggie's Farm" recast as a 25¢ number featuring a bare-chested hunk at his plow wiping the sweat off his neck with a red polka-dot bandanna and a dark-haired woman in boots and an unbuttoned white blouse sitting on a log nearby. She's giving him the eye; he's wondering whether to take her up on it now or later. As I remember, that wasn't exactly in the song.

5–8 ▪ Bob Dylan, *Live 1962–1966: Rare Performances from the Copyright Collection* (Columbia Legacy) Twenty-nine tracks on two discs; often when the passion rises out of a performance it's so intense it can be hard to credit. Sometimes it's a matter of craft, as on "Seven Curses" (New York, 1963), an original song cast as a Child Ballad: the beginning is so arresting you're sucked in in an instant, transported back hundreds of years, to times when events turned into fables. "When the judge saw Reilly's daughter / His old eyes deepened in his head"—you can feel the writer inhabiting both the woman and the man, the tension is already building, and the final countdown of curses comes on like Dracula descending a staircase, from the prosaic "That one doctor will not save him" to the supernatural: "And that seven deaths shall never kill him." With "It Ain't Me, Babe" (London, 1964), it's the singer reaching through a song to grasp something that seems beyond words and music. With "Mr. Tambourine Man" (London, 1964), it's the play of melody, the way Dylan slows down the harmonica solo in a way that the shifting sound so completely creates its own ambience you don't care if he ever gets back to singing the song. And there is the force and brutality and scorn in the last verse of "The Lonesome Death of Hattie Carroll" (New York, 1963), as if to disguise the singer's own shock at his own tune—it's horrifying, and when the crowd applauds at the end of the song it feels all wrong, a violation, as if the audience thinks the song was congratulating them, as if when Dylan sings "Those who philosophize disgrace," he's talking about someone else. Did he ever put more into this song? Did the song ever get more from him? Compared to this, "The Times They Are A-Changin'" (London, 1964) is a dog braying.

9 ■ **Bob Dylan, "I Got a New Girl" (YouTube)** From 1959, at a friend's house in Hibbing. Though the words are too obvious for any professional recording, the feeling is very Bobby Vee. "Suzie Baby," not "The Night Has a Thousand Eyes."

10 ■ **Laurence Osborne, *Only to Sleep: A Philip Marlowe Novel* (Hogarth)** Osborne has to do a little cheating to get the seventy-three-year-old retired private eye into 1988, but not more than Raymond Chandler himself did, who in seven mysteries from 1939 to 1958 had Marlowe born anywhere from 1903 (for *The Big Sleep*, his first) to 1914 (for *Playback*, his last). The payoff is the chance to listen in as Marlowe muses on "the strange music of Tina Turner," shakes his head over Guns N' Roses, and sets a scene that in its very blankness carries a hint of something slightly off, telling the reader something about the characters that they don't know themselves: "When I was opposite the gangplank I saw that it was not a party at all but just a middle-aged man with a Mexican girl and a boat's captain of sorts in a cream-colored uniform. The middle-aged man—Black, I assumed—had a sunburned pirate's face with a ridiculous dyed goatee and eyebrows painted on with a calligrapher's brush. The man fighting signs of aging always has a touch of sinister vaudeville about him. But his threads were impeccable. The three of them were playing cards at a glass table with a bottle of Jav's rum and listening to Bob Dylan."

It's a literary impersonation that actually works, even if Osborne has Marlowe say "It is what it is" once and "Back in the day" at least twice—the kind of cant phrases Chandler would have never used, because they smear specifics of motive, mood, time and place and replace morality with *Whatever*. I hope there's a sequel. Seventy-three is not that old, and "I stopped the car to let a tarantula make its way across the road in the same way you would stop for an old lady" is just what a seventy-three-year-old Marlowe would say.

November 27, 2018

1 ▪ Fernando A. Flores, *Death to the Bullshit Artists of South Texas* (Host Publications) After reading the ten singular tales in this book, Flores's first, I have no idea who the bullshit artists of South Texas are. The characters in these stories about people in the punk scenes of the Rio Grande Valley, or people on their margins, or people who pass through on their way to somewhere else, are drawn with affection and wonder, as if every time Flores came up with a musician—the members of "The House Band for the Hotel Cuerpo de la Paz" or "Pinbag" or "Bread8," or "The Lead Singer for the Short-Lived Band ERIKKKLAPTON"—you can feel him saying, *OK, now who is this really?* and then pushing until he and you find out.

This isn't the typical rock novel, which is fundamentally no different from *Behind the Music*—and I do miss that absolutely addictive show, probably because it was as formulaic as any program in the history of television. Flores creates a milieu of EPs run off at a copy shop, most of which end up in nobody's hands, of audiences of ten or fifteen, of bands you can't be sure even the people who were in them remember. The drama, again and again, is a moment of discovery, when a person finds his or her nascent, hidden gift. It's an epiphany of self-realization, or a sudden need to write five songs a day for two weeks, real songs, good songs that other people want to play, and Flores can let you hear them—almost alone among writers making up bands to write about, when Flores puts the lyrics he's made up for Pinbag or Bread8 on the page they read like something people would actually sing. That the revelation fades, that people who for a brief time put something new into the world—one of Flores's titles, and fundamental ideas, is "The First-Ever Punk Band in the World (Out of Raymondville)"—go back to the alcoholics and layabouts they always were, takes nothing away from their accomplishments, which glow on the page, making you wish you'd been there. Sometimes Flores does this simply;

sometimes he pulls out all the stops, and you might gasp, wanting to believe it all happened just like this, Bobby Lou on guitar, Sandy on the drums: "It was past midnight when they got back to the house, and neither Beth nor Fizzcakes were around. Sandy and Bobby Lou got behind the same instruments and summoned a sandstorm from a secret 1002nd Arabian Nights tale—an old wine bottle fell from the sill, rolled on the ground, hit the bass amp, and when the cork popped off it released a mob of cheering fans taking pictures and yelling their names, quickly turning into protesters waving picket signs, men on megaphones calling them sluts, and Molotov cocktails waiting to be ignited—it became clear that they were here for Sandy and Bobby Lou, the world was out of balance and the mob had chosen them to be burned at the stake for their false greater good."

2 ▪ Lil Wayne with Halsey, "Can't Be Broken," *Saturday Night Live* (NBC, November 10) Wizened, his face tattoos fading, he looked sixty years old, and generated a pulse of brittle jeopardy that made those who've supposedly sidelined him feel lazy.

3 ▪ Jon Bream, "Cyndi Lauper has fun while Rod Stewart coasts at St. Paul concert," *Minneapolis Star-Tribune* (October 16) "His biggest misstep was including a video clip of him being knighted in 2016 by Prince William along with footage and headlines of World War II warriors while he crooned 1991's 'Rhythm of My Heart.' What war did Sir Rod serve in? The British Invasion?"

4 ▪ *Women Who Rock: Bessie to Beyoncé. Girl Groups to Riot Grrrl*, edited by Evelyn McDonnell (Black Dog & Leventhal) An oversize book with 103 essays-with-new-paintings-or-drawings of individuals and a few groups (i.e., June Millington but not Fanny), and with that a who's-in-who's-out is inevitable. Joan Baez but not the Shangri-Las? Fiona Apple and not Kleenex? Anybody but not the Slits? For that matter, June Millington and not Etta James? But the problem is the conventionality of the writing, by thirty-four different women—and the artwork, by five women, plus Grace Slick's self-portrait, which ranges from flat (Janelle Monáe by Winnie T. Frick won't tell you anything the photo it's based on doesn't) to impenetrable: for Sleater-Kinney, by Anne Muntges, Carrie Brownstein looks like—who knows. The only way you can tell which woman is which is by a process of elimination, and even then you're not sure if the band kicked someone out and brought in somebody else.

This isn't exactly a missed chance. At $35 for more than four hundred pages, it's a gift that could make a difference in a lot of lives. But there's something too finished, too sunny, too you-can-make-it-if-you-try here, an attitude that makes even the entry on Amy Winehouse feel like a success story.

5 ▪ Fred W. McDarrah, *New York Scenes* (Abrams) McDarrah (1926–2007) from 1950 to 1980, and with a warm but frank introduction by the historian Sean Wilentz ("I never saw her again, and a few years later she died, a casualty of the counterculture," he says of a sixteen-year-old first cousin, glimpsed here dancing at a gathering in Central Park in 1967. "So thinking about that whole part of the Sixties still makes me ache and still makes me mad") that the work of the long-time *Village Voice* photographer rarely lives up to.

6 ▪ *black-ish*, "Purple Rain" (ABC, November 13) The series creator Kenya Barris came up with the idea, but Anthony Anderson as Dre seems on top of this from the beginning—twelve-year-old twins Jack and Diane have no idea who Prince was—to end, when after family members re-create Prince videos with utter shamelessness, Anderson picks up a lap keyboard and begins to pick out "Nothing Compares 2 U." The twins want to know why they're doing Sinéad O'Connor (they've heard of her and not him?), and within a moment each member of the family sings a line as if it's a personal memory. It's sentimental, but it's theirs, as the videos are not. It's right up there with the "Tiny Dancer" scene in *Almost Famous*. Is Diana Ross next?

7–9 ▪ Elvis Costello and the Imposters, *Look Now*, with *Regarde maintenant* EP (Concord), and at Northrop Auditorium, University of Minnesota (November 15) *Look Now* is twelve songs baked in a cake. Even with a fourteen-piece string section on the last track, the four songs on the EP that comes with the expanded edition aren't burdened by the curlicues and sprinkles of the album numbers. The gem of the entire enterprise, from the EP, is "The Final Mrs. Curtain." A gauzy, disorienting melody leads you into a story that takes place somewhere in the half-worlds of, say, Cole Porter's "Miss Otis Regrets" and Costello's own "Sleep of the Just" and "My Dark Life." It's not altogether clear who the murderer is, or the victim, or how many there are. The mood isn't menacing. It's not any kind of satire, but an untangling of the pun in the title as if it were a clue—to some other mystery, maybe.

Despite a request, Costello didn't play the tune in Minneapolis. For a crowd of more than 2,500 where it was hard to spot anyone under forty, he opened with a harsh "This Year's Girl" that couldn't break through the echoey, muddy sound; brought songs from *Look Now* down to earth, and ended the eleven-song encore set with "(What's So Funny 'Bout) Peace, Love and Understanding." The performance I'll keep thinking about was "Deep Dark Truthful Mirror," which turned into the kind of epic "I Want You" once was: a performance that can come back and trip you up, change your day, invading your memory without warning, and a song that, as a performance, felt as if it could go on forever without exhausting what it had to say. I have no idea how long the song was this night—six minutes? Ten?—but it dwarfed every-thing else Costello played. As it went on, his voice got bigger, then seemed to double in reach, range, intensity, and desire—desire for the song itself, desire for the mirror to reveal all his secrets, or all of yours. It wasn't a scary prospect. When the song did end, it felt as if he should have gone right into part two.

10 ▪ **"Suspicious package reported at Duke Energy building in Char-lotte," FOX 46/WJZY newsbreak, Charlotte, North Carolina (October 31)** Just five days after the arrest of Cesar Sayoc for mailing pipe bombs to Democrats and critics of Donald Trump, with no certainty about what might still be on its way: "Reports of a suspicious package Tuesday morning prompted evacuations and road closures in uptown Charlotte. The package ended up being a Journey cassette tape, police said."

Thanks to Andrew Hamlin and Cecily Marcus.

December 26, 2018

1 ▪ **Rich Kreuger, "Kenny's (It's Always Christmas in This Bar)," from** *NOWThen* **(RockkinK Music)** Years ago in Chicago, in the middle of winter, my friend Bill Wyman was taking me to a bar: "Chicago's a really friendly town," he said. "You'll like it here." As we approached the place, two burly guys came out and one fixed me, as if trying to figure out what I was doing there. "You haven't been here before, have you?" he said. His tone wasn't threatening, but—"You're going to like it in there," he said. As Rich Krueger sings in this deliriously happy song, "a stranger's just a stranger here/For less than one half a beer." That was the place.

I can't remember the last time I said yes to a song out loud in its first three seconds. In the instant when I realized that Krueger—a neonatologist at the University of Chicago—was something different, I also felt as if I'd been listening to this song half my life. Krueger catches the feel, the cadence, of ordinary talk as he jumps the waves in the sound. He's rushing inside music that never hurries, as if for him time's running out but the music knows the place never closes. "It's like trying to tell a stranger about rock 'n' roll" except he's trying to tell you about this bar. You believe him, you want to be there. He sounds like he's been all around the world without ever leaving home.

2 ▪ "Trump bestows Medals of Freedom on Adelson, Babe Ruth, Elvis and others," CNN headline (November 16) "The King of Rock and Roll—the true king, and you have to say that," Trump said at the White House, to reassure his followers that there'd be no truck with any claims for Chuck Berry, Little Richard, Fats Domino, or Bo Diddley. Not that the award Trump gave Elvis Presley was worth anything: given that you can now buy a Medal of Freedom, as Miriam Adelson did, the only way it can convey honor now is when someone refuses it.

Still, you have to watch the video of Trump's presentation to realize how sordid it was. He stands at the podium smirking. "How Great Thou Art"—which Trump will say he chose—comes up. As the instrumental passage beginning the song plays, Trump smiles, preens, as if he knows a punch line no one else does. Then Elvis sings the first words of the song: "Oh, Lord—" and Trump's grin widens. He touches his tie, and puffs himself up more than he already has. He looks down on himself, admiringly, as if he's surveying a national park, then looks around the room, all in one studied movement, as if accepting a silent wave of applause, to acknowledge that that opening was meant for him: he is the Lord. The song was cut after those two words.

3 ▪ Lady Gaga on *The Late Show with Stephen Colbert* (CBS, October 5) Lost in the news cycle: The night before Brett Kavanaugh was confirmed by the Senate as a Justice of the Supreme Court by a vote of 50–48, after being accused by Christine Blasey Ford of sexually assaulting her when she was in her teens, Lady Gaga described the process of repression, denial, and self-protection that follows such an attack. "The brain changes," she said. "It takes the trauma, and it puts it in a box, and it files it away, and shuts it, so we can survive." She joined the drama that at that moment was convulsing the nation, speaking with deadly seriousness in an almost pedagogical mode, pointing her finger, jabbing it in the air, saying: "But what I believe I have seen, is that when that woman saw that Judge Kavanaugh was going to be put in the highest position of power in the judicial system of this country, she was triggered. And that box opened. And when that box opened, she was brave enough to share it with this world: to protect this country." *To protect this country*: those words were said with a vehemence so strong it could have cracked the Liberty Bell all over again.

4 ■ Aidin Vaziri, **"Sheeran does bland pub show for 40,000," on Ed Sheeran at AT&T Park,** *San Francisco Chronicle* **(August 22)** "For a little over 90 minutes, fans were treated to just Sheeran, his rotating cast of acoustic guitars and something called a loop station—an effects box that allowed him to sample and overdub his vocals and guitar chords live, layering everything until it sounded like Coldplay minus a billion dollars."

5 ■ *Chicago Plays the Stones* **(Raisin' Music)** Aren't tribute albums terrible? The Rolling Stones' 2016 *Blue & Lonesome*, their Chicago blues album, certainly was, and this, a Stones-blessed project (Mick appears with Buddy Guy on what I'm just going to call "Heartbreaker" to save space, Keith with Jimmy Burns on "Beast of Burden"), bringing together players who made their mark in the 1950s with musicians born then, is much worse. You'd think that Billy Boy Arnold—whose rickety 1955 "I Wish You Would," with what sounds like a teenage vocal, is as primitive as Buddy Holly's "Not Fade Away"—could bring some restraint, a sense of timing and suspense, to "Play with Fire," but it's as rushed, as trashed up, as everything else here. The music is like a cut-rate neon sign that's about to burn out.

6 ■ **"Rock & Roll Hall of Fame Class of 2019 Inductees" (RockHall .com)** The Zombies: two effectively Beatle-style Top 10 hits in 1965 (think of "She's Not There" and "No Reply"—which one disappears in the face of the other?) and another one, boring even if the radio loves it, four years later. But when the Shangri-Las—"Remember (Walking in the Sand)," "Leader of the Pack," "Give Him a Great Big Kiss," "Out in the Streets," and "I Can Never Go Home Anymore"—three of them Top 10 in 1964 and 1965, one of them Number 1, all of them not merely hits, but iconic—have never been nominated, let alone voted in, how can this mean anything at all? I don't know if Janet Jackson or Def Leppard would agree, but I'd bet Stevie Nicks and Bryan Ferry would.

7 ■ **Dr J. Gérard, *La Grande Névrose (The Great Neurosis*, 1889), in "Sigmund Freud: Du regard à l'écoute (From Looking to Listening)," Musée d'art et d'histoire du Judaïsme, Paris (through February 10)** In a vitrine near the beginning of this labyrinth-like exhibition (for the narrow gallery spaces, but also the back-and-forth, leaps-and-bounds discoveries of psychoanalysis—of the discovery *of* psychoanalysis) was this book from Freud's library. It held the most frightening and suggestive image in the show: a woman, naked except for black stockings and heels, wrestling with an octopus, whose head was her own brain.

8 & 9 ■ **John Simon, *Truth, Lies & Hearsay: A Memoir of a Musical Life in and out of Rock and Roll* (available on Amazon) and the Band, *Music from Big Pink: 50th Anniversary Edition* (Capitol)** In the late 1960s, John Simon may have had the keenest ear of any record producer. He also had the most open heart, the most self-deprecating ego—the horn parts he and Garth Hudson designed and played on *Music from Big Pink* in 1968 are almost invisible, not so much inaudible as pure texture, a daydream inside an argument. That is why, moving on from the fellowship of the Band—of which as their first producer he felt so deeply a part that "One day I asked Robbie if could join up. He said, 'We've already got two piano players.' And that was that"—he was able to make his way through the music business without accusations of betrayal, manipulation, and theft trailing behind him, and why he could write a book without a hint of rancor, complaint, whine, or resentment. There is a profoundly Jewish sense of irony here, something you find in comic Jewish novels and memoirs from the 1940s—a conviction that life is a cruel joke and that any escape from tragedy is a matter of undeserved luck. He produced Big Brother and the Holding Company's first album, *Cheap Thrills*, which made Janis Joplin a world star. "Did she die in bed?" he writes. "In the bathroom? On the floor? Or was that Elvis? Or Jimi? Jim Morrison? Sid Vicious? Kurt Cobain? Michael Jackson?"

The fiftieth anniversary edition of *Music from Big Pink*—with only two of the Band left to see it—comes in a box set with a remixed CD, a Blu-ray version, LPs, a book, for all I know paint chips from the Band's rented pink house where the music took shape. All you need is the single CD as remixed by Bob Clearmountain, which you can get on its own, and it's a shock.

It's displacing how much there is to hear that was never there to hear before, but nothing that was there before is elided or erased. *How would Ray Charles sing this song?* Richard Manuel seems to asking as he begins "Tears of Rage," and the answer is at once physical and mystical. You can hear "The Weight" as never before. The opening guitar figure and strum is loud; then the sound steps down a level, as if to say, "Hey, now that I've got your attention with a little melodrama, we'll let the story play out at its own pace." Levon Helm's voice is so strong you can feel the muscles in his throat—you realize that here, on the fifth song on the album, you're hearing him for the first time, and, with Rick Danko and Manuel not behind him but around him, hearing how complete the brotherhood not of the group but of the music itself truly was. As Helm goes on, you hear that the brotherhood comes out of the notion that each person has something to give that others can't, something they can envy, something they can love. The others' voices, which have crooned and barked and chirped through the first four songs, were soft and quizzical, soulful and plaintive, but Helm is from another country: tough, humorous, experienced, a roughneck straight out of Mark Twain, someone who's been around and taken his knocks, and somehow can't bring himself to knock down anyone in turn—after all, he knows he's going to spend the rest of his life trying to figure out what Miss Fanny really wanted from him, and if he came through.

10 ■ **Chuck Berry, *Chuck* (Dualtone); Sturgill Simpson, *High Top Mountain* and *Metamodern Sounds in Country Music* (High Top Mountain/Thirty Tigers); Sam McGee, *Grand Dad of the Country Guitar Pickers* (Arhoolie); *Doors in Mexico* (Goldtone bootleg); Elvis Presley, *Way Down in the Jungle Room* (RCA); *Fleetwood Mac* (Columbia); Bettye LaVette, *Interpretations: The British Rock Songbook* (Anti-)** I walked into Down Home Music in El Cerrito, where you always find stuff you can't

find anywhere else or didn't know existed at all, and walked out with this. The Doors record looked interesting because when they played in Mexico City they were barred from playing anywhere else, except it turned out to be an earlier show in Toronto. The Elvis I had, but this version had seventeen outtakes. The only one with any life in it at all was *Chuck*, which came out last year, after he died, and didn't include a rewrite of "Dear Dad," when it appeared in 1965 a letter to Henry Ford from his son Edsel, with the name of a different tycoon's son at the end.

Thanks to Aidin Vaziri.

January 18, 2019

1 ▪ **Dirty Denim, "Meant to Be," from *Dirty Denim Demo Tape* (7″ EP)** This is the most arresting thing I've heard come out of the radio—in this case, KALX, the University of California station in Berkeley—since Lady Gaga's "Bad Romance" and Train's "Hey Soul Sister." A four-woman band from San Francisco starts up, as if Sleater-Kinney, or more accurately the Corin Tucker-Sarah Dougher-sts spin-off Cadallaca, had fallen head first into the Shangri-Las. Punk wham in place, one person starts up with screechy *eeeees*, another with high *ooooooos*, a third with *dop-wop-wahs*, all running around an I-saw-him-on-the-street-and-I-had-to-have-him plot. The lead storyteller, in a tiny, troll-like voice, makes him a promise he can't refuse: "Gimme a ride on that motorcycle / If you treat me right, I will not go psycho." These people are having so much fun, turning all of rock 'n' roll into one little tin-foil-wrapped joke and meaning every sound that isn't a word with all their hearts.

2 ▪ **Sharon Van Etten, *Remind Me Tomorrow* (Jagjaguwar)** Going back to at least the 1890s, there has always been a claque of New York writers to insist that the last flowers of bohemia are still pushing up through the concrete.

3 ▪ **Cat Power, *Wanderer* (Domino)** Chan Marshall has been making records for more than twenty years, but there's still something

tentative and unsure in her tone, in the way she feels her way into a song, in their fraying endings. At her best—and along with her worst title, this might be her best album—those qualities can seem mystical, as if she's receiving a song, accepting it, not making it, not even finding it. That's most distinctive on the first and last numbers here. With "Wanderer" you can feel Blind Willie Johnson hovering in its clouds, whispering "Dark was the night, cold was the ground" into the singer's ear. With "Wanderer/Exit," Lead Belly's "Black Girl," or anyone else's "In the Pines," seems to drift in between the trees. You can sense it, but you can't catch it, can't fix it, can't say, *there*.

"Horizon" creates the illusion that you're waking up to hear it; it makes a shift in dimensions. When the voice is doubled, a kind of unreality sets in. It's as if two sides of the same person, each with a different set of memories, is questioning the other about the same events, the same family. The chiming piano that carries the music is distracting in its precision, but nothing like that happens with "Robbin Hood," where a plain strummed guitar and a nearly invisible bass creates the ambiance of an empty room. You can't tell if the singer is afraid to leave, or—the song is only two minutes long, it doesn't tell you enough, it seems to have been cut off by someone who doesn't want you to hear it.

This is music that creeps around baseboards, feeling for tiny holes in the wood, because they make great echo.

4 ▪ **Jeff Jackson, *Destroy All Monsters—The Last Rock Novel* (FSG Originals)** I'm suspicious of anyone who claims to have done the last anything. It's like they're telling everyone else to shut up. Jackson does have an end-of-story premise: people are loose in the land, seemingly independent of each other but following the same script, massacring bands onstage. The book is two novels back-to-back, with different dead heroes but the same story. "My Dark Ages" is direct, "Kill City" metaphorical.

Apparently, with everybody in a band, almost every band is terrible. "The killers wanted music to matter again, she says. They wanted to purify it." This is not convincing; it's not even interesting. But the scenes of carnage, every one presented plainly, without pumped-up adjectives and gory effects, are absolutely devastating.

5–7 ▪ **Van Morrison, *Live in Boston 1968* (vanmorrison.com); Alan Torney and Tim Desmond, producers, "The Summer of Astral Weeks"**

(RTE 1); Van Morrison, *The Prophet Speaks* (Caroline/Exile) Research-ing the book that appeared last year as *Astral Weeks: A Secret History of 1968*, Ryan Walsh spent months looking for a rumored tape of Van Morrison playing a Boston club called the Catacombs that summer, trying out some songs that later that year would make up the core of his album *Astral Weeks*—a record that, as the critic Lester Bangs once put it, would over time take on the quality of a beacon for people who needed that and nothing less. Walsh found the tape; while he wouldn't copy it, he would play it for friends. It was a revelation. Here was Mor-rison on acoustic guitar, Tom Kielbania on bass, Joe Bebo on drums, and John Payne on flute, in the dankest obscurity. Morrison was in Bos-ton hiding out from mobsters who had their hands on rights held by Morrison's late producer, Bert Berns. And here was "Cyprus Avenue" whole, complete, those first notes raising a curtain that, in Morrison's music, has never come down, a single performance affirming the au-thority of someone who ruled the world. "Beside You" was almost as strong, but the music wasn't exactly about the songs. There was a new aesthetic of suspension, between experience and dream, love and death, whispering and miming, that in Boston made Morrison's 1967 hit "Brown-Eyed Girl," which could have been Tommy James and the Shondells, or "He Ain't Give You None," from Morrison's grunge album *Blowin' Your Mind* from the same year, sound—now, fifty years later—as if they were written for the next album, not the last.

Last fall, the tape appeared on Morrison's website, likely as a copy-right protection. It was taken down almost before anyone could notice. This was fitting: what began as a rumor went right back there. You can find it if you look; it's a signal document, but also a kind of mystery story. What if this music happened once, this night, and then, for what-ever reasons, good, bad, unspeakable, was never heard again?

As enthralling is Torney and Desmond's radio documentary on both Morrison's Boston combo and the team of first-rank New York jazz mu-sicians, assembled by the producer Lewis Merenstein, who with Mor-rison and Payne would make *Astral Weeks*. Whether one is listening to Joe Smith of Warner Bros., who signed Morrison and released the album, to the New York engineer Brooks Arthur, or the Boston and New York musicians, what comes through is professional detail, a de-votion to craft, and, overwhelmingly, a sense of having received, and still possessing, a kind of gift: *We were in the right place at the right time. If anything had been different, none of it would have happened. It was the kind of chance that comes to no one more than once.* They're as joyously mystified by their own actions as anyone coming across their music hundreds of years from now might be.

Most striking of the witnesses to right place, right time, is Janet Morrison Minto, Morrison's then-wife, at the time traveling as Janet Planet. She is precise, clear, thoughtful, emotional. She sounds simultaneously and consistently as she would have been in 1968, young and girlish, frightened and thrilled by her own memories, and like an old woman for whom there are no borders between past and future: "I still love him to death."

Lately, Morrison has been collaborating with the jazz organist Joey DeFranceso on remakes of jazz and R&B standards and productions of his own new songs. For me, jazz organ is a crime against nature, and nothing on *The Prophet Speaks* (not as pretentious as it sounds: the sleeve shows Morrison shushing the ventriloquist's dummy on his lap) makes an argument to the contrary. Morrison has been down this road before, a road where everyone you meet offers a dead fish for a handshake. It turns, sooner or later.

8 ■ **Andrew Shaffer, *Hope Never Dies: An Obama Biden Mystery* (Quirk)** With details that lead you right into the story (Jill Biden upstairs watching *Law & Order* reruns—what else), the tale of the ex-vice and the ex-president, both bored out of their minds, teaming up to solve a Delaware crime, falls into place quickly. What emerges more slowly is a novel about friendship, told in Biden's voice and spinning on his resentment and near-worship of Obama, which hits its peak when Biden is facing down a clubhouse full of bikers with guns drawn. He tells them he was vice-president. They're blank. "I was your state's senator for 36 years," he says. They have no idea who he is. Then Obama strolls in through the back door with a sawed-off shotgun over his shoulder. The bikers lower their guns. "'Looks like you all know who my pal is,' I said with authority. 'He's the guy who killed Bin Laden,' one of the bikers blurted. They all nodded in agreement. The awe in their eyes was, frankly, embarrassing. 'Actually, SEAL Team Six—' I started to say, but Barack cut me off with a stiff pat on the back. '—is waiting outside, in case there's any trouble,' he finished." You can bet that if Biden runs, Shaffer will have the second installment out by May. If Biden doesn't, he ought to anyway.

9 ■ **Alexandria Ocasio-Cortez, "War" (Twitter)** "I hear the GOP thinks women dancing are scandalous," she wrote. "Wait till they find out

Congresswomen dance too!" To the old Edwin Starr hit, which sounds as fresh today as it did in 1970, nineteen years before she was born, she pranced up to her office door, pointed her finger, did a pirouette, backstepped in front of her plaque and the flag, and went in. It felt like an oath of office: as if she were breathing in the Constitution and whistling it out.

10 ▪ Bumper sticker, Berkeley (December 22) "EVERY TIME I CHANGE LANES," read the top of a two-line message, the two levels separated by a thick black rectangle, which kept your eye from going down so quickly that you can't think up the tag line before you do. I expected something like "IT REMINDS ME OF MY PLACE IN THE GREAT CHAIN OF BEING." "I THINK OF SANDRA BLAND," it ended.

Thanks to Ryan Walsh, Jim Lockhart, Alan Torney, and Doug Kroll.

February 27, 2019

1 ▪ Nobody's Baby, "Life of a Thousand Girls" (Bandcamp) "All the ingredients to an American classic, the Teenage Death Song," says this San Francisco foursome of itself. "Noboby's Baby formed around the idea of capturing the raw honesty buried in early 60's cheese schlock." Fair enough, but that doesn't touch the dramatic hesitations or the pathos that Katie Rose, also of Dirty Denim, puts into the music. It's as if her absolute seriousness is fighting off her own self-mockery. "I-I-I've lived the life of a thousand girls," she sings to trebly guitars, through a tricky doo-wop change, to a high, chirpy chorus, in a voice that's simultaneously rich and poor, a thousand years in the line each of the six times she lets it out.

2 ▪ *Green Book*, directed by Peter Farrelly (Universal) Yes. But what does Little Richard think?

3 ▪ Lt. Col. Ralph Peters (Ret.), *Anderson Cooper 360* (CNN, February 21) Bill Brown writes in: "'It comes down to money!' Peters says. A changed man—he used to appear on Fox News—he's talking about the transactional relationship between Putin and Trump. 'In the immortal words of that American neo-Marxist philosopher Cyndi Lauper,' he says, '"money changes everything."' Cooper is smiling. 'I'm trying to get the image of you sitting in a room,' he responds, 'analyzing the music of Cyndi Lauper from the neo-Marxist perspective.' 'Actually, I'm really more of a Velvet Underground guy,' Peters says."

4 ▪ Elvis All-Star Tribute Hosted by Blake Shelton (NBC, February 17) Part re-creation of Elvis's 1968 *Singer Special* (as in the sewing machine company, which sponsored it), known ever since as the '68 Comeback—footage from the original show was intercut continually, to the point of Shelton dueting directly, and not badly—and part crapshoot—"Heartbreak Hotel" asks for understatement, but Jennifer Lopez's only answer to any question is histrionic—this was not embarrassing. With a few more turkeys—Pistol Annies, Josh Groban, Yolanda Adams—most performers seemed honored by the songs, to be saying that only their best would do. Darius Rucker came on like an amateur for "One Night," except that his voice is too good: he made you realize how big the song is, how much it wants, from the world or whoever sings it. Steve Binder, producer of the 1968 show, told a scary story about Elvis learning the finale for the night, "If I Can Dream," the ballad that never mentioned the assassinations that year of Martin Luther King Jr. and Robert F. Kennedy, but carried them as if each word was a pall-bearer—a story so strong it didn't fade when Shelton led Rucker, Post Malone, Carrie Underwood, and more through the number against footage of Elvis's physically clumsy and emotionally harrowing original. Priscilla Presley and daughter Lisa Marie were zombies, but Don Was led a subtly nimble rockabilly band that gave those who could use it a perfect setting, and no one was better than Adam Lambert, of 2009 *American Idol* infamy, with "Blue Suede Shoes." He looked to be having the time of his life. He sang with limitless pleasure without missing a step. He wore blue suede shoes. He wore blue nail polish. He made the song new.

5 ▪ Steve Binder, *Comeback '68/Elvis—The Story of the Elvis Special* (Meteor 17 Books) With redundant titling reminiscent of a mid-'70s Elvis budget album, this handsome, LP-size book is not what anyone might have expected. For a very short time, Binder broke Colonel Parker's hold on Elvis—he allowed Elvis to set himself free, and after that Binder was treated like a disease. There is great heart here, moment-by-moment detail, a sense of suspense, and also bitterness. Never again

allowed in Elvis's presence, in the seventies, well after Elvis's cataclys-
mic debut at the International Hotel in Las Vegas, which Binder attended ("At my own expense . . . he was fantastic"), Binder went to Las
Vegas to see him again: "I knew right then that it was over." Elvis didn't
die of drugs, he died of boredom, Binder says, even if that amounts to
the same thing. "The Colonel had his final victory. An empty and
shameful one at that." And Binder gets an eloquent last word.

**6 ■ Drew Harwell, "Fake Porn Videos are being weaponized to harass
and humiliate women: 'Everybody is a potential target,'" _Washington
Post_ (December 30)** Scarlett Johansson, on having been "superimposed
into dozens of graphic sex scenes" posted on porn sites: 'The internet
is a vast wormhole of darkness that eats itself.'"

**7 ■ _The Killer Inside Me,_ directed by Michael Winterbottom (Revolu-
tion Films, 2010)** I'd seen this precise adaptation of the 1952 Jim Thompson novel before. I'd never noticed that as the psychopathic small-town
Texas deputy sheriff Lou Ford, Casey Affleck pitches his voice to precisely match Bill Clinton's. It's a hunch on his part, a joke, an argument:
listen for two minutes and try to deny it.

**8 ■ Plagiarists theater group, _Münsterspiel,_ written by Gregory Pe-
ters, directed by Jack Dugan Carpenter (February 22)** Jon Langford reports: "Behind the Albert E. Berger mansion on the shores of Lake
Michigan we gather in a Chicago Parks District coach house to witness time collapse. It's 1534, OK, and all your punk rock hopes and
dreams are bursting into brilliant flame in the German city of Mün-
ster. The Anabaptists are radical, heretical and sexy and they've taken
over the town. Using buckets of hyper-protestant love power they've
kicked out the Bishop/Prince for being a drag and punched a hole in
the space-time continuum _Doctor Who_ style. This isn't going to end
well. Peters based his play on literary and theatrical dramatizations of
the proposition that long-suppressed histories of seismic social eruptions create non-linear cultural connections across all borders—so here
the Stooges and Pistols provide the soundtrack as the big man in the
big hat with the big chair teams up with an epoch-straddling black ops
force of ultimate cosmic negativity to quell the dissent with B-52s and
some old-fashioned testicle-slicing. When the reluctant and useless
smart-aleck Anabaptist leader John of Leyden gets branded (physically

and figuratively) with corporate logos by a hooded Xbox shooter game assassin, it reminded me of Peter Cook's disillusioned George Spiggott/ Devil character in the movie *Bedazzled:* 'I thought up the seven deadly sins in one afternoon. The only thing I've come up with recently is advertising.'"

9 ■ Benvenue, "Days to Years" (Benvenue/Tunecore) The pauses in the harsh noise, not far from Bush's "Glycerine" but more metal, the clear tone of the singer's voice—"Truth be told, you were never there— never there"—the desperation of the reach in the music: for four mostly former Cal football players who named themselves after the one-mile Berkeley-Oakland street where some of them had their first student apartment, this song would have sounded at home on the soundtrack to *Blindspotting*, not only the best Oakland movie released in 2018, but also the best American movie. I had my own first student apartment on the street myself, at the Berkeley end—now I live on the same street a block over the Oakland line. It's a quiet street with rose bushes; it doesn't feel remotely like the sound the band makes. Until you remember it's also the street where Patty Hearst was kidnapped.

10 ■ Loose Wing, *Loose Wing* (Loose Wing) A Seattle band led by singer and guitarist Claire Tucker. Out of nine songs, "Learn Your Lines" sticks hardest. There's a thinking-it-all-over feeling that calls up "Angel of the Morning" by Merrilee Rush and the Turnabouts— another Seattle band, from fifty years ago. They walked the same streets, and maybe some of the same dirt rubbed off. Nothing can be rushed, both songs say, but Tucker goes farther when she lifts up for the last word of a verse: "I hardly ate my sophomore year / Learned to get a failing grade / I didn't come back from winter break / But I knew that I was right."

March 15, 2019

1 ■ Amy Rigby, "The President Can't Read" (amyrigby.com/bandcamp) With a jangly sound that places it right where all the half-Beatles/half-Byrds L.A. bands were in 1966—the Leaves, say, or Jackie DeShannon *with* the Byrds—the same year he managed his way out of Fordham and into the Ivy League.

2 ▪ Chelsey Minnis, *Baby, I Don't Care* (Wave Books) 240 pages of one-page poems, mostly double quintets, of film noir dialogue, fractured—fractured as if the actress is stepping in front of the cameras so drunk she can only say what she wants her lines to say, or what they really say: "I'm a pair of diamond earrings away from sleeping with you." "The word for what I want is money." The book is deliriously entertaining, and the screws get tighter. "That was terribly decent of you," Minnis begins on page 193. "I have to run along now. / I'm beginning to catch on. / You're a very good person but you can't get away with it forever."

3 ▪ Mick LaSalle, review of *Mapplethorpe*, San Francisco Chronicle (March 8) In one of several Friday reviews, an essay on reductionism in culture in fifty-three words: "How does a movie depict what can't ever be identified to anyone's satisfaction, that might be a mystery to the artist himself? This is just the limits of the biopic form. Did Ray Charles and Johnny Cash really become great musicians because their brothers died? Maybe. Sure. But then again, *of course not*."

4 ▪ *Streets of Fire: 35th Anniversary Edition*, directed by Walter Hill, written by Larry Gross (Shout Factory DVD) "A rock 'n' roll fable where the Leader of the Pack"—Willem Dafoe, with Lee Ving as his so-evil-you-can-barely-look-at-him enforcer—"steals the Queen of the Hop"—Diane Lane—"and Soldier Boy"—Michael Paré—"comes home to do something about it," Hill described the movie when it was released in 1984. It was met with critical derision and public indifference.

It ends with Lane's character and her band performing "Tonight Is What It Means to Be Young" at a triumphant final concert—the music, produced by Jim Steinman and actually sung and played by a huge, faceless assemblage credited as Fire, Inc., is dead coming out of a speaker but so big on screen it's convincing that the single song *is* the concert: nothing could set it up, nothing could follow it. It's the most emotionally complete rock 'n' roll performance footage, real or fictional, I've ever seen.

"When he was writing *Hamlet*," Bob Dylan wrote in 2016 in an acceptance speech for the Nobel Prize read by the American ambassador to Sweden, "I'm sure he was thinking about a lot of different things. . . . His creative vision and ambitions were no doubt at the forefront of his mind, but there were also more mundane matters to consider and deal with. 'Is the financing in place?' 'Are there enough good seats for my patrons?'"

"Tonight Is What It Means to Be Young" is of a piece. It was, as so much of movies are, about money and rights and time and improvisation: how do we solve this problem? "We were looking for a title" for the movie, Hill said when I asked him about how the song happened. "I was blissfully ignorant of the Springsteen song"—a small, powerful ballad from the second side of Springsteen's 1978 *Darkness on the Edge of Town*. "Maybe it was in the back of my mind. I was looking in the Book of Leviticus—you can always find imagery in the Old Testament. There was 'Seven Days of Fire'—I had figured out over how many days the story took place. 'Seven Days of Fire'? 'No,' people said, '"Streets of Fire"!'"

Hill and his team were negotiating with Universal; the film producer Joel Silver brought in the music producer Jimmy Iovine to do the soundtrack: "He was close to Springsteen, he can get the song. It was a matter of getting the movie made—this wasn't going to be a movie-star movie. The title: the commercial power of Springsteen put us over the top."

"We shot 'Streets of Fire' as the ending song, as the end of the movie," Hill said. "But Springsteen didn't want to give up the rights. Maybe there was some resentment that the title of the movie had already been announced. But Jim Steinman had come in. When Springsteen didn't want to do it, I was—'Hosannah!' I didn't want the movie to be seen as a movie of the Springsteen song. And most importantly, I liked the song Jim wrote.

"He had already seen the finished film. We shot 'Tonight Is What It Means to Be Young' four or five months later. We had to bring Diane back from *Cotton Club* and work around her. Jim came in with 'Tonight.' I thought it was a terrific recapitulation of the idea of the movie—it had an intensity and a melancholy, graceful and hopeful: youth isn't going to last. I told the studio—I did some of my best acting—I was the wounded artist forced to do something he didn't want to do, which was not at all true—because this was not going to be a one-day shoot. We took four days for it. With Diane on loan, we didn't have much time for rehearsals." ("I had great respect for people like Minnelli," Hill had said in an earlier interview. "MGM in the old days, everybody was on contract and they would rehearse for weeks. We don't get that. We would stage it and shoot it.") "Everything evolved out of the music. It came from repeated listening to the song. My statement came out of that—the deep melancholy as opposed to surface ideas about youth. I was going to shoot the shit out of it. Lots of angles. As much prelighting as we could. Three cameras—shooting the whole song three times."

As you watch, now, you can find your way into the song. You're the drummer, shot from below. You're in the doo-wop group high-stepping into the show from the wings and taking it away. You're the guitarist in a zoot-suit, whirling to meet Lane back to back as if she's the picture and he's the frame. You're in the audience, trying to make the song last forever. You're singing the song as it comes out of Lane's mouth, wondering who the six or seven people who seem to be actually singing really are, and then not caring.

5 ▪ Alphaville, *Strange Attractor* (Polydor) Anyone who attended grade school or high school graduations in the nineties had to sit through the processional of the slow version of Alphaville's "Forever Young," a pumped-up but self-doubting anthem that quickly became unbearable. The band was always sharp—"Big in Japan," from their first album, is as sardonically defeatist as anything from Steely Dan—and even if only singer Marian Gold remains from the original group, and this came out in 2017, it took Gold and four new members five years to make, and in the middle of the album—"Enigma," "Mafia Island," and "Handful of Darkness"—the sound is as twisty and shrouded as it always was. "Heartbreak City" is more—a riff, somehow hidden in a swirl, that seems to run from day to night.

6 ▪ *Russian Dada, 1914–1924*, edited by Margarita Tupitsyn (MIT) As the twentieth century began, the order that had held Europe together since the 1870s and 1880s was beginning to come apart, but the first manifestations came not in politics, but in art: art that said that life as everybody understood it, as everybody expected to go on just as it had, no longer made sense. It didn't make dada sense, didn't reflect the truths artists were fooling with that said that ordinary language was insufficient to say what had to be said, that a view of the world could only be depicted in fragments, that chance had to replace intent—and while the word dada wasn't discovered until the spring of 1916 in

Zurich, as part of the experiments going on nightly at the Cabaret Voltaire, other artistic effusions took the name after the fact. One, as detailed in Tupitsyn's "Putting Russia on the Dada Map," a hurricane of a long first essay in this catalogue of an exhibition at the Reina Sofia in Madrid in 2018, was Ilia Zdanevich's Shoeism—launched in 1912 when he announced that the *Mona Lisa*, at the time missing from the Louvre, was, as Tupitsyn writes, "not worth finding and claimed that a cheap ready-made such as a shoe should supersede it." Zdanevich doubled down in 1914 with a lecture titled "Adoration of a Shoe," attacking "Italian futurism's fascination with progress and technology" with the prediction, in his own words, that "in thousands of years, to those who think of the twentieth century there will appear a specter not of an airplane . . . not of futurism . . . not of wireless telegraph . . . not of Marinetti or of Tolstoy, but of a shoe." The book is illustrated as thrillingly as Tupitsyn writes—an opening two pages of the actress Lev Kuleshov in the 1925 film *The Death Ray* show a woman laughing so freely it's a shock to go to YouTube to watch the movie and find out she's a witch—and if the essays that follow are standard academic exegesis, Tupitsyn's opening shot, 150 pages with art, is out of a cannon.

7 ■ Mekons, "Weimar Vending Machine," from *Deserted* (Bloodshot) You put your money in, you reach for what you paid for, and the machine pulls you in, until your face is right there next to the sandwiches and candy bars. If you're lucky the next person will buy you out, but it's 1929, and it's time that's running out. Forty-two years after it formed in Leeds, England—can that be?—the group is more contemporary than bands that formed last week: more focused on the present moment, on the history of the world, the history of their shared U.K.-U.S. homelands, the history of their own band. With this number the music is as confused as they can make it—a melodramatic "This Wheel's on Fire" introduction on guitars, a slyly whispered vocal from Jon Langford, a quote from Kurt Weill's "Alabama Song," chirpy women going "Nyaa nyaa nyaa" between the lines, then the whole city shouting that it's all over, that the world as they know it is going down, and then screams, which make history into a present moment. You are there; you can feel it.

8 ■ Dignity Health Found Footage ad (Eleven, Inc.) The thirty-second spot shows a man lifting a colt that's wandered onto the road back over a fence to its mother as two lines from Patsy Cline's 1958 "Just Out of Reach (Of My Two Empty Arms)" play in the background. But that's format language: the sound is so preternaturally bright it makes Cline almost physically present. Really, she's in front of what you're seeing—and her always slightly stiff delivery, a reach for gentility as a veil over her own chaotic life that provides a pathos that was all her own, sweeps away what you're seeing, leaving her voice in the air.

9 ▪ **Jewel, "Body on Body," from** *Johnny Cash: Forever Words* **(Sony Legacy)** Kris Kristofferson, Willie Nelson, Brad Paisley, Kacey Musgraves, T Bone Burnett, Rosanne Cash, Elvis Costello, many more, make songs out of poems and lyrics Cash left behind. It's earnest and you can hear people trying to convince themselves the material is better than it is. But remember Jewel? After selling tens of millions of records in the late nineties she hasn't had a hit for more than fifteen years, and maybe the producers thought she'd say yes to anything. She breaks through—through the piety of the occasion, the song, her career, through herself. She sounds like the greatest movie sunrise ever filmed—the one in F. W. Murnau's 1927 *Sunrise*, and that movie was silent. And then comes I'm With Her and Aoife O'Donovan turning "Chinky Pin Hill" into the smile almost everyone else seems to be faking.

10 ▪ **David M. Halbfinger, "For Netanyahu, Trump Offers Election Boost"** *New York Times* **(March 11)** "Yet as much as Muddy Waters anticipated Mick Jagger, Mr. Netanyahu was thrilling Israeli audiences with a visceral blend of populism, ethnic resentments and media-bashing fully 20 years before Mr. Trump took that brand of politics to the big time."

"Bibi, who's Muddy Waters?" Trump asked. "The Hoochie Coochie Man," Netanyahu said. "That's me!" Trump said. "No, Donald," Netanyahu said. "I came first. You're the prodigal son."

April 25, 2019

1 ▪ **"Lana Del Rey and Jack Antonoff Debuting New Country Song at the Ally Coalition Talent Show" (YouTube)** From December—and can this performance really have had less than nine thousand views? There's no title: with Antonoff strumming an acoustic guitar, then hinting at a figure, the song refers to Hank Williams in its first verse, but that's as close to what's sold as country as it gets. In the melody as it slowly takes shape, in the forest mood, in the faraway lilt of the voice pitched high, as if walking a rope bridge over a gorge, without any details this is a nineteenth-century murder ballad, half "Poor Ellen Smith," half "Danville Girl." The musical intensity once the theme is set—the "I'm unprepared to die you see" line repeating from ballad to ballad and not sung here, but wordlessly acted out—is hard to take; the shouts from the crowd are shouts of recognition, of the thrill and the fright of seeing your own face in the mirror of the song. Will it be on the long-promised *Norman Fucking Rockwell?* If it is, will anything on *Norman Fucking Rockwell* be half as good?

2 ▪ **Billie Eilish, *When We All Fall Asleep, Where Do We Go?* (Darkroom/Interscope):** Catchy. But the *New York Times* has invested so much ink and picture space in this performer you might fairly wonder what it expects in return.

3 ▪ ***Billions,* "Overton Window" (Season 4, Episode 4, Showtime, April 7)** In someone's mind, there was an emblematic subtext in both opening and closing the show with a remixed version of Bob Dylan's 1993 cover of the Mississippi Sheiks' 1931 "World Gone Wrong"—for this continuing investigation of Manhattan money-tower nihilism, with guitar chords shooting out of the song like bone fragments.

4 ▪ **"Kentucky Fried Chicken and Waffles, 'Dance Is the Hidden Language of the Stomach'" (W+K Agency), seen on Golden State Warriors vs. Los Angeles Clippers, NBA Playoffs (ABC, April 21)** The current Colonel Sanders, the one with the grating and bullying voice—but here silent, as, whiter than white, he approaches a life-size brown Mrs. Butterworth syrup bottle, shaped and colored as a grotesque Aunt Jemima parody, and, to Bill Medley and Jennifer Warnes emoting on "(I've Had) The Time of My Life," sweeps her off her feet and lifts her into the air in a gesture of absolute ownership: *I'm gonna pour you, baby.* Unbelievable.

5 ▪ **"Dream Bigger" (Mazda North American Operations and Garage Team Mazda), seen on Virginia vs. Texas Tech, NCAA Men's Basketball Finals (CBS, April 8)** For Mazda, a version of the Cranberries'

"Dreams" just over a year after their singer Dolores O'Riordan was found dead in a hotel bathroom—clueless, or was that the hook? It was followed by a sound-alike Beatles' "Help"—as with the first number, you buy rights to the song, not the performance, you hire mimics to make it sound as close to the real thing as possible, which is very close, but not close enough to keep you from realizing you're being fooled, that what you're hearing is real fake news, not close enough to keep you from feeling not only that the commercial wants your money but that it's already stolen it. But after that, a Gatorade ad positing a seventies disco battle between Indianapolis Colts quarterback Andrew Luck and Los Angeles Angels outfielder Mike Trout was just fine.

6 ▪ James Lasdun, *Afternoon of a Faun* (Norton) As a rape accusation from long ago surfaces, a frame of the 2016 election is thinly drawn around the story, until the last pages, at a party to watch the second Clinton-Trump debate, the one following the it's-all-over release of the "Grab them by the pussy" tapes—when Trump rounded up a rack of women who had accused Bill Clinton of worse and sat them in the front row, and then left his place onstage to menace Hillary like a stalker, and everyone knows it's in the bag for Hillary, and the frame is hardened and the picture is blacked out. "The nightmarish possibility of his presidency was slipping, mercifully, into the realm of bullets dodged, disasters averted. Some day no doubt novelists would write dystopian alternate histories in which he won, but it was becoming clear, if one had any doubts, that in the real world rationality and basic decency were going to prevail, as they usually did."

7 ▪ NC/Northern Coffeeworks, Minneapolis (March 28) When I opened the door in the late afternoon, the place was nearly empty. Sinéad O'Connor's "Nothing Compares 2 U" was playing, and for a second or two it was simply right, like being wrapped in a blanket after coming in from a storm. But as it never quite had before, what came across was the violence in the performance: the way O'Connor spits out the last two words of each chorus, cutting off *"to you"* as if she's cursing her own memory. Then the John Maybury video, that almost-absolute five-minute close-up of O'Connor's face, appeared as if it were playing on the walls of the shop, and for the first time I realized where that image came from: the end of Carl Dreyer's 1928 *Joan of Arc*, holding on Falconetti's face as she's burned at the stake.

8 ▪ Jenny Lewis, "Rabbit Hole" (Warner Bros.) From her all-breasts-no-face album, *On the Line,* a dim version of the Primitives' "Crash." She sings "the Rolling Stones" as if she's heard of them, which means David Bowie got it right with "My brother's back at home with his Beatles and his Stones / We never got it off on that revolution stuff," in "All the Young Dudes," in 1972, four years before Lewis was born.

9 ▪ "Warpaint: Live Score + Films of Maya Deren," San Francisco International Film Festival (Castro Theater, April 19) Gina Arnold reports: "Cinematically groundbreaking though they may be, Maya Deren's experimental black-and-white films from the 1940s and '50s can be difficult to parse when viewed on YouTube (or in a stuffy graduate-school classroom, which is where they're usually seen). But blown up to fit the massive screen at the Castro and then sonically jet-propulsed by the Los Angeles–based band Warpaint's tense score was a different story entirely. As on their own collaborations, like the song 'Elephants,' which was featured on the soundtrack of the horror film *Siren,* or the equally haunting 'Love Is to Die,' from their second album, *Warpaint,* the band (or half of it, Stella Mozgawa on drums and Theresa Wayman switching between keyboards and guitar) created a lush, percussive moodiness that perfectly accentuated Deren's dreamy and beauteous, but often frightening, subjectivity. Hence, what once had to be painstakingly explained by some antic film professor was now made plain: the sinister image of a statue leaping from a plinth to pursue the filmmaker, the horrifying reaper hurrying down the path to the sea . . . these and other arresting images were dramatized by Warpaint's work so strongly that, for those who were there, the films may now be impossible to watch in any other way."

10 ▪ Cheyenne Roundtree, "EXCLUSIVE: Hey, Mr. Trampoline Man! Bob Dylan, 77, makes sporty updates to his Malibu compound—purchased for $105,000 in 1979—but keeps true to his folk roots with wood cabin on grounds," *Daily Mail* (March 12) From a drone photo, there is a trampoline; the cabin is built like a sharecropper's shack, something out of Walker Evans, if not Marie Antoinette's farm at Versailles. There seem to be dogs on the porch. It looks like a place the Mississippi Sheiks would be renting if they weren't all somewhere else.

Thanks to Michael Robbins and Steve Perry.

June 24, 2019

1 ■ Overheard at "The World of Bob Dylan" symposium, University of Tulsa (May 30–June 2) "I'm seventy-one years old. *When* will excruciatingly boring fat men cease trying to hit on me?"

2 ■ Erin Durant, *Islands* (Keeled Scales) I've played this album a dozen times over the last two months. Sometimes Durant's piano seems to be drifting in from a neighbor's window; then it might all but fade out as she plays. From Brooklyn by way of New Orleans, Durant has a tiny voice that never presses; it can feel as if it's been under your skin, in the back of your mind, for years, and then you might not be able to remember it. But her playing and singing can call you back, trying to hear what she's not saying. The first number here, "Rising Sun," opens one verse with "There is a house in New Orleans," another with "Take me to the river," but neither connects to an old song as deeply as the way Durant faintly admits she's "a little drunk"—there's a movie of a whole life in her few words, running backward.

3 & 4 ■ Bruce Conforth and Gayle Dean Wardlow, *Up Jumped the Devil: The Real Life of Robert Johnson* (Chicago Review Press) and *Remastered: Devil at the Crossroads—A Robert Johnson Story*, directed by Brian Oakes (Netflix) Robert Johnson, 1911–38; as the title of the 1961 album that introduced the twenty-nine songs he recorded in 1936 and 1937 to the world put it, "King of the Delta Blues Singers." He has traveled down to our time with the legend that he sold his soul to the devil for the right to outplay anyone who was ever born. Despite their devil-mongering title, the longtime blues researchers Conforth and Wardlow claim to have settled the matter against the underworld—and you don't have to believe a ghost of the story to be appalled by what they've done to it. Ignoring the testimony of the blues scholar Mack McCormick (1930–2015) and the blues guitarist Mike Bloomfield (1943–81) that the tale of Johnson's deal with the devil was a widely shared and dispersed story going back to the 1940s, Conforth and Wardlow source the claim solely to the blues critic (at the start, that was his beat at *Rolling Stone*), researcher, and record producer Pete Welding (1935–95), and his quote from Johnson's older compatriot Son House: "He sold his soul to the devil in exchange for learning to play like that." In a cowardly manner, not naming Welding but unmistakably fixing him, the authors imply that he both plagiarized his supposed interview with House and made up House's supposed statement out of whole cloth. Running the previously impossible trick of proving a negative, Conforth and Wardlow insist that House never said any such thing—because, as one reader of the book who has himself weighed in on Johnson over the years puts it, "Well—he just *couldn't.*" That the book is marred by all kinds of errors, some of them merely sloppy, some of them mind-boggling—stating that Johnson's 1990 *Complete Recordings* "has sold more than fifty million copies in the United States alone," which, as a two-CD set, would make it by far the best-selling album in history, not to mention amounting to one copy for nearly every sixth American, including infants, undocumented immigrants, and racists who would never let an object with the face of a black person on its cover into their houses—makes it difficult to trust any given particular in the vast and humbling trove of biographical information the authors have assembled, let alone this.

It's an epic labor of devotion to facts large and small—and that, harvested especially from interviews with Johnson's contemporaries (many of them, going back to 1967, conducted by Wardlow), is where the value of the book lies, to the point that one can imagine the loudness of the dismissal of the deal-with-the-devil as most of all a commercial hook. Detail upon detail of family life, love affairs, marriages, education both formal and in the blues, apprenticeship, musical partnerships, travel, hoodoo practice, composition, recording, popularity, career pursuit (it's wonderful to read that while passing through New York, Johnson tried to get on the national CBS radio showcase *Major Bowes Amateur Hour*—and that "Frank Sinatra originally appeared on the show as part of the Hoboken Four quartet in 1935"), craft, money, and death does demystify the always mystified and for that matter self-mystifying artist in an accumulatingly powerful and valuable way. But while Conforth and Wardlow can explain Johnson's music, they can't convey anything of its novelty or daring—of the shock, on the part of people in Johnson's time or ever since, of encountering the music. The prose rarely rises above lumpiness: "Robert's rambling had become both his main way of traveling from one job to the next and his way to satisfy the need to just 'get up and go.'" There is more than a hint of a certain animus, or distaste, for the way Johnson lived his life: "They frolicked," the authors write, describing a single Mississippi night, "until

Robert went home with one of the women or collapsed drunk on the floor," which means they have no idea what Johnson actually did that night—he could have stayed up reading Walt Whitman. They find nothing more gratifying than being able to reduce art to biography: for the meaning of "Dead Shrimp Blues," recorded in San Antonio in 1936, "it might not be necessary to look any further" than the fact that San Antonio was a good place to eat shrimp. And even that kind of reduction leads to a greater reductionism: that of the essential hollowness in the sensibility that is brought to bear in what is finally a charmless book. "One can," they say of "Hellhound on My Trail," "sense a certain angst in this song. It's not a happy piece." To which the world shakes its head in awe: *Really? I never thought of that!*

For all of its self-presentation as an exercise in exploitation, the *Remastered* documentary, with animated sequences of the devil granting Johnson his powers and, of all people, Bruce Conforth as the principal walk-through narrator, may ultimately be more sophisticated about the old story, which, I think, no one ever really believed, but which has taken so many so far. "It's a metaphor," says Keb' Mo', "for a person to go ahead and become who they are."

5 ▪ Kelly Hunt, *Even the Sparrow* (Rare Bird) Growing up in Memphis, now in Kansas City, Hunt plays a soprano banjo, which sometimes jumps right out of a song as if it wrote it and is demanding credit. She's not exactly afraid of song titles, or taking on—or taking down—whatever one might bring to them: on her first album her own songs include "Across the Great Divide," "Back to Dixie," "Men of Blue and Grey," "Delta Blues," and "Gloryland." "Oh Brother, Where Art Thou?" opens with plucked notes on the banjo; Hunt lets the instrument shape her syllables. From the first instant you know you're in a place where there is no sense of time, where anything can happen and no one will ever have to admit to a thing: "You go to your pasture, I'll go to my field." The high voice snaps; the mood insists you're listening to a murder ballad, but no matter how often I go back to the song I can't tell you if anybody dies—the faraway drift of the song as it begins to give up on itself, to give up on life, sweeps me away from whatever the story might be every time.

6 ▪ 13th Floor Elevators, "You're Gonna Miss Me," in *Charlie Says*, directed by Mary Harron (IFC) In the only film treatment of the Manson saga that captures the bone-rattling nightmare of Ed Sanders's *The Family*, which is credited as source material, this 1966 song finds a new voice. It always had a dark, doomy feeling, and it was always sort of a cartoon. Here it feels like a wolf running over a hill in the dark with a hand in its mouth.

7 ▪ *Her Smell,* written and directed by Alex Ross Perry (Bow + Arrow Entertainment) Who knew that Gloria Swanson, who in 1966 appeared on an Avalon Ballroom poster for a Big Brother & the Holding Company show—the 1924 Edward Steichen portrait, her eyes burning through a veil—would turn up half a century later as the face of riot grrrl? Sixty-nine years after Swanson shot William Holden in *Sunset Boulevard*, Elisabeth Moss's Becky Something is Norma Desmond from first to last.

8 ▪ Timothy Hampton, *Bob Dylan's Poetics: How the Songs Work* (Zone Books) Forget the main title; the subtitle describes what happens here. With a style that turns analysis into a form of suspense, Hampton can walk you through "Visions of Johanna" or "Summer Days" the way the art historian T. J. Clark can walk you through Manet's *Olympia*. There's the same generosity of spirit, the same love for the work and the social meanings it absorbs, transforms and sends back, as with Hampton on Dylan's so-called Sinatra albums of the last few years: "Dylan suddenly became a 'folksinger' who turned songs that"—like the nineteenth century–composed and –copyrighted parlor songs that A. J. Carter re-copyrighted and turned into what everybody embraced as Carter Family songs—"were initially thought to be the very opposite of 'folk songs' into folk songs." Which doesn't begin to catch the delight Hampton takes in criticism, as with his account of "Tombstone Blues" and the line "Ma Rainey and Beethoven once unwrapped a bedroll" as "a rewriting of Chuck Berry's 'Roll Over Beethoven' (now know we who Ludwig was with when he rolled over!)."

9 ▪ DJ Khaled, *Saturday Night Live* (NBC, May 18) The Emperor's New Clothes, with, lining the streets and cheering him on, John Legend, Lil Wayne, SZA, Big Sean, and Lil Baby—not to mention LeBron James, Al Gore, Felicity Huffman, Tiger Woods, Beto O'Rourke, and an ultrasound of a six-week fetus.

10 ▪ **Trip Gabriel, "Pete Buttigieg (It's 'Boot-Edge-Edge') Is Making Waves in the 2020 Race,"** *New York Times* **(March 28)** "'I think there's still an attitude in some parts of the party that what we have to do is find the final proof that Trump's a bad guy and show it to everybody,' Mr. Buttigieg said in an interview. 'What it misses is there's a lot of people where I live who were under no illusions about his character. They already get that he's a bad guy, but they made a decision with their eyes open to vote to burn the house down.'" Didn't Chris Stapleton say that?

Thank to Emily Marcus, Robert Cantwell, Elijah Wald, and Ramona Nadaff.

July 24, 2019

1 ▪ **Aisha Harris, "Lion Queen (Beyoncé) Has Her Say,"** *New York Times* **(July 20)** New Horizons in Democratic Theory Dep't: "To hear Beyoncé speak is such a rare occurrence that any instance of it, no matter how fleeting, feels special, like catching a glimpse of a shooting star."

2 ▪ **Bruce Springsteen,** *Western Stars* **(Columbia)** Battle of the Bands: Harry Nilsson v. Glen Campbell. On the record, it's a draw, and really, who cares? Off the record, the world is smaller without Glen Campbell. It isn't without Nilsson. And it isn't bigger with this.

3 ▪ **Pere Ubu,** *The Long Goodbye* **(Cherry Red)** With bandleader, singer, and writer David Thomas looking at death, he went back to 1975 and Pere Ubu's first song, "Heart of Darkness," inspired not by Joseph Conrad—Thomas has always loved putting classic titles (as here "Fortunate Son") on songs that have nothing to do with what they're supposedly referring to—but by Raymond Chandler. For what he expected would be his own long goodbye, as if his whole life had been a kind of farewell, Thomas chose the title of Chandler's 1953 novel, itself a kind of rewrite of *The Great Gatsby*, which as a detective story has more corpses than Chandler's *The Long Goodbye*. And this time the title is not a false clue: putting a generic noir image on the album cover, Thomas digs down, inhabiting Philip Marlowe, looking for the streets he walked.

Thomas composed the songs, set them to music with synthesizers and drum machines, and sent the tracks to the rest of the band. The result is on the first disc here, which is not quite there. It's all there on the second disc, a live performance of the album from Montreuil, just outside of Paris. Beginning with "Heart of Darkness," moving with jumps and stalls through "Flicking Cigarettes at the Sun," "Marlowe," "Skidrow-on-Sea," the band is severe and brittle, with Thomas, in his cracker-barrel philosopher mode, explaining the music: his favorite movie Marlowe is Robert Mitchum, he says, but the song he's going to play next is based on Elliott Gould's Marlowe in Robert Altman's version of *The Long Goodbye* . . . It's game, a great circle of a band's story, which might have made its best album.

4 ▪ National Delivery, *A Plurality of One: The Song of Walt Whitman*, a dramatic presentation written and staged by Joe Christiano, with sound ambiance by Justin J. Jones, Timbre Folk and Baroque (Berkeley, July 20, with a reprise August 3) Before a semicircle of twenty-three in a stringed instrument space, Stanley Spenger strolled in as Whitman's ghost, dressed in rough-looking clothes—he hasn't slept since 1892—and a broad-brimmed leather hat, remarking that he was on leave from his usual haunts in any given branch of the New York Public Library. Soon enough in the hourlong production he was orchestrating "Song of Myself"—"Not all of it"—and instantly, it rang. Throwing out lines for people to shout back either together, or, with a pointing Whitman finger, any given person on their own, the poem began to echo over the whole of the American discourse that Whitman was calling up and that, since he wrote, has called up him. You could hear that the opening of the poem was purposefully following the cadence of the beginning of the Declaration of Independence ("We hold these truths to be self-evident" . . . "You shall assume what I assume"). As the poem stepped toward its last lines with "Look for me under your boot-soles" you could hear Tom Joad's testimony as he disappears from *The Grapes of Wrath* ("Then I'll be all aroun' in the dark. I'll be ever-where—wherever you look"). In Whitman's "The kept-woman and sponger and thief are hereby invited" you could hear the witnessing in Bruce Springsteen's revision of "Gospel Train" in "Land of Hope and Dreams": "This train carries whores and gamblers," which, presumably, Spenger's

Whitman, checking out *Wrecking Ball* at the Williamsburgh Library on Division Avenue in Brooklyn, had already heard.

5 ▪ Rails, *Cancel the Sun* (Thirty Tigers) Two musicians flailing about, except when Kami Thompson does an ethereal float through "Save the Planet," a punk song disguised as a soft, comforting ballad: "No one likes you, and you know why . . . Save the planet, kill yourself."

6 ▪ Colson Whitehead, *The Nickel Boys* (Doubleday) It takes nerve, or a blunt disregard for what the world expects, to follow the hugely honored best-seller *The Underground Railroad* with a small-sized novel of barely two hundred pages and not a lot more than half as many words as the supposed game changer. Small novels don't sell like big novels, because they seem small—too small to carry the weight of the world. But despite a story that posited a somehow completely believable real, actual underground railroad, with real stations, real conductors, and tunnels worthy of John Henry, and accounts of slavery and racism so brutal, so true to history, and so starkly, poetically written they can be as hard to read as Kara Walker's silhouettes can be to look at, *The Underground Railroad*, which did everything it could to escape the escaped-slave and slave-catcher genre, remained a genre novel. There was a way in which you had read it before.

The Nickel Boys, following two boys in their late teens, Elwood Curtis and Turner, in the Nickel Academy, a segregated boys' reformatory in Florida in 1963 and 1964, is not a genre novel. There is nothing in it that is mandated by its form, because it doesn't inhabit one. There is nothing predictable. The sense of jeopardy is like a curse, and the most foreboding moments are those in which Whitehead lets both his characters and the reader relax, lets them and you almost off the hook, where for at least a moment they and you can forget what has already happened and what might come next.

At Nickel, boys who don't know how to get along are beaten and whipped. Those who engage in some small, even semiconscious refusal, like failing to throw a fight that is supposed to be fixed, are tortured and starved, and then executed: "Sometimes they take you to the White House," second-timer Turner tells the green Elwood, "and we never see your ass again."

Eight years after *Brown v. Board of Education*, in his segregated high school in Tallahassee, with textbooks discarded by white schools and defaced with racist taunts by the white students when their new ones arrive, Elwood is studious, hard-working, breaking no rules. Whitehead could have called the book "The Sixties Without Music": while there are snatches of Chuck Berry and Elvis and the theme song from *The Andy Griffith Show* from radios in the Nickel infirmary or a Nickel van, Turner picking up each as a whistle, the only album Elwood's grandmother, who has raised him, will allow him is *Martin Luther King at Zion Hill*, which he finds as inspirational, as soul-filling, as *Life* magazine: "He knew Frenchtown's piece of the Negro's struggle, where his neighborhood ended and white law took over. *Life*'s photo essays conveyed him to the front lines, to bus boycotts in Baton Rouge, to counter sit-ins in Greensboro, where young people not much older than him took up the movement. They were beaten with metal bars, blasted by fire hoses, spat on by white housewives with angry faces, and frozen by the camera in tableaus of noble resistance. The tiny details were a wonder: how the young men's ties remained straight black arrows in the whirl of violence, how the curves of the young women's perfect hairdos floated against the squares of their protest signs. Glamorous somehow, even when the blood flowed down their faces." Whitehead's reach back to magazines published before he was born is its own wonder: his homing in on those tiny details, bringing them into the present like shaming ghosts.

Elwood is in Nickel because, hitch-hiking to special classes at a nearby college, he caught a ride in a stolen car, which got him charged with car theft. Turner is full of rage, his talk is rough compared to his new friend's, but he's if anything more thoughtful, more attuned to what he doesn't know, because unlike Elwood he doesn't believe there are answers to every question. When you begin to feel that one of the two may not survive the story, you try to worry Turner out of it.

The variety of the books that sound through *The Nickel Boys* testifies to how and why, like Whitehead's first three novels, *The Intuitionist*, *John Henry Days*, and *Apex Hides the Hurt*, which in just over two hundred pages is as ambitious as *Moby-Dick* and as precise as *The Scarlet Letter*—and unlike his next two, the coming-of-age *Sag Harbor* and the zombie-killer thriller *Zone One*—*Nickel Boys* negates category. There are the Hardy Boys books, which make Elwood a reader. Even before the fight scene in *The Nickel Boys* you may have already thought of Ralph Ellison's 1952 *Invisible Man*, which Elwood wouldn't have read yet—and echoing just as strongly are books Whitehead himself may not have read, though given the research that went into *John Henry Days*, where it seems impossible that there is anything in the realm of fact or myth about John Henry that Whitehead hasn't read twice he almost certainly has: Haywood Patterson's devastating 1950 *Scottsboro Boy*, and beyond that Robert Elliott Burns's 1932 *I Was a Fugitive from a Georgia Chain Gang*. Beyond that there is *Tom Sawyer, Detective* and *Adventures of Huckleberry Finn*. *The Nickel Boys* has part of all of them in it while being not like any of them.*

7 & 8 ▪ **Bob Dylan, "The Lonesome Death of Hattie Carroll" and "This Land Is Your Land,"** *Rolling Thunder Revue: The 1975 Live Recordings* **(November 19, 20, 21, two shows, December 4, Columbia)** Over sixteen CDs, along with rehearsals and songs not often performed, the shows collected here are standard: in the first set "The Lonesome Death of Hattie Carroll" comes third, in the second "This Land Is Your Land" comes last, and without variation and a doggedly uninspired band— with the exception of Scarlet Rivera on violin, the faceless musicians back Dylan, but they don't play the songs—I found myself waiting for those to come around.

Hearing "Hattie Carroll" again and again, you realize it could be Bob Dylan's best-written song, and structurally his most original, with all the different parts—the direct opening line of each verse, then the music opening up for a detailed narrative, then the chorus undermining what you've just heard and speeding you into the next verse— speaking a different language, almost becoming a different language. In the last performance, at the Forum in Montreal, you feel that in every previous attempt Dylan has been holding back: here there is a rush, a desperation, behind every syllable, each one building up to an intensity that throws the reality of the story Dylan is telling, and the art with which he's telling it, straight in your face. It suggests that one direction Dylan's bootleg series could take would be discs of versions of songs Dylan has performed from the beginning of his career on, in different times, settings, election nights: "Masters of War," "Blowin' in the Wind," "Young but Daily Growing," "The Lonesome Death of Hattie Carroll."

"This Land Is Your Land" is interesting because it's absolutely horrible. It's a hoedown with big names each taking a verse—Jack Elliott! Roger McGuinn! Bob Neuwirth! Joan Baez! Joni Mitchell!—and if

* In 2020, like *The Underground Railroad* in 2017, *The Nickel Boys* won the Pulitzer Prize for fiction.

you've ever wondered what hell is like, it's Joan and Joni singing this song as if it's opera and they're opera singers, night after night. Glen Campbell used the same arrangement in his TV show a few years later, duetting with Andy Williams. It was better. "This Land Is Your Land" was written by Woody Guthrie as an answer to Kate Smith's pompositous rendition of Irving Berlin's "God Bless America." That was better.

9 ■ *Diane,* **written and directed by Kent Jones (IFC)** Set in decaying rural Massachusetts with snow on the ground and Mary Kay Place's Diane in every scene, this is a movie about aging, death, addiction, poverty, religion, and bad food. Especially bad food: the people in this story live lives without pleasure. The most spectacular event shown is an argument at a dinner table; repeatedly, you see Place and others serve food to the homeless and indigent in a church basement. You can't look away from anything. In a performance that echoes Robert Duvall in *Tomorrow* in 1972 and Melissa Leo in *Frozen River* in 2008, across an hour and thirty-five minutes Place's expression barely seems to change, and so it's the moments when it does, or almost does, that might stay with you. Place sits stone-faced in a holiness church while everyone around her is in a trance of deliverance; in the kind of bar where they never take down the Christmas lights, she drinks herself into a resolute oblivion, dancing at the jukebox to Bob Dylan's "Tonight I'll Be Staying Here with You," which in this setting sounds trashier than Leon Russell's "Out in the Woods"; in a displacement of her own son's addiction that seems at once a willed nightmare and everyday life at its limit, she goes to see a man to get shot up with heroin, for the first time, in her seventies, maybe the last time, maybe not, and here, most strikingly, her expression does change. A whisper of a smile crosses her face as the man plunges the needle; it's as if she's gone to see a priest to confess and without saying a word leaves feeling blessed.

10 ■ **Mekons, Music Hall of Williamsburg (Brooklyn, July 19)** Shannon McArdle writes in: "Sally Timms's brown purse plunked in front of Steve Goulding's kick drum, a harbinger that she, the bag, and the remaining seven Mekons would be coming and going a few times during the two-plus hour affair. There was warm teasing and loving surrender in Jon Langford's oral interludes. Just before a more rocking, still reggae version of 'Tina,' he acquiesced: 'Even the setlist has arthritis!' Expression of such feebleness has long been there, far before the

members themselves confessed to any of the personal physical manifestations of it.

"When Sally sang 'I Love a Millionaire,' the mordant, mournful
tone—a woman mourning herself and the world, too—'Dreaming of
a creature who is too pale and large to stand and only feels the terror
of his vain flight from earth'—the words portended a sickness where
they stood now that the band dared to imagine over twenty-five years
ago. Tom Greenhalgh presented a more personal exploration of what
plagues us currently, collectively. 'Father, father, dig my grave, for I am
pickled, I am done / Upon my hand, a velvet glove to show them all I
died for love,' he implored, studying his open hand in the air, not one
star in sight."

Los Angeles Review of Books

2019·2021

August 23, 2019

1 ▪ Lana Del Rey, "Looking for America" (Interscope) This airy, at times almost a cappella ballad is being called a protest song about the massacres in Gilroy, El Paso, and Dayton. I'd call it a song of refusal, and what makes it go in like a knife in the heart is the specificity of place—the way the singer floats over Fresno or Lake Placid, looking down as if they could be wiped out in an instant, if they haven't been already. "It was quite the scenic drive"—the cynicism in the way she tosses off the line carries the whole sense of what the whole country has surrendered.

2 ▪ Sleater-Kinney, *The Center Won't Hold* (Mom + Pop) It makes too much sense that after twenty-two years drummer Janet Weiss, the center of the band, quit. She's here, and you can hear her being told what to do. It's a producer's record; everything sounds like a special effect.

3 ▪ Peggy Sue Gerron and Glenda Cameron, *Whatever Happened to Peggy Sue?* (Togi Entertainment, 2007) She died last year; at eighteen in Lubbock, Texas, she let Buddy Holly's drummer Jerry Allison bully her into marrying him. Holly met Maria Elena Santiago in New York and proposed to her on their first date. And then Holly tells Peggy Sue that he's getting a divorce and she should too, since they should have married each other. Then he dies and she has to go on living.

4 ▪ Bill Wyman writes in "So I'm several hundred miles south of Darwin, Australia, hanging out in a park with an Aboriginal guide, who's telling our small tour group about her family's ancient lands and taking us back several generations in her family line. Her grandfather was a noted person, she tells us—a fierce activist for Aboriginal rights and a noted author. Turns out he was also white. At a certain point she gets to her own parents, and shows us a picture of her dad.

"'Everyone called him Elvis; I don't know why,' she says.

"'Wait a minute,' I say. 'You don't know who Elvis is?'

"'Well, yes,' she says.

"'But you don't know why someone would call him Elvis?'

"'No,' she said, sincerely.

"'Maybe because he's incredibly handsome and is riding a fucking alligator looking like Marlon Brando in *The Wild One?'*

"She shrugged. 'I thought it was because of his hair.'"

5 ▪ Quentin Tarantino, *Once Upon a Time in . . . Hollywood* (Sony Pictures) Los Angeles, 1969—when, according to this movie, there wasn't a single good song on the radio. When well into more than half-way through the Rolling Stones' 1966 "Out of Time" comes on—not playing via the agency of any character, just dropped over a scene—the relief is like a wave that started in Japan coming down on the beach at San Pedro. Then it's back to the sludge.

6 ▪ Geoff Dyer, *"Broadsword Calling Danny Boy"—Watching "Where Eagles Dare"* (Pantheon, 2018) Step by step through the greatest action movie ever made, with Richard Burton and Clint Eastwood behind German lines and passing as Nazi soldiers "so fluent in German that it sounds indistinguishable from English."

7 ▪ Robbie Robertson, *Sinematic* (UMe) The accompaniment, both by other musicians and other singers, is restrained and subtle, almost spectral—except on "I Hear You Paint Houses," a hit-man duet with Van Morrison where by the end Robertson, barely a singer, and Morrison, perhaps the purest singer of the last sixty years, are intersecting with each other within single words, with Morrison sounding like himself and Robertson like a character who's listed in small type in the cast of a 1950s noir. That allows the best songs—"Dead End Kid," where Robertson's own background as a teenager on the fringes of the Toronto Jewish mob is the background, or "The Shadow," starring (both on the 1930s radio show and here) Lamont Cranston and Orson Welles—to breathe and move. But ultimately the album comes down to "Once Were Brothers," from the documentary *Once Were Brothers: Robbie Robertson and the Band,* an adaptation of Roberston's 2017 autobiography, *Testimony,* premiering next month at the Toronto Film Festival.

In *Testimony,* Robertson recounts his discovery of a brotherhood within the brotherhood of the Band: Levon Helm, Rick Danko, and

Richard Manuel were all using junk, creating a closed circle that shut Garth Hudson and Robertson out. With "Once Were Brothers," the Protestant-funeral-procession cadence carries the story but allows you to forget the music; it's something Robertson, as a singer, or more completely a witness to his own tale, can pace himself to. The song starts out harsh—"Once were brothers/Brothers no more . . . There'll be no revival/There'll be no encore"—and there shouldn't be, the song says, even if we were all here for it: "We lost our connection/After the war." As the song approaches the middle-eight, with both the music and Robertson pressing down just slightly, but enough to let you feel as if something is about to change, there's a feeling of suspense. The war Robertson is talking about is a civil war, with the Civil War draped over it: "We already had it out/Between the north and south/When we heard all the lies/Coming out of your mouth"—with who *you* is left to the listener. Levon, lying to Robertson about heroin? Naysayers, whoever they might be? Robertson, lying to himself? The whole idea of the Band? Or whoever loves their music?

8 ▪ Erica L. Green and Stacy Cowley, "For-Profit Failure Clouds Education Dept.," *New York Times* **(July 24)** Randy Newman has made no secret of his delight in licensing: "I sold it to toothpaste companies, mule-packing teams," he once said of his "I Love to See You Smile," from the 1989 movie *Parenthood.* I wonder if he got paid for the cover of "You've Got a Friend in Me," from the 1995 *Toy Story,* recently put out by a lawyer for the Dream Center Education Holdings college chain, which despite the best efforts of Betsy DeVos and Co. collapsed in January: "We've got a friend in Trump . . . Too many regs, were way too tough/After so many years/We'd just had enough, but/Now, we've got a friend in Trump."

9 ▪ Andrew Shaffer, *Hope Rides Again: An Obama Biden Mystery* **(Quirk Books)** It's March 2019, just a little more than a month before Joe Biden announced his candidacy for the Democratic nomination. He's almost but not quite made up his mind, and he and Obama are in Chicago for a connection that might help—who turns up dead. The real story, as with *Hope Never Dies* from last year, is in Biden's attempt to untangle his psyche from the awe that overtakes him whenever he gets within a foot of Obama, and if Obama as walk-on-water, even in Shaffer's Biden's eyes, isn't quite believable, Shaffer's Biden is. It's his narrative voice telling the story, all doubts and hesitations, as if you're as trapped inside Biden's head as he is, as if you want to burst out of it and into the light, into the race, as badly as he does. "Forward," he says at the end, looking over the Chicago skyline, thinking about a city still acting out the legacy of slavery. "Barack looked at me sideways. 'What's that?' 'Our campaign slogan, from 2012. Forward. We keep moving forward, even if the current keeps pushing us back.' I paused. 'I'm paraphrasing from *The Great Gatsby*,'" Biden says, maybe thinking of the plagiarism scandal that sank his first run, back in 1988. "I've read it," Obama says. "I suppose you have," Biden says—someday, if only in this series, he'll drop a line Obama can't pick up.

10 ▪ **Richard Russo, *Straight Man* (Random House, 1997)** "I was about to achieve glory, and now I never will," says the hero, a fifty-year-old English professor who thinks that if he acts as if life is but a joke it won't be on him; he's just awakened from a dream where he's starring in the big game. "Someone left a cake out in the rain, I think, my dream sliding away on greased skids, and I'll never have that recipe again. I've always feared the day would come when that lyric made sense."

Thanks to Steve Erickson, Emily Marcus, and Steve Perry.

September 20, 2019

1 & 2 ▪ **Bryan Ferry, Fox Theater, Oakland (August 31) and Bryan Ferry and his Orchestra, *Bitter-Sweet* (BMG)** At the Fox, the music playing between the opening act and Ferry was interesting, and a cue: Little Eva's "The Loco-Motion," from 1962, the Shirelles' "Will You Love Me Tomorrow," 1960, the Chiffons' "He's So Fine," 1963, Betty Everett's "The Shoop Shoop Song (It's in His Kiss)," 1964—a series Sly and the Family Stone's "Everyday People," 1968, closed perfectly. As the show unfolded, a nine-piece assemblage of musicians and singers and Ferry himself picking up a harmonica or sitting down at a keyboard, with spectacular extravaganzas from Bob Dylan's "Just Like Tom Thumb's Blues," which seemed to fill ten minutes without a sense it was even beginning to use itself up, to Wilbert Harrison's "Let's Stick

Together" as a closing roller coaster, what came into view—with "Out of the Blue" yielding to "Slave to Love" followed by "While My Heart Is Still Beating," "Dance Away" moving into "My Only Love," "More Than This" dissolving into "Avalon"—was the performance of a single romantic ballad, all of it finally revealing itself as a version of "Will You Love Me Tomorrow." Each part seemed to make every other bigger, richer. Were you to hear them an hour or a day apart, "Slave to Love" is nothing compared to "More Than This"—but here they were discovering the same language, each a note in a song that's still unfinished. Though his voice could be all silk, Ferry hid nothing of his age— he'll turn seventy-four this month—and that added to the authority he brought to the songs, or the song: not someone who's seen it all, but someone who still knows how much he hasn't fully understood, which is why the songs remain alive, unsatisfied.

Bitter-Sweet takes off from Ferry's cameos in the series *Babylon Berlin*—and his absolutely convincing performance at the end of the second season of a German-language version of the 1974 Roxy Music number "Bitter-Sweet" as it would have been done in a 1929 Weimar cabaret by a singer born in about 1858. Here everything that flowed from Roxy Music comes stepping to a Kurt Weill beat, jerky New York jazz you can imagine being played by puppets, and it feels like the tune the songs wanted all along. Especially "Dance Away": in 1979 it seemed like a mandatory disco number on Roxy Music's dispirited *Manifesto*. Now, as an instrumental over far too soon, it's an unfolding of how many shapes and colors the melody can open up, like Gatsby throwing his shirts in the air.

3 ▪ Tom O'Neill with Dan Piepenbring, *Chaos: Charles Manson, the CIA, and the Secret History of the Sixties* (Little, Brown) Steve Perry writes in: "After seeing the Tarantino movie I reread Ed Sanders's book and then started O'Neill's new one. Here's the strangest passage I've read in a while"—on record producer Terry Melcher using Manson to supply girls for his "executive parties" in exchange for a recording contract; when that didn't come through, Manson supposedly ordered the massacre at 10050 Cielo Drive, where he had once met with Melcher and Candice Bergen, which is old news. But this, from one Bob April, whom O'Neill describes as "a retired carpenter who'd been a fringe member of the Family," isn't: "'That's why everybody got killed,'" April said: Melcher was going to put Manson on ""Day

Labels," his mother's imprint. But Doris Day took one look at Manson and laughed at him and said, "You're out of your mind if you think I'm going to produce a fucking record for you." Said it to Charlie's face.'"

4 ▪ Tui, "Make Me a Pallet on Your Floor," from *Pretty Little Mister* (tuiband.com) From Maryville, Tennessee, fiddler Libby Weitnauer's softly twisting voice makes the sexiest version of this previously done-to-death song I've heard. There's an edge in the vocal: you don't know how this story is going to turn out once the song is over. The rest of the album, with fiddler Jake Blount from Takoma Park, Maryland, on vocals, is fine, but this is harder. "Make me a pallet on your floor"— there's a hint of apology, not come on. "I'm going to my long, lonesome home": as Weitnauer sings the line, she lets you hear that in the language of folk music and blues it sometimes means not peace of mind but death, or that as far as she knows they're the same thing.

5 ▪ David Thomas, *Baptized into the Buzz* (Ubu Projex) A companion to Pere Ubu's recent album *The Long Goodbye.* Included for the colophon: "An Irony-Free™ Book."

6 ▪ Yes We Mystic, *Ten Seated Figures* (DevilDuck) Silent movie gestures: ten people from Winnipeg make a better Alphaville album than the last Alphaville album Alphaville made.

7 & 8 ▪ Shirley Collins, "Adieu to Old England" in Jonathan Coe, *Middle England* (Knopf) As the novel opens in 2010 just after his mother's funeral, Benjamin Trotter thinks of the 1974 recording by the British traditional singer. "If the world had been ended when I had been young/My sorrows I'd never have known": it's a tragic prisoner's ballad that for Trotter strikes a chord of memory he can't still. ". . . Yes," Coe writes, "it was possible to extract this meaning from the words, to infer a story of loss, a loss of privilege, that resonated across centuries, but in reality everything that was beautiful about the song, everything that reached inside Benjamin now and clawed at his heart, came from the melody, from this arrangement of notes which seemed so truthful and stately and somehow . . . *inevitable.*"

The book is about how in six years, with the impossibilities of the United Kingdom voting to leave the European Union and the United

States electing a sadistic game-show host as president, the song will be a screaming headline.

9 ▪ **Lana Del Rey, *Norman Fucking Rockwell!* (Interscope)** One test of a good album is that your favorite songs keep changing—and another is whether one song drops away as another replaces it, or if each song that first drew you to it reemerges to let you hear something you didn't hear before. That's what happens on this record. Lana Del Rey crafts tunes the way Coe's Benjamin is caught by Shirley Collins's "Adieu to Old England": whatever the words, it's the melody that takes you down. Like Bryan Ferry, Lana Del Rey makes atmospheres, and in the slow-motion miasma of her Southern California, where all of life feels like an attempt by people born in the 1980s to escape a past sketched out by pop songs and never filled in, all the street signs are from old Top 40 charts or FM playlists, California Dreaming Avenue, Dream a Little Dream of Me Drive, Crimson and Clover Boulevard, Summertime Street, Crosby Stills and Nash Alley, I'm Your Man Frontage Road, Ladies of the Canyon Cul de Sac, Girls Just Want to Have Fun Dead End.

At more than nine-and-a-half minutes, "Venice Bitch" will stand as this album's match for the Rolling Stones' "Goin' Home," which for what it's worth was recorded in Los Angeles—it begins to fade out after about four minutes, and that's when the real song begins. But it was the swooning "California" that pulled me in first; then it seemed to pale against "How to Disappear" and "Happiness Is a Butterfly," which gets out from under its sappy theme in seconds. Then it came back; then "Cinnamon Girl" (you must be kidding) seemed far more subtle, more faraway, and then "California" was a state I didn't know regardless of having lived here all my life.

Despite changing her name, as has been known to happen in Hollywood and New York, there's no persona; this is no cute Manhattan art statement where Susan Thompson "performs as" the Impossible Dream and then goes shopping as a real person. On *Norman Fucking Rockwell!* there are echoes of Julianne Moore in *Far from Heaven*, Lindsay Lohan in *The Canyons*, Barbara Stanwyck in *Double Indemnity*—the singer is an actress acting out characters in fictions of her own making, feeling her way through what they can barely admit to themselves.

10 ■ Jon Caramanica and Jon Pareles, "What Do Rally Playlists Say About the Candidates?" *New York Times* **(August 19)** Jon Pareles plays the songs and he plays the candidates: his account of Elizabeth Warren's list reads like the bullet-point summary of a Warren position paper. Jon Caramanica would like you to know he's hipper than Cory Booker.

Thanks to Emily Marcus.

October 25, 2019

1 ■ Don Juan, "Gimmie Shelter," Lutsen Resort, Lutsen, Minnesota (October 4) It could have been taken from a particularly bland track on a José Feliciano album—but the soft treatment emphasized the words, they locked into the present day, and in this hotel lobby the song was still somehow irreducible.

2 ■ Faiza Mahamud and Jessie Van Berkel, "'I didn't know we were hated like that,'" *Minneapolis Star Tribune* **(October 13)** Philip Roth wrote this story in *The Plot Against America* in 2004, when it was the early 1940s, the president was the Minnesotan Charles Lindbergh, "the only ones against him were the Jews," and the witness was an eight-year-old boy named Philip Roth. Today it's a twenty-two-year-old Minnesota-born Abubakar Abdi, watching the October 10 Minneapolis rally where Donald Trump denounced the Twin Cities Somali-American community and the crowd joined him with catcalls and jeers. "What if my former classmates were among the ones booing?" he said. "What if it was my former teachers booing?" The show will be coming to your city soon.

3 ■ Jon Savage, *This searing light, the sun and everything else: Joy Division—The Oral History* **(Faber & Faber Social)** In their few brief years before singer Ian Curtis's suicide in 1980, the Manchester band left behind music (*Unknown Pleasures* and *Closer*), images (four young men from a distance, on a bridge under the overcast sky), and countless legends. With guitarist Bernard Sumner as the singer, bassist Peter Hook and drummer Stephen Morris, with Gillian Gilbert on keyboards, they went on to a career of undimmed brilliance as New Order; all but Gilbert have written their own books, following the first, *Touching from a Distance,* by Curtis's widow, Deborah Curtis, and *24 Hour Party People* by the late Tony Wilson of Factory Records. None approach this assemblage of testimonies from musicians, friends, producers, drivers, journalists, photographers, designers, and others. With Curtis missing save stray words from music-paper interviews, in Savage's hands everyone who had something different to say about a story that, it seems, made a poet of anyone who struggled to tell it speaks with a startling eloquence. As with Stephen Morris: "There were arguments. I mean, everybody argues, but we were almost a democracy. You were influenced by your limitations." As with the photographer Daniel Meadows on Curtis onstage: "It was unlike anything I'd ever seen. It was strangely private. He was doing something I suppose a lot of young men sort of do in front of a mirror. It had that private feel to it, made public." Or Bernard Sumner on Curtis: "He had a shadow on his personality that was so dark that I don't think even he could see into it."

4 ■ **Hanif Abdurraqib, *A Fortune for Your Disaster* (Tin House)** From the Columbus, Ohio, pop critic and author of *They Can't Kill Us Until They Kill Us* and *Go Ahead in the Rain: Notes to A Tribe Called Quest,* fifty-one poems, thirteen of them titled "How Can Black People Write About Flowers at a Time Like This" (mostly love poems, almost all of which lack gravity and play on predictable rhythms, you're not surprised by anything they say, until the last one, with changes so hard you're never ready for the next line), three titled "It's Not Like Nikola Tesla Knew All of Those People Were Going to Die," and, as the heartbeat of the book, seven titled "The Ghost of Marvin Gaye" followed by a verb, as in "The Ghost of Marvin Gaye Sits Inside the Shell of Nikola Tesla's Machine and Builds Himself a Proper Coffin," plus "One Side of an Interview with the Ghost of Marvin Gaye" (all answers, the last being "A: anyone who thinks of death as a peaceful place is still alive").

So the book is playful and serious, and you can't always tell—you can't always feel—what's happening when. There are rhythms line to line, but deeper rhythms running through the collection as a whole. In "The Ghost of Marvin Gaye Plays the Dozens with the Pop Charts," the seeming non sequitur "your mouth so wide / all the black people in Detroit don't remember what they parents danced to" becomes the almost literal "everybody wanna make soul but don't nobody wanna chew a hole through the night small enough for a bullet to pass through"—literal until a last line kicking off its ampersand, "& pull each of their lovers into it"—which is still laying the ground for "your mouth" shifting into "your mama" and a stinger you can imagine not even the form could top: "your mama so black she my mama too." But the entire series, the whole conversation, finds its perfect balance, the balance between love and death, only more than fifty pages later. "The Ghost of Marvin Gaye Mistakes a Record Store for a Graveyard"— the kind of mistake a dead man might make, or a person who still uses the word record—is a switchback so quick you barely need a poem to follow it, until the poem does, and you realize where Abdurraqib was reaching all along, but not until he's made his subject fully present, looking at you looking at him: "they burned the disco records / and from the smoke I heard / my mother's voice or was it / that my father once wore / my mother's dresses spun in front of a mirror."

Like a song, the poems here pull you back, to listen to them over and over again, until you can play them in your head.

5 ▪ Avengers at Fine Line, Minneapolis (October 14) West Coast punk: the Avengers came together in 1977 when guitarist Greg Ingraham of Orange County joined singer Penelope Houston of Seattle and others in San Francisco. They were at the center of the scene, and always different. When Houston shouted, "*We are not fascist! . . . Capitalist! . . . Communist! . . . We are the one!*" she made the first three labels sound as eternal, and as mystical, as the last.

With Hector Penalosa of the Zeros, which formed in Chula Vista in 1976, on bass and David Bach on drums, all but Bach in the range of sixty, they did the same this month. Houston wore a black T-shirt reading "Punk Rock Sewing Circle," Ingraham a *REsearch* cover T-shirt showing William Burroughs with a rifle, Bach a black number advertising Randy's Record Shop in Gallatin, Tennessee—you couldn't tell with Penalosa, because his leather jacket was zipped to the neck. There were no visible tattoos to prove that anyone meant what they said. That was the last thing they needed.

Houston and Ingraham's commitment to "Open Your Eyes" and "The American in Me," songs they were performing more than forty years ago—the way they performed how real the songs remain to them—was a little shocking, but "Car Crash" was written as shock treatment. It was epic: like dreaming yourself into the car chase in *Bullitt* and then trying to dream your way out of it.

What is punk rock? It's the fact that Houston and Ingraham still can't play "Paint It, Black," which fell down on their 1983 *Avengers*, which came out long after the band had broken up, and fell down at the end of their set. The rhythms are too complicated, too ornamented. Their timing disappears. It's all wrong. It's not a parody: to them, this song says what they want to say. But they've already said it, in their own language. That they can't play the song is a negative affirmation that punk is a thing in itself; it isn't transferrable, and it's not a translator.

6 ▪ Kim Gordon, *No Home Record* (Matador) West Coast punk: after the Avengers came Sonic Youth, which Kim Gordon, from Los Angeles, formed with Thurston Moore in New York in 1981. Her singing on "Shaking Hell" on their first album, the 1983 *Confusion Is Sex*, could have been an imaginary soundtrack to Ingmar Bergman's horror movie *The Virgin Spring*; what she did with "I Wanna Be Your Dog" could make you think the Stooges had no idea what they were saying when they wrote it. It's as physically present as any music I know.

After Sonic Youth dissolved in 2011, Gordon made two studio albums with the guitarist Bill Nace as Body/Head, and both were far more head than body. *No Home Record* is not. With Gordon leading as singer and guitarist, the harshness that has always been her most convincing tongue amplifies the stop-beat cadences of "Sketch Artist." It feeds the way the scattered vocals in "Don't Play It" burn off each other until a stray phrase—maybe "Don't swing it!"—can feel like a dare. It turns the guitar in "Hungry Baby" into a gun firing tracer bullets and makes the song feel like a hit. It opens up the six-and-a-half minutes of "Cookie Butter" until from line to line in the chant that counts down the music—"I . . . fucked / I . . . think / I . . . want / I was born / I fell" is just the start—you can't tell if you're hearing a confession or a simple, measured *fuck you*, which as no surprise was the title of an Avengers song.

What is punk rock? It's Kim Gordon, at sixty-six, back in Los Angeles, sounding as if she can't blink.

7 ▪ Sleater-Kinney at the Palace Theater, St. Paul (October 15) West Coast punk: guitarists Corin Tucker and Carrie Brownstein formed Sleater-Kinney in Olympia, Washington, in 1994; drummer Janet Weiss joined in 1996 and left this year upon the release of *The Center Won't Hold*, an album produced by the New York musician St. Vincent. With new drummer Angie Boylan, and, at either side at the back of the stage, Katie Harkin and Toko Yasuda alternating between guitars, keyboards, and singing, Tucker and Brownstein gave off an instant wave of glamour, pleasure, and heedlessness. They opened with "The Center Won't Hold," which, as if to prove it meant what it said, felt as if it lasted barely a minute. The stage was dark; Tucker hit a drum pad with a stick in one hand with the other on her guitar. There were no visible tattoos; the clothes were black and shiny. The show broke open with "Jumpers," from the 2005 album *The Woods*; it was huge, as if without boundaries of loudness, speed, direction. "They were so serious," Corin said later of the crowd at the start. "But the first eight songs are so dark—*catastrophe.*"

Some of the newer songs, which on record are decorated, were hobbled by fancy beats; with some you heard contrivance before anything else, and a kind of psychedelic pointlessness. But no lull spilled over. It became a game, wondering who of the five would do what, and when Tucker put down her guitar, picked up a hand mic, and came to the front of the stage like a torch singer—especially with the new song "Broken," accompanied only by Brownstein on a small electric keyboard—you knew you were seeing a band you hadn't seen before. Even if "Dig Me Out," their last of five encore numbers, from 1997, still sounded as if it were being played from inside a collapsed mine—the collapsed mine of sexism and racism, plutocracy and domination, without a word naming anything of the sort—that was no clue as to how it might sound two, five, or ten years from now.

What is punk rock? Carrie from the lip of the stage, to someone pressed up against it with his cell phone in his hand: "You filmed the whole show. How many times are you going to watch this later?"

8 ▪ Aleksandar Hemon, "Why Reward an Apologist for Genocide?" ***New York Times*** **(October 16)** On Peter Handke being named a Nobel laureate in literature: it's not surprising that some people still consider Bob Dylan's Nobel Prize a crime against the Enlightenment. One *New Yorker* writer compared it to the election of Donald Trump less than a month later. Hemon calling Peter Handke, the author of *A Sorrow Beyond Dreams*, *Offending the Audience*, and *A Moment of True Feeling*, a supporter of the Serbian mass murderer Slobodan Milošević, and someone whose record collection, I would bet, includes the likes of *Highway 61 Revisited* and *Time Out of Mind*, "the Bob Dylan of genocide apologists" says more about another writer's contempt for Dylan than it does about his loathing of Handke.

9 ▪ **Hanif Abdurraqib, "It Is an Entirely Different Thing to Walk into the River with Stones," from *A Fortune for Your Disaster* (Tin House)** Especially when the stones are the Rolling Stones and Merry Clayton is taking the third verse of "Gimmie Shelter," because Mick Jagger "needed someone to sing the word *murder* like they were trying to squeeze it through a barbed wire fence without opening a wound on their own fingers"—which is a writer trying to escape a tired phrase with a grace note that only highlights how obvious the tired phrase is. But that's also a writer warming up, then hitting almost as hard as Merry Clayton did: "& when her voice tears at the air on the second syllable of *murder* Jagger whispers *wow* & the song must hold up despite death & it must still be able to sell a car or a sandwich or a war."

10 ▪ **Don't Fret, poster in restroom at Cafe Alma, Minneapolis (September 19)** By the Chicago street muralist, loosely hand-lettered, all caps, in blue, green, red, and black:

> YOUR OPTIONS
> INCLUDE
>
> —BECOMING YOUR
> FATHER
>
> —JOINING THE
> ARMY
>
> —MAKING
> CONCEPTUAL ART
>
> —DYING ALONE
> IN THE WOODS

Which, among other things, is punk rock.

November 29, 2019

1 ▪ "Blues & the Soul of a Man": An Autobiography of Nehemiah "Skip" James, from interviews with Stephen Calt, edited by Stefan Grossman, with an introduction by Eddie Dean (Mel Bay Publications and Stefan Grossman's Guitar Workshop) The Mississippi blues singer Skip James (1902–69) first recorded in 1931; in 1964 blues devotees found him in a hospital in Tunica and brought him north to perform at the Newport Folk Festival, where despite not playing for decades he shocked the crowd with the ghostly curse of "Devil Got My Woman." He was a difficult man who considered himself a great artist and most others pikers or pretenders—and he was a great artist.

The blues scholar Stephen Calt (1946–2010) spent countless hours with him, with the intent of compiling an autobiography; instead he published *I'd Rather Be the Devil: Skip James and the Blues*, a deeply researched book that at times spilled over into near dementia, as if what Calt wanted to say was that unlike Robert Johnson, who supposedly merely made a deal with the devil, James *was*.

By editing Calt's interviews into a coherent and startling narrative, Stefan Grossman has produced a historic and invaluable addition to the story not only of the blues but of the American tradition of radical individualism, a book that despite less than seventy-five pages of narrative can be placed next to Theodore Rosengarten's *All God's Dangers: The Life of Nate Shaw*, a big, indomitable book of the voice of the Alabama farmer Ned Cobb (1885–1973—Rosengarten changed his name to protect his family from reprisals from whites), who would have had a lot to say to Skip James.

"You're talking to the walking encyclopedia," James says at one point, and in tale after tale he brings you into his life, often shaping his stories around lyrics from his songs, not as if the songs are autobiography, but as if they're philosophy lessons. "But you take guys like John Hurt and Son [House]," James said of the two Mississippi blues singers from the twenties who he was often paired with in the sixties, "they're just shaky. A white could tell 'em: 'Go ahead and put your head in that hole nigger,' and they'll cower to that extent."

Calt made much of the people he says James murdered as a younger man, and James does describe one fatal shooting, as self-defense, a death that in his account brought no charges or even blame—it happened at a work camp, and James didn't even leave. But Calt also lied. At one point he takes James's song "All Night Long" as proof that James was wanted for murder in Louisiana, and implies that James hinted that was so. What James actually said is not just a corrective, or, you can hope, the righting of a literary blues crime. In its way, it's another version of the song.

"If it had been just a few Negros like my daddy and myself and a uncle or two I got, this riot"—the Civil Rights movement: James was found the same day the SNCC voting rights activists James Chaney, Michael Schwerner, and Andrew Goodman disappeared, murdered in Mississippi by the Ku Klux Klan—"wouldn't been existin' now: everything woulda been settled fifty years ago. . . . You know, the Southern white folk at that time didn't wanna see the colored fellow with nothin' but a shovel or a hoe-handle or plough-handle in his hands, and a mule to pull it. Some places, they tell me, down in Louisiana there, they made the Negroes pull ploughs. And they wouldn't give 'em no place to lay down; just put 'em in a stall like they did mules and give 'em so many ears of corn. Sure! That was long about 1910 or 1912; I was just a kid when I heard all that kinda stuff. . . . Now, I never did go down there and investigate. If I hadda did, they woulda had to kill me, understand. Just like I sang in All night long:

I'm goin', I'm goin', comin' here no more
If I go to Louisiana mama, they'll hang me sho'

"That's the time this riot oughta been organized," James said. "It should have originated right then. If you speak for yourself, and you know you're right, it's always best."

2 ▪ Dwight Garner, "When Literature Mattered," review of D. H. Lawrence, *The Bad Side of Books: Selected Essays of D. H. Lawrence,* edited by Geoff Dyer (NYRB Classics) Noting that Lawrence died in 1930 at forty-four: "It is curious to consider that Lawrence, had he not been unlucky, might have lived to see Chuck Berry and the Kennedy assassination and maybe even to write about them." So perfect: in a new edition of his 1923 *Studies in Classic American Literature,* following the original last chapter, "Whitman," with the new "Chuck Berry's America: No Money Down."

3 ▪ Duracell Optimum, "Gamer x Toothbrush" (Wieden+Kennedy, directed by Tom Kuntz) In the living room, Asian-American woman holding a remote and jumping all over her video game. What does she want out of a battery? "Extra Life!" African-American man in the bathroom, about to turn on his electric toothbrush: "Extra Power!" But now, with Optimum, you can get both . . . but this ad is coded. As it goes on, she burrows into the sofa, and a huge white smear of toothpaste cream takes over the bottom of the man's face—precisely as if he were a Negro blackface performer from the turn of the twentieth century, his face made darker than whatever shade it really was, and gross white lips painted over his mouth, as with Bert Williams and George Walker, who, to put themselves a cut above the simple white man's blackface worn by Irish and Jews, billed their act "Two Real Coons."

Black people loved it; whites did too. So what kind of cultural memory is being summoned here? Unconscious throwback image retrieval on the part of the ad directors, or the suggestion that black people are already being pulled back to a different time, in the same place?

4 ▪ *Motherless Brooklyn,* written and directed by Edward Norton (Warner Bros.) These days, everything and its mother is called film noir, but noir is more than plot, attitude, and shtick—or rather it's not that at all. Noir is tone, texture, pacing, a matter of walk and talk—ambiance, and a certain sense, not delivered directly, not even something you can name, that the world is out of joint. In *Motherless Brooklyn,* inspired by Jonathan Lethem's 1999 novel but departing from it by a long stretch, this comes from setting, a grimy late-fifties New York that radiates the affection people have for it, from the ratty features of Edward Norton, playing the private detective Lionel Essrog, and from the holes in Essrog's brain, which give him both a photographic memory and the uncontrollable tic that causes him to react to any transitional situation, like encountering someone or opening a door, with a jerking burst of words that sound like something between obscenity and nonsense but are in truth violent word-associations as pointed as puns, or guns.

They must have been hell to write. "I'm sorry," Essrog keeps saying, but nobody seems put off, even irritated—given that everybody else in the film lies, his outbursts come off like indecipherable truths. They pull you in. You wait for the next one. You wonder how you'd handle it if you had the same problem. You worry that if his affliction goes away he'll lose his edge and never solve the case.

Norton's picture has echoing affinities with Carl Franklin's exquisite 1995 film of Walter Mosley's *Devil in a Blue Dress* (down to Michael K. Williams in a version of the Don Cheadle role)—and it may stand as that good. Aside from *This is how the world works, buddy* monologues from Alec Baldwin's all-powerful master builder and Willem Defoe's cast-aside bug of Baldwin's younger brother—as Mosley has written of hard-boiled language, "it is elegant and concise," not didactic and explaining—the movie doesn't slip. God knows Essrog's language is concise, and it shares a mission with the hard-boiled as Mosley fixes it: "To describe an ugly and possibly irredeemable world . . . it is a blunt object intent upon assault and battery." That is how *Motherless Brooklyn* works: Essrog is the only one who gets the joke that the scrambled eggs that jump out of his mouth are really weapons.

5 ▪ Matthew Frye Jacobson, *One Grain of Sand* (Bloomsbury Academic) A 33⅓ book on the 1963 Odetta album, made up of deep-diving and unlabored social histories of five songs, most strongly "Midnight Special" and "Cotton Fields," all based in the idea that as a singer Odetta was a social historian. "Folk songs," Jacobson quotes her from 2007, the year before she died, "were the anger, the venom, the hatred of myself and everybody else."

6 ▪ "2020 Grammy Nominees: Complete List," *Billboard* (November 20) Halsey denied shocker: she's white, she has a lot of tattoos, she has a bullying style, any given song is no more than a marketing strategy—what isn't she doing right?

7 ▪ Gordon Sondland testifies before the House Intelligence Committee (November 20) "Well, the whole thing sort of came back to me after he mentioned A$AP Rocky," he said of his July 26 call with Donald Trump from Kyiv. Kim Kardashian and Kanye West were pressuring Trump to get a rapper out of jail in Sweden, where he and members of his entourage were charged with beating up a man who had annoyed them. Sondland, the ambassador to the European Union, was attempting to talk Trump out of intervening directly—which he did anyway, calling the Swedish prime minister. "You can tell the Kardashians you tried," State Department official David Holmes, who heard both sides of the call, testified Sondland told Trump. "Let [him] get sentenced, play the racism card, give him a ticker-tape when he gets home."

The hearings are meant to demonstrate that when it comes to the interests of Donald Trump, the United States has a private foreign policy. But the lodestar of an American ambassador's memory of a call with an American president about the subversion of Ukraine was the centrality of the fact that, with the entire force of American policy working to serve the desires of two famous people who might give an American president a leg up with black voters, we now have a private government.

8 ▪ Bob Dylan (featuring Johnny Cash), *Travelin' Through, 1967–1969: The Bootleg Series,* Vol. 15 (Columbia Legacy) The two discs of material with Cash are poor; the real stories are in the disc of outtakes from *John Wesley Harding* and *Nashville Skyline.* From the first, there's a slow, burdened attempt at "As I Went Out One Morning," the song coming across anonymously, as if it's a lost Child Ballad the singer is merely passing on—but the artistry in the piece, the way "my voice" floats into "the center of her mouth," can glide past a listener in the released version, and here it rises to the surface with a slithering delicacy. The portent of doom, of fate in your hands, in the opening strums of "All Along the Watchtower" in a version that can make you feel you're less listening to a song than overhearing it, made me think of *Butch Cassidy and the Sundance Kid* from a year later. Imagine, if this was playing during the bicycle scene instead of "Raindrops Keep Fallin' on My Head," then with the words "two riders were approaching" fading into your head, as the movie goes on, into the Pinkertons who follow Butch and Sundance even to South America. There's no such drama in takes on "Peggy Day," "One More Night," "Tell Me That It Isn't True," "Country Pie"—this could be a Brill Building songwriter banging out Bobby Vee B-sides, with "Lay Lady Lay" and "I Threw It All Away" A-sides for Elvis or Tom Jones.

9 ▪ Freakwater, "Sway," on *Too Late to Pray: Defiant Chicago Roots* (Bloodshot) Twenty-two acts fill this twenty-fifth anniversary celebration of the back-alley Second City country label, and the lithe, long-lasting combo of Catherine Irwin and Janet Beveridge Bean—

here just a banjo and two voices—step past even Big Sadie, Kelly Hogan, and the Handsome Family. "Should the days of solitude run into years," the late Nick Tosches once wrote about the notion of being stranded on a desert island with nothing to listen to but the Rolling Stones' *Sticky Fingers,* "I might even figure out the lyrics to 'Sway.'" Even though you can hear the words the women are singing, there's a damning bluegrass dip in the melody as Irwin plays that takes the song all the way back to what you don't want to know.

10 ■ **Nell Zink, *Doxology* (Ecco)** This is a coyly written, hateful novel about how some people are better than others. But when you start off making a joke out of one lead character's mother dropping dead at a college picnic ("The students mimed heartbreak while her husband mimed CPR"), or have another character who "personally had first heard of John Lennon the day he died" play "post-sensitive" while doing an inside-baseball mental jigsaw puzzle over Mark Chapman, it's kind of hard to convince the reader you're serious that the death of your idiot savant pop star the first time he tries heroin is some kind of tragedy that casts a shadow of inspiration and legacy over everybody else. Even if it happened on the day of the terrorist attacks in 2001, the cheapest touch of all.

December 27, 2019

1 ■ **Rachel Harrison, "Life Hack," Whitney Museum of American Art, New York (through January 12)** As a sculptor, Harrison is playful, tough, funny, a visually promiscuous found-object maven whose aesthetic is rooted in the double-take. This vast, full-floor show breaks out all the way in the last gallery, with an untitled circular grouping of twelve big pieces which often—especially a huge pink green and white mottled rectangle named *Al Gore*—loom up like the Neolithic standing stones you can still see in Brittany, the Orkney Islands, or the Isle of Skye. With among the others *I'm with Stupid, Panama Papers, Life on Mars,* and *Sculpture with Hot Sauce,* and a circle of forty-four folding chairs facing outward, this is Harrison's Stonehenge.

2 ▪ Sasha Frere-Jones, "New as Foam, Old as Rock: The Music Criticism of Ian Penman" (*Bookforum*, December–January 2020) A review of the U.K. critic's essays on James Brown, John Fahey, Elvis Presley, Donald Fagen, Charlie Parker, Prince, and Frank Sinatra. It could not be more fulsome, and I'm looking forward to finding the book, but from what Frere-Jones quotes from Penman I doubt I'm going to find anything as good as his own "With Nelson Riddle's string arrangements, Sinatra found the heartache in every dream home and then sang the doors shut."

3 ▪ Tony Conrad, *Writings*, edited by Constance DeJong and Andrew Lampert (Primary Information) Conrad (1940–2016) was a New York drone musician, a filmmaker, and much more—over the years he moved from the Theater of Eternal Music (aka the Dream Syndicate) to the Primitives (with Lou Reed and John Cale) to work with Jim O'Rourke, Faust, and Animal Collective. But from the time he was twenty-one into this decade, he wrote, and what he wrote—collected in a compact, quietly elegant volume, nearly six hundred pages that in your hand feels like something much more modest—is unparalleled in postwar arts criticism for its lack of affect, its clarity, and a coolly surprised humor that seems to run beneath every line.

Revelations are everywhere. I went to "Sacred Harp Heterophony" (from 2003, and like much here previously unpublished) almost randomly, and after Conrad's invocation of Orwell's *Nineteen Eighty-Four* "SLAVERY IS FREEDOM / FREEDOM IS SLAVERY" found an account of how Louis XIV invented both the modern state and modern music. The tool was the centralization of administrative power and the nationalization of taxes, thus turning directorates into provinces, which led directly to the erasure of the ancient practice of heterophony, where, as in the Sacred Harp music of the American South in the nineteenth century, many voices sang their own tunes at the same time, and its replacement with homophony, where, in musical ensembles, discipline and a single focus both reflected the new political order and reinforced it, thus instituting an aesthetic order "that was to become the hallmark of genteel Western music, from Moscow to Boston." But in a society with a democratic charter, it didn't quite work: "It is all too easy to transfer one's disciplined attentiveness from one's own feelings and thoughts to the authority of another person—a teacher, maestro, or composer.

Can we be surprised that most black Americans didn't fall for this slavery?—for the classic double bind that is latent within the deepest paradox of composed music: 'You are ordered to express yourself!' 'Be free!'?"

4 ▪ Incident at a Minneapolis Lower School (November) "I turned the gym teacher on to Lana Del Rey," said a third-grader. "He went to the principal and said he wanted to play Lana Del Rey during gym, and she was like, '*No!*' He said, what if he made sure none of the songs he played had swear words, and she said [in a fed-up voice]: '*Fine.*'" "So he went and listened to everything again to check?" "No, he just googled Clean Lana Del Rey."

5 ▪ Henry Rollins and Cyndi Lauper, "Rise Above," the Novo, Los Angeles, December 10 (YouTube) In a black T-shirt, short white hair, and armfuls of tattoos that still look fresh, Rollins kicked off the Black Flag anthem with harsh gestures. In a huge yellow Mohawk, black jacket, and a plaid skirt held up by a square yard of petticoats, Lauper came on as if wired to open current. If one dance went back forty-five years in a time machine to invent punk, this was it.

6 ▪ *Marriage Story*, written and directed by Noah Baumbach (Netflix) It starts out with a hilariously affected, pretentious bit of downtown New York avant-garde theater (soon to go to Broadway!—in some Broadway producer's worst sadomasochistic fantasy of a play closing on opening night). The movie picks up its own cue: in a picture as emotionally predictable as any you've ever seen, there's never a moment when you don't know the actors are acting—when you're taken out of the dictatorship of the film and are living alongside the characters. Scarlett Johansson's actress and divorcing wife is written cold; her role is finished with a supplicating gesture, which makes her human. Theater director and divorcing husband Adam Driver, often a magnet, here never more dour, is written as heroic (he bleeds!). The movie reaches its height when Driver takes the mike at the piano bar where his company hangs out and, in an increasingly mellifluous voice, sings Stephen Sondheim's "Being Alive" for forty minutes.

7 ▪ Randy Newman, *Marriage Story—Original Score* (Lakeshore) Teasingly allusive—to other Randy Newman soundtracks.

8 ▪ **The Band, *The Band: 50th Anniversary* (Capitol)** From the over-stuffed box set (though the full performance from Woodstock that same year is flaming: Richard Manuel hangs the moon as he all but laughs in falsetto on "I don't think I'm gonna *last*" from "Chest Fever"—"*very much longer!*" Levon Helm comes down like a hammer), available on its own, and you don't need it. Where for *Music from Big Pink* the Bob Clearmountain remix from last year found accents and textures that could make some songs sound not merely reissued but rediscovered, here the revision offers a thin, trebly, brittle sound. Single elements are brought out far too strongly, and all sense of "a mutual, joint-stock world," as Ishmael puts it in *Moby-Dick*, describing the essence of the Band's sound more than a hundred years in advance, is wiped away. Second and third voices that in John Simon's original production were all taking part in the same conversations—the Band's version of heterophony—are now backups; what you might have called simply the first voice is now a conventional lead. On Manuel's ineffable "Whispering Pines"—he could be singing asleep, any sense of self-consciousness is that distant—the delicacy and soulfulness of his voice, and the slipstream organ, is brought out as never before. But Levon Helm's singing behind him, or hovering above him, is now stark, intrusive, not as in John Simon's original production the first singer's second mind, his unconscious, or his conscience, but merely half of a formal duet, and here a half plus a half equals zero.

9 ▪ **Paul Solman, interview with Pete Townshend, *PBS NewsHour* (December 5)** "As an artist, I feel very, very lucky to have, what do they call it, a patron. And the patron is my audience. What I do has worked for them and *continues* to work for them. And I want to keep doing it, if I can."

10 ▪ **Martin Chilton, "'Up on Cripple Creek': The Story Behind the Band's Song," *uDiscoverMusic* (November 29)** "Robertson has admitted that the song is not dealing with particularly sophisticated people." Yeah, right. The song is about a trucker and his prostitute girlfriend. Who heard this guy talking about them and voted for Trump.

Thanks to Elisabeth Sussman, Rose Perry, Stan Draenos, and Andrew Hamlin.

January 24, 2020

1 ▪ *Queen & Slim,* **directed by Melina Matsoukas, written by Lena Waithe, with Daniel Kaluuya and Jodie Turner-Smith (Universal)** The black-Bonnie-and-Clyde plot is so oppressive that at one point a character has to step in and apologize for it—after which the movie doubles down to the point of restaging the iconic outlaw-lovers-and-their-car photo.

But the real movie is in its ambiance, its barely shifting tones, the feel for shadows, faces, settings: "There were scenes that seemed lit only by their eyes," said a friend.

2 ▪ **Fran Lebowitz on Toni Morrison in the** *New York Times Magazine's* **annual "The Lives They Lived" issue (December 28)** In the first paragraph, the word "I" appears ten times. Plus one "me."

3 ▪ **Steve Perry writes in on Paul Schrader's "Notes on Film Noir"** (*Film Comment,* **Spring 1972) and Lana Del Rey** "As a description of the way her music admits of no vision of a future, this passage, on what Schrader calls 'the overriding noir theme,' stopped me cold: 'The *noir* hero dreads to look ahead, but instead tries to survive by the day, and if unsuccessful at that, he retreats to the past. Thus *film noir's* techniques emphasize loss, nostalgia, lack of clear priorities, insecurity; then submerge these self-doubts in mannerism and style. In such a world style becomes paramount; it is all that separates one from meaninglessness.'"

4 ▪ **Big Thief,** *Two Hands* **(4AD)** The second 2019 album by the Brooklyn band led by Adrianne Lenker, their second for the tony U.K. label, and like most performers on 4AD—Bauhaus, Dead Can Dance, Modern English, Throwing Muses, the Breeders, St. Vincent, Deerhunter—not really anywhere.

5 ▪ **Drive-By Truckers, "Thoughts and Prayers," from** *The Unraveling* **(ATO)** As an attack on what people who don't think and have never prayed say about school shootings, it's all concept, music and voice, and the concept is a twang so encompassing it turns everything it addresses into corn.

6 ▪ **Adrienne Miller, _In the Land of Men: A Memoir_ (Ecco)** At twenty-five, Miller became the literary editor of _Esquire_, a job she held for nine years. This cool, careful, enraged book about condescension has quiet humor ("I would come to note some regional peculiarities such as the appearance of John Denver in a great number of the stories from Aspen, Colorado"), perfect pitch ("Like so many other of David's most deliberately self-deprecating one-liners, this mordant comment has the character of something rehearsed, rehashed"), and an unfashionable stoicism, especially for someone writing a memoir ("Most people leave no legacies"). When finally the fuse that's been burning under her desk for nearly a decade of literary gate-keeping and risk-taking goes off, you don't even feel as if Miller is raising her voice, only saying what she means, editing out, as was her profession, whatever doesn't need to be there: "What I really wanted to do was write manifestos, organize opposition parties, pick fights, scream obscenities into a bullhorn."

7 ▪ **"Same Game, Different Smokers: A Look at the Tobacco Industry's Footprint on Black Lives and Black Lungs," San Francisco Public Library (through February 6)** Opening with a note that the first African slaves brought to the English colonies in 1619 were sold to tobacco planters, this small exhibition on the marketing of cigarettes to African Americans, curated by Tracy Brown, is full of bombs. You're first caught by Brown's signature juxtaposition: a circa 1830 image of the white minstrel Thomas Rice in the midst of his "Jump Jim Crow" jig, a prancing-knee, arms-akimbo performance that set off the blackface craze that dominated American entertainment before and after the Civil War, up to Al Jolson's _The Jazz Singer_ in 1927, with a 2007 Newport ad showing a band onstage, the black singer jumping in Thomas Rice's shoes, miming his every move as Rice, he said, mimed a crippled black stableman, as his white bandmates gape and point at him as if he's from another planet.

As with the current Duracell blackface ad, this isn't a matter of the ad-maker's subconscious cultural memory: it's the ad-maker's conscious cultural memory playing on the subconscious cultural memory of the people who are supposed to be attracted to the product. But this is nothing compared to the ads, from around the turn of the twentieth century, for Nigger Hair Long Cut Tobacco ("long, curly shreds makes it slow-burning and cool smoking") and Coon Skin Cigars (copy is a poem featuring sexual innuendo between a black couple around "de coon skin," which seems to be both their skin and what they might be doing with their cigars). The images and text may seem quaint, but not Brown's own copy: "These ads evoke the idea of separating pieces from the Black body and ingesting them through smoking. One cannot ignore the connections of this idea to the history of public lynching of Black people as a social activity in the United States, a popular practice at the time these ads were running. One of the many disturbing aspects of the public lynching was the collection of pieces from the body of the human being who had just been brutally murdered by savage white supremacists. Attendees would cut off feet, skin, fingers, toes and genitals and then display them in jars in shop windows or even mail them, along with commemorative picture postcards, to their loved ones who may not have been able to make the 'social event.'

"In addition to portraying humans of African descent as subhuman savage buffoons, Black bodies and the very lives they live are portrayed as chattel or property to be used, exhausted and tossed aside like cigarette butts."

Which is a story you can follow today on signs reading BLACK LIVES MATTER.

8 ▪ **Steve Miller Band, *Welcome to the Vault* (Capitol)** From 1967 to 2016, three CDs of live recordings, alternate takes, official releases, many of them blues, whether "When Things Go Wrong (It Hurts Me Too)" or "Double Trouble," deeply felt and far less than great, plus a DVD of performances, and what they leave behind is the warm sense of a hit-maker who continues to live out an honest career without taking himself more seriously than he might. Even if he means every note he plays in the devastating outtake of his 1970 "Jackson-Kent Blues"—an answer record to two student massacres—he really is the joker he claimed to be.

9 ▪ **Santo & Johnny, "Sleepwalk" (1959) in *The Irishman*, directed by Martin Scorsese, music by Robbie Robertson (Netflix)** For the long Joey Gallo sequence, what always seemed like a dreamy stroll becomes perfect music for big black cars on dark big-city streets. It's the constantly high, piping organ sound, a sense of action within the famous guitar lines that are now mere foreshadowing, that makes the difference—something that was never in the song before. "Just added some sounds," Robertson says, as if reimagining and then remaking a song that has lasted more than half a century was the most obvious thing in the world.

10 ▪ Algiers, "Hour of the Furnaces," from *There Is No Year* (Matador) From a band that in its sound does what Adrienne Miller really wanted to do, utter fury—with a chorus of what sounds like real people having fun making music. For a would-be revolutionary protest song, this isn't easy to pull off.

February 21, 2020

1 ▪ Sarah Vowell writes in (February 11) "I just heard a guy on cable news say that last night at a rally in New Hampshire the Sanders campaign was handing out stickers that say, 'Solidarity Forever.' The other day I heard him asking a crowd which side they were on. I think he's got the posthumous Pete Seeger vote sewn up."

2 ▪ Luke Combs, *What You See Is What You Get* (River House Artists/Columbia Nashville) and "Lovin' on You" on *Saturday Night Live*, February 2 (NBC) In *American Humor: A Study of the National Character*, published in 1931, Constance Rourke wrote about archetypes. So here she is today on a North Carolina country singer: "Like the Yankee in the Revolution the backwoodsman had leapt up out of war as a noticeable figure—the War of 1812; in the scattered western country his portrait had taken shape slowly. Once on the national horizon, however, he made up in noise what he had lost in time. . . . He was not only half horse, half alligator, he was also the sea-horse of the mountain, a flying whale, a bear with a sore head. He had sprung from the Potomac of the world. He was a steamboat, or an earthquake that shook an enemy to pieces, and he could wade the Mississippi. 'I'm a regular tornado, tough as hickory and long-winded as a nor'wester. I can strike a blow like a falling tree, and every lick makes a gap in the crowd that lets in an acre of sunshine.'"

That's Luke Combs, who's also a better Big Bopper than the Big Bopper because he has more than one song (though if J. P. Richardson were alive today he couldn't resist a stab at Combs's "I don't have to see my future ex-mother-in-law anymore" from "When It Rains It Pours"). But while *What You See,* only his second album, ought to be a knockout—the songs are good, Combs knows how to lift a rhythm past itself, when he crosses over the Valley of the Shadow of Death you can believe him—the sound is busy and cluttered, and he feels constrained. Too often the rhythms are guardrails. You have to see him live—and he clearly took the *Saturday Night Live* showcase, so often a setting for the precious, the jejune, the self-impressed, as a chance to say it all. "Lovin' on You" uses the country form of verses full of clack-a-lacka verbiage wrapping around each other with a chorus that brings the song down to earth: on record, Combs tries to break out of the cliché but he doesn't make it. Here the verses were a springboard, a warm-up, and when the chorus came he grabbed it out of the air and launched it as a missile. It was such a thrill it was hard to believe he ever got back to the song, but he did, and then he did it again. The right song, the right place, the right time, ghosts smiling in the background, watching as he did what they did: "Heels cracking, he leapt into the air to proclaim his attributes against all comers . . . as a preliminary to a fight he neighed like a stallion or crowed like a cock."

3 ▪ Pedrito Martinez, "Loco Amor," in *The Marvelous Mrs. Maisel,* Season 3, Episode 5, "It's Comedy or Cabbage" (Amazon Prime) Miami 1960: Lenny Bruce takes Midge to a Cuban nightclub where elegantly dressed hookers take up every seat at the circular bar, dancers prance in what look like voodoo masks, and a singer strolls through the place, flanked by a guitar player as a second guitarist plays with a small combo on a stage in the background. It's a deep, nearly unbearably romantic doo-wop number with blues notes trailing every vocal phrase: transporting, with the singer moving slowly, as if thinking through every beat. The mood seems to pass through: as the night ends, Mrs. Maisel promises Lenny she'll sleep with him before he dies. She has six years to keep her promise.

4 ▪ Elizabeth Pepin Silva and Lewis Watts, *Harlem of the West: The San Francisco Fillmore Jazz Era* (Heyday, 2020) A handsome new edition of a book first published in 2006—page upon page of well-dressed people having a good time framed by a blunt and lucid history of postwar San Francisco as a viciously segregated city. There are almost no white faces here, a testament to how fully people cast into a ghetto created their own world. One striking note among many: five people gathered in front of Rhythm Records on Sutter Street in 1947, behind them a poster advertising Andrew Tibbs's smooth, after-hours 78 "Biblo Is Dead"—a number about the infamous Mississippi racist so slick you can't even hear the sarcasm as Tibbs runs through the "One Meat Ball" melody to tell you how he's not sure he'll ever get over the death of his "best friend." The poster adds a *!* to the title of the record—thus turning the record into news, and a celebration.

5 ▪ New Pornographers, *In the Morse Code of Brake Lights* (Concord) When Simi Stone, Kathryn Calder, and Neko Case weave their voices around each other, they find the sound of a fairy tale that begins with an embrace, a warmth that seems to flood your veins, and that ends with a wave as the three pass over a hill, leaving you behind, but feeling as if life is a gift. There is no sense of realism here; maybe that's what the music is for.

6 ▪ Mr. Wrong, *Create a Place* (Waterwing) And the joy of *this* band—drummer Ursula Koelling, guitarist Lindsey Moffett, and bassist Leona Nichts—is in the clatter their three voices make when they create the ambiance of people walking into each other as if they're birds flying into plate glass windows, as if that's their way of saying, *What's new? Anything happening? You're kidding!* On their second album—nine songs on a 45 rpm 12-inch—the playground shouts of the Slits and Kleenex are still there, but just try to untangle the three friends battering back and forth at each other. "Too much work," sighs one. "So much fun," says another. What's different is the swirl of the rhythm in "Overstimulation"—the feeling you're about to be taken somewhere you haven't been before (you don't get there; you just feel it is there)—and a certain determination to catch the true black humor of everyday life, as in "Holding for Healthcare," where "getting older" (*Your call is very important to us. The average wait time is approximately four hours*) is the last rhyme.

7 ▪ *The Assistant*, written and directed by Kitty Green (Bleecker Street) The last pages before the first pages of "Bartleby."

8 ▪ Bryan Ferry, *Live at the Royal Albert Hall 1974* (BMG) By 1974, Ferry had released his first two solo albums, mostly of covers, with a taste in selection that both delighted and shamed any fan of any of the songs he chose, many of which should have been *un*coverable: Elvis's "Baby I Don't Care," the Beach Boys' "Don't Worry Baby," Bob Dylan's "A Hard Rain's A-Gonna Fall." His approach was loving, heretical, absurdist; he could make you feel stupid, as if you'd never had the nerve to sing along to Lesley Gore's "It's My Party" yourself. Here, facing the crowd, he crafts a version of "The 'In' Crowd" that all but puts triple scare quotes on the word—he makes the scene feel cheap, pathetic, even dirty, and he lets you feel how invaluable it is. But he was born to sing "Smoke Gets in Your Eyes."

9 ▪ "DISCOUNT MORTGAGES," *New York Post* **(February 12)** A grimy-looking half-page ad, with three endorsements: "It's Now or Never," from "Elvis Presley, rock star," "Great Rates and Great Programs" from "Keith Kantrowitz, Power Express President," a mortgage broker and presumably the brains behind this, and "Closing Is Our Business," from "Mariano Rivera, Hall of Famer," also pictured to the side, looking very sincere for "Let me help you SAVE money," with his name and honorific repeated, lest you doubt it's really him. Too bad: Elvis sightings aren't what they used to be. Neither, apparently, are Hall of Fame endorsement opportunities. Or maybe Elvis and Rivera need better agents.

10 ▪ Terry Gross on *Fresh Air* **interviewing Martin Scorsese, NPR (January 15)** On *The Irishman*, but also focusing especially on Ray Liotta's Henry Hill in *Goodfellas*. She plays a clip of a Liotta voice-over: "As far back as I can remember, I always wanted to be a gangster. To me, being a gangster was better than being president of the United States." "And now," said a person listening, "you can be both."

Thanks to Bill Brown.

March 27, 2020

1 ▪ Walter Mosley, *Trouble Is What I Do* **(Mulholland Books)** Walter Mosley plays the blues: as the African-American private eye Leonid McGill talks with a client in his office, he hears music coming through a door. He finds his own eighteen-year-old son Twill, his nineteen-year-old receptionist Mardi Bitterman, and the client's great-great-grandson Lamont, leading on guitar, making a song. "*I'm gone after that rabbit, but she don't wan' none'a me,*" sings Lamont. "*I'm gone after that rabbit,*" Twill answers: "*She don't wan' none'a me.*" "'*They wanna pull my long hair,*' Mardi added in a voice that was from another day, another time, '*drag me down in infamy*'"—and they all break up laughing, if only because it's not likely anyone has ever sung a blues with that last word before. The most acute and dangerous of Mosley's Easy Rawlins detective novels were mysteries of race; the sixth in his Leonid McGill series enters the same territory. He moves out from that office scene until finally a woman descended from a Mayflower daughter and ninety-four-year-old Mississippi blues singer end the tale on their own terms—and with 165 pages carrying less than 40,000 words, Mosley has completed *Juneteenth*, the novel Ralph Ellison left unfinished at his death.

2 ■ **La Serenissima, Adrian Chandler, director and violin, Antonio Vivaldi, Presto movement, "Summer," from *The Four Seasons,* in *Portrait of a Lady on Fire,* written and directed by Céline Sciamma (Lilies Films)** Years after the end of their love affair, Marianne spots Héloïse from the opposite balcony of a concert hall. Both are oddly alone—isolated not only from each other but from the world. The overpowering opening notes of the music are a shock. The camera remains on the second woman's profile: she struggles to absorb the music, to merely listen to it, but she can't. As the excruciatingly thrilling piece goes on, every shade of separation crosses her face: every degree of regret for what can never be recovered. It's not that the music orchestrates or even prompts the response. As you watch, the woman's response expands the music.

3 ■ **Orlons, "I Caught My Jeans" (Cameo, c. 1964)** I was changing stations and caught just the last forty seconds of this, there was no ID, but it had to be them, in Philadelphia, a year or two and a lifetime after they had three hits in the top five and never again, by 1964 just trying to keep up with what everybody else was doing, so it's the lead singer chasing her boyfriend down the street, screaming at him to stop, and just as she's almost there she scrapes against something that stops her as if she's been lassoed: "I caught my jeans! I caught my jeans!" but he jumps on his motorcycle and roars off, the vroom-vroom special effects making the record a cross between their own "Don't Hang Up" and

the Shangri-Las' number one "Leader of the Pack" from the same year as this absolute obscurity I'd never heard before. Then I woke up.

4–9 ▪ Fleetwood Mac Fleetwood Mac (4) was a blues band at the start, and no one before or since ever matched their sound at its most distinctive: light, clean, uncluttered, emotionally and sonically transparent, with a sense that there is a place for every note, if you can find it—a tone that called up fated blues, if you could feel the edge of fate. The guitarist, singer, and songwriter Peter Green (5) formed the group in London in 1967 with the drummer Mick Fleetwood and, soon after, the bassist John McVie; when the guitarist Jeremy Spencer came on to make it Peter Green's Fleetwood Mac featuring Jeremy Spencer, Green cut back and named the band after the rhythm section, which meant as long as Fleetwood and McVie stuck together the band could go on forever, which it has—after Green left in 1970 after a mental collapse, after Spencer in 1971 disappeared into the Children of God, where he remains to this day, after they kicked out Lindsey Buckingham in 2018, after whoever is next is spun off into the rings traced by those the band has forgotten.

But Green cast a long shadow. He survives today as a ruin; he was unique in the history of the blues. His songs "Oh Well," "Rattlesnake Shake," "The Green Manalishi," and "Black Magic Woman" shot through the charts in the U.K., but in his deepest work he took the music to places Robert Johnson would have recognized, but never described. "I just wish that I'd never been born," Green sang in "Man of the World," in his plain English voice, no down-home mannerisms, no drawl, and he could stop you dead with that line, the song going on but you not hearing a thing, frozen in contemplation of how a line that first took shape in the fourth century BC in Sophocles's *Oedipus at Colonus*—"Not to be born prevails over all meaning uttered in words; by far the second-best for life, once it has appeared, is to go as swiftly as possible whence it came"—had traveled the millennia whole until they found a voice that could make them seem at once like words spoken for the first time and the end of history. Even Green's playing seems to have an English accent: clipped, precise, lucid, each line an aphorism, all governed by a sense of restraint, as when after the shockingly loud first note in his almost unbearably sustained, nearly two-minute closing solo in "Love That Burns" he pulls back and over the next measures leads the song into silence. There are many Fleetwood Mac collections where, among Spencer's ridiculously satisfying Elmore

James covers, Green seems to arrive from some blues country not on any map—the most recent is (6) *Before the Beginning: 1968–1970 Live and Demo Sessions* (Sony). It can stop you anywhere: "Worried Dream," "Trying So Hard to Forget," "Have You Ever Loved a Woman." If his most indelible songs aren't here, it hardly matters: what you hear now is that it was all one song, a song no one else could sing.

On February 25, Mick Fleetwood hosted a concert at the London Palladium (7) to celebrate Peter Green, though Green did not play. There was a train full of famous names, from David Gilmour of Pink Floyd to Billy Gibbons of ZZ Top to Steven Tyler of Aerosmith (did he really need to tie all those signature scarves to the microphone at a show that was supposedly about somebody else?) to Pete Townshend of the Who and so many more, who added nothing, and nothing of themselves; the one exception was (8) Noel Gallagher, late of Oasis. Carrying an acoustic guitar, he came on to sit down with a small band for "The World Keeps on Turning." "I know what some of you are thinking," he shouted at the crowd. "What does he know about the fucking blues? Well, you're about to find out." After that it wouldn't have mattered if he'd played "Wonderwall," but he crawled into the song, and every word rang true: "I need her like the sky needs the sun."

Mick Fleetwood was seated next to him, tapping sticks on a block. "Did you learn a lot from Peter Green?" he was asked last year on the *Raised on Radio* podcast (9), and he spoke with an eloquence that you can read back onto any Peter Green song: "Did I learn a lot—I learned pretty much everything as a player. I learned, one, that someone believed that I could actually play—which was a huge help. And he found whatever trigger that was that I could identify with being okay with myself playing. Which is the perfect slot to be suited—a sort of simple, groove drummer, that maybe thought I didn't think I was very *good*, or I thought I wasn't clever enough. And he saw, and had the perfect music, sort of diagnosis for it, which was playing blues, as long as you listen like a hawk, and you know how to swing, and you are on the edge of collapse, and therefore vulnerable—which leads you to empathizing with feeling. It was the perfect lesson that I learned from Peter Green."

On the edge of collapse—that was it. That's what Peter Green reached for, over and over again, and what he left behind.

I never saw it happen. I could have: the band played its first show on August 13, 1967, at the Windsor Music Jazz and Blues Festival in Berkshire, England. But I was there to see Donovan, then deep into his shimmering Pre-Raphaelite period, with a small band at his right, a string quartet to his left—and, to its left, a helipad, where a machine carrying musicians landed and took off throughout his set, which didn't do a lot for the sound.

10 ▪ **Elliott Chaze, *Black Wings Has My Angel* (1953, republished by NYRB Classics, 2016)** Lovers on the run after the big score, with a line a man named Peter Greenbaum could have written: "I was too stinking rich and bloody and scared to listen to my real name."

Thanks to Charles Taylor and Bart Bull.

April 24, 2020

1 ▪ **Chris Murphy, *Vulture* (April 17)** Headline: "Rising Star Bob Dylan Is Back with New Single 'I Contain Multitudes.'" Ending with "Check out Bob Dylan's 'I Contain Multitudes' and keep looking out for this kid, because he seems to be really going places."

2 ▪ **Bob Dylan, "Murder Most Foul" (bobdylan.com)** His first release of self-written music since the devastating *Tempest* in 2012, a seventeen-minute fever dream of the first Kennedy assassination—and really, the true story of this song, before it's barely begun to live its life, to make its way into the world, is in the noise around it. "Rock 'n' roll forms its own society," Dylan said to Ron Rosenbaum in 1978. Here it's as if a single song has done that. The have you heard's. The what do you think's, from all over the world, from people you'd never imagine wanting to talk about a Bob Dylan song. The hundreds of instant and definitive Captain Midnight Decoder Ring analyses of every word, among the most representative tying the entirety of the performance down to its last syllable to (a) a specific online JFK conspiracy lecture (with references in the song to sliding down a banister and Gerry and the Pacemakers' "Ferry Cross the Mersey" deciphered as references to the Jim Garrison assassination suspects Guy Banister and David Ferrie) or (b) the immemorial Masonic conspiracy (with a reference to watching the Zapruder film thirty-three times signifying the overriding significance of the numeral three in Masonic lore—though, maybe because it was just too obvious, the author neglects to mention that in 1965, in

an interview with *Disc Weekly*, Dylan claimed to have thirty-three guitars), each piece completely convincing and all of them dedicated to
the proposition that there is a one-dimensional explanation for anything. The videos of historical footage people have laid over the tune
(clips from the Zapruder film and *Tommy*, photos of Etta James and
Jelly Roll Morton), all of which seem to diminish it, to bring it back to
that one dimension. The cover version that went up on YouTube the
day after the number appeared for free on Dylan's website, and the day
after that a serious publisher proposing a book on the song with a word
count up to 40,000 words and a publication date in twelve months.
Gideon Coe's three-hour April 9 BBC radio "Bob Dylan Murder Most
Foul Themed Show"—"Bob Dylan Bingo!" Coe crowed before turning the litany of performers and songs called out in "Murder Most
Foul" into a hydrogen jukebox where the line "Play John Lee Hooker"
came out as more than ten minutes of "Boogie Chillen" from Hooker
and Canned Heat, Elvis Presley's "Mystery Train" never sounded more
like a miracle, and newsbreaks on the coronavirus cracked the sense
of time of singers calling out to each other from their graves (Presley,
1935–77; Bob "The Bear" Hite, 1943–81; Al "Blind Owl" Wilson,
1943–70; Henry "Sunflower" Vestine, 1944–97; Hooker, 1917–2001;
Larry "The Mole" Taylor, 1942–2019) but didn't break it. A singer barely
two months short of his seventy-ninth birthday reaching number one
on the *Billboard* singles chart for the first time in his fifty-eight years
as a recording artist. Like the release of the Beatles' *Sgt. Pepper's Lonely
Hearts Club Band* in 1967, a one-record pop explosion, where a record
appears and in an instant it can feel as if the whole world is listening,
talking back, figuring it out, and playing with it as if it's a cross between
the Bible and Where's Waldo. In the strange way the song can hardly
be heard once without sparking anyone's need to hear it again, a world
gathering around a campfire of unanswered questions, and it takes
everyone around the campfire to hear the whole song.

   **3 & 4 ▪ Neil Young with Crazy Horse, "Shut It Down 2020" and John
Legend and Sam Smith, "Stand By Me," from *One World: Together at
Home* (Global Citizen, ABC-CBS-NBC, April 18)** When Young gets to the
list of What about the's in the middle of the number—"What about
the animals, what about the birds and bees?" is mandatory, "What
about the bookshelves, what about the histories?" isn't—this repurposed
2019 climate change protest is frightening and absolute: you really can

feel it all slipping away. And when Legend reached the heart of Ben E. King's seemingly inexhaustible 1961 love ballad—"If the sky, that we look upon, should tumble and fall / And the mountains, crumble to the sea"—the song suddenly changed, as if it had never before been sung when you could hear those lines not as a nice romantic metaphor, but as a fact.

5 ▪ Randy Newman, "Stay Away" (KPCC-FM, Los Angeles) When the weary misanthrope says, "Stay away from me," it can feel as if you're hearing him tell his own honest truth. But as a social-distancing PSA this is really a love song, where love is a balm to resignation, and resignation is part of love.

6 ▪ LiberationAsOne, "San Francisco—Sheltered in Place" (YouTube) Set to Radiohead's "4 Minute Warning," a three-minute-and-fifty-five-second bird's-eye view of San Francisco freeways and streets: the car chases from *The Lineup* and *Bullitt* with no cars.

7 ▪ *Hamilton* Original Broadway Cast Zoom Performance, "Alexander Hamilton" (YouTube) With the hit within the hit the "Bay Area Toile" wallpaper behind Daveed Diggs—a very genteel nineteenth-century parlor design by Matt Ritchie and Jorma Taccone—featuring among other Bay Area faces Too $hort, Joe Montana, Angela Davis, Alice Waters, and Mac Dre.

8 ▪ Knnackk, "My Corona," tribute vocals by Kanye West and Kid Rock, new lyrics by Jared Kushner (#Liberate) No reunion, as Knack leader Doug Fieger died in 2010 of cancer, but this homage—

> Ooh, my little pretty one, my pretty one
> When you gonna give me some time, Corona
> Ooh, you make my motor run, my motor run
> I've gotten a lot smarter about this, Corona
> Never gonna stop, in this life you're on your own, I guess

—fully lives up to the sensitivity of the 1979 number one. No royalties to the Fieger estate, though, because the song has been requisitioned on an emergency basis for morale-building purposes under the 1950 Defense Production Act.

9 ■ **Barry Franklin writes in (April 8)** "After a lengthy phone call—replete with the usual frustration—to Apple this evening, to determine how they could possibly sell us an iPhone without a SIM card, rendering it a non-iPhone, and having been stuck on hold several times (where we opted for classical music), I asked the Service Rep if the 'This call may be monitored or recorded for quality purposes' also applied to the music-while-on-hold, because I was pretty sure the first violin, third chair's (on whoever's version of the Vivaldi's *The Four Seasons*) instrument was out of tune."

10 ■ **Bob Dylan, "I Contain Multitudes" (bobdylan.com)** A second new single in under three weeks: set to the melody of Dylan's own "Nettie Moore," from *Modern Times* in 2006, but trading that song's parlor-tune gentleness for a hard-boiled defiance. But only on the surface. The way he sings the title phrase at the end of the last verses, in its tone, its inflection, what the song says is direct: everybody does.

Thanks to Lee Brackstone, Linda Mevorach, Doug Kroll, Cecily Marcus, David Thomson, and Daveed Diggs.

May 22, 2020

1 ■ **Little Richard, "I Don't Know What You Got but It's Got Me" (Vee-Jay, 1966)** "You can only carry 'Tutti Frutti' so far," said Bob Dylan in 1984 (his "We'll remember always" page in his 1959 high school yearbook featured "Margaret Spinelli: forever having her seat changed," "Shirley Zubich: not least, but usually last," and "Robert Zimmerman: to join 'Little Richard,'" as if Little Richard were not a person but some sort of fictional construct, which among other things he was), but heaven help anyone who thinks he or she can go further than this deep doo-wop blues. Requiescat in Pace? Requiescat in Conturbet. He should have lived forever.

2 ■ **Geico commercial, "RATT Problem" (Martin Agency)** First they had the band Europe playing in an office lunchroom. Now it's the creepy eighties hair band Ratt imitating vermin in a kitchen. Next up:

Whitesnake in the bathroom down the hall. "We've played some real toilets lately," David Coverdale says, "but this place is actually pretty clean."

3 ▪ **X, *ALPHABETLAND* (Fat Possum)** When X's *Los Angeles* appeared in 1980, three years after the group formed—singers John Doe and Exene Cervenka, guitarist Billy Zoom, drummer Don Bonebrake—they stepped past every other punk band in town, or the state (the Avengers had already broken up), or the country. There was nothing to match their perversity and bite: the five last notes of the title song felt like a story being cut off at the neck. This, with all four back in the band, could be that first album. The solipsistic, nihilist disgust might be replaced by a refusal that's more social, but "Goodbye Year, Goodbye" is the best song here, big, fast, complex, all bad weather. The record ends with a beat poem by Exene, which you could have found on a 45 in 1957, never mind 1977. It taps into the occult side of Los Angeles: the way that there are still pockets of the city where you can find people living out everything that ever happened there, adepts even of cults of one.

4 ▪ **"Wartime," *Ozark*, Season 3, Episode 1, written by Chris Mundy, directed by Jason Bateman (HBO)** Laura Linney's Wendy may be Lady Macbeth, but there's no stain that doesn't wash right off. Here she's trying to talk a middle-aged dentist into holding his group's convention at her family's new money-laundering riverboat casino at Lake of the Ozarks rather than at entertainment hub Branson. "Have you ever visited?" says the dentist. "It's not just country. That's a misnomer." His eyes light up with awe: "We saw Molly Hatchet open for 38 Special"—and you can't tell if he's more astonished that a band as great as Molly Hatchet was *fucking opening for 38 Special* or that two bands this great appeared on the same bill. As if setting up a murder, Wendy wants to know just what it's going to take to make it happen for her Missouri Belle. "REO Speedwagon," says the dentist, gazing off into the middle distance as if he's just seen the Virgin Mary. She gets it done, too.

5 ▪ **Bob Dylan explains "Murder Most Foul" to John Cohen and Happy Traum, *Sing Out!* (October–November 1968)** "The thing about the ballad is that you have to be conscious of the width of it at all times, in

order to write one. You could take a true story, write it up as a ballad, or you can write it up in three verses. The difference would be, what are you singing it for, what is it to be used for. The uses of a ballad have changed to such a degree. When they were singing years ago, it would be as entertainment . . . a fellow could sit down and sing a song for a half hour, and everybody could listen, and you could form opinions. You'd be waiting to see how it ended, what happened to this person or that person. It would be like going to a movie. But now we have movies, so why does someone want to sit around for half an hour listening to a ballad? Unless the story was of such a nature that you couldn't find it in a movie. And after you heard it, it would have to be good enough so that you could sing it again tomorrow night, and people would be listening to hear the story again. It's because they want to hear that story, not because they want to check out the singer's pants. Because they would have that conscious knowledge of how the story felt and they would be a part of that feeling . . . like they would want to feel it again, so to speak."

6 ■ Guy Trebay, "No Prince Without the King," _New York Times_ (May 11) "'There would be no Prince without the King,' the costume designer Arianne Phillips wrote in an Instagram post last weekend after Little Richard died at age 87," Trebay says, and, while carefully noting Richard's "pompadour adapted from the R&B singer Esquerita," marches dead ahead: "no Mick Jagger," "no Madonna," for that matter likely no Janelle Monáe, H.E.R., or Tyler, the Creator, or a thousand other names you could toss out at random. It's typical of the mindless reductionism sucking the life out of criticism in any field: the disbelief in the notion that there might be something new under the sun—or that God forbid anyone should ever feel as if there were without someone to set them straight before it goes too far.

The dullest question any journalist can ask a musician is "What are your influences?" which means _What box can I put you in_. Run the same game Trebay is playing on, say, Prince's "When You Were Mine." It's a perfect record no one else would have made, but dig between the notes and: no "When You Were Mine" without the Beatles' "I'm Looking Through You" and Robert Johnson's "Love in Vain"! And no "I'm Looking Through You" without Sam Cooke's "Wonderful World" and no "Love in Vain" without Leroy Carr's "When the Sun Goes Down"!

Gotcha! And all it does is erect a screen between you and the object of your delight.

7 & 8 ▪ **Bob Dylan, "False Prophet" (bobdylan.com) and Tom Moon, "Trickster Treat: Bob Dylan's New Song Sounds Awfully Old . . . and Familiar," NPR (May 12)** "False Prophet" is the most musical, the most sung of the three songs Bob Dylan has released this spring, and the funniest: a nineteenth-century Mike Fink brag, from the Colorado River to the source of the Missouri, a drunk standing on a table swearing he rassles with wild cats, sleeps with thunder, drinks the Mississippi dry, and takes the Ohio for a nightcap. As others have done (where do these people find the *time?*), Moon sources the song to a number called "If Lovin' Is Believing," the B-side of a single by the supposedly everybody-knows Sun singer Billy "The Kid" Emerson, now ninety-four—with Jerry Lee Lewis one of the last people still on earth who recorded for Sam Phillips in Memphis when he and others were inventing or discovering rock 'n' roll. "If Lovin' Is Believing" is as obscure as the music gets; Emerson was never famous. He was a fairly colorless singer who wrote indelible songs: "Red Hot" was cool for Emerson and red hot for Billy Lee Riley, "When It Rains It Pours" was a weather report for its composer and an odyssey across more than eleven minutes for Elvis Presley in 1955.* Nobody knows this stuff more minutely than Bob Dylan: "False Prophet" does have Emerson's arrangement, defined by his lurching beat. But it's nothing like the way Dylan draped Gene Austin's 1928 "The Lonesome Road" over his 2001 "Sugar Baby." With that you couldn't not wonder where the magical tone of Dylan's recording came from; "False Prophet" doesn't ask that question. Moon may offer what seems like a reasonable accounting of how "popular music is an ongoing conversation between the creators of the present and those who came before," and of how Dylan has made "tweaks or modifications": "Dylan truncates the form to 10 measures instead of 12." But you can hear *Thief! Thief!* between every line.

If you read through Dylan's interviews from the start of his career to the present, it's striking how consistently he insists that he's "not a melodist," that over and over, often citing specific records and perform-

---

* With the stronger title "When It Rains It Really Pours."

ers, he has built his tunes on songs from folk music and early rock 'n' roll, sometimes speaking in religious terms: "The songs are my lexicon," he said in 1997. "I believe the songs." This comes out in the way that, from high school to now, people playing with Dylan have said that songs they thought were his weren't and those they thought weren't were. The filmmaker D. A. Pennebaker told the story of a few minutes Dylan had him cut out of *Don't Look Back:* in a hotel room after-party, Donovan, in 1965 celebrated and shamed as the latest New Dylan, playing "Mr. Tambourine Man," convinced it was an old folk song he just hadn't found before, and how disappointed Dylan was to hear it. "Most of my songs aren't original," he said to Pennebaker in the moment. "But that is."

9 ▪ *Once Were Brothers: Robbie Robertson and the Band,* written and directed by Daniel Roher (Magnolia Pictures) A convincing film about regret, with thrilling onstage performance footage from their days as the Hawks in the early sixties. Of the talking heads, bandleader Ronnie Hawkins is a firecracker in his eighties; Dominique Robertson, Robbie's former wife, is a savant. You believe everything they say, even if in Hawkins's case the tall tale is his first language. The picture lights up every time they come back on the screen.

10 ▪ Glenn Danzig, *Danzig Sings Elvis* (Cleopatra) Maybe not quite as far back as his punk days with the Misfits, but Glenn Danzig has threatened this record for decades. He falls short, or apart, with Sun rockabilly or well-known RCA material ("Baby Let's Play House," "When It Rains It Really Pours," and "One Night"), but with his voice as full and deep as it can go, on ballads—not the ballad as Bob Dylan talked about it, but straightforward manufactured pop love songs—he inhabits levels of subtlety, doubt, certainty, and despair that Elvis didn't allow himself.

The accompaniment is minimal, a fuzz guitar and backing vocals removed to a faraway, echoey dankness, and Danzig stills the room. "Is It So Strange" is not of this world; it seems somehow suspended between Elvis's death and whenever the singer's might be.

The heart of the music is in the many ballads slipped in as filler on Elvis soundtracks and throwaway albums that now live lives they never lived before, even when you could hear in Elvis's own singing an implicit admission of how little he cared about the songs, or a listener's apprehension of how much the songs wanted more: "Lonely Blue Boy," "First in Line," "Pocketful of Rainbows," "Loving Arms," "Young and Beautiful," which closed *Jailhouse Rock* in 1957—a song it's hard to credit anyone would try again after the way Aaron Neville sent it to heaven in a live performance included on the bizarre 1990 tribute album *The Last Temptation of Elvis: Songs from His Movies*. But "Love Me," played so slowly it's hard to take, could be the one. The bridge— the *I would beg and steal*—so barely varies the song it doesn't actually register as any kind of musical shift. The song is all on one plane, as if there is only one truth in life, as if for a moment someone glimpsed it.

Thanks to Jean-Martin Büttner.

June 8, 2020

SPECIAL ALMOST ALL QUOTATION EDITION!

1 ▪ **Taylor Swift, Twitter (May 29)** "After stoking the fires of white supremacy and racism your entire presidency, you have the nerve to feign moral superiority before threatening violence. 'When the loot- ing starts the shooting starts'??? We will vote you out in November."

2 ▪ **Killer Mike of Run the Jewels, at a press conference in Atlanta opened by Mayor Keisha Lance Bottoms (CBS, May 29)** "I've got a lot of love and respect for police officers, down to the original eight police officers in Atlanta that, even after becoming police, had to dress in a YMCA because white officers didn't want to get dressed with niggers. And here we are, eighty years later, I watched a white officer assassi- nate a Black man, and I know that tore your heart out.

"I'm duty-bound to be here to simply say that it is your duty not to burn your own house down for anger with an enemy. . . . I woke up wanting to see the *world* burn down yesterday because I'm tired—of seeing—Black—men—die. He casually put his knee on a human be- ing's neck for nine minutes as he *died*, like a zebra in the clutch of a lion's jaw, and we watch it like murder porn, over and over again, so that's why children are burning to the ground. They don't know what else to do. And it is the responsibility of us to make this better *right now*. We don't want to see one officer charged. We want to see four officers prosecuted and sentenced. We don't want to see Targets burning. We want to see the *system* that sets up for systemic racism burnt *to the ground*. And as I sit here, in Georgia, home of Stephens of Georgia, former vice president of the Confederacy, white man said that law, fundamental law, stated that whites were naturally the superior race, and the Confederacy was built on a cornerstone—it's called the Cornerstone Speech, look it up, the *Cornerstone Speech*—that Blacks would always be subordinate. That officer believed that speech because he killed that man like an animal.

"In this city, officers have done horrendous things, and they have been prosecuted. This city's cut different. In this city, you can find over fifty restaurants owned by Black women. I didn't say minority, and I didn't say women of color. So after you've burned down your own home, what do you have left but char and ash?"

3 ▪ Lizzie Johnson, Trisha Thadani, Chase DiFeliciantonio, and Kevin Fagan, "Protests, violence shake Bay Area," *San Francisco Chronicle* (June 2) "[San Francisco] Mayor London Breed said city leaders 'feel the hurt and the pain' of those outraged at Floyd's death. But she also denounced people she said were 'coming to our city for the sole purpose of destroying our city.'

"Protestors gathered outside Breed's home Saturday night, shouting and setting off fireworks.

"Breed said the protestors outside her home 'were all white people yelling, "Black Lives Matter." But that didn't bother me as much as the taunting of me coming outside with firework torches in their hands looking like what used to happen when the KKK would show up to black people's houses to burn their houses down.'"

4 & 5 ▪ Eddie Glaude Jr., on *The Last Word with Lawrence O'Donnell* (MSNBC, June 1) and Annye C. Anderson with Preston Lauterbach, *Brother Robert: Growing Up with Robert Johnson* (Hachette) Glaude, chair of the Department of African American Studies at Princeton: "There's an old blues metaphor. You know, Robert Johnson found his sound at the crossroad when he made a deal with the devil. It seems to me that the country is at a crossroad, whether we are going to continue to invest and double down on the ugliness of our racist commit-ments, or we're finally leave this behind."

Anderson was twelve when Johnson died in 1938. "He's been gone so long, over eighty years. I think of saying goodbye to him. Walking with him to Third Street, Highway 61, where he'd hitch a ride across the Harahan Bridge, going over the Mississippi River. I still think of how it felt to hug him. He put his skinny arms around me. His clothes felt starched and pressed. His face felt smooth. He smelled like ciga-rettes and Dixie Peach."

6 ▪ Dina Peone, "The High Notes and Hard Knocks of My Traveling Karaoke Family," *narratively* **(April 13)** Her parents ran a company called Star Tracks Entertainment. She began performing in public at the age of four: "Before I learned to spell my name I was memorizing lyrics and rehearsing choreography. . . . I faked every word on the blue screen, watching the ball bounce in rhythm with the light swelling inside the hieroglyphics." Her father was an adulterer, but even as the family was falling apart her parents still sang together onstage: "Although I had been impersonating my idols throughout elementary school"—her big-gest number was Loretta Lynn's "You Ain't Woman Enough"—"I was still shocked to learn that karaoke could be a medium for insincerity, that my parents didn't mean it when they looked into their eyes and sang, 'There ain't no hill or mountain we can't climb.'"

At sixteen, after her father had been kicked out, she woke up in the middle of a fire. She and her younger sister and her mother escaped just before their house exploded. Her sister was in an induced coma for more than two weeks, she for nearly three months. When she came to she learned that "I was held together by stapled pig skin, cadaver skin, and skin from my shaved head." One hand was missing two fin-gers; the rest were frozen. She couldn't write and a tracheotomy had left her with a hole in her throat and no voice.

After a year most of her voice came back: "Due to smoke inhala-tion, I could no longer hit high notes. . . . I felt resigned to the idea that my vocal range was now limited to songs sung by men." She practiced with a karaoke machine in her family's new kitchen.

For her comeback, "my first live performance as a burn survivor took place under a pop-up tent in a veteran's backyard. It was the summer I turned 18, and my wavy hair had grown back in wild curls."

She sang "Light My Fire."

7 ▪ Joe Biden, speech in Philadelphia (ABC, June 2) "'I can't breathe. I can't breathe.' George Floyd's last words. But they didn't die with him. He's still being heard, echoing all across this nation. They speak to a nation where too often, just the color of your skin puts your life at risk. They speak to a nation where more than 100,000 people have lost their lives to a virus and 40 *million* have filed for unemployment—with a disproportionate number of those deaths and job losses concentrated in black and brown communities. And they speak to a nation where every day millions of people, millions, not at the moment of losing their life but in the course of living their life are saying to themselves, *I can't breathe.*"

8 ▪ Jackson Browne with Bruce Springsteen, "Running on Empty," at Vote for Change, Continental Airlines Arena, Rutherford, New Jersey, October 13, 2004 (YouTube) I stumbled on this looking for something else and played it for half an hour. I've always loved the song, but at a time when the country is running on empty, it felt like a national anthem.

9 ▪ Michael Corcoran, illustrations by Tim Kerr, *Ghost Notes: Pioneering Spirits of Texas Music* (TCU Press) With short chapters and rich drawings covering the territory from the 1920s gospel singers Arizona Dranes and Blind Willie Johnson, from Hattie Burleson's 1928 "Dead Lover Blues" (in 1918 she had shot and killed the editor of the African-American newspaper *Dallas Express*) to the Austin rocker maudit Roky "I Walked With a Zombie" Erickson, ending with Don Robey, who founded the Duke/Peacock record company in Houston in 1949: "Half black, half Jewish, all gangster"—an "entrepreneur whose very name started with R-O-B." "Robey did have a heart, it turned out," Corcoran finishes up. How could anyone tell? "It stopped beating in 1975."

10 ▪ Noel King, "Black Female Lawmaker in Minnesota Worries About Teenage Son's Safety," on *Morning Edition* (NPR, June 2) State Representative Ruth Richardson, DFL-Mendota Heights, on why it isn't safe for her high school sprinter son, Shawn, to run alone in their neighborhood: "You can't do the same things that your white friends do." "If I can't run in the neighborhood," Shawn says to King, "it's like I can run on a track or something. You know, it's not the end of the world." "It is the end of the world," Richardson says. "Because if you can't run in our neighborhood, if you can't walk out into the world, and just be seen as a 17-year-old boy who loves to run, there's something deeply wrong with that." "What do you think the right response is?" King asked later. "To address racism in our country?" Richardson said. "I mean, that's a really big question because, look: you can change legislation, but you can't change hearts and minds. When I visited the site of George Floyd's death, there was a sign that said, SMASH WHITE SUPREMACY. And as I was watching the sign just kind of blowing in the wind—it was on a white sheet and spray-painted with red letters—it was like the answer is literally blowing in the wind at the site of where George Floyd was murdered."

"The systems that we have built within this country have been built with racism at the core," she said. "People talk about our systems being broken. Our systems are working just the way that they were designed to work."

Thanks to Robert Christgau, Jon Landau, and Paul Bresnick.

Correction: In my last column, on the Geico commercial featuring RATT as the "rat problem" in an otherwise nice new house, I hadn't watched it carefully enough. They aren't playing in the kitchen, where I put them: they're in the basement, the laundry room, and the bathroom down the hall. Which I guess leaves Whitesnake in the Porta-Potty in the backyard.

June 19, 2020

SPECIAL ALL ROUGH-AND-

ROWDY-WAYS EDITION!

1 ▪ Alexis Petridis, "Bob Dylan: *Rough and Rowdy Ways* review—a testament to his eternal greatness," *Guardian* (June 13) First sighted piece on the new Bob Dylan double album. Would it make you want to read past the headline? With all conceivable questions erased in advance by trumpets of jubilee?

2 ▪ **David Hepworth, "The Invisible Man," _Q_ (October 1986)** Hepworth opened by contrasting a fifth annual Dylan imitation contest at a MacDougal Street bar with Dylan's own show with Tom Petty's Heartbreakers at Madison Square Garden the same night. At the bar people were "clicking their tongues in disapproval when a competitor tried to pass off Bringing It All Back Home material with a Nashville Skyline intonation—but they were probably having a better time than those who'd paid twenty dollars and more to watch a distant silhouette act out the fiction of his rebirth for the umpteenth time."

He had a new album out but he didn't play a single song from it: "Oh, he found room for Ricky Nelson's Lonesome Town and ancient gospel corn like That Lucky Old Sun but apparently wasn't ready to play Brownsville Girl or any of the other tracks that the American press were dutifully hailing as a Return to Form. (He'd probably read the CBS handout calling Brownsville Girl 'a masterpiece'; all Bob Dylan songs of more than five minutes duration are 'masterpieces')."

3–6 ▪ **Bob Dylan, "I've Made Up My Mind to Give Myself to You," "Black Rider," "Goodbye Jimmy Reed," "Mother of Muses," from _Rough and Rowdy Ways_ (Columbia)** Hepworth is writing from the nadir of Bob Dylan's career—that stretch from _Street-Legal_ in 1978 to the first years of the 1990s, when Dylan reinvented himself onstage as a lead guitar player and went back to the ballads and blues of his first discovery of folk music with _Good as I Been to You_ and _World Gone Wrong_. But his sour tone is a tonic when everything on this epochal album is being drowned out with hosannas—and the middle of this ten-song, nearly seventy-one-minute album is a long trough of dead air.

The rhythms are slack and the melodies cookie-cutter, vague whispers, or convoluted. With "Mother of Muses" the title phrase is out of reach—Dylan can't rise to the _u_ in the third word, the song curdles, and it never takes shape. What could conceivably be an interesting idea—that the Civil War liberated Elvis Presley and World War II set the stage for Martin Luther King Jr.—dies when Dylan is unable to get through the word "Presley" and tries to come back by reciting "Martin Luther King" so heavily he sounds as if he's reading the name off the wall of a public building. Just as music can make a trivial line feel profound, music as weak as that infecting these tunes can turn good lines flat. But here the songwriting itself is off. If "Sherman, Montgomery, and Scott" "cleared the path for Presley to sing," whether they

did or not, they really didn't, because the words aren't real speech: Elvis Presley may be a one-word figure, but the word is "Elvis," not "Presley." (Though the more I listen, the more I hear that the certain
distancing in the use of the last name grants Elvis the dignity he's usually denied, making him an actor, a person of intelligence and will,
not just a phenomenon.) It's the same at the beginning of what will
turn out to be as rich an epic as Dylan has ever fashioned, the closing,
seventeen-minute "Murder Most Foul." The song almost dissolves before it starts with "It was a dark day in Dallas / November '63 / A day
that will live on in infamy"—again, even disregarding the Vincent Price
intonation, it's not real speech. The day entered history, and more
important common memory, as its own day: people say, people think,
"November 22, 1963," so "November '63" signifies less than nothing—
it'd be like saying "Pearl Bay" instead of Pearl Harbor. And Dylan
sounds embarrassed repurposing Roosevelt's words on Pearl Harbor,
as if he can feel how moving the phrase from one event to another di-
minishes both. But "Murder Most Foul" recovers not four lines later,
when Dylan, making his way into John F. Kennedy's deep subconscious
in the instant the first bullet hits him, speaking in Kennedy's voice,
addresses his assassins with the instinctual reaction of the rich, the famous, the powerful: "Do you know who I am?" It's a stunning moment, and it brings you into the song. "Mother of Muses" never recovers,
and, running up to it, "I've Made Up My Mind to Give Myself to You"
and "Black Rider" barely start and "Goodbye Jimmy Reed," a big body
in an ill-fitting suit bought online, empties out before it's over.

**7 ▪ Bob Dylan, "My Own Version of You," from *Rough and Rowdy
Ways* (Columbia)** The album begins with "I Contain Multitudes" and
"False Prophet," two of the three songs released earlier in the year on
Dylan's website; the first seems to fade from its first impression and the
second seems made for the long haul. Dylan has developed an interesting way of singing words placed either at a turning point in a line
or at the end of it, maybe first surfacing as the "I don't *care*" in "High
Water (For Charley Patton)" on *"Love and Theft"* in 2001—where once
he dragged out such words, or honked them, giving Dylan imitators
an automatic hook, now he drawls them with such a delicious tear in
his voice it's as if he's laying a dead hand on the word, and that touch
is all over "False Prophet." Then comes "My Own Version of You":
more inspired, more seemingly emerging out of its own forehead than

either. Like Dylan's exquisite versions of the standard "Once Upon a Time"—on the Tony Bennett ninetieth birthday telecast in 2016 or in 2017 on *Triplicate,* the third (or third, fourth, and fifth) of Dylan's so-called Sinatra albums—the music gathers itself, and as it rides up at the end of a verse, it begins to sway. That back and forth lets you hear the singer telling you what he wants out of life with an earned, pleasurable cynicism, someone whose main pleasure these days seems to be getting something right. And the mood takes on such body that everything seems right, or fated: with the quietly gruff "You can bring it to St. Peter, you can bring it to Jerome," the notion of the founder of Christianity passing the baton to Bo Diddley's maracas player feels sublime, as if history has completed itself.

8 & 9 ■ **Bob Dylan, "Key West (Philosopher Pilot)," from *Rough and Rowdy Ways* (Columbia) and Charlie Poole, "White House Blues" (Columbia)** "McKinley hollered, McKinley squalled/Doc said to McKinley, 'I can't find that ball'"—so sang D. H. Lawrence in 1915, entertaining friends: "He set our brains jingling," wrote one, "with an American ballad on the murder of president McKinley with words of brutal jocularity sung to an air of lilting sweetness." Lawrence wasn't recording, but in 1926 the North Carolina banjo player Charlie Poole put out "White House Blues" in precisely the same spirit, history as a cosmic joke that this time just happened to fall on a president instead of the ordinary Joe who didn't even vote for him, but who now gets the last word: "Roosevelt's in the White House, he's doing his best/McKinley's in the graveyard, he's taking his rest/From Buffalo, to Washington." The song carried over into John Mellencamp's 2002 "To Washington": in the face of the disaster of George W. Bush ("A new man in the White House, with a familiar name"), he couldn't muster the glee.

Dylan doesn't try. Coming off of "Crossing the Rubicon," which comes on strong but is captured by its own cliché, "Key West (Philosopher Pirate)" begins with a chord so light and golden, a reverberation of the spirit, that you're all but suspended in its glow. You don't want the song to move on from that moment, and it barely seems to. When the singer comes in, sixteen seconds later, with the same old lines, just slightly shifted—"McKinley hollered, McKinley squalled/Doctor said, 'McKinley, death is on the wall'"—the balance between tone and pacing is so elegant the assassination from 120 years ago seems present, the event unfinished, a moment in history that is not resolved, that we're still living out. It's a sensation that carries over into the next, final song on the album, beginning with the assassination of another president—not in the first clumsy measures of that song, but as it turns its corner into the playlist for the ages, when the singer knows the country needs to hear the right songs to live up to the violation, the unclosed breach in history that opened when Walter Cronkite announced, "From Dallas, Texas, apparently official, President Kennedy died at 1:00 P.M. Central Standard Time," to live up to it, and, as long as the signal stays in the air, bear the violation away. "Sing it to me," Dylan sings—speaking to Charlie Poole or history itself, and the road of the song opens up.

The song—the arrangement, the performance—seems to hover over itself, moving slowly over its more than nine-and-a-half minutes toward a receding utopia. This Key West has no Hemingway drinking in Sloppy Joe's, no Santo Trafficante bringing in heroin, no Cuban exiles plotting their ninety-mile trip back. This is the territory of the most luminous and least obvious songs Dylan has made this century: "Sugar Baby" from 2001, "Ain't Talkin'" from 2006, "Forgetful Heart" from 2009, "P.S. I Love You"—not the Beatles song, but the 1934 hit for Rudy Vallée—in 2017. An accordion lifts the music again and again. You could be listening to one of David Lynch and Angelo Badalamenti's songs for Julee Cruise—how in "Falling" and "Questions in a World of Blue," notes are held up to a distant light in a dark nightclub, the singer listening for the echo of her own voice.

Here whatever story is being told, whatever old friends and heroes are named, slip away into the moral rhythm of the song, the way it seems to unfold and fold back, unfold and fold back, until the way the singer casually, or with a resignation so complete it brings its own satisfaction, lets "Such is life" hang in the air of the song. In the most distant manner, the moment swings. You might not even have to notice it for it to stay with you, the words "Such is life" playing in your head for no reason, with no apparent source, years later, not the words at all, really, but the mystery in the way they're sung.

10 ▪ Bob Dylan, "Murder Most Foul," from *Rough and Rowdy Ways* (Columbia) The piece never does settle down, pitching back and forth between history and 78s and 45s and tracks off old LPs, even after the singer calls in to Wolfman Jack, the disc jockey dead like Kennedy, dead like Etta James and John Lee Hooker, dead like Marilyn Monroe and Glenn Frey and Carl Wilson and Warren Zevon and Chet Baker and Charlie Parker and the countless others the singer has on his request list, *You do play requests, don't you, and who said I had to get off the line, just write it down, play "Key to the Highway" and "Anything Goes," and I'm just getting started, I'm going to go all night.*

What you might sense—after you've played this record a dozen times, if you do, over a dozen years, if you do, wondering, now, as you imagine doing that, if the person who made it will still be around, if you will be—is a reckoning, someone, or a whole country, or the whole of an era ("I'm a spokesman for our generation," Dylan said in Rome in 2001, when someone asked him about the words "The future for me is already a thing of the past" in his song "Bye and Bye" on *"Love and Theft."* "I'm speaking for all of us"), taking stock. What is there to leave behind? What is it worth? As the singer says at the very end, "Play 'Marching Through Georgia' and 'Dumbarton's Drums' / Play darkness and death will come when it comes"—and if you do what he says, go to YouTube and listen to Jean Redpath sing "Dumbarton's Drums." Her song, like "Murder Most Foul" across its last long minutes, will silence the world around you, and for a minute or an hour you may not be able to hear anything else.

Thanks to Anne Margaret Daniel and Sean Wilentz.

July 31, 2020

1 & 2 ▪ Bettye LaVette, "Strange Fruit" (Verve) and H.R. 35 Emmett Till Antilynching Act, carried by Representative Bobby Rush (D-Illinois) Abel Meeropol wrote "Strange Fruit" in 1937, as part of the campaign to make lynching a federal crime: to pass a law that had been blocked in Congress since 1918. Billie Holiday recorded it in 1939 and made it part of American history.

Bettye LaVette sings the song as if she'd just heard it, out of the blue, and could not but put her voice to it, as if no one ever had. There's shock hiding in the burr of her voice, as if she's seeing what she's singing about for the first time, as if the bulging eyes and the twisted mouth were never quite as real for her as they are now.

This year the House passed Bobby Rush's antilynching bill 410–4; with the backing of 99 members, it was set to pass the Senate in June when Rand Paul put a hold on it (he wanted to make it "stronger," he said, but that was complicated, and—). The bill remains in limbo. There's so much more to focus on: the virus, the next relief bill, federal agents in disguise disappearing people into unmarked cars, but Rush has a record of persistence. He was a founder of the Chicago chapter of the Black Panthers; in 1992, decades after the murder of Panther chairman Fred Hampton by the Chicago police, he was elected to Congress. I will never forget the little item in the paper about his being challenged in the 2000 Democratic primary by a former editor of the *Harvard Law Review.* "What a carpetbagger," I remember thinking. Rush defeated Barack Obama by two to one.

3 ▪ Mekons, *Exquisite* (bandcamp) A socially distanced album, or in Mekon Jon Langford's words "long distance file sharing: Sally and I in Chicago but did not meet up during the process. Tom was looking after his Dad for much of it down in Sussex with only a cell phone. Rico in Aptos CA. Steve played drums in a basement in Brooklyn into a cell phone. Susie and Lu on either side of the Thames—not meeting up as Susie and her husband both had full on COVID. The saving grace was Dave Trumfio our bass player isolating in Silver Lake with a full recording studio so he was the final stop for all the files. I decided to see what I could do with my phone to encourage the others even though I have a home studio in the basement."

What they came up with is stirring and incomplete. "Nobody," with Tom Greenhalgh leading, calls back the despairing isolation of "King Arthur" in 1986—there it was political, here it's a social, physical fact that won't hold still. The song is like its own lost chord, drifting too far from the shore: it's scary. But "What Happened to Delilah" is the other side of the story: quick, a leap, another leap, a punk ring shout, first made of affection between friends, then a sign of community.

4 ▪ Peggy Noonan, "The Week It Went South for Trump," *Wall Street Journal* (June 25) "The real picture at the Tulsa rally was not the empty seats so much as the empty faces—the bored looks, the yawning and phone checking, as if everyone was re-enacting something, hearing some old song and trying to remember how it felt a few years ago, when you heard it the first time."

5 ▪ **Eric Church, "Stick That in Your Country Song" (UMG Nashville)**
Can you be cool and inflamed at the same time? This is Church's
"Born in the U.S.A." written in 2015, recorded in January, released at
the end of June. There's no reference to a pandemic or a man being
slowly tortured and killed in public on an American street, not literally, but you can't not see all or any of that as the song plays. This is
the country turning its back on every promise it ever made, until rage
rolls over every concise, pungent, necessary argument: "Rock me hard,
stop my heart/And blow the speakers right out of this car." The song
gets louder as it goes on, but the real volume is there in the start, the
very first time Church spits out the title phrase, so coolly, so inflamed,
that he puts a silent word on it: "Stick that in your country song,
motherfuckers."

6 & 7 ▪ **Lady A, "Dear Fans" (Instagram and comment, June 11)** As
many have, you can call Lady Antebellum's announcement that they'd
changed their name to Lady A to rid it of the stain of slavery trivial,
and you can say they put the name right back when they sued a black
blues singer who performs under the same name. But the Instagram
comments following the announcement show it was anything but trivial, this being only one of the more articulate responses (the most articulate was "Bravo!"): "Unbelievable! Who exactly are you pandering
to? EVERY LIFE MATTERS!! Go ahead Keep the race narrative alive. Sorry
I was a fan. Not anymore. Ask the DIXIE CHICKS HOW PANDERING WENT
FOR THEM. Good luck."

8 ▪ **clipping., "Chapter 319" (bandcamp)** The art for this precise, short,
withering stomp by the techno-hip-hop-Afro-futurist-whatever-they-
will-not-call-themseves-next trio—Daveed Diggs, voice, William
Hutson and Jonathan Snipes, machines—beautiful as it is (and I don't
mean righteous-beautiful, I mean its digital sleeve art: with flames and
graffiti on a city street framed like an old master it's a perfectly composed image that you can't help but respond to aesthetically, consciously or not) only grounds the music, it doesn't speak for it.
    clipping. is the perfect name for this group: Diggs seems to clip a
split-split second off every line-closing consonant, while Hutson and
Snipes seem to trim their beats from the front, kicking them forward
into the music a split-split second before you're expecting to hear them.
Diggs can rush past his lines—"Fuck the history lesson you know you

know by now," says the man who played Jefferson and Lafayette in the original cast of *Hamilton* ("The fact that we were all here playing the founding fathers and mothers of this country implies a sort of ownership over our country's history that I had never felt before," he's said). He can bring the song to a halt, a cop flashing his lights and shining his flashlight in its face: "Donald Trump is a white supremacist—*full stop*. If you vote for him again you're a white supremacist—*full stop*." The record shows up, says its piece, and leaves.

9 ▪ *Hightown* opening credits, produced by Jerry Bruckheimer (Starz) They use "Vacation" by the Textones (the unglossy, unprofessional 1980 recording of the song Kathy Valentine brought to the Go-Go's) over the opening montage, a portrait of Provincetown, the end of Cape Cod as the end of the earth. You see a utopia of gay bars, fishing boats, transvestites dancing in the street, a multisex Poseidon leading a parade and unfolding his arms as if he's inviting you into the future. It's irresistible, so sensuous you can't take your eyes off of it, so fast in its humor—a bag of shrimp is dumped in one quick cut, a bag of syringes in the next—that the very good crime show that follows never quite catches up to it. But the first season only just ended.

10 ▪ Ted Widmer, *Lincoln on the Verge: Thirteen Days to Washington* (Simon & Schuster) American presidential historian, Bill Clinton speechwriter, and Lord Rockingham in the 1990s band Upper Crust, Widmer throws you into a cauldron of jeopardy and suspense and never lets go. Abraham Lincoln is leaving Springfield, Illinois, by train, with Indianapolis his first of the sixteen stops it will take him to reach Washington, D.C., for his inauguration—if he makes it, if the capital is still there. At the same time, Jefferson Davis is on his own train from Mississippi to Montgomery, Alabama, to assume the presidency of the Confederacy, and if Maryland goes, the U.S. government will have to flee. An assassination plot in Baltimore has been uncovered, but not contained, and in fact Lincoln is facing assassination every time he gives a speech, not that the speeches are hobbled and stiff. In Indianapolis, where everything—whether Indiana too might secede—is riding on it, he compares secession to one of the free-love cults that had been outraging Christian society throughout the century. "The refusal to fall apart in 1861 made a difference," Widmer ends quietly, echoing Melville's daunting "The Declaration of Independence makes a difference," just a line in a letter to his editor in 1849. Finally the book is an act of fraternity, subject and writer as democratic brethren—not that Widmer would make such a claim for himself. "It's definitely about Lincoln," he says of the 13 days 159 years ago, "but some small piece of this story came from the experience of being in a band, traveling around the country between low-paying gigs."

Thanks to J.-M. Büttner and Steve Weinstein.

August 28, 2020

1 ▪ Fundraising email from Mike Pence on Joe Biden's selection of Kamala Harris as candidate for vice president of the United States, as reported in the *New York Times* (August 14): "This is YOUR country, not THEIRS." This is the ruling social fact of life in the United States today. Everything else takes meaning from this fact, or fails to.

2 ▪ Steve Weinstein writes in on June 5 "I don't know if you get these emails from Folkways. I found this one especially annoying in the same way that I find much folk music annoying, in that it just assumes the audience for folk music is white people, disaffected though they may be. Lead paragraph: 'This week we challenge Smithsonian Folkways listeners to do more than listen. Educate yourself and begin dismantling the white supremacist narrative which has deferred justice in our country for over 400 years. The Smithsonian Folkways catalog is abundant with recordings from groundbreaking Black thinkers, poets, musicians, storytellers, and activists, past and present, who have much to teach us.'

"'Us.' If there actually were a young black fan of folk music, and she read this, how would she feel? Pretty excluded, is my guess."

3 ▪ Emma Swift, *Blonde on the Tracks* (Tiny Ghost Records) Aren't tribute albums terrible? Yes, except apparently when they're made by one person about one other person, as in the Nashville singer from Australia taking on Bob Dylan. This doesn't rise to the level of Bettye LaVette's similar project, but her *Things Have Changed* was for me the

best album of 2018 and the best of LaVette's own career—and she released her first record the same year Bob Dylan released his. Here, Swift's precise, slow-moving voice highlights lyrics, making you realize how musical Dylan's own version of, say, "I Contain Multitudes" is—not that what Swift offers is a recital. As she picks her way through the words as if she's walking barefoot on rocks, she orchestrates how the song was written as carefully as she's singing it. At the same time, you can hear how contrived "Simple Twist of Fate" always was, as if it were meant to flatter the singer, to show you what a good writer he is. The song has no room for Swift—she doesn't so much sing it as find herself modeling it. The real transformation comes with "One of Us Must Know (Sooner or Later)," from *Blonde on Blonde,* released fifteen years before Swift was born. In Dylan's own performance, undeveloped, scattered lyrics sung with increasingly terrifying intensity left the song stranded on the album, out of place. Swift somehow reconstructs it. Her high, clear voice highlights each syllable, letting you hear the words form, one seemingly following inevitably from the other, until they feel handed down, fragments of old songs now speaking to each other. And the more you listen, the more you hear Robyn Hitchcock's guitar, never in the way, always on the verge of fading out, making you say, no, no, not yet. As tributes go, it may not reach the gold standard—"When I sing it," Dylan once said of Jimi Hendrix's version of "All Along the Watchtower," "I always feel like it's a tribute to him"— but it's honorable work.

4 ▪ Senator Charles Schumer, D-New York, press conference (August 16) On Postmaster General Louis DeJoy: "So that's why I say we should stamp him with 'Return to Sender' if he won't appear before the hearing. And I might add that it is appropriate to say today. Does anyone know why? It's appropriate to call to tell him he should be stamped 'Return to Sender' today because today is the 43rd anniversary of Elvis Presley's death." Reporters: "What's 'Return to Sender'?" "What's that have to do with Elvis Presley?" "Who's Elvis Presley?" "He was on a stamp."

5 ▪ Beyoncé, *Black Is King* (Disney+) "If you trace back the DNA in the maternally inherited mitochondria within our cells," as *New Scientist* summarizes current thinking about who we are and where we came from, "all humans have a theoretical common ancestor. This woman, known as 'mitochondrial Eve,' lived between 100,000 and 200,000 years ago in southern Africa." This is the character Beyoncé embodies as her latest extravaganza begins, with a bit of Pharaoh's daughter rescuing Moses thrown in. Some years ago I heard a deeply respected and also puckish music writer refer to "Beyoncé, the mother of us all"—I didn't think she was kidding, but Beyoncé definitely isn't.

6 ■ **"To play or not to play the national anthem; Chronicle readers respond," *San Francisco Chronicle* (July 23)** More than 640 people wrote in in reaction to sports columnist Bruce Jenkins's suggestion "that perhaps the time had come for the national anthem to not be played before every sporting event in this country." There were reasoned and fulminating yeses and noes, along with predictable calls to replace "The Star-Spangled Banner" with "America the Beautiful" or "This Land Is Your Land." Others actually rose to the challenge. "The 'Marvin's-late-Marvin's-late-whoa-Marvin-got-all-of-that-one' anthem at the 1983 NBA All-Star game is not walking through that door," wrote Bill Devine of Mountain View. "Marvin Gaye's performance appears to be a once per half millennium experience. I vote with you." "Personally," wrote Kevin O'Brien of San Mateo, "I like the theme from *Rawhide*."

7 ■ **Pretenders, "Didn't Want to Be This Lonely," from *Hate for Sale* (BMG)** Could be a track on the new X album. Or the Pretenders' first album. Or the first X album.

8 ■ **"Your Favorite Rock 'n' Roll, Country and R&B Legends as Marionettes" (Dangerous Minds)** The Glasgow musician George Miller had nothing better to do during his virus lockdown, so he played Punch and Judy with Chuck Berry, Wanda Jackson, Gene Vincent, Little Richard, Link Wray, Buddy Holly (who came out looking exactly like Elvis Costello), and a glorious Bo Diddley. You can't buy them, but you can look, with the figures sometimes in action, most often in their matchbox-like containers, which means you get to see them sitting up in their coffins, as if they're about to stand up and go looking for blood. Especially Jerry Lee Lewis, who isn't even dead.

9 ■ **Allstate "Burger Joint" (Starcom)** In this ubiquitous commercial, which is really a commercial within a commercial, its self-referentiality subsuming any other reality, Allstate "Safe-Drivers-Save-40-Percent" pitchman Dennis Haysbert walks into a restaurant. The host does a double take, then excitedly welcomes him by name: "Safe Drivers Save 40 Percent!" (Shouldn't he have said "Mr."?) The place goes quietly bananas: it's that guy they've seen on TV, in their restaurant, breathing the same air they're breathing, which means they get to breathe the same air he's breathing. "Safe Drivers Save 40 Percent!" "Safe Drivers Save 40 Percent!" "Safe Drivers Save 40 Percent!" everyone says to each other. "That's totally him," says a man to a woman, as if he's just won the lottery of life.

Dennis Haysbert is a big man, a first-class actor with a deep, ineradicable presence, a presence as powerfully moral as it is physical: as President David Palmer in *24*, a great, complex role, as the gardener Raymond Deagan in Todd Haynes's hard, heartbreaking *Far from Heaven*. Nobody in the burger joint—a very genteel, upscale burger joint—sees him as those people, The-Guy-Who-Was-Almost-Assassinated-but-Became-the-First-Black-President, The Guy-Who-Was-Run-Out-of-His-New-England-Hometown-Because-He-Was-Seen-in-Public-with-a-White-Woman, even if they actually did watch him as David Palmer or Raymond Deagan—those people have been erased, which means Dennis Haysbert, even in the fictional roles he's inhabited, is erased, appearing in a little commercial drama as if the rest of his life never happened. BLACK LIVES MATTER really means IN THIS COUNTRY BLACK LIVES DON'T MATTER—and the black lives that don't matter, that in Allstate's commercial never happened, are of a piece with what one Rob Bliss found when this July he stood by a street in Harrison, Arkansas, a Klan haven, holding a homemade BLACK LIVES MATTER sign, filming what people shouted at him as they passed by. "Explain to me why a coon's life matters," said one—an unspoken line in the episodes where David Palmer's cabinet invokes the 25th Amendment and removes him from office, when white kids chase Raymond Deagan's daughter after school and pelt her with rocks. Why does a coon's life matter? Because in a burger joint a guy without a name walks in, and he's been on TV.

10 ▪ Cinder Well, *No Summer* (Free Dirt) A woman from California moves to Ireland to find how folk songs are sung. That transports her back to the Kentucky highlands a hundred years ago, and then a hundred years before that. She opens her mouth and she still sounds like she's from California; a hum rises up behind her, as if the whole murderous tradition is waiting to hear if she can get out of the song. She sings very consciously as a haint: when she says she's far from home, you don't believe she ever had one. So the tradition sits back and listens to see if there's anything here it hasn't heard before. "California?" it says when the record is over. "Where in California?"

Thanks to Bill Brown and Charles Taylor.

September 25, 2020

1 ▪ Eric Burdon, on the use of the Animals' "House of the Rising Sun" at a Trump rally in Wilmington, North Carolina (Instagram, September 5) "A tale of sin and misery set in a brothel suits him so perfectly!"

2 ▪ Robin Wright, "Is America a Myth?" New Yorker (September 8) An altogether vile, intellectually empty little piece about how America never existed—and, given Wright's "fairly explicit Calhounism," as Sean Wilentz writes in, why it shouldn't. It may be a giveaway that Wright—a New Yorker staff writer, not President Claire Underwood—adopts Nazi race theory to press her argument for division over commonality: "The American promise has not delivered for many Blacks, Jews, Latinos, Asian-Americans, myriad immigrant groups, and even some whites as well."

3 ▪ Spoon, "The Fitted Shirt," on the Current (KCMP-FM, Minneapolis/St. Paul, September 12) From the backseat: "Is there nothing to write about now?"

4 ▪ Benjamin Taylor, Here We Are: My Friendship with Philip Roth (Penguin) Benjamin Taylor certainly knew Philip Roth infinitely better than I did. He was, he writes, Roth's best friend and closest confidant for over twenty years: "Wait till you go well and truly to sleep where the body forks. A great peacefulness, yes. But it's the harbinger of night," he quotes Roth, speaking of joining "the ranks of the sexually abdicated." I only had dinner with Roth a few times. But I do know he didn't speak in engravings.

5 ▪ **Cristiano Bianchi and Kristina Drapić,** *Model City: Pyongyang* **(MIT Press)** Soundtrack to this account of Ozymandian capital city architecture, with full-page photos rendered in pastels: David Bowie, "Life on Mars?" To which the book replies: Of course! Aren't buildings life? Even if they look like they were put up thousands of years ago?

6 ▪ **Bruce Springsteen, "Letter to You" (Columbia)** There's nothing new in the sound of the title song from the forthcoming album—if someone were playing it on the street on their phone you'd say "Bruce" from half a block away. What is new is the trust in abstraction in the story the song is telling. What does the letter say? The song doesn't say, and that can suck you right in.

7 ▪ **Early James, "The Night They Drove Old Dixie Down," with the Marcus King Band's "Four of a Kind from Nashville" virtual concert, August 3 (Fantasy Records)** Aren't tribute albums terrible? Especially when they condescend to their material, in this case by enlisting Robbie Robertson and Levon Helm into Lost Cause mythology, as if the Band's song were a statue of Robert E. Lee and had to be pulled down. Which, by gesture, the country singer Early James—if country singers can actually have their records released by the chamber music label Nonesuch—is going to do with this rewrite: "Depraved and powered to enslave, I think it's time we laid hate in its grave / I swear by the earth beneath my feet, monument won't stand no matter how much concrete." If the philistinism of this verse doesn't make you cringe, what might is the fact that regret over fighting a war that deserved to be lost fills every word of what used to be the song as Helm sang it.

8 ▪ *The Harry Smith B-Sides* **(Dust to Digital)** Flips of the eighty-four selections of 1926–34 78s the anthropologist Smith compiled for his revolutionary 1952 art project—as the historian Robert Cantwell called it, his American "Memory Theater"—*Anthology of American Folk Music.* Except when white artists use the word "nigger," as black artists like the Memphis Jug Band were doing with their uproarious "On the Road Again," which for its 1928 beat could almost have reappeared in the Bronx in 1980 as an answer record to the Funky 4 + 1's "That's the Joint" without sounding out of place. Which means you can't hear Uncle Dave Macon's "I'm the Child to Fight," from the same year, which even without the word would still be one of the most outrageous American records ever made, if there were such a thing as America.

9 ■ Hoyt Ming and His Pep Steppers, "Indian War Whoop," from *Anthology of American Folk Music* (Smithsonian Folkways) Again from 1928, and as a Redface example of a white band not only stealing but, by the very act of white people identifying themselves as other, mocking what they're stealing, eminently censorable, though the B-side was "Old Red," which wasn't a reference to Native Americans, so it's included on *The Harry Smith B-Sides*. Which in any case justifies its existence with Jim Jackson's 1927 "I Heard the Voice of a Pork Chop," which you don't even have to hear to have it make your day.

10 ■ News Break, CNN (September 8) "President Donald Trump launched an unprecedented public attack against the leadership of the U.S. military on Monday, accusing them of waging wars to boost the profits of defense manufacturing companies. 'I'm not saying the military's in love with me—the soldiers are, the top people in the Pentagon probably aren't because they want to do nothing but fight wars so that all of those wonderful companies that make the bombs and make the planes and make everything else stay happy,' Trump told reporters at a White House news conference." Great. But you probably shouldn't expect "Masters of War" on the playlist the next time the Trump show comes to your town.

Thanks to Steve Perry, Pearl Perry, and Lance Ledbetter.

October 30, 2020

1 ■ Bruce Springsteen, *Letter to You* (Columbia) An eighties or even seventies Springsteen album with a decades-older self-questioning voice—the best of both worlds.

2 ■ Robert Johnson, *Phonograph Blues* (Pristine Audio) Ten transfers from "ultra-quiet" test pressings prepared for the release of *King of the Delta Blues Singers* in 1961, and a lost mine for anyone touched by

Johnson's music before or since. Listen once, and the sound is most of all familiar, even if there are odd accents, stronger highs and lows: the progression of notes near the end of "If I Had Possession over Judgement Day" is now a flurry. But listen three times, and it's as if you've never heard these performances before. And you hear it immediately: there is more depth in the recordings made in 1937—"Stones in My Passway," "Love in Vain," "Hellhound on My Trail"—than those made just a year before. There is more consideration, more thought, more intent, to the point that, in the right mood, or the wrong one, the intensity is almost unbearable. Once I couldn't turn it off but I had to leave the room. Here the revelation might be "I'm a Steady Rollin' Man," which before could have come across as little more than another got-to-ramble commonplace. Now the line "I am the man that rolls" lifts the singer above the ground as a pillar of air. You can see a colossus watching the whole of the earth unfold before him, half-heroic, half-cursed, a cloud fated to drift forever. And you can imagine it's a deal some people might take, if they could just once speak this fully, and find at least one person to hear them.

3 ▪ **JoAnn Mar, *Folk Music and Beyond*, KALW San Francisco (October 10)** A celebration of the late John Prine. Most interesting: bandmates and compatriots taking up Prine's songs, rising to them every time. Least interesting: the songs themselves, curdling with the cheapest nostalgia, from the unbearable "Paradise" on down.

4 ▪ **Chuck Bromley writes in on *The Harry Smith B-Sides* (September 27)** "I turned on the TV this morning to see the runner 'Harry Smith celebrates 34 years of charity concert.' It was Harry Smith the reporter talking about Farm Aid, of course, but for a second I had an image of an Ur-Woodstock, with Uncle Dave opening and Rabbit Brown singing at sunrise, 'I've seen better days . . .'"

5 ▪ **TK & The Holy Know-Nothings, "Hard Times," from *Arguably OK* (Mama Bird)** A Portland cowboy bar band recording in a theater that sounds like a bar, and after a string of low-key, low-stakes numbers that don't stand out from each other, right from the start the feeling of a never-ending story—as maybe anything that takes in the Stephen Foster song and all songs about going down to the river that aren't about baptism but about murder and suicide take on by right and fate. Plus

an echo of "Season of the Witch," and a lurch toward the chorus that tumbles into the refrain in the Beatles' "I Want You (She's So Heavy)." "When I was lowered onto the cold cement," Taylor Kingman sings as if he's still on it, with yearning horns on the bridge, "I hung my head by the river and prayed my eyes would close." But his prayers aren't answered, and he has to finish the song.

6 ▪ Dave Alvin, Facebook (September 10) "While my beloved California burns to the ground, I've been stuck on hold with the NOT beloved California DMV for the past two hours or so (their website has been unresponsive for at least 24 hours). After about 20 minutes of waiting and listening to the repetitive soft-rock and smooth jazz Muzak, I decided to make the best use of my time by practicing guitar along with the bureaucrat approved, inoffensive yet maddening garbage. After an hour and a half, I'm getting pretty good at playing this junk. Seeing how there are no live gigs in the foreseeable future, maybe I should consider changing musical direction and start recording easy listening, mind numbing pablum to make a little cash in the 'waiting on hold' music market . . . WAIT! Quick! Please someone slap me back to my senses! I may be losing it."

7 ▪ Bettye LaVette, _Blackbirds_ (Verve) Except for "Strange Fruit," the songs aren't strong enough. She's a counterpuncher and they don't give her anything to push back at. All she can do with the tunes is stylize them.

8 ▪ Neil Young, _The Times_ EP (Reprise) If you found yourself in a coffeehouse in Santa Cruz sometime in the early seventies and a sort of stumblebum folk singer with a guitar was doing mostly Neil Young protest songs, "Ohio," "Southern Man," "Alabama," and not really bringing them off, after four or five efforts you'd probably go somewhere else. But a week later, or a month later, you'd remember something odd, a broken riff in "Campaigner," or the slow lilt of the voice in "The Times They Are A-Changin'," and you'd wish you could remember the guy's name.

9 ▪ Peter Guralnick, "Robert Johnson and the Transformative Nature of Art," in _Looking to Get Lost: Adventures in Music and Writing_ (Little,

Brown) "To say that Robert Johnson sold his soul to the devil is to pay him the highest compliment we can pay any artist—which is to say that his art defies explanation."

10 ▪ **Street art, Lyndale Avenue and West 24th Street, in front of Misfit Coffee, Minneapolis (September 21)** On a bright red free newspaper dispensary box, a large white paste-on with a blank, pinkish eye staring out at nothing. On a mailbox a few feet away, a blue-and-white sticker showing a woman with short dark hair, fierce eyes, and a lettered bandana over her nose and mouth: "RESPECT MY EXISTENCE OR EXPECT MY RESISTANCE."

If Donald Trump achieves four more years—and I'd give him about a 75 percent chance, holding his wins from 2016 except for Michigan and Wisconsin, Trump 280–Biden 258: polls don't correct for voter suppression, where, to start at the scene of the art crime, post office self-sabotage, GOP suits against vote-by-mail, falsely invalidated ballots, polling place intimidation, disinformation online and on the streets, could mean a swing of three to five percent—this may be the only dissident form of speech left. Effaceable, replaceable—disable the security camera, sneak back into the long American night.

Thanks to Emily Marcus.

November 16, 2020
SPECIAL ELECTION EDITION!

Written November 12, though when it appears, the country will most likely still be attempting to exhale, or debating what it means that the sitting president fired General Mark Milley as chairman of the Joint Chiefs of Staff and replaced him with Michael Flynn.

1 ▪ **Larry Krasner, Philadelphia District Attorney (October 28)** "The Trump Administration's efforts to suppress votes amid a global pandemic fueled by their disregard for human life will not be tolerated in the birthplace of American democracy. Philadelphians from a diversity of political opinions believe strongly in the rule of law, in fair and free elections, and in a democratic system of government. We will not be cowed or ruled by a lawless, power-hungry despot. Some folks learned that the hard way in the 1700s."

2 ▪ Haim Shweky, "A Hollow Response to a Hallow Threat," forthcoming in *City Journal*, passed on by the author (November 1) On the murder of the schoolteacher Samuel Paty on October 16 in Conflans-Sainte-Honorine outside of Paris: "Free speech does not preserve itself, but is prolonged in the exercise thereof. Inevitably, some will think otherwise. For the moral equalizers, an attack on our institutions is a chance to quickly and reflexively point to *ourselves* as the originators of our troubles, 'reaping what we sow,' evil begetting evil. This comes instead of the natural revulsion to militant illiberalism one might expect from privileged civilians of the freest societies. . . . The tendency to redirect blame from Islamists to their victims might be explained by a deeper kinship: the fringe left denounces the West as rapacious, materialistic, upheld on the twin pillars of racism and slavery, comprised of a provincial populace and imperialistic government. Islamic terror groups justify their rage based on a kindred version of history, adopting the idea of a sinful West to then assume their role as rectifiers. Murder as a response to a cartoon tells us something of our enemies; rationalizing it tells us something of ourselves."*

"*Je Suis Samuel* now holds the place once occupied by *Je Suis Charlie*," Shweky goes on, but after a few more paragraphs the tone shifts. "So let us continue with the hashtag crusades—as if our enemies quiver from our balloons and candles and hugs—lest we show some true outrage, lest we express ourselves beyond 140 characters, lest we remember tomorrow what was the most important thing in the world today. And besides, a new cause is currently trending and has taken its place. Je Suis desuetude. But of course I still care about the dead of Thursday, but today is Friday. And Je Suis . . . Everybody! Beheading is the new black."

---

* Haim Shweky's piece was never published in *City Journal* or, save for this column, anywhere else.

3 ▪ **Don DeLillo, *The Silence* (Scribner)** With a few people gathered in New York two years from now to watch the Super Bowl, Seahawks versus Titans (Seattle by 3—I added that), the digital grid that envelops the globe dissolves. One character starts calling the game to a blank screen, commercials included: *"Wireless the way you want it. Soothes and moisturizes. Gives you twice as much for the same low cost. Reduces the risk of heart-and-mind disease."* "All my life I've been waiting for this without knowing it," says another. The vise so tightens that *"Ere the sockson locked at the dure,"* a line from *Finnegans Wake*, translates itself.

Reading on November 2, halfway through the 116 pages I realized I was getting very tense: I was associating the no-future of the novel with the world as it might be if the next day, as I expected, Trump won the election. It was the impossibility of thinking even one day ahead.

A first review said this wasn't really a book, but a couple of warm-up chapters for a book the writer didn't bother to write. For a novel that crystalizes DeLillo's work since *Cosmopolis* in 2003—his best work, I think—you couldn't miss the point by more. This book is about a world where there will be no plots, no stories.

4 ▪ **Eddie Muller, email (November 3)** "I am attempting to maintain some level of energy. Sanity went a couple of years ago. Half of our fellow citizenry are OK being governed by Lex Luthor."

5 ▪ **"News of the Day," *San Francisco Chronicle* (November 4)** "Cemetery vandalism: Michigan police are investigating vandalism that left several headstones at a Jewish cemetery in Grand Rapids spray-painted with 'TRUMP' and 'MAGA' before President Trump held his final campaign rally in the western city."

6 ▪ **Grzegorz Kwiatowski, email (November 7)**
> congratulations!
> finally it happened!
> hooray!
> greetings from the free city of Gdansk
> to free country
> free USA

7 ▪ Steam, "Na Na Hey Hey Kiss Him Goodbye" (Fontana, 1969/November 7) For one day, on street parades across the country, a new national anthem. "I love that song," Doug Kroll wrote in on hearing the news, "because it is impossible . . . even if you hate it . . . to not sing along."

8 ▪ Joe Biden, victory speech, Wilmington, Delaware (November 7) He came onstage like a combination of Gary Cooper in *Meet John Doe* and James Stewart in *The Man Who Shot Liberty Valance*, either of whom could have delivered the line in the speech, on the past four years, that will linger: "This grim era." Given the campaign to nullify the election, it lingers now.

9 ▪ Lana Del Rey, "On Eagle's Wings," YouTube (November 7) "Folks," Biden said that night, "in the last days of the campaign, I began thinking about a hymn that means a lot to me and my family, particularly my deceased son, Beau. It captures the faith that sustains me, and which I believe sustains America. And I hope—and I hope it can provide some comfort and solace to the 230,000 Americans who've lost a loved one to this terrible virus this year. My heart goes out to each and every one of you. Hopefully, this hymn gives you solace as well. And it goes like this: 'And he will raise you up on eagle's wings, bear you on the breath of dawn, and make you shine just like the sun and hold you in the palm of his hand.' And now together, on eagle's wings, we embark on the work that God and history have called upon us to do, with full hearts and steady hands, with faith in America and each other, with love of country, a thirst for justice."

"I thought I would just give a little version of that as we took a break in the studio," Del Rey wrote a few hours or a few minutes later, under a video showing her recording a cappella for half a minute in what looked like a closet. Was it great? No. Rather than someone singing it was really someone listening.

10 ▪ Andrew Shaffer, email (November 11) In 2018 and 2019, Shaffer published *Hope Never Dies* and *Hope Rides Again:* "An Obama Biden Mystery," each was slugged. The stories of the out-of-office team could be hard to follow, but not the real story: the attempt of Joe Biden to escape Barack Obama's shadow, and his struggle to convince himself he was worth it.

Given that *Hope Rides Again* was set in early 2019, with Biden on the edge of declaring for the presidency but not there yet, I asked Shaffer if he had another one on the way. "I 'hope' so . . . we're talking about it now," he said. "Joe sort of threw a wrench into the plot I had for the third book."

Thanks to Steve Perry.

December 17, 2020

1 ▪ Yard sign, 6100 block of Hillegas Avenue, Oakland (November 8) Designed just like a BIDEN-HARRIS sign, reading:

PRESIDENTS ARE TEMPORARY

WU-TANG IS

FOREVER

2 ▪ Walter Mosley, *The Awkward Black Man* (Grove Press) None of the stories here is predictable, even if the reader might begin to notice how large amounts of money turn up at the end of many of them. The characters surprise themselves. An alcoholic homeless man named Albert ("I live in a hole in the ground," he says, "but I'm not homeless") is picked up by a white woman named Frankie, who hires him as a decoy while she shoplifts ("I won't steal," he says, "but I don't mind walkin' around in a store"). Like the other Frankie, she has a gun and uses it. Unlike the other Albert, he ends up with peace of mind, and $83,000 he's put away from begging on the street.

3 ▪ David E. Kelley, writer and producer, *The Undoing* (HBO) A sleepwalking suspense thriller without suspense or thrills, though Nicole Kidman's hair does give a whole new dimension to over the top. I reread the novel it was based on—or you could maybe say platformed on—Jean Hanff Korelitz's *You Should Have Known* (2014). It's about a well-off, middle-aged woman living out the unthinkable, and even more skin-crawling the second time around.

4 ▪ Andrew Martin, "A Dog Named Jesus," in *Cool for America: Stories* (Farrar, Straus and Giroux) Dialogue—

"Oh man," Clyde said, deliberately shifting the conversation. "Today a guy came into the store asking for a book to give to his girlfriend. He says, 'What's the one about the famous magician? The one with Leonardo DiCaprio?' And I'm thinking, I'm thinking."

"Oh no," Allison said.

"And suddenly I realize what he's talking about. I ask him, 'Do you mean . . . *The Great Gatsby*?' And he's all relieved. 'Yes! Dude, thank you!'"

"It *is* a pretty misleading title," Jake said.

"It should be about a magician," Leslie said. "A magician who hypnotizes women into thinking he's Leonardo DiCaprio."

—that's pretty typical of the attitudes Martin's people use to work their way into a future that barely seems like an idea. Plus a nice invocation of "The old, fake America"—"People in cities." "I should move back to New York and be a brand consultant or whatever." "Yeah, follow your dreams," Jake says.

5 ▪ *Eternal Beauty* (2019), written and directed by Craig Roberts (Samuel Goldwyn) Sally Hawkins goes nuts. Since her whole career is about someone balancing on a knife with sanity on one edge and insanity on the other, to have her go all the way in either direction isn't interesting. The way songs are used in the film is. The blandness of Ricky Nelson's "I Will Follow You" makes it ordinary, giving the characters just a thin layer of believability. The madness around the edges of Beth Orton's "Blood Red River" creeps over everything as nothing on the screen quite does. Willie Nelson's "Blue Skies" can make you think everything in pop music is a lie.

6 ▪ Nobody's Baby, "Acid in Marin" (Spotify) "I don't fucking remember!" This unclassifiable San Francisco four-person combo—I'll call them hardcore tattooed doo-wop, today—starts at the top. Every time you think Katie Rose, with a shade of Grace Slick in "Somebody to Love" in her voice, but with a warmth Slick was never interested in, can't go any farther, she does. But the bass might draw you into a song that under the noise you can barely follow. Or the guitars. And then Rose is back, shouting, *No! Listen to me!*

7 ▪ The Doors, *Morrison Hotel: 50th Anniversary Deluxe Edition* (Elektra) As these now inescapable expensive reissues go, this is very discreet. There are no facsimiles of concert tickets or hardbound art books picturing Doors T-shirts from every country on earth. What there is is the original album as LP and CD, and one disc of outtakes and rehearsals on the two most interesting songs. There is the jazz ballad, "Queen of the Highway"—you can almost picture Jim Morrison composing it, mouthing it to himself as he writes lyrics on a bar napkin somewhere in Santa Clarita. And there's "Roadhouse Blues"—and that, after nine stabs and versions, with at one point Morrison declaiming, as if in an old-man alkie bar in Hollywood where he can be sure no one will pay any attention to him, on the real meaning of roadhouse, blues, and everything else, could go on forever. The song doesn't so much get better as it gets more—grabs more musical geography, sets you down in any town off any highway, and lets you, for a while, feel at home. The song becomes more of itself, wrapping around itself like a snake, tense, scared, and thrilled to be right where it is, where it can say anything, dive into be-bop-a-lula glossolalia, shout "Save our city!" as a patriotic oath. "I woke up this morning and got myself a beer/The future's uncertain and the end is always near"—it's pretentious, but Morrison can make you feel as if you're doing just what he's describing and feeling just like he says.

8 ▪ "Daydream at the DMV," Geico Insurance commercial (Martin Agency/Horizon Media) Guy in his sixties waiting in line but deep in a reverie where he's a biker heading up a mountain with the Troggs' "Wild Thing" coming out of his mouth. "Wild thing/I think I—" he says in his own voice, letting the "—love you" hang in the air, before realizing he's at the head of the line and the clerk, played by Bonnie Hellman, looking about the same age, maybe older, is waiting for him to remember where he is. She stares up at him—way up at him; she seems to be about five feet tall—amusement playing over her face. "You know what I think? I think you owe us $48.50—*wild thing*," she says mordantly. But there's just a hint she wouldn't mind a ride.

9 ▪ *Hillbilly Elegy,* advertisement (Netflix) Glenn Close in an American flag T-shirt six sizes too big and looking mean and indomitable, Amy Adams bulging out of her cut-off overalls and looking *Fuck you looking at?* Absolutely fulfilling the Firesign Theatre on their 1970 *Don't Crush That Dwarf, Hand Me the Pliers:* "Presenting stories of honest working people as told by rich, Hollywood stars . . ."

10 ▪ Uptown Theatre marquee, Hennepin and Lagoon, Minneapolis It went up months ago, the election has come and gone, it hasn't changed: YOU'RE STILL HERE? IT'S OVER. GO HOME GO.

January 15, 2021

1 ▪ Joe Biden, address to the nation (January 6) Against Donald Trump's Capitol Death Trip oration rallying his troops to march on Congress to break the government and burn the Constitution, president-in-waiting Biden gave his most eloquent speech since he threw his hat in the ring in 2019. It wasn't any particular words. It was his tone of quiet vehemence, something that felt stronger than anything said by the destroyer he was facing down. And as Biden spoke—"At this hour, our democracy is under unprecedented attack"—and quoted Lincoln—"we shall nobly save, or meanly lose"—as the news flashed the picture of a man with a Confederate battle flag parading through the halls of the Senate as the tribune of abolition and Reconstruction Charles Sumner looked down from his portrait, and the champion of disunion John C. Calhoun looked down from his, you could hear that same tone carrying Walter Benjamin: "Even the dead will not be safe from the enemy if he wins." But not quite like that. Biden sounded like a real person talking. And so you could hear a real conversation, two people at a bar watching the television overhead, if there were bars where you could do that, one saying, "You know, not even the dead are gonna be safe from these assholes if we let them win." As much as anything that the House and Senate were prevented, in this moment, from putting into the historical record of the country, in both the Puritan and republican meanings of the word, Biden sounded elected.

2 ▪ Wire, *Mind Hive* (pinkflag) Wire is a very old band. They formed in 1976, played the Roxy in London sharing the stage with the most piercing punk combos of the day, and three of the original four—Colin Newman, guitar and vocals, Graham Lewis, bass, keyboards, and vocals, and drummer Robert Grey—are still there. What's so striking is that whenever they have resurfaced over the decades, on a new album, on stage, even if one looks as if he hasn't aged a day and another looks as if he's done the other one's aging for him along with his own, they feel new, as if the idea of the band occurred to them a few weeks before. Their music never feels reprised, never seems to carry its past with it. If you're a fan—maybe follower is a better word—if the music feels familiar, it's because that's a quality you've brought to it, not them. The songs are intricate, spectral, hints, not statements, and you pick your way through them; nothing settles quickly.

That is perhaps more true than it's ever been with the last track on this album, which song to song does not feature a flat moment: a quiet, peaceful, fatalistic mystery called "Humming." It's theme music for any neurotic British TV detective series, whether it's Helen Mirren in *Prime Suspect* or Paddy Considine in *Red Riding* or a hundred others. There's just a wisp of story: "Someone was humming a popular song." But what happens in the music pulls against any story, and then, in the music's argument that peace of mind is what the dead get, begins to suggest one. It's the held chord on an organ, or a synthesizer, with the bass counting behind it, then walking around it. Newman, in his small voice, talking to himself, thinks it over, but wherever he tries to go he's walking in circles: when the band started, they were cheeky enough to have called this "Huis Clos." The song plays: when the case is over and nothing has been solved, no one has been caught, and all that's left is what the body looked like when you found it, you have to go on living. And this is what that sounds like, for the rest of the life of the person who has to do it. You can't think about it too much. You can't dwell on it. You can't sleep. So you paint the ceiling with your eyes.

3 ▪ Charles Taylor writes in (January 4) "When you work retail, being a customer in another store gives you freedom with difficult customers you don't have in your own place of work. I was in the record department of Barnes & Noble just now and there was a guy drawing out an absolutely simple order with the clerk. It's bad enough that he was sputtering on about nonsense without, some of the time, wearing a mask. It's bad enough he said 'good girl' to her when she did something that pleased him. But what really cheesed me off is that this poor kid has to risk her life so this useless motherfucker can order the first Jonathan Edwards album on CD."

4 ▪ Fiona Apple, *Fetch the Bolt Cutters* (Clean Slate/Epic) Arch. And despite the title, for that matter the name of the label, there isn't a whisper of free air anywhere on the record. Though there is, as always, a lot of whispering.

5 ▪ AT&T, "A Little Love Goes a Long Way," January 1, College Football Playoffs, Alabama vs. Notre Dame (BBDO) Among them LeBron James, looking like the nicest guy on earth, people Facetiming each other singing Jackie DeShannon's 1969 "Put a Little Love in Your Heart" all over town. Presumably the message—i.e., what they're selling—is something to do with "communication." But what actually takes place is people all over town celebrating a song, and a songwriter.

6 ▪ Scott Simon, "'The Great Gatsby' Enters Public Domain but It Already Entered Our Hearts," *Weekend Edition* (NPR, January 2) That I-don't-have-to-raise-my-voice-for-you-to-hear-it attitude: "As we think of this past trying and tragic year, we might all imagine some names, many in high places, of those who disdained wearing masks and brushed aside guidelines to hold events when Fitzgerald writes of 'careless people' that 'smashed up things and creatures and then retreated back into their money or their vast carelessness, or whatever it was that kept them together, and let other people clean up the mess they had made.'"

7 ▪ PJ Harvey, *To Bring You My Love—Demos* (Island) *To Bring You My Love* was a harrowing, entrancing album when it was released in 1995, and as it was re-released it still is. But this—with Polly Jean Harvey playing whatever instrument she needs, a fluttering organ, flat, dead drums, and dubbing it over whatever she needed before—is much scarier. The voice can be ugly, an organ like a kidney or a liver, but hanging outside the body. "C'Mon Billy," "Long Snake Moan," "Down by the River," "The Dance"—you can see Charlotte Gainsbourg singing any of them as she walks through the woods naked in Lars von Trier's *Antichrist*, or acting them out.

8 ▪ **Kim Gordon, *No Icon* (Rizzoli)** With a foreword by Carrie Brownstein (catching Gordon's "playfully sinister" voice in Sonic Youth's "Kool Thing," taking the song "like the rest of the band suddenly required an invitation to be there along with her") this is an autobiography in images: photos of Gordon, her paintings, sculptures, album art, gallery installations, bits of writing, full page self-quotes (her indelible "People pay money to see others believe in themselves" from *Artforum* in 1983). There are a lot of performance photos—and performance photos are almost always boring because there are so few moves to draw on. Those collected here aren't boring, because what they depict are not moves but variations on a stance: as shown in a blurry shot from 2008 on the first page of the book proper, a woman in a short striped dress, short-heeled shoes, shoulder-length blond hair, holding a bass, one foot forward, establishing tension, one foot back, as if holding back, establishing uncertainty—from there to the end, the nearly forty-year-story of a stance. That's not a move, that's a novel—and inside that story is another one, a story of abandonment. These are portraits of Gordon lying onstage and singing—rendered best in her own 2018 ceramic sculpture *The Pitch 21*, a woman in a black dress lying on her stomach, legs bent upward, one black, one white, no head. Look long at that, look at photographs, and you can glimpse someone for an instant turning into something else.

Placed all through the book are full-page presentations of Gordon's 2010 "Noise Paintings"—mostly names of noise bands painted in big black letters on a white background ("The Stooges," "Pussy Galore," etc.). What makes them work—what makes them seem almost alive—is that they're also drip paintings, with squirming, dirty black lines descending from each letter like strings for marionettes out of the frame. The most threatening is probably the one that looks most like an accident, or a mistake, or an artist giving up and throwing the paint at the canvas and stomping on the picture and leaving the room: *The Promise of Originality*, though it's too smeared to read in a glance. And maybe that was the name of a band, for a day.

9 ▪ **clipping., "Say the Name," from *Visions of Bodies Being Burned* (SubPop)** Reaching a high point with the faster than sound "Something Underneath," ending with the nearly gospel vocal yearning in "Entrancing" and a chamber-music rendering of Yoko Ono's 1953 "Secret Piece"—how little sound can you make if you're still making sound?—

you realize that track by track this album is made to defy expectations. That's a formal goal and it's pursued with a deadly serious sense of try-anything. But "Say the Name," anchored by a distorted deep voice chanting a line from the Geto Boys' bottomless "Mind Playing Tricks on Me," from 1991—"Candle sticks in the dark, visions of bodies being burned"—is the bedrock of the record. With a pace that touches the "Don't push me" cadence of "The Message" from Grandmaster Flash and the Furious Five in 1982, it's constructed out of plain, straight dis-course on social collapse from Daveed Diggs, the clatter of planks peeling off buildings, a steady, round bass, and a rising synthesized theme that makes you want to see the movie it's calling up from Wil-liam Hutson and Jonathan Snipes. Lines flash up, not explaining them-selves but claiming history, saying this band can rummage through the attic of the twentieth century and use it to decorate the twenty-first century house: "Guernica blood on the wall." "That train left the station with the great migration." Or as the Chaucer scholar and Dylan fan Betsy Bowden put it in a year-end letter to friends, "We must never forget the year 2020, which emptied the ashtrays on a whole lotta levels."

10 ■ Conor Lamb on *The Last Word with Lawrence O'Donnell* (MSNBC, January 7) The Democratic congressman from western Penn-sylvania after calling out Republican colleagues on the floor of the House as liars: "I really don't think you have to be very partisan to look at yesterday and be insulted the way we would be if we had been in-vaded by a foreign power. I mean, there were essentially foreign flags, Trump flags, being posted and hung from some of the most sacred square inches of ground in the United States"—and so the Trump proj-ect ends as it began, as it was supposed to, leaving the country discred-ited before the rest of the world, giving Vladimir Putin, collecting the interest on the loans to the Trump company, the free field he paid for. It's the id surfacing as a person looks for the words to say what he means in a fraught moment, when the everyday unconscious limits on speech don't work, and what comes out is not an argument, but a realization, the child realizing the emperor has no clothes: "Foreign flags, Trump flags."

Thanks to Sean Wilentz.

•

February 26, 2021

1 ▪ Inauguration of Joe Biden and Kamala Harris (January 20) When Garth Brooks actually took his hat off to sing "Amazing Grace" without accompaniment, I felt as if I'd never heard the song before. Every word stood out like a star, unmoving in its own light. Lady Gaga so mastered "The Star-Spangled Banner" she made it human, not abstract. She made it speak as strongly to history as it ever had. The tremor she gave to "Proof through the night" put you in the war it was written for, or any war. It put you in jeopardy: only fourteen days removed from America's own Kristallnacht, it made you feel the jeopardy of the moment. *She's up there with Marvin Gaye*, I thought—until I watched him again at the 1983 NBA All-Star Game. No, that was once in a lifetime—"I asked God," Gaye said later, "if when I sang, it would move me in my soul"—the lifetime of the song.

2 ▪ Heather Digby Parton, "Trump lawyers make a mockery of Republican senators," Salon (February 10) On the opening impeachment trial presentation by Bruce Castor and David Schoen: "The two of them could have come out and done an interpretive dance to 'YMCA' and it wouldn't have made any difference."

3 ▪ "The Middle" (Doner Agency), Bruce Springsteen for Jeep, CBS Super Bowl telecast (February 7) "NO SONGS WERE HARMED IN THE MAKING OF THIS COMMERCIAL" reads the disclaimer—well, it might have, since there weren't any songs in it. But given the opening lines— "There's a chapel in Kansas, standing on the exact center of the Lower 48"—I wanted to hear Bruce quietly reading Allen Ginsberg's "Wichita Vortex Sutra" in the background. He could have. In 2000, he attended an undergraduate seminar at Princeton on the poem. Like the students, he'd read it and listened to a 1994 recording of Ginsberg performing the forty-three-minute jeremiad-cum-Lenny Bruce routine while backed by downtown New York musicians from Philip Glass to Lenny Kaye to Christian Marclay. He came in with an argument he wanted to make, which with his preternatural ability to put people at ease he made only by responding to what others said: that "Wichita

Vortex Sutra," which is insistently about finding oneself in the exact center of the country, was Ginsberg's affirmation of his place, his burden and his duty, as a full citizen of the United States. That said, the only commercial of the day worth remembering was the BBDO M&Ms spot "Come Together," where it was about people offering packets of M&Ms to people they've offended, as in one woman saying to another, "Sorry I called you Karen." "That's my name." "Sorry your name is Karen."

4 ▪ *On the Rocks*, written and directed by Sofia Coppola (A24/Apple TV+) Rashida Jones is so half-dimensional even in a sitcom she could be out of her depth. Marlon Wayans's role is so impoverished he might have more to do in a commercial. Bill Murray seems to think he's Gene Hackman in *The Royal Tenenbaums*. Coppola has made exquisite movies, with a touch that's both light and hard, kill-you-with-a-velvet-pillow movies—that this tepid comedy of errors opens with Chet Baker's "I Fall in Love Too Easily" is the real proof of its cheapness. The song is meant to cast a veneer of seriousness, even impending tragedy, over everything to come, and what it does is expose that the only art in this picture once fit on a 45.

5 ▪ *One Night in Miami*, directed by Regina King, written by Kemp Powers (Amazon) Sam Cooke (Leslie Odom Jr.), Jim Brown (Aldis Hodge), Malcolm X (Kingsley Ben-Adir), and the future Muhammad Ali (Eli Goree) really did meet in a Miami motel room on February 25, 1964, just after Cassius Clay shocked the world by defeating the undefeatable Sonny Liston. What happened only Powers knows, and he made it up: surrounded by many more themes, a battle between Malcolm and Cooke over the value of Cooke singing his music to white people and Bob Dylan's own version of "Blowin' in the Wind." Odom brings some of the defensiveness and resentment of his Aaron Burr in *Hamilton* to his role; Ben-Adir makes Malcolm X a haunted, hunted man who can't dance and could out-argue the devil. "That movie made me feel good," said one person watching, even though it's 114 minutes of tension and both Cooke and Malcolm X would be shot to death within a year. That's because the picture doesn't insult anyone's intelligence: not the characters', not the actors', not yours. It engages it. It demands it.

6 & 7 ▪ *Tesla,* written and directed by Michael Almereyda (IFC) and Ethan Hawke, *A Bright Ray of Darkness* (Knopf) As someone so trapped within himself that his most evident human attribute is smoking, with Almereyda and Ethan Hawkes's reconstruction of the visionary inventor Nikola Tesla (1856–1943) it somehow seems inevitable, after his finally dead-end entanglements with Thomas Edison (1847–1931, Kyle MacLachlan), J. P. Morgan (1837–1913, Donnie Keshawarz), and Sarah Bernhardt (1844–1923, a slithering Rebecca Dayan), and his outliving them almost into the postwar modern world, dying alone and forsaken in a New York hotel, that in some karaoke bar of the mind Tesla will finally stand up to croak out Tears for Fears' "Everybody Wants to Rule the World." The first-person narrator of Hawkes's *A Bright Ray of Darkness,* one William Harding—a movie star whose marriage has broken up after he was caught on the covers of tabloids around the world with another woman, and who's about to make his Broadway debut in *Henry IV*—runs through the pages of this backstage/onstage novel as if he expects, deserves, wants, *no-no-no-no I don't!* the same fate as his Tesla. The book shivers with suspense and excitement: suspense backstage, over the first rehearsal, the first preview, opening night, over what the *New York Times* review will say, and excitement onstage, with the actors throwing Shakespeare's lines in the air and watching them explode time, place, and, in Harding's case, what he thought was his personality. When, following a fraught performance that has shown Harding he has never understood his character, his Hotspur is hammering Henry as he never has before ("—*by the* CHANCE OF WAR!"), and the actor playing Henry hits back with even greater force ("*Mighty and to be fear'd!*") and then drops dead on the stage of a heart attack, the audience thinks it's part of the play, and Harding actually has to ask "IS THERE A DOCTOR IN THE HOUSE?" The last line of the chapter seems as unavoidable as Tesla singing 1985's most memorable song forty-two years after his own death, and just as funny: "The King had left the building."

8 ▪ The Band, *Stage Fright 50th Anniversary* (Capitol) For $19.98, you get *Stage Fright* remixed by Bob Clearmountain to bring out startlingly acute and yet warming accents, with a booklet of photographs, effectively brief liner notes, and Robert Hilburn's original *Los Angeles Times* review. There's a new, deeply more effective track order, supposedly the once-intended arc of the album (opening with the now almost stomping "The W. S. Walcott Medicine Show," the head-on "The Shape I'm In," and the spinning "Daniel and the Sacred Harp" instead of the far more modest "Strawberry Wine," "Sleeping," and "Time to Kill"). On the same disc there are "Alternate Mixes" of "Strawberry Wine" and "Sleeping"—which are in fact irresistibly rough solo demos, as full of feeling as anything here, the first with Levon Helm on acoustic guitar, the second with Richard Manuel on piano. There are Robbie Robertson, Rick Danko, and Manuel in a hotel room, working out songs and fooling with a few oldies, but what you really hear is friendship, trust, fun—music that doesn't have to mean anything, that needs no consequences, new songs that could be left off the next album, as the small, glowing "Get Up Jake," which they try to get twice, was. On a second disc you get a very hot 1971 Albert Hall show—the singing is diminished by a recording that doesn't approach *Rock of Ages* or *The Last Waltz*, but you can ride the music by itself. For $129.96 more, you get that plus a cardboard box that may hold up better than a CD case, a Blu-ray, the revised album as an LP, a 45, a larger-size booklet, and a slipcase of three suitable-for-framings.

I always liked *The Godfather Part III*, but it wasn't until last year's revision—a few cuts, a few scenes transposed, a slightly different ending—that it too felt like a masterpiece, that it escaped the first two movies and spoke in its own voice, told its own story. The burden of the epic hung over the 1990 original, making it seem tacked-on and contrived. The new version lets you watch the film as a chamber movie, or Chekhov as opposed to Verdi, each actor moving around another with small gestures, which now took on affection, fright, foreboding. After *Music from Big Pink*, full of epic songs, and *The Band*, an epic in itself ("We could have called it 'America,'" Robertson once said), *Stage Fright* could feel constricted, the songs separated from each other, and as mostly a set of solo or separated vocals, diminishing each other—without the community of voices in a single line, or Huey, Dewey, and Louie finishing each other's sentences. The new version of the album (with what now feels like a nearly religious ending of "The Rumor," the whole congregation shouting out for the good and the right) says, yes, that's all true—but step back, and see if a walk down the street might not be just as interesting as climbing a mountain and jumping off. And the remastering of the one epic song here—"Daniel and the Sacred Harp"—brings out a totality in the indecipherable parable of the tune, a great melodic sweep. It was always there—but as an idea, not a body. Now it gets up and runs.

9 ▪ **Barack Obama, *A Promised Land* (Crown)** Blast from the past, on one of his rivals for the nomination in 2008: "Though I didn't know him well, I'd never been particularly impressed with Edwards. Despite the fact that he had working-class roots, his newly minted populism sounded synthetic and poll-tested to me, the political equivalent of one of those boy bands dreamed up by a studio marketing department"— or like a K-Pop star with his very own sex scandal.

10 ▪ **"The Rock & Roll Hall of Fame Foundation announced today the following Nominees for 2021 Induction" (February 10)** Mary J. Blige, Kate Bush, Devo, Foo Fighters, the Go-Go's, Iron Maiden, JAY-Z, Chaka Khan, Carole King, Fela Kuti, LL Cool J, New York Dolls, Rage Against the Machine, Todd Rundgren, Tina Turner, Dionne Warwick— yeah, I guess. I'll probably vote for the female nominees who aren't already there. But like Cato ending every speech with "Carthage must be destroyed!": *What about the Shangri-Las?*

Thanks to Michael Almereyda.

Acknowledgments

MY FIRST THANKS GO TO those who gave my column a home, no matter that I kept finding that what I thought was my own room was more like couch-surfing from one place to another: at the *Barnes & Noble Review*, Jim Mustich, Nick Curley, and Bill Tipper; at *Pitchfork*, Mark Richardson; the staff of the *Village Voice*; at rollingstone.com, Jon Dolan; at the *Los Angeles Review of Books*, Boris Drayluk, Cord Brooks, Tom Lutz, and Steve Erickson. I owe a special debt to Joe Levy, the real editor behind the column's space at the *Village Voice* and *Rolling Stone*—a special irony, given our history with the thing. And I thank with continuing surprise at my good fortune all of those who accepted assignments to cover shows I couldn't attend, who took the column as a forum for whatever they might have to say, who had as much fun with it as I did: Bruce Jenkins, Molly Gallentine, Joe Christiano, Cecily Marcus, John Rockwell, Michael Zilkha, Doug Kroll, Jo Anne Fordham, Andy Bienen, Tamar Newberger, Corin Tucker, Joshua Clover, Joel Selvin, Michael Robbins, Steve Perry, John Shaw, Lucy Gray, Robert Fiore, Elizabeth Flock, Mia Hanson-Løve, Rob Hatch-Miller, Pearl Perry, Rose Perry, Gina Arnold, Bill Brown, Eddie Muller, Grzegorz Kwiatowski, Barry Franklin, Ted Widmer, Peter Guralnick, Betsy Bowden, Joerg Haentzchal, John Langford, Uhuru Comix, Daveed Diggs, Shannon McArdle, Bill Wyman, Sarah Vowell, Emily Marcus, Sean Wilentz, Steve Weinstein, Chuck Bromley, Haim Schweky, and Charles Taylor. With some exceptions (the White House, a few more), the "friend," or "the person listening," or "the person watching" who appears in these pages is Jenny Marcus.

At Yale, I again had the generous counsel of John Donatich and Susan Laity (above and beyond), the never-falling-a-day-behind collaboration of Abbie Storch, the resourcefulness of Jennifer Doerr, and the care of the designer, Sonia Shannon. I thank as well Rich Black, who designed the jacket, based on a photo by the probing and generous Fred Kihn (Paris); the indexer Meridith Murray; and especially the peerless raconteur as copy editor Dan Heaton. At Brandt and Hochman, I can never thank Emily Forland enough—and I thank too Marianne Merola, Henry Thayer, and John Spano.

And thanks to Steve Wasserman, who thought of it first.

Index of Names and Titles